CW00969904

SACRED KŌYASAN

PHILIP L. NICOLOFF

SACRED
KŌYASAN

A Pilgrimage to the Mountain Temple of

Saint Kōbō Daishi

and the

Great Sun Buddha

STATE UNIVERSITY OF NEW YORK PRESS

COVER: A class of seminary students chant in veneration of the Five Buddhas enshrined in Kōyasan's Western Stūpa. *Photo by author.*

Published by
STATE UNIVERSITY OF NEW YORK PRESS, ALBANY

© 2008 State University of New York

For information, contact
STATE UNIVERSITY OF NEW YORK PRESS, ALBANY, NY
www.sunypress.edu

Production and book design, Laurie Searl
Marketing, Susan M. Petrie

Library of Congress Cataloging in Publication Data

Nicoloff, Philip, 1926-
  Sacred Kōyasan : a pilgrimage to the mountain temple of Saint Kōbō Daishi and the Great Sun Buddha / Philip L. Nicoloff.
    p. cm.
  Includes bibliographical references and index.
  ISBN 978-0-7914-7259-0 (hardcover : alk. paper) — ISBN 978-0-7914-7260-6 (pbk. : alk. paper) 1. Koyasan Monasteries (Japan) 2. Kukai, 774–835. I. Title.

BQ6353.K7N53 2008
294.3'435095219--dc22

                                              2007002070

10 9 8 7 6 5 4 3 2 1

To my wife, Maggie,

who shared the whole Kōyasan experience

CONTENTS

ACKNOWLEDGMENTS

The writing of this book has been a deep pleasure for me, in good part because of the encouragement and assistance I have received from so many people.

I wish initially to thank Professor Mori Haruhida, formerly of Kobe University, through whom my wife and I were first able to visit Japan. At Kōyasan there was Abbot Soeda Ryūsho of Rengejō-in, at whose temple we stayed so often. Abbot Soeda was unfailingly helpful and opened many doors. I thank him, his mother (Soeda Kiyomi), and the Rengejō-in staff. We stayed at fifteen other Kōyasan temples as well. In this regard I especially thank Abbot Fujita Kōkan of Daien-in, who early in my Kōyasan experience provided a personal tour of the Okunoin and assisted me in other ways.

For their generous help I thank Professor Takagi Shingen, formerly president of Kōyasan University, Zengan Aritano Kōgi of Yōchi-in, Rev. Yamamoto Chikyō of the Reihōkan Museum, Rev. Gomi Hōdō of Daishi Kyōkai, Rev. Hashimoto Eizui of Shinnō-in, Professor Hinonishi Shinjō of Kōyasan University, Professor Inui Hitoshi of Kōyasan University, Rev. Kamei Eishō of Nishimuro-in, Rev. Konishi Shoho of Kongōsanmai-in, Rev. Kuraoka Hiroyoshi of Daishi Kyōkai, Rev. Nagao Sōtoku of Daishi Kyōkai, Professor Okamitsu Kinji of Kōyasan University, Rev. Nakata Ryūō of the Nyonindō, Sugaya Atsuo of General Affairs at Kongōbu-ji, Nagasaka Yoshiaki, Nagasaka Yoshimitsu, Nishimoto Fumio of Nishiri and Co., Kise Michiyo of the Kōyasan Tourist Association, Shimada Momoyo of Sōji-in, and Hamada Sumiko of Hamada-ya. I also thank warmly Prof. Namai Chishō, now president of Kōyasan University, who assisted me both at the start and at the finish.

Among nonresidents of Kōyasan I express my gratitude to Abbot Kōno Seikō of Daian-ji (Nara), Bishop Miyata Taisen of Kōyasan Betsuin (Los Angeles), Rev. Takata Ryūkan of Zentsū-ji (Shikoku), Rev. Taniuchi Seigaku of Jingō-ji (Kyōto), Rev. Hashizume Masahiro of Tō-ji (Kyōto), Rev. Matsuzaki Kōzui of Ube City, Shigefuji Etsuo of Seifu Senior High School (Ōsaka), Hirayama Sumie of Daigan-ji (Miyajima), Shiotani Ayako of Jizō-ji (in Shiide), Saitō Kazuo (of Sidney, Australia), and Wang Han Ging of Ch'inglung [Qing Long] temple (Xian, China).

I thank Chancellor Kurozawa Kazuaki of Kobe Shoin Women's University and all my colleagues at both Kobe Shoin and Kobe University for responding to my frequent requests for help—especially professors Hamamoto Hideki, Haruki Takako, Inazumi Kaneaki, William Atwell, Dorsey Kleitz, Mitsuboshi Kenichi, Niiro Takuya, Shirakawa Kazuko, Takagi Toshikimi, Toda Masaru, and Mizukoshi Hisaya. I am particularly grateful to Professor Aoki Nobukazu, Professor Matsudaira Yoko, and Professor Richard Jambour for their sustaining friendship and counsel during my project. I thank Inagaki Fumiko and Masui Keiko of "English Island," and my assisting students, among them Shimizu Yuka, Inoue Kanako, Konishi Yumiko, Maeda Yasuko, Ro Senkei, and Tsubakimoto Kayoko. My gratitude goes to the Kobe Shoin staff, especially to Mori Akiko, Komoto Kazuko, and Nakagawa Hiroe.

Many others provided help, among them Professor Okamura Sachiko, Tsuno Fumi, Ikawa Sayoko, Morgan Gibson, Aoki Kazuyo, Paula Di Felice, Emily Nicoloff Horning, and David Gardiner and Mikael Adolphson (both at that time graduate students doing research in Japan).

I thank the administrations and staffs of the research libraries at Kōyasan University (especially professors Teratani Tomoyuki and Okamitsu Kinji), at the NCC Center for the Study of Japanese Religions in Kyōto (especially Dr. Martin Repp and Professor Yuki Hideo), at Ōtani University in Kyōto, at the Japan Foundation in Kyōto, and at the University of New Hampshire.

I received a series of research grants from Kobe Shoin Women's University over a period of four years, and a sabbatical leave from the University of New Hampshire. These were very helpful.

Kato Yoko served as a brilliant guide to Kōyasan and to Daian-ji in Nara. Hiroko Jackson provided invaluable help with scholarly Japanese texts. Professor Mori Michiko twice accompanied us to Kōyasan and was endlessly supportive. Tamakoshi Tokie was a generous translator and benefactor. Shimada Ikuko wittily shared her encyclopedic knowledge of Japanese language and culture and twice accompanied us to Kōyasan. Our Austrian friend Professor Herberth Czermak read the opening of an early draft and gently suggested some necessary adjustments.

I am especially indebted to Rev. Eko Noble, ācārya and abbot of Radiant Light Temple Kōmyōji in Washington state, who has been an inspirational support from the beginning. On the quite practical side she generously clarified for me a number of difficult points of fact and interpretation. She also provided the Japanese/Chinese characters and the scholarly transliterations of Sanskrit for the Glossary.

I thank Professor George J. Tanabe Jr., who graciously responded to my inquiries with invaluable advice.

I thank editors Nancy Ellegate, Allison Lee, Cathleen Collins, and Laurie Searl of SUNY Press for their expert help.

And now back to my wife, Maggie, to whom I am most indebted. *Sacred Kōyasan* had its beginning in the fall of 1989, and I've worked on it rather steadily down to the present moment. In all that time, during which I evaded so many obligations because of "the book," she never once hinted that I was taking too long or just might have made a wrong turn back on the road somewhere. Instead, she wishes to return to the mountain, and grows a little weepy when she reads the pages about the days and nights in the temple.

INTRODUCTION

The Japanese medieval epic *Heike Monogatari* relates that when retired Emperor Shirakawa (1053–1129) expressed a desire to embark on the ultimate religious pilgrimage—that is, to travel to distant India, the land where the historical Buddha had preached—adviser and scholar Ōe Masafusa suggested a less hazardous but equally exalted destination. "You may find an incarnation of the Great Sun Buddha on Mount Kōya here in our own country," Masafusa declared. "Shākyamuni in India and Kōbō Daishi in Japan both attained Buddhahood while still alive. Kōbō Daishi's virtue gave light to the darkness that had long ruled the world. Even after his death he continues to sustain his flesh on Mount Kōya in wait for the appearance of Maitreya Bodhisattva, the Buddha of the Future."[1]

So the pious ex-emperor changed his plans. With a glittering retinue of nobles and courtiers he journeyed southward from the capital to Mount Kōya in the heart of Japan's Kii wilderness. Near the mountain's summit he purified himself in the water of the Tamagawa, the "Jewel Stream" that flows past Kōbō Daishi's tomb. He knelt at the door of the burial chamber and prayed directly to the still living saint. Afterward the priests of Kōyasan set before Shirakawa the golden three-pronged *vajra* Kōbō Daishi had thrown from the shore of China in 806 and which traveled miraculously to the mountain where the temple was to be founded. The priests then unrolled an early history of Kōyasan on which Kōbō Daishi's handprints appeared. In gratitude the ex-emperor donated funds for rebuilding the mountain's central Great Stūpa, the primary shrine of the cosmic Great Sun Buddha.

Even before Shirakawa's time pilgrims had begun making their way to Kōyasan, drawn by a belief that it was a type of Buddhist paradise and that Kōbō Daishi still sustained his life there. The flow of visitors has continued to the present day. Pilgrims now travel more swiftly, of course. They journey by bus or by automobile over modern mountain roads, or on a remarkable train that climbs halfway up the mountain, then transfers its passengers to a cable car that continues the ascent. Beliefs, too, have altered somewhat. Perhaps only a minority of today's two million annual visitors strictly believe that Kōbō Daishi remains physically alive in fulfillment of his pledge to serve as savior to the Japanese people. Some also question his radical teaching that each person can, with proper disposition and discipline, achieve Buddhahood in his or her present lifetime. Many do believe these things, however. In every season, in all kinds of weather, they walk the forest path to the tomb. There they light three sticks of incense and a votive candle and chant the mantra *Namu Daishi henjō kongō*. "I take refuge [*namu*] in the Great Teacher [*Daishi*] whose light shines everywhere and is as eternal as the diamond." *Henjō kongō* is the esoteric ordination name of Saint Kōbō Daishi. It also is a secret name for the Great Sun Buddha. In essence the priest Kōbō Daishi and the cosmic Dainichi ("Great-Sun") are one.

Today's visitors often remain on the mountain for at least one night, choosing among the fifty monastery temples that accommodate guests. They eat the temple meals and soak in the temple baths and walk at dusk in the temple gardens, gazing at stars rarely observed in the crowded cities down below. They attend the early morning sūtra readings in the temple sanctuary. They chat with Shingon priests and student monks and strike up friendships with other visitors. A typical itinerary will include a visit to the forest cemetery and tomb on the afternoon of the first day. On the morning of the second day visitors likely will pray at the Great Stūpa (Daitō) and the Golden Hall (Kondō) and tour Kongōbu-ji, the mountain's headquarters temple. After lunch they might examine the magnificent collection of Buddhist art in the Reihōkan museum and shop in the temple town for souvenir gifts for friends back home. Some of the more earnest will arrange to take courses in meditation, sūtra copying, or sacred music, and resolve to return to the mountain in early spring or early fall to participate in a Shingon ceremony of mystical bonding to the Buddha known as *Kechien-kanjō*. A few visitors will have brought with them the ashes of their dead for blessing and interment near Kōbō Daishi's tomb, and may themselves return to the mountain one day in the form of ashes.

Even as it has become one of the most popular destinations of modern Japanese "tourist Buddhism," Kōyasan has managed to preserve its basic purpose as a holy place for religious study and practice. Its rich ceremonial life continues virtually without interruption from predawn to dusk. The mountain supports a Buddhist university, a major Shingon seminary for men, a seminary for women, and a large lay religious education center.[2] Kongōbu-ji serves as the administrative and spiritual headquarters for more than three thousand affiliated Kōyasan Shingon temples spread around the nation and overseas. Above all, the mountain continues to be a venue of divine Wisdom and Compassion, symbolized by Saint Kōbō Daishi seated in his tomb and the golden Great Sun Buddha seated in the Great Stūpa.

We begin our own Kōyasan pilgrimage as do many modern Japanese, riding toward the holy mountain on the Nankai Railroad's Kōyasan Express.

CHAPTER ONE

GOING TO THE MOUNTAIN

THE CELESTIAL RAILROAD

It is mid-morning. The four-car electric Kōyasan Express, now nearly an hour into its southward journey from Ōsaka's Namba Station, has reached Kimi Pass in the Izumi Range. As the train exits the last tunnel and begins its descent into the valley of the Kino River, we rise from our crowded bench seat and go to the car's front window. The view from this height is one of the trip's important opportunities. Spread before us are the mountain ridges and river valleys that make up the storied peninsular region known as the Kii Hantō. Somewhere out in that purple haze is the burial cave of the goddess Izanami, co-creator with her brother of the islands of Japan. There also is the route followed two and one-half millennia ago by Japan's first emperor, the legendary Jimmu, grandson of the sun goddess Amaterasu, as he trekked northward through the Kii to found a new nation.[1] Jimmu's guide on that occasion was a three-legged

1

crow, a gift of the sun. The whole region is filled with ancient shrines and ancient legends. Young Kōbō Daishi retreated into this wilderness when he abandoned his college education in order to seek the transforming power of mountain meditation. At some point during that experience he discovered the high summit valley where he later would establish his greatest temple.

Kōyasan is straight ahead of us now, its dark irregular profile lifting over the fronting foothills just beyond the Kino River. The round bulge at the western end of the ridge is Mount Benten. The more pointed silhouette at the eastern end is Mount Yōryū. Extending between these two summits lies the high level valley, or *kōya*, that gives the overall mountain its name. *Kōya-san*. Such locations were thought in Kōbō Daishi's time to be ideal for spiritual practice and study of the Dharma.

Back in our seats, we continue talking with a woman who has been sitting across from us ever since we left Ōsaka. It is rare to see a Westerner on this train, she tells us. They usually take the later and more comfortable Limited Express. She explains that she has visited Kōyasan at least once each year since she was a small child. She turns her shoulders to show us the faded image of Kōbō Daishi printed on the back of her white pilgrim's smock. This garment is more than twenty years old.

When we arrive I will go first to the forest cemetery to pray at the graves of my mother and my grandparents. Then I will pray at Odaishi-sama's tomb, asking him to protect my husband's business and the health of our children and grandchildren. After lunch I will visit the Karukaya-dō. That is my favorite place on the mountain, despite the crowd of tourists. The story of Ishidōmaru climbing Kōyasan to search for his lost father meant a great deal to me when I lost my own father in the war. Sometimes I imagined that my father had not been killed, but instead had escaped to Kōyasan to live near Odaishi-sama, just like Ishidōmaru's father.

The train crosses the wide but shallow Kinokawa and pauses at the little riverside village of Kamuro. In past centuries Kamuro was a bustling place with inns and teahouses that served foot travelers bound for Kōyasan along the Kyū-Kōya Kaidō ("Old Kōya Path"). But Kamuro no longer bustles. No one is getting on the train or getting off. Our woman friend points out the window at a sign that pictures a little boy in ancient aristocratic dress. This is Ishidōmaru. The sign advertises a local temple shrine, the Kamuro Karukaya-dō, that is dedicated to the story of Ishidō-maru's search. Ishidōmaru began his climb here in Kamuro, leaving his mother at a local inn because women were not permitted on the holy mountain. When he reached the temple near the summit he met a gentle, sympathetic priest who told him the father he sought had recently died, and pointed to a freshly dug grave as proof. Ishidōmaru sadly descended the mountain, only to discover that in his absence his mother too had died. So, now an orphan, he sorrowfully re-climbed Kōyasan, had his head shaved, and became a disciple of the gentle priest. The two spent their lives together worshiping the Buddha, and never did the older man reveal to Ishidōmaru that he in fact *was* his father.[2] The poignant story may date back as far as the twelfth century.

Our train passes a spread of rice fields just coming into ripeness, then stops at the village of Kudoyama, or "Nine-times Mountain," also on the southern bank of the Kinokawa. The unusual place name is construed locally to be a reference to the number of times Kōbō Daishi descended from Kōyasan to visit his mother here. Her residence presumably was at or near the village's Jison-in temple, Kōyasan's earliest supply depot. A carefully laid out footpath, twenty-one kilometers in length, extends from Jison-in to Kōyasan's summit. This path, still the official pilgrimage route up the mountain, is the one ex-Emperor Shirakawa took.

From Kudoyama Station the single-track line turns sharply away from the Kino River and we begin climbing up the narrowing gorge of the rushing Fudō-dani-gawa. Ahead lie fifteen tunnels and five mountain village stations. The last station, still only half way up Kōyasan, is the Gokuraku-bashi Eki, "Station of the Bridge to Paradise."

Upon exiting from the first brief tunnel we stop at Kōyashita ("Below Kōya") Station in the village of Shiide. Not so long ago Shiide supplied *kago* carriers for pilgrims who wished to be taken up the mountain by litter. The village is little noticed now, but on August 16 substantial crowds gather for the "Dance of the Shiide Demon," an ancient ritual designed to protect the local children from disease and assure the success of the fall harvest.[3]

As the train pushes forward the scenery becomes more dramatic, a constantly changing landscape of forested ridges and steeply terraced persimmon and *mikan* orchards. The wheels screech as we cross trestles and turn in and out of narrow tunnels. The cascading Fudō-dani-gawa recedes steadily deeper into the ravine below. In 1885 the Nankai railroad's founder, Matsumoto Jūtaro, vowed to construct a track capable of carrying pilgrims from the heart of Ōsaka to the summit of Kōyasan. That endeavor took forty-five years to complete.[4]

At last, after thirty more minutes of climbing, we reach Gokuraku-bashi Station. Forested slopes rise abruptly on all sides. Nankai's engineers could push the track no farther. A few meters below the station is the arched, red-painted "Bridge to Paradise," the footbridge for which the station is named. If we wish we can continue on by our own power, climbing to Kōyasan's Fudō Entrance along the paved and graded Fudō-zakka trail. On the way we would see a legendary waterfall and visit the trailside Fudō chapel where Ishidōmaru sought shelter when overtaken by darkness. A vast crowd of other climbers would join us, at least in spirit—centuries of student monks, zealous pilgrims, despondent lovers, soldiers in flight, emissaries from the shōgun, *hijiri* carrying ashes to place near Kōbō Daishi's tomb.

But the cable car offers a less strenuous way to paradise. And we already have our ticket. A clanging bell. We rush through a sheltered passageway and up steps to the second of the linked cars. Only a few empty seats remain. The bell clangs again and the cars slide into motion. Soothing music begins to pour from the public address system. We welcome the music, for the track ahead seems absurdly steep. We understand this to be the steepest cable track in the nation. And the oldest. But no matter, we are ascending smoothly and rapidly. Gokuraku-bashi Station falls farther and farther below us. We notice two small distant figures moving slowly along the Fudō-zakka trail. Foot pilgrims. Next time we may wish to join them.

At the upper terminus, Kōyasan Station, we step out into air that is sharply cooler. We are now at the altitude of the Kōyasan temples, but still must travel a couple kilometers or so through mountain forest to reach the valley's Fudō Entrance. A bus already is waiting for us, also supplied by Matsumoto's Nankai company.[5]

The bus starts off down the narrow, twisting, deeply shaded forest road, tightly following the contour of the mountainside. This road is for the exclusive use of buses that shuttle back and forth between the valley and the cable car terminus. Over the PA system a motherly Japanese voice describes some of the attractions that await us, followed immediately by a much younger female American voice that relates the same information in English. Suddenly the trees separate up ahead, sunlight splashes down, and the two voices call out the first stop: "Nyonindō." The Hall for Women. We press the bell, grab our backpacks, and, as the bus slows to a stop, step down to the pavement. Our Japanese friend waves through the window at us as the bus continues on through the Fudō Entrance and down the sloping road into the sacred valley. She will remain on the bus until its last stop, number eleven, "Okunoin-mae," at the far eastern end of Kōyasan. There she will find the shortest path to the "inner temple" and Kōbō Daishi's tomb. As for ourselves, we are going to spend the next half hour right here, just outside the gate.

OUTSIDE THE FUDŌ ENTRANCE:
THE WOMEN'S HALL

A welcome silence encloses us, the first real silence we have experienced since rising in darkness at four a.m. in Kobe. Sharp edged sunlight fills our little opening in the forest. The air is damp and spicy. Unlike Kōyasan's main western entrance, with its massive and intricate Great Gate, this Fudō Entrance is marked only by two large stone lanterns, one on either side of the road. On the lantern post at the right are carved the three Chinese characters for *Kō-ya-san*. On the lantern post at the left are the characters for *Kon-gō-bu-ji* ("Diamond Peak Temple"), the name selected by Kōbō Daishi for the overall monastery. Beyond the entrance we can just make out the wall of the first temple, about fifty meters distant.

In former years the Fudō Entrance (*Fudō-guchi*), although geographically a side gate to Kōyasan, was the busiest entrance to the valley, for it was the terminus of the Fudō-zakka trail, the last segment of the Old Kōya Path that came through Kamuro. Gate keepers were constantly alert, checking credentials, assigning visitors to the various temples, watching out for women. Before the twentieth century no woman, regardless of age or connection, was permitted to pass through any of Kōyasan's seven entrances.

We can imagine one such woman. She looks down the entrance road into a world she is forbidden to enter. The two strongest yearnings of her religious life, to speak to Kōbō Daishi at his tomb and pray before the Great Sun Buddha in the Great Stūpa, are both thwarted. With soft voice she tells the gate keeper that she has a brother who is a resident of Kōyasan. Might he be permitted to come out to meet her here at the gate? No, he says, that is not possible. She thanks him for not speaking to her in an insulting way, then turns toward the massive bronze statue of Jizō Bodhisattva (Sk. Kshitigarbha) that sits in meditation just outside the gate.[6] Jizō has a shaved head and is dressed as a simple monk. His assignment is to protect all travelers, both in this world and in the next, both male and female. He has a compassionate, dreaming face, almost the face of a woman. She now crosses the road to the Women's Hall, the Nyonindō. She wishes to rest for a time before starting back down the mountain. Perhaps another woman will be waiting there. Perhaps they will share their experiences and drink some tea together.

Nyonin-kinzei: *No Women Allowed!*

From the very beginning the *nyonin-kinzei* prohibition was a common part of Japanese monastery discipline. A woman's presence would be a distraction to celibate males engaged in spiritual study. It also might remind the monks of powerful ties that once bound them to the secular world: to parents who counted on the blessing of grandchildren and on receiving support in their old age, to sweethearts or wives (and sometimes children) who had been left behind as a precondition for entering the religious life.[7] Kōyasan was famous for applying the *nyonin-kinzei* policy with particular severity. Do not attempt to communicate with our men. Do not come to our gates in the hope of obtaining interviews. Your loved ones are dead to you.

According to popular tradition the woman who served as the basic model for Kōyasan's gender exclusion was Kōbō Daishi's own mother.

Near the end of her life Lady Tamayori, then a widow, is described as taking up residence at the foot of the mountain near Jison-in temple, her intention being to devote her remaining years to the care of her son. When Lady Tamayori attempted her first climb, however, Kōbō Daishi intercepted her on the path and forbad her to proceed beyond a point marked by two barrier rocks. When his mother protested, Kōbō Daishi removed his *kesa*, the most sacred article of priestly dress, and placed it across the path. "Mother, if you wish to climb higher you will have to step over my *kesa*. When she attempted to do just that there was an earthquake and a descent of fire balls from the sky. As a ledge of rock slid down to crush his mother, Kōbō Daishi stepped forward, seized the stone, and held it up to shield her against the fire.[8] Clearly both the law of Buddhism and the will of the native gods supported the principle of *nyonin-kinzei*. Lady Tamayori never again attempted to climb the mountain.

Through the centuries, however, Japan's women kept pressing closer to Kōyasan's summit, until by the time of the Tokugawa shōgunate they were allowed to proceed all the way to the entrance gates, of which there now were seven. There they might pause and pray, perhaps bid farewell to a spouse or loved one, or leave ashes for later burial near Kōbō Daishi's tomb. If these women pilgrims were accompanied by a man he would be permitted to pass through the gate to register at a temple. After signing his own name he could write the woman's name, adding *tono* at the end to indicate her temporary status as an honorary male. In this way she might receive spiritual credit for her journey.[9] If the man elected to remain overnight at Kōyasan, the woman had the option of staying in one of the crude women's shelters that sprang up outside each entrance gate or of retreating to a traveler's inn part way down the mountain—perhaps at Kamiya, a small village not far from the Gokuraku-bashi.

Inevitably a degree of sisterhood built up among these excluded women, and soon a path was worn along the summit ridge that connected the seven women's shelters. This encircling path, known as the *Kōya-nana-guchi-nyonin-michi* ("Women's Path to the Seven Entrances to Kōyasan"), is still maintained and provides the mountain with one of its more attractive day hikes. Signs identify the original site (*ato*) of each shelter. From several locations along the path a hiker can look down into portions of the valley, see the upper roof and spire of the Great Stūpa (Daitō) and hear the throb of the ancient Daitō bell.

The first significant initiative to allow women to pass through Kōyasan's gates came in 1872 when the new Meiji government in Tōkyō ruled that all of the nation's "sacred mountains" must be opened to pilgrims of both sexes. About a month after this edict, in a still more drastic move, the government decriminalized priestly marriage and the eating of meat, two of the most fundamental Buddhist clerical vows. Monks also henceforth might let their hair grow and wear secular clothing when not performing religious duties. The government's motive for taking these measures was in part to demonstrate to the nation and to the world that Japan was modernizing its social policies. The rulings also were an expression of the early Meiji hostility to the Buddhist establishment. Kōyasan, however, largely ignored these edicts. For the next thirty-four years its application of *nyonin-kinzei* did not change, at least not officially.

Then in 1906 the exclusion was lifted. By that time a generation of Kōyasan's priests had observed their fellow Shingon clergy "down below" enjoying the privilege of marrying and having children. Some wished this opportunity for themselves. A few already had wives and children, although secretly, and desired that these unions be made public and the banned wives and children brought to live on the mountain.[10] An eldest son could then be trained for the priesthood with the expectation that he eventually would take over the father's temple, a practice that was becoming the norm elsewhere. On the other hand, many of Kōyasan's priests were scandalized by the prospect of such laxity. Even today there are Shingon priests who believe the lifting of the ban on marriage forever destroyed an essential element of priestly discipline and culture.[11] "Our priests worry about their children's education," one priest told us. "They worry about their automobiles. Some take up golf. How are these men different from other men?" But the debate now is largely theoretical. Women have entered the valley to stay—as wives, daughters, mothers, teachers, temple employees, business clerks and managers, as university students, as students in the seminary for priests. And as pilgrims and visitors.

Today more than one million women, young and old, from every station of life, pass annually through the gates of Kōyasan. The discomforts and sorrows of *nyonin-kinzei* are matters of the past. But they are not entirely forgotten. An aid to memory is the Nyonindō itself, the Women's Hall that stands just outside the Fudō Entrance. It is the only women's shelter that still survives, although, strictly speaking, it no longer serves as a shelter. It is closed at night. During daylight hours, however, women come here to remember and to pray.

The Women's Hall

The Nyonindō, most recently rebuilt in 1871, is a traditional wooden Buddhist hall with a large shingled roof that sweeps up slightly at the eaves. Across the age-darkened facade are twelve sliding doors, two of which are now open. We enter without removing our shoes, for the hall's stone floor is made for the rough use of travelers. Once inside we perceive immediately that this is a place for supplication and prayer. Displayed side by side behind racks of flickering votive candles are the sculptures of three divine figures. Each image is in shadow, but the one at the center, a small Great Sun Buddha, is covered with gold and therefore glows brightly in the candlelight. This sculpture of Dainichi Nyorai (Sk. Mahā-vairochana Tathāgata) is the Nyonindō's primary object of worship. In fact, in esoteric Buddhism he is the ultimate recipient of every possible act of worship, now and forever. Dainichi sits with his hands resting open in his lap, the right hand placed on top of the left. This "concentration" *mudrā* is most appropriate for a Women's Hall, for it expresses among other things the "female" energy that gives birth to the phenomenal world and oversees it with compassion. We won't feel the full significance of this image until we visit Dainichi's primary shrine, the Great Stūpa.

The carving to the left of Dainichi is so dark in hue and set so far back in the shadows that at first we see only a pair of staring eyes. But gradually the figure of a man emerges. He is sitting stiffly upright in a rocky cave. His face is gaunt. He wears a pointed beard. His body is thin to the point of emaciation. The right hand grips a ringed walking staff. The left hand holds a single-pointed *vajra* or *dokko*. This intense figure is En-no-Gyōja (En-the-Ascetic), a seventh-century Buddhist mountain mystic who is believed to have opened hundreds of Japan's mountains to the Dharma, including Kōyasan itself. Legend tells us that En's wilderness austerities were so successful that they gained him the power to subject demons to his bidding and to fly. His presence in the Nyonindō reminds us that Kōyasan is a place consecrated to the mountain intoxicated.

En's connection with the needs of women is not obvious, but we do know of his famous attachment to his mother, who conceived him after swallowing a *dokko* in a dream. Like Kōbō Daishi, En prevented his mother from entering the terrain of the mountains where he practiced his austerities. He did, however, again like Kōbō Daishi, frequently descend to visit her. According to one legend En ended his career by his placing his mother in a Buddhist alms bowl and flying off to China with her, where they still enjoy an immortal existence together.[12]

But En is only a sideshow here. Sitting to the right of Dainichi Buddha is the queen of the Nyonindō, the goddess Benten (also known as Benzaiten or Daibenzaiten). Benten, who evolved from the Indian river goddess Sarasvatī, is one of the most potent figures in the Japanese esoteric pantheon.[13] She easily is Kōyasan's most powerful woman. In her most beautifully aggressive manifestation she appears with furrowed brow and eight arms, each arm displaying a distinctive symbol of conquest and benefit (a sword, arrow, *vajra*, eight-spoked wheel, etc.). This is the form we later will see in Kōyasan's Golden Hall. There Benten serves as the primary muse of Shākyamuni's enlightenment. Here in the Women's Hall we find her in her less intimidating two-armed form. She is dressed is the robes of a Heian-era noblewoman. She is seated and is playing a short-necked lute. This lute, known in Japan as a *biwa*, reminds us that Benten is a goddess of music. She equally is a goddess of wealth, of beauty, of eloquence, of learning, of science, of intuitive insight. Her intellect is profound. One story has her inventing Sanskrit, the sacred language of the gods.

The most fundamental of Benten's many powers, however, is her mastery of water, the "ground and mother-body of all life." As such Benten is the deity of "flowing things," of all that nourishes and is compassionate. She is an embodiment of the ideal female, is the "best of mothers." The forested mountain that rises immediately to the south of the Nyonindō, and which provides Kōyasan with its primary source of water, is named Mount Benten (Bentendake). On its summit, just a twenty minute climb along the Women's Path, is Kōyasan's most important Benten shrine. Legend says the shrine was initiated by Kōbō Daishi when he buried a set of prayer beads there as a device to attract the goddess.[14] Benten has six other shrines in the valley. Altogether the seven shrines form a protective, snake-shaped loop about the mountain's most important temple halls. Water-producing snakes are a definitive manifestation of the goddess.[15]

When we first stepped inside the Nyonindō a woman and a young man already were standing in front of Benten. They are still there, heads bowed, chanting softly and rapidly. We have seen these two worshipers before, not here in the Nyonindō but down along the Fudō-zakka trail near the Kiyome (Purification) Waterfall. On that occasion they were crouching in front of a mossy embankment chanting just as they are now. Later, when we looked for the object of their devotion we discovered a small wooden shrine about the size of a cigar box beneath a falling trickle of water. Inside the shrine was a tightly coiled ceramic white snake with the head of a bearded man. The two had placed before this snake an offering of a single hen's egg.

Which reminds us now to take notice of the golden tiara on the Benten sculpture's head. Behind the arc of the tiara is a miniature *torii*, or Shintō gate. And within this gate coils the miniature body of a white snake with the head of an elderly bearded man. This man-snake is an esoteric form of Benten known as *Uga-jin*.[16] Kōbō Daishi is said once to have carved just such an image, but with the head modeled after the wife of Emperor Junna, a woman who became a nun and one of his disciples.[17]

And now we notice one more thing on the altar. Someone has placed a small *ihai*, or memorial tablet, directly in front of Benten. On it is written this accusatory prayer in Japanese: "For consoling the anguished spirits of foreign women, now dead, who were forced to serve the Japanese military as comfort women in China, the Philippines, Burma, and the Dutch East Indies." Goddess Benten, assuage the grief of your suffering sisters!

Three women have entered the hall. They are wearing white pilgrim smocks and clearly have been traveling together. We guess they are mother, daughter, and granddaughter. The eldest goes to the small office at the east end of the hall and asks Reverend Nakata to enter the Nyonindō's seal in the book she is carrying (the hall's seal features the name of its *honzon*, Dainichi). Such seals provide a souvenir record of visits to pilgrimage destinations. The other two women have lit candles and are beginning to pray.

We look around the hall. Obviously it no longer serves as an overnight shelter. There is hardly a place to sit. But the Nyonindō remains a center for women's concerns. A recent visitor has left a pile of pamphlets that protest the suppression of women in Japan's political life. Among several books stacked on a shelf is Ariyoshi Sawako's *Kinokawa*, a novel that describes four Japanese women—mother, daughter, grand-daughter, great-granddaughter—who struggle with the dramatic social changes of the first half of the twentieth century. One prized element of continuity in the women's lives are visits made during pregnancy to the shrine of Kōbō Daishi's mother at Jison-in. At the novel's close the great-granddaughter chooses not to marry and have children, a decision reen-forced by the death of an ancient white snake that had been living in the family storehouse.[18] We find a loose page of sheet music on the shelf with the books. The song's lyrics describe a woman making a pilgrimage to Kōyasan in the hope of finding liberation from the pain of a lost love.[19] She crosses the Kinokawa, the "river of farewell," then climbs the sacred mountain, praying all the while that her agony will end. But the pilgrim-age brings no relief. In the last stanza she enters the Women's Hall and calls out in despair, "I love him still!" The title is "Nyonin-michi." Women's Path.

There are several pictures on the wall. One is a painting of a woman leading a child to Kōbō Daishi's tomb. Another is a faded photograph of Akuno Shizuka. Shizuka-san is thought to have been the first person, either male or female, to have been born within the precinct of Kōyasan. In 1896, well before the official admission of women, her mother secretly entered the valley to visit her husband, a forest worker, and unexpectedly gave birth.[20]

It is time to leave. We go to the office to exchange greetings with Reverend Nakata Ryūō, the friendly host of the Nyonindō. He is head priest of a small Shingon temple down in the mountain village of Nosegawa, but with only thirty local families to support his temple he must find further employment. So he comes up the mountain each morning to welcome visitors to the Nyonindō, to provide them with information and other services, including selling them a variety of talis-mans and amulets (*o-fuda* and *o-mamori*). He has been known to offer us coffee and cookies, and on one occasion a bag of forest mushrooms.

We step outside into the patch of sunlight. Near the Nyonindō, to our left as we exit, is a glassed-in shrine dedicated to the Jizō of traffic safety. This shrine was a gift from a Korean enthusiast named Kin. For many years Kin visited Kōyasan regularly, even building a small residence for himself part way down the Fudō-zaka trail near the hall of the Purification Fudō Myō-ō and the Purification Waterfall.

To our right is a second, more important, shrine. It is dedicated to a woman named Kosugi who is said to have provided the funds that built the first women's hall at this spot. Kosugi's story is a tale of personal tragedy and uncomplaining persistence. After suffering unspeakable abuse from a cruel father and treacherous stepmother, she set off on foot from the northern province of Echigo with an infant son tied on her back. Her half-delirious hope was to find protection for her child at the distant Kōyasan monastery. The infant boy died during the journey, however. So upon reaching the Fudō Entrance Kosugi surrendered the only two things of value she had left in the world—her baby's hair, for burial near Kōbō Daishi's tomb, and a small pouch of gold, the baby's birth gift, for the building of a shelter for women outside the Fudō gate. A sign at the shrine says only, "[Kosugi's] life was very unfortunate, but Kōbō Daishi saved her." Rev. Nakata has a pamphlet for those who wish to learn more.[21]

Our time outside the gate is ended. We are heading into the sacred valley.

CHAPTER TWO

STAYING AT A *SHUKUBŌ* TEMPLE

OUR MIDDAY ARRIVAL

We walk past the entrance lanterns and down the forest-lined road. Within fifty meters we reach the first temple wall on the left and continue on until that wall angles in, revealing a temple gate. The name of this temple is *Rengejō-in*. "Temple of the Lotus-Flower Meditation." This is where we will stay for the duration of our visit.

Rengejō-in is located in an area of Kōyasan known as Gonomuro-dani, one of the valley's nine officially designated neighborhoods (*dani* means "little valley").[1] Within Gonomuro-dani are seven large *shukubō* temples ("lodging" temples that take in overnight guests), eight small "residential" temples, a dozen lay residences, several commercial shops (such as the Imanishi Shōten *tōfu* and fish shop and the Hana-asa flower shop), four or five small manufacturing establishments (among them Mr. Iwatsubō's woodworking Sanko-sha that makes such religious objects as

ema, o-fuda, and *sotoba*), three small *tahōtō*-style pagodas (including Kōyasan's only surviving "exterior" guardian pagoda, the Kinrin-tō), a half-dozen shrines (including a hilltop Inari shrine and a local shrine to the guardian native mountain gods), a small public park with children's swings and picnic tables, several small but ancient cemeteries, a telephone office, a gasoline station, and, for those seeking evening entertainment, the Mika ("beautiful song") Karaoke & Pub.

It sounds like a busy place, but in fact Gonomuro-dani is quieter than most of Kōyasan's neighborhoods, largely because it contains only two notable attractions for visitors. One attraction is the opulent Mausoleum of the Tokugawa, a shrine for the deceased spirits of the first and second Tokugawa shōguns, Ieyasu (1543–1616) and Hidetada (1579–1632). Not many of today's Japanese take much personal interest in these once all-powerful figures.[2] The second attraction, a small carving of a fierce-looking god in the sanctuary of Nan-in temple, is an object of much greater devotion. The sculpture is said to have been executed by Kōbō Daishi when he was in China. Its popular name is Nami-kiri ("Wave-cutting") Fudō, and it is credited with having saved Kōbō Daishi's life and the lives of his shipmates by quieting a violent ocean storm on the return voyage. Even more famously, again in response to prayer, this wind-conquering Fudō is credited with having produced the *kamikaze* ("divine wind") that destroyed Kublai Khan's invasion armada off Kyūshū in the thirteenth century. Today's visitors to Nan-in ask the Nami-kiri Fudō for help with personal problems, especially intractable ones such an addiction to alcohol or gambling. The scowling, half-naked god, armed with sword and binding rope, is most tenacious and severe, but he is a manifestation of Dainichi's love.

Homage to the great fierce one! Annihilate all evil enemies! Exterminate all defilements! Hām Mām!

We will return to the history of the Nami-kiri Fudō in a future chapter.

We enter Rengejō-in. Just inside the main gate is the front garden, a calming expanse of immaculate white sand bordered by cherry, maple, plum, Indian lilac, and a dozen other varieties of small trees and shrubs, all now showing their early fall colors. The garden is enclosed on two sides by temple porches and on a third side by the temple's exterior wall. Over this wall rises a shoulder of Mount Benten, its misty forest providing "borrowed scenery" for the garden. The sand's white surface has been raked into wave patterns, at the center of which is a carefully formed Sanskrit syllable *hrīh*. A small sign informs the visitor that *hrīh* is the *bija*-letter for Amida Buddha, the Buddha of love and compassion to whom this garden is dedicated.[3] Amida Buddha is the *honzon* (chief object of worship) enshrined in Rengejō-in's main sanctuary, which borders the west end of the garden.

Carefully arranged on the main hall's entrance steps are the appropriate number of temple slippers. The staff expects us. We remove our shoes, slide into the slippers, and climb the steps to the front corridor. There we place our street shoes in a storage cabinet. Seichō-san, who already has spotted us from the temple office, hurries out with his greeting. Next year Seichō will begin formal training for the priesthood. Everyone agrees he will make an excellent priest.[4] Two barefoot student monks appear. They are "blue heads," young men with freshly shaved pates. Seichō gives them instructions and off they go down the polished front corridor, loose temple fatigues flapping, while we follow as best we can. We pass the *hondō* (main sanctuary) and the Fudō chapel and climb the rear stairway that overlooks the waterfall and carp pond of Rengejō-in's inner garden. At the door of our room we step out of our slippers. The slippers are for corridors only, never to be worn on the delicate woven *tatami* that covers the floors of temple rooms.[5] The two young monks promise to return shortly, then hurry off.

Except for one low table our room is entirely bare of furniture. If we wish to sit we must sit on the *tatami*, or on a flat pad-like *zabuton* that is placed on the *tatami*. At night the low table will be pushed off to a corner and *futon* spread in the middle of the floor for sleeping. There is no closet or anything resembling a chest of drawers, so we place our backpacks in a corner. The aesthetic focus of the room is its *tokonoma*, a small alcove in which a scroll painting and a small arrangement of flowers are displayed. This alcove is a sacred area. It is no place for a pile of underclothes or toilet kit or an alarm clock. If we were carrying pilgrim staffs, however, we could put them in the alcove, for such staffs represent the spiritual presence of Kōbō Daishi.

The room's windows are covered with Japanese *shōji*, sliding screens made of one thickness of translucent paper stretched over a wooden lattice. The paper lets in a pleasant, softly diffused light. We slide back one of the *shōji*. Outside the window is a small sand and stone garden.[6] Kōyasan has hundreds of gardens, both large and small. Most are strikingly beautiful. A few are quite famous.

The two side walls of our room are made up largely of *fusuma*, sliding doors constructed of two thicknesses of opaque paper stretched over wooden frames. By removing these doors we could unite our room with adjacent rooms. A traditional Chinese scene has been painted on each *fusuma*. In one a small boy is watching a flute player riding on a donkey. In another two men are meditating beside a stream. In a third an artist is painting a dragon while two assistants mix paints. Each of the scenes is set in mountainous terrain. We will ponder their mysterious beauty tonight while waiting for sleep.

A low voice at the door. One of the young monks slides the door open from a kneeling position, a mark of deference and courtesy. They have brought us a pot of tea and a plate of *manjū*, rolls of sweetened bean paste covered with buckwheat dough. The *manjū* will be our emergency lunch.

"When do you wish dinner?" the taller monk asks in careful English. The question is largely for politeness, for temple meals are served on a fixed schedule. We agree that the evening meal (*ban-gohan*) will be served at six. We ask when the honorable bath (*o-furo*) will be available. From five to eleven. And at what time is the morning sūtra service (*Rishu-zammai-hōyō*)? Six. Breakfast (*asa-gohan*) will be at seven.

We converse for a while in a mix of weak English and weak Japanese. These cheerful young men are students at Kōyasan's Buddhist high school. Each comes from a Shingon temple family. The taller is an eldest son who anticipates someday taking over the position of head priest at his father's temple. He expects to complete all his training for the priesthood here at Kōyasan. The shorter boy is a middle son and has no expectation of becoming a priest. All the same his family thinks the discipline he will receive at Rengejō-in will profit him in the future. At the very least he will learn good manners.

Rengejō-in is made up of six major buildings, all connected by covered corridors. The sanctuary hall, the *hondō*, dates back some five hundred years. The "big roof" main hall is about two hundred years old. The main hall contains the public rooms where major banquets and ceremonies are held. It also houses the temple offices, the temple kitchen, a private chapel, and living quarters for the head priest's family and a dozen or so resident monks and priests.

The four other primary halls contain rooms for temple guests. These guest rooms, nearly fifty in number, vary between eight and fourteen *tatami* mats in size. In theory Rengejō-in could sleep and feed and bathe a couple of hundred guests at one time. Several other *shukubō* temples at Kōyasan could accommodate twice as many. A few are quite small, with room for no more than a dozen visitors.

Shukubō temples vary somewhat in the amenities they provide.[7] The recently rebuilt Sōji-in—a temple that burned a few years back—has the most luxurious facilities. Each of its guest apartments has air-conditioning, a vanity table with mirror and chairs, in-room hot and cold running water, a private Western-style toilet, a closet with hangers, a color TV. Four of the apartments have small attached penthouse gardens. Additionally, Sōji-in's public baths are gorgeous, with thick towels, herbal soaps, and fresh orchids floating on the steaming surface.

But Sōji-in is not typical. At the average Kōyasan *shukubō* the rest rooms are large, public, and unisex, with Japanese-style flat-to-the-floor toilet stalls along one wall and urinals along another (although Western-style toilets are almost always available). One washes one's hands and face and shaves while standing with others before a single long sink, usually located in a hallway. Hot water? Usually not. Be grateful that there is a small mirror. In the cold winter dawn, with the taps left dripping all night to keep the pipes from freezing, one might have to break through a skim of ice in the water trough in order to wash up. The hot baths are wonderfully hot in all seasons, but the towels won't be much larger than a washcloth. And no floating orchids.

For most visitors, especially for the foreign ones, a little austerity is a desired part of the temple experience. Washing together, men and women, friends and strangers, is a good way to begin a day. It is a step toward social awareness and away from private self-pampering. Sometimes nature intrudes in a delightful way. One summer morning at Sannō-in, where the washing area is outdoors, a bright green tree frog climbed up on the rim of the water tank not six inches from my nose as I splashed my sleep-numbed face. Some of the water splashed on the frog as well, but it held its place, iridescently beautiful and calm.

EVENING

Toward the end of each afternoon the forest paths leading to Kōbō Daishi's tomb become deserted. Shoppers along Odowara Street vanish from the stores and sidewalks. Custodial monks in the Garan close the heavy doors of the Golden Hall and Great Stūpa and head home. At 5:30 p.m. (thirty minutes earlier during the short days of winter) a lullaby-like melody plays over the town loudspeakers. The lyrics are not sung, but everyone knows the familiar message. Children, stop your outdoor play and hurry home. Dinner is ready. Darkness is coming. Mother is waiting for you.

> The bell of the mountain temple is ringing.
> By the time the small birds start their dreaming
> The stars will be twinkling in the sky.

On hearing this music we hurry home, too, back toward Rengejō-in, our thoughts on the evening meal, the hot bath, the comfort of the *yukata*, the oblivion of the *futon*.

Promptly at 6:00 p.m. a young monk knocks at our door and we follow him down the stairway past the inner garden to one of the old rooms of the main hall. At the center of this room, displayed on low red-lacquered tray tables (called *zen*), is our evening meal. The surroundings are quite resplendent here. The *fusuma* are richly detailed. The transom screens (*ranma*) are filled with intricately carved images of plants, birds, and animals. Several temple treasures are arranged beneath the scroll in the *tokonoma*.

Each of us sits before two tray tables loaded to their margins with small bowls and dishes, ten containers in all. No two containers have the same decorative pattern. The largest of the bowls, a casserole, sits over a candle flame. Another bowl, tightly lidded, contains heated broth. Two of the bowls lie face down. These we will fill ourselves, the larger one with rice, the smaller one with tea.

The temple kitchen staff has composed for us a calculated medley of shapes, colors, ingredients, tastes, and methods of preparation, using two traditional organizing principles. The first principle is the law of *shōjin ryōri*—literally, "a diet in pursuit of enlightenment." No animal product has been used: no meat, no fish, no milk, no cheese, no egg, no gelatin. *A person who eats flesh kills the seed of compassion*, warned the Buddha on his deathbed. Neither is there any food with a strong taste or smell: no onions, no pepper, no hot curry. Strong tastes and smells stir sensual appetites.

The second organizing principle is known as the "system of five." Our meal includes the five basic tastes: sour, salty, sweet, tangy, and fermented. The preparers also have employed the five basic methods of cooking: raw, boiled, baked, fried, and steamed. Finally, there are the five basic colors: red, black, yellow, white, and blue/green. The number five is no arbitrary choice, for it unlocks much of the sacred world the Buddhist inhabits: the Five Precepts, the Five Wisdoms, the Five Meditations, above all the Five Buddhas of the Dharma Body.[8]

We say the traditional Japanese Buddhist grace, *Itadaki-masu*. The words mean, literally, "I will eat," but in context they convey much more. "I accept responsibility for eating this meal; I express gratitude to the Buddha and to those creatures (the vegetables, the water, the fire) and those persons (the farmers, the cooks, the monks) whose sacrifice and labor have made it possible."[9]

We begin with the bowl of broth. With our *hashi* (chopsticks) we pick out the warm gingko nuts, the snow peas, the curls of *yuba*, then drink the mild liquid directly from the bowl. The broth is just what our dehydrated bodies seem to need. Next comes the golden *tempura*, its crisp batter still warm from the cooking oil. Slices of burdock root, lotus root, sweet potato, green pepper, mushroom. Next the little bowl of black beans. Then the salad, a mixture of several finely grated vegetables, mostly *daikon* (a mild Japanese radish) and carrot. By this time the *mikutaki* casserole is hot and bubbling. The pale cabbages, mountain mushrooms, dark *kombu* (seaweed), and squares of *momengoshi-dōfu* ("cotton" *tōfu*) have been simmering for a full fifteen minutes. We eat each delicious item, keeping to the last a small piece of kneaded wheat gluten called *fu*.[10] This evening's *fu* has been colored and stamped out in the shape of an autumnal maple leaf, much like the maple leaves outside in Rengejō-in's front garden. *Fu* follows the seasons. In spring it will be given the shape and color of a cherry blossom.

Next up is the bowl of oozing, frothy *yama-no-imo*, a "mountain potato" celebrated as a cure for high blood pressure and much else that ails the aging body. One hopes these health claims are true, for *yama-no-imo* is not a particularly pleasant dish. Nor is the next one, *konnyaku*, a starchy extraction from Devil's Tongue that has the appearance of congealed dishwater. But take heart. *Konnyaku* has been a standard ingredient of the Japanese diet for a thousand years.

We turn to the *goma-dōfu*, a *tōfu* made from ground sesame and potato starch. A large cube sits jiggling in a shallow puddle of sweet sauce. At one time *goma-dōfu* also presented a challenge, but no longer. We boldly slice the cube with the *hashi* and slurp it down, quivering piece by quivering piece. Next up, the *kōya-dōfu* (the evening's third *tōfu* variation), so named because it is an ancient invention of the monks of this mountain. By allowing the liquid content of regular soybean *tōfu* to evaporate in the dry winter air the monks produced a spoilage-resistant product with the appearance and texture of a dry sponge. *Kōya-dōfu* is restored to palatability by immersion in a sweetened liquid.

For dessert we have the world's sovereign citrus fruit, the tangy *mikan*. At this time of year the *mikan* orchards below the mountain are heavy with harvest. Pyramids of the golden fruit stand before every deity of Kōyasan. We are eating like gods tonight.

The meal is nearing its end. We have another cup of tea, then a final serving of rice. Every meal is concluded with tea and rice.

Back in our room we find the *futon* laid down for the night, positioned so that our sleeping heads will be pointing toward the east. That direction is the one used by the emperor and recommended by Confucius. It is associated with strength and vigor. The south and the west also have merit, but one should never sleep in a northward position ("north pillow"). That is the direction assigned to the dead. It is the position assumed by the historical Buddha, Shākyamuni, at the time of his *parinirvāna*.

Ah, blessed bath time. We strip down in our room, put on a freshly ironed blue-and-white *yukata*, pick up a thin temple towel, and head up the hall. At Rengejō-in the entrances to the men's and the women's baths are next to one another, so we check the signs carefully. The *kanji* for man includes the character for strength. The *kanji* for woman looks like a seated stick figure with crossed legs. They are not at all alike. But one can blunder. This is my story. In the anteroom of what I thought was the men's bath I removed my *yukata* and eyeglasses, then happily entered the steamy bathing area. A single hunched figure was soaking in the pool. I spoke my usual friendly greeting. The soaking figure rotated toward me and gestured with a wig-wag of the hand. But I kept coming. At this point the figure rose up majestically from the water, like Venus at her birth, and pointed in the direction of the men's bath. Just another crazy foreigner.

I slide open the glass door to the bathing room. Three middle-aged Japanese gentlemen are sitting beside one another on the washing deck, sudsing and talking. I select a stool, sit down facing the long row of cold and hot taps, fill a wash basin, splash water over my head and body, then begin soaping up. The men ask if I'm an American. I say that I am, that I teach in Kobe. They are from Okayama. Sensing that my Japanese may not support a useful conversation, they go back to talking among themselves. All the same we're on good terms. They can see I know the bathing routine. I will scrupulously rinse off every bubble of soap before entering the bath.

Almost in unison we four stand up and walk to the brimming, steaming pool. For them this is an almost daily event, one they've enjoyed since childhood. For me it still retains some terror. I watch them slide in—legs, rumps, torsos, arms, into the water right up to their chins—all without a gasp or murmur. They watch as I seat myself on the tile and tentatively dip in one foot. Good grief.

I will not fail and I will stay silent. My left foot goes in up to the calf. Now both legs. Slowly, slowly. The hips. The delicate skin of the waist. How amazingly delicate that skin is. And the equally tender chest. My heart is pounding. Only my head and hands are above the surface now. I let out an involuntary moan and the three men laugh. Actually it isn't so bad. Slowly the heat works deeper. Everything relaxes. I begin to dissolve. I grow spiritual. We four are spiritual brothers.[11]

At nine o'clock, back in our room, we hear a nightbird singing. *Bup-pō-sō!* We hurry to the window and open it on the rear garden. Moonlight is falling in patches through the trees. *Bup-pō-sō!* The bird that voices this song is said to nest only on sacred mountains. More than a thousand years ago Kōbō Daishi wrote of its strange cry.

In a quiet forest, sitting alone
in a grass hut at dawn,
"Bup pō sō!" I thought
I heard a bird cry.
Was it a bird's cry?
I heard it in my mind.
The sound, stream, clouds, and mind
diffuse brightly in the morning rays.[12]

Actually the birdsong we are hearing now is coming from the town's loudspeakers. This is the Kōyasan community's way of bidding everyone goodnight and suggesting some final thoughts for the day. *Bu*, for the Buddha who loves us. *Pō*, for his precious Teaching. *Sō*, for the monastic Community of which we are now temporarily a part. Kōbō Daishi imagined this sacred trinity being announced to him by a forest bird. Shingon Buddhism teaches that every thing in nature instructs us in the path to enlightenment.

"A MIND OF RAPTURE": THE MORNING SŪTRA SERVICE

At a few minutes before six the next morning we descend to the front porch of Rengejō-in's *hondō*, drawn by the rhythmic clanging of the temple announcement bell. We slip quietly through sliding doors into the dark, incense-fragrant hall and seat ourselves on the *tatami*. A dozen other temple visitors have arrived ahead of us, several of whom were washing up with us just fifteen minutes ago. Especially noticeable are two middle-aged women, dressed in black, who appear to be sisters. They have a young man sandwiched between them and are whispering in his ear. Our guess is that the woman on the left is the young man's mother, the other his aunt, and together they have brought him to Rengejō-in for a memorial service for his father. He sits slumped and frowning in his dark suit. He dreads everything about this too solemn place. The three men from last night's *o-furo* are not here. They did some after-bath drinking and are still asleep. Also absent are the six pilgrim ladies who occupied the room next to ours. Well before dawn we heard them rise and slip away, their bells tinkling softly, heading off toward the distant Okunoin and an early call on Kōbō Daishi.

Placed quite close to us, just outside the altar railing, is an incense bowl on a low table. A narrow thread of smoke rises upward from its center and vanishes in the darkness. At the proper moment in the ceremony one of the monks will invite us to come forward to add a pinch of incense in veneration of the Buddha. A popular notion suggests that the Buddhas are sustained by this smoke. It is their celestial food.

Overhead hang two large golden canopies (called *tengai*), one positioned over the inner altar area (the *naijin*), the other over the outer space (the *gejin*) where we are seated. Several lamps and candles illuminate the rows of golden cups, *vajra*, and other liturgical instruments that rest on the altar table. All but invisible in the darkness beyond the altar is the form of the compassionate Amida Buddha, a primary Buddha who promises to welcome to paradise all who called on his name. To either side of the altar sit the temple monks, six in all, who will assist in the sūtra reading. They are waiting for the head priest.

And here he comes. He is a tall man with a commanding presence. He seats himself quickly on the elevated cushion before the *dan*, adjusts his clothing, then checks each of the altar instruments. The six monks have risen to their feet. They make several rapid half-bows toward the altar, then a single full prostration (*gotai-tōchi*) with hands, knees, and foreheads touching the floor. *Om, I prostrate myself at the feet of all the Tathagatas.* They seat themselves again and open their texts. One of the monks begins striking the large floor bell in a slowly increasing crescendo of *bongs*, ending with a pause and three measured strokes. The head priest reaches out with his wand-like *sanjō*, dipping it three times into a small altar vessel that holds purifying water. *Plink. Plink. Plink.* We are ready—the presiding priest, the attending monks, the lay worshipers, the myriad dead whose *ihai* fill the shelves that surround the room.[13]

The *Rishu-zammai-hōyō* is the primary daily ceremony of Shingon Buddhism, so designated by its greatest champion, Kōbō Daishi. Its benefits are diverse. It helps destroy bad *karma* and advances individuals toward enlightenment. It solicits material benefit. It assuages the suffering of the dead. It is a vehicle for meditation.[14] It also teaches some central Buddhist truths, for at the heart of the Rishu-zammai-hōyō is the chanting of the *Hannya-rishu-kyō*, one of the most profound of Esoteric

Buddhism's instructional sūtras. The sūtra's wisdom, and indeed its very language, is understood to have been dictated by the Great Sun Buddha. That is, it is a weaving together of the mind and voice of ultimate reality.

Prompted by the sounding of the bell the monks have begun chanting a slow melodic verse dedicating the service to Dainichi. Other introductory verses follow, each concluded by the striking of cymbals (*nyōhachi*). This is *shōmyō* we are listening to, the art of chanted Sanskrit invocations for which Shingon is famous. The tempo of the chant suddenly quickens, the tone flattens, and the male voices mesh in a single deep resonance. "Thus have I heard." The *Hannya-rishu-kyō* begins.[15]

The preamble of the sūtra relates that "at a certain time" the Cosmic Buddha took up residence in the jeweled palace of Paranirmita-vasha-vartin (J. *Take-jizai-ten*), the loftiest of the physical heavens. In that resplendent setting, before a vast body of Bodhisattvas (among them such figures as Kongōsatta, Kannon, Kokūzō, and Monju), he expounded the teaching of unrivaled merit that we are now going to hear. The first section of the sermon is startling, for in it Dainichi proclaims that the human passions—lust, covetousness, gluttony, sloth, and the rest—should not be despised or eradicated. Quite the contrary. Each passion is pure in its own "self-nature" and serves as an essential device for attaining the summit of Bodhisattvahood. "Binding one another in love [that is, in sexual relations]," for example, "being pure in itself, deserves the rank of Bodhisattva." Seventeen appetites are identified by name: "male" eroticism (lust, touching, love-bond, sovereignty), "female" eroticism (seeing, rapture, craving, pride), natural gratification (adornments, mental abundance, sunlight and moonlight, bodily ease), physical senses (sight, hearing, smell, taste). These carnal passions are transformable engines that carry one toward enlightenment. "Whoever receives and retains this teaching, and recites and contemplates it daily, shall in this present life receive the joy of innumerable blisses, pass through the lives of the sixteen Great Bodhisattvas, and attain the stages of the Buddha." The opening section ends with the Bodhisattva Kongōsatta promising that he will convey the message to all sentient beings everywhere. In demonstration of his commitment Kongōsatta smiles, strikes a pose, and expounds the essence of the teaching in a single syllable. *HŪM.*

The floor bell is sounded, and part two of the teaching is chanted (there are seventeen parts in all, each prompted by the bell). This second passage is largely an elucidation of part one. Part three addresses more explicitly the "three poisons" that inhibit human spiritual development: greed, hate, and delusion. These poisons are not to be eradicated but instead transformed with their energy kept intact. Upon hearing this challenging message, the fierce Bodhisattva Gōzanze bares his fangs, strikes a pose of conquest, and elucidates the teaching. *HŪM.*

Part four again addresses the unstained nature of existence. Though in superficial appearance all human beings are born of corruption, they remain inherently untainted like the lotus flower that generates in filth and darkness. The Bodhisattva Kannon strikes a pose and expounds the essence of this wonderful teaching. *HRĪH.* Part five explains that the sacramental power of compassion is able to bestow every physical and spiritual treasure. Bodhisattva Kokūzō smiles, places the wish-fulfilling *mani* jewel on his head, and expounds the essence of the teaching. *TRĀM.* Part nine proclaims that the three best ways to worship Dainichi Buddha are to perpetuate this teaching, labor toward personal enlightenment, and seek the salvation of all sentient beings. *OM.*

Such are the arguments of the sūtra. Essentially they are three in number. The passions of human beings are pure in their essence. Human beings are fundamentally enlightened just as they are. Human beings are living in paradise just where they are. But how can one awaken to these astonishing truths? One way is to rise early each morning and receive the sermon we have just been hearing.

> [Kongōsatta], if anyone hears this original guiding principle of wisdom, and rising early every morning recites it or listens to it, he will attain peaceful bliss in everything and a mind of rapture.[16]

The chanting slows for the Coda. *Zen-zai, zen-zai.* "So good! So good!" The monks recite Dainichi's name eleven times, asking the cosmic Buddha to assist them in the search for enlightenment. May all the heavenly and earthly guardians of the Dharma increase in power. May Kōbō Daishi increase in power. May the emperor escape harm and live a long life and the nation enjoy peace and harmony. May knowledge of the Dharma increase here and everywhere. "We wish that the vow of enlightenment never cease, guiding all beings equally toward the attainment of the ultimate world—and that we may all enter together into the land of the Buddha Dainichi, for it is His nature that we share."

The *Kōmyō Shingon*, or "Light Mantra," follows: "*Om* O unfailing Dainichi! Great *mudrā*! Turn the flame of the jeweled lotus! *Hūm.*"17 Then the Kōbō Daishi mantra: *Namu Daishi Henjō Kongō*. The monk strikes the floor bell in the same rhythmic pattern that began the service. The Rishu-zammai-hōyō is over. The six monks bow three times to the altar, then hurry off to their remaining morning duties. The head priest rises and comes forward to speak to the young man in the dark suit, then to his other guests.18

Whether one understands the import of the text or not, the time spent at the ceremony is deeply moving. The Rishu-zammai-hōyō is thought to open the soul in the same way that dawn light opens a clenched lotus flower.

Back in our room we find breakfast fully laid out and waiting. As at dinner there are two tray tables of food for each of us, although now the dishes are fewer. We begin with the *misoshiru*, a broth flavored with fermented soybean paste. Next is the *hirosu* (called *gammodoki* in Tōkyō), a mixture of *tōfu*, carrot, burdock, and seaweed made into a patty and deep fried. *Hirosu* smells and tastes like a waffle and is delicious. We proceed to the several dishes of crunchy vegetables, most of them pickled. The boiled rice, eaten plain at dinner, is dressed up a bit for breakfast. First we open a cellophane package containing small sheets of black toasted seaweed called *yakinori*. One by one these sheets are wetted in soy sauce to make them less brittle, then wrapped around a mouthful of warm rice. The combination of tastes is subtle and perfect.

As we drink more tea we mull over our plans for the day. Before leaving the temple we want to call on the mother of the head priest, a woman who has done much to make Rengejō-in a second home for us. We will sit before her on low cushions and listen to her observations about the past and the present. She is a native of Kōyasan. When she was seven she started attending a school in faraway Wakayama, walking down the Fudō-zakka trail each day to catch the train at Gokuraku-bashi Station. After spending her childhood and young womanhood at Kōyasan, she attended a Christian college in Tōkyō. There she perfected her English. When American air raids over the capital intensified, her family insisted she return to Kōyasan. She married Rengejō-in's head priest and quickly assumed responsibility for much of the practical operation of the temple. Now her eldest son is the head priest. Little about the social, liturgical, and political life of Kōyasan seems to have escaped her.

We also hope to meet with her son, although that may take some arranging. His days are packed with responsibilities: ritual worship, religious study, administrative duties, preparing lectures, giving instruction to his monks. Additionally, he has the duties of a husband and father. Even as we linger here over our breakfast tea he is performing a full program of morning obligations. Following the six-o'clock Rishu-zammai-hōyō service he enters the nearby chapel of Fudō Myō-ō to chant the *Kannon sūtra*. He then goes to the *jibutsu-dō*, the private sanctuary in the main hall, where he recites a succession of *darani* before the *ihai* of the previous abbots of the temple, now including his father. He asks these holy men for help in his work as a priest. While there he also prays to Kōbō Daishi, to the temple protectress Benzaiten, and to Aizen Myō-ō. Finally he offers prayers of supplication to the gods of fire and water in the kitchen. Only then does his regular work day begin, a day spent much like that of any other busy professional.[19] In the evening, before having his dinner, he sits for forty minutes in a private meditation on the Sanskrit seed syllable *A* (the *A-ji-kan* meditation). During this sitting he visualizes the primordial *A*, the sound of which is the luminous Dainichi of the Womb Realm. At the climax of the meditation he imagines Dainichi's sacred light entering his mouth, flowing into every cell of his body, and radiating outward through each pore of the skin. For that instant the priest becomes the Buddha. Afterward, he vows to employ the discovered indwelling Buddha Nature in every aspect of his life.

Once we have called on both the head priest and his mother, we are going to make a visit to Kōyasan's oldest temple, Ryūkō-in, located near the Great Stūpa and just a ten minute walk from Rengejō-in. Ryūkō-in is famous for having been Kōbō Daishi's Kōyasan residence. It is where he lived his final years and where he "died."

At present, however, we are still at our breakfast, still basking in the affirmative glow of the morning Rishu-zammai-hōyō service. Are you going to eat the rest of your *yakinori*? Would you like another cup of tea? So good. *HŪM*.

CHAPTER THREE

THE LIFE AND LEGEND
OF KŌBŌ DAISHI (KŪKAI)

The name Ryūkō-in means "Temple of the Dragon Light." This is not the temple's original name, but one adopted in the sixteenth century when a monk observed a luminous dragon rising skyward from out of the temple pond. Prior to that event the temple was known simply as Chū-in, or "Middle Temple," a reference to its physical location at the center of the earliest residence halls of Kōyasan.[1]

We are now at Ryūkō-in, standing in a small chamber known as the *Kōbō Daishi go-nyūjō-no-ma*, or "Honorable Room of Kōbō Daishi's Entrance into Continuous Meditation."[2] The room is dimly lit, with no furnishing other than a single low table with bell, book, and incense bowl. The table faces a shrine alcove protected by closed lattice doors. On the shrine shelf sits a small dark figure enclosed in protective glass. The light is much too dim for us to make out any sculpted detail, but we know already that the figure is Miroku Bosatsu, the Buddha of the

Future.[3] Kōbō Daishi sat before this carving during his final hours, or so it is believed.

Two lamps hang in front of the shrine. The lamp at the right supports a flame that reportedly has burned without interruption since the time of Kōbō Daishi's departure, a stretch of more than eleven and a half centuries. The lamp's oil level is checked twice daily, once in the morning and once in the evening.

Death, or what most people would have called death, came to Kōbō Daishi at four a.m. on March 21, 835. The texts tell us that seven days earlier, on March 15, he had given a final message to his disciples and then retired to this room. Here he seated himself before Miroku Bosatsu. Outside the room, in the next apartment, his anxious disciples began to recite the Miroku mantra. Word spread to the lower villages that the Master, who had been ill for some time, was now certainly dying. Over the next several days hundreds climbed the mountain to stand vigil outside in the courtyard. Early in the morning of March 21 the watching disciples noted that the Master's eyes had closed, but beyond that there was no discernible change. He continued to sit firmly upright. Seven agonizing days passed with the Master's position unchanged. At that point it was agreed a memorial service should be held. After seven more days a second memorial service was held, and another service seven days after that. But no formal funeral ceremony was conducted, for in all respects the Master had the appearance of continuing his deep meditation.

On the forty-ninth day six of the disciples entered the room (or perhaps the burial cave at Okunoin; the sources are ambiguous) to prepare the body for interment. When they touched the body they discovered the skin was still warm and moist. They noted also that Odaishi-sama's hair and beard had continued to grow. They shaved his head and beard, then proceeded with preparations for a funeral ceremony, which was held on the fiftieth day, May 10, at four p.m. Later that evening (or perhaps earlier; again the sources are ambiguous) the disciples lifted the platform on which the Master sat, placed the platform on a litter, and solemnly carried the Master to his predetermined place of burial near the bank of the Tamagawa at the eastern end of the valley. Upon returning to the room at Chū-in they decided not to extinguish the lamp that was burning there, but to refill it with oil.

The chamber also is called the *Yōgō-no-ma*, or "Room of the Turning Shadow," because of occasional reports of Kōbō Daishi's shadowy appearances here. Such appearances seem to have been especially frequent in the eleventh century when large numbers of the aristocracy and nobility made pilgrimages to Kōyasan, many of them staying at this temple. At the moment, we have no sense of anything apparitional taking place, but we do have a fresh awareness of the importance of Kōbō Daishi's remarkable life. That awareness is a constant on the mountain.

From Ryūkō-in's front porch we again look out into the bright fall sunlight. Directly ahead of us here, observed through the branches of giant cedars, rises the massive vermillion and white form of the Great Stūpa. The Great Stūpa is the mountain's single most dramatic physical expression of Kōbō Daishi's religious vision. To the right of the Daitō is the low dark Miedō, where Kōbō Daishi's sacred portrait is enshrined (the Miedō too is a candidate for the physical location of Kōbō Daishi's Kōyasan residence). Several hundred meters to the left, hidden from us by a wall of trees, is the Dai Kōdō (Great Lecture Hall), another major "church" where Kōbō Daishi is enshrined.

In time we will visit all these places, but for now we will proceed with Kōbō Daishi's personal history. It is a life that visitors to Kōyasan cannot escape. Cherished details are recounted in brochures, in temple murals, in narrative scrolls, in cartoon books, in videos, in movies, in ceremonial parades, in sermons. Much of the life is fully documented history. Much is pious legend. Usually, little attempt is made to separate the factual from the legendary, for both are essential.[4]

THE EARLY YEARS

Kōbō Daishi was born to Lady Tamayori and Saeki Tagimi on the island of Shikoku in 774. The precise day of birth is unknown, but later tradition selects June 15 as probable, for on that day in 774 the sixth of the eight Shingon patriarchs, Amoghavajra, died in China. The matching of dates lends credence to the notion that Kōbō Daishi was Amoghavajra's reincarnation. As a small boy he was called Mao ("True Fish") and, as an endearment, Tōtomono ("Precious Child").[5] Since for most of his adult life he was known by his ordination name, Kūkai, we will use that name in this review of the life.

The site of Kūkai's boyhood home is within the grounds of Zentsū-ji, an expansive Shingon temple located in Zentsūji city in northeastern Shikoku. Today Zentsū-ji is designated temple number seventy-five on the island's famed eighty-eight-temple pilgrimage, and is the largest and busiest temple on the circuit. Local faithful claim Kūkai himself founded Zentsū-ji in 807 shortly after his return from China, naming it in honor of his father (whose Buddhist name was Zentsū). The priests of Zentsū-ji refer to their temple as Japan's first Shingon institution.

At the center of Zentsū-ji's western court is a large hall built near the presumed site of the birth. This hall, known as the Miedō, or "Portrait Hall," enshrines a "self-portrait" said to have been painted by Kūkai as a keepsake for his parents prior to his voyage to China. The Miedō is a primary goal of pilgrims. Beneath its floor is a circular tunnel through which visitors walk in total darkness, moving past unseen paintings of sacred images until reaching an illuminated shrine directly beneath the birthplace. This shrine, described as a *Gokuraku Jōdo*, or Buddhist paradise, represents the light of deliverance that overcomes spiritual darkness. On the shrine altar sits a hidden Dainichi, the cosmic sun of the Shingon faith, surrounded by visible deities of both the Womb Realm and the Diamond Realm mandalas.

Not far from the Miedō is a small pond said to have been used by young Kūkai as a mirror when he painted the self-portrait. At the pond's center now stands a statue of Kūkai dressed as a pilgrim ascetic, a form known as *Shugyō Daishi*. Seated in front of the Shugyō Daishi is a small statue of Miroku, the Buddha of the Future, for whom Kūkai becomes a special harbinger. Stone images of Kūkai's parents are set on pedestals at either side of the pond—the father on the left, Lady Tamayori on the right. This couple had several other children, although the precise number is uncertain. We know definitely of a younger brother, Shinga (801–879), who became one of Kūkai's disciples. There also is evidence of a sister and at least one older brother.

Not much is known factually about Kūkai's childhood, but tradition proposes several events that convey his precocity in religious matters. At the age of three he is said to have fashioned a clay figure of the Buddha, then knelt before it while the Four Heavenly Kings, the *Shitennō*, surrounded him like protecting angels. These same Four Kings also stood guard over the youthful Shākyamuni.

A more audacious childhood event is said to have taken place on the highest of the three steep mountains that rise with increasing elevation behind Zentsū-ji. According to the story, at age seven Kūkai impulsively walked to the highest cliff edge, turned his face toward India, and cried out to the Buddha:

> *In order to save many people I make a vow to devote my life to the pursuit of Buddhahood! If I am not capable of fulfilling this vow, then I do not deserve my existence!*

With this challenge he cast himself over the precipice.

The event is featured in nearly all pictorial accounts of Kūkai's life. As the child plummets downward through space, his hands pressed together in *gasshō*, his eyes clenched in prayer, up from the bottom of the frame floats Shākyamuni (or in some cases the Bodhisattva Kannon). In the next instant the Buddha will catch the falling child and carry him to safety, preserving him for a life of service to the Dharma. A refinement of the story proposes that during their brief aerial embrace Shākyamuni preached to the child the key Shingon principle of *sokushin jōbutsu*, the attainment of Buddhahood with one's present body. The precipice described in the story is popularly known as the Shashin-ga-take, or Cliff of Jumping, and may be reached by climbing a well-marked trail. The temple at the foot of the mountain, number seventy-three on the Shikoku pilgrimage, is called Shusshaka-ji, "Temple of Shākyamuni's Appearance."[6]

When Kūkai was fifteen his maternal uncle, Atō Ōtari, a tutor to the emperor's eldest son, took him from the family home on Shikoku to Nagaoka-kyō, the improvised new national capital where the emperor recently had brought his court. There, under the uncle's direction, Kūkai intensified his study of Chinese language and literature. At eighteen he entered the national college in the old capital of Heijō-kyō (today's Nara), where in the company of other young men of good birth he studied the standard Confucian curriculum designed for future employees in the government bureaucracy, the career proposed by his family. By his own testimony Kūkai was a diligent student. Nevertheless, after as period of schooling that may have been as long as two years or as short as a few months, he left Heijō-kyō.

Kūkai later described his departure as being precipitated by a Buddhist monk's showing him a scripture called *Kokūzō-gumonji-no-hō*.[7] "In that work," writes Kūkai, "it is stated that if one recites the mantra one million times according to the proper method, one will be able to memorize passages and understand the meaning of any scripture." Kūkai retreated to a mountaintop (Mt. Tairyū in Shikoku) and there performed the demanding *gumonji-hō* ritual. Each day the purification, the offerings, the incantation, the visualization, the sought-for fusion with the deity Kokūzō. Each day and each night for fifty or one hundred consecutive days, his mind, spirit, and body strained to make the infinite journey. The effort was rewarded. On one occasion Kokūzō's sword appeared to fly at him at the climax of his meditation. At Cape Muroto, on Shikoku's eastern shore, as he recited the mantra while facing the open sea, the star Venus, Buddhism's celestial image of Kokūzō Bodhisattva, rushed at him like an arrow and entered his mouth. "From that time on," he writes, "I despised fame and wealth and longed for a life in the midst of nature."[8]

At this period in Japan a young man who wished to pursue the Buddhist priesthood was expected to enter a government monastery, study the approved Buddhist curriculum there, and pass qualifying examinations administered by government-appointed monastic officials. Kūkai chose a different course. The general belief is that shortly after leaving college he became a lay monk (a *shidosō*) attached to an unaffiliated, outlaw mountain temple located in the mountainous area of Yoshino-Tenkawa just west of Kōyasan. There he embraced such practices as meditating in the wilderness for long stretches of time, punctuated by periods of wandering in rags through rural villages with a begging bowl. His parents had counted on his restoring the family's name and fortune. Instead young Kūkai seemed bent on a life of shameful eccentricity.

The most detailed information we have about Kūkai's behavior during the period is found in his first major literary production (probably completed when he was twenty-four), an intense, showy, semi-fictional *apologia* entitled *Sangō shiki*, or "Indications of the Goals of the Three Teachings."[9] Composed in Chinese, the *Sangō shiki* is the length of a short novel, which it somewhat resembles. In it Kūkai both explains and proclaims his sudden decision to reject Confucianism and embrace Buddhism. He also rejects Taoism, a third option. "Can anyone now break my determination? No, just as there is no one who can stop the wind" (*MW*, 102). The intended audience for the document seems to have included his family and teachers.

Kūkai's biographers generally agree that the central character of the *Sangō shiki*, an itinerant Buddhist monk named Kamei-kotsuji, is in good part a self-portrait. Like Kūkai, Kamei, whose name means "anonymous beggar," was born on Shikoku at a place famous for its camphor trees. The beggar is described as laughably haggard and unkempt, a man thoroughly despised by the citizens of the secular world. "If by chance he entered the market place, people showered him with pieces of tile and pebbles; if he passed a harbor, people cast horse's dung upon him." Such rejection makes it easier for Kamei to live a life aloof from the destructive appetites that the world celebrates. Even the problem of celibacy, a troubling matter for him, is resolved.[10] "Once he was attracted by a beautiful girl, Undō, and his determination was somewhat relaxed, but on meeting the nun Kobe he was encouraged and his loathing for the world was intensified" (*MW*, 121).

Kamei has one close friend with whom he shares his aspirations. He also has a spiritual sponsor. But intimacy with nature when isolated in the mountains is what he loves most:

> . . . brushing aside the snow to sleep, using his arms for a pillow. The blue sky was the ceiling of his hut and the clouds hanging over the mountains were his curtains; he did not need to worry about where he lived or where he slept. . . . [He was] quite satisfied with what was given him, like a bird that perches on a single branch, or like the one who subsisted on half a grain a day.[11]

In the primary discourse of the book Kamei becomes involved in a debate with two learned opponents. One is a self-assured Confucianist, the other a devotee of Taoism. The Confucianist recommends the career enjoyed by a government official, which includes a handsome wife, possessions, marvelous dinner parties that go on for days, and "a beautiful posthumous name." The Taoist demurs, pointing out that any happiness gained from wealth and position is evanescent, as "unstable as floating clouds." A cure for this evanescence can be found in secret Taoist incantations and elixirs. "When you realize the Way and master this art, your aged body and gray hair will be rejuvenated and life prolonged." You will enjoy the eternal privileges of the gods (*MW*, 112, 118–20).

Kamei's rebuttal to both men is unequivocal. Confucianism is no more than a "dusty breeze of the secular world" and Taoism but "a petty seeking for longevity." The storm of impermanence overlooks no one. "No matter how much of the elixir of life one may drink, nor how deeply one may inhale the exquisite incense that recalls the departed soul, one cannot prolong one's life even for a second" (*MW*, 132). The only way to escape from the endless cycle of birth and death and rebirth is to pursue the Self beyond all individual selves, the grand Dharmakāya, the final unchanging Reality that waits for us. The *Sangō shiki* ends with these lines of poetry that declare Kamei's (and Kūkai's) liberation.

> Eternity, Bliss, the Self, and Purity are the summits on which
>   we ultimately belong.
> I know the fetters that bind me in the triple world;
> Why should I not give up the thought of serving the court?
> (*MW*, 139)

Kūkai joined the Buddhist priesthood in two formal stages. The initial ceremony, the head shaving, took place at Makino'o-san-ji temple in the Izumi mountains not far from where the Kōyasan Express passes through. Kūkai may have been as young as twenty at this time, or as old as twenty-four. The general assumption is that his primary mentor, Abbot Gonzō of Daian-ji, presided. As part of the ceremony the name Mao was changed to Kūkai. *Kū* meant "sky." *Kai* meant "sea." Together the two *kanji* may have signified something like "the ocean of emptiness," a profound Buddhist concept. The character for *kū* probably was derived from Kokūzō, Kūkai's sponsoring Buddhist deity. Kokūzō's wisdom was as large as the sky—that is, was infinite.

Kūkai's final initiation into the priesthood, with its five additional precepts, likely occurred on April 7, 804, at famed Tōdai-ji monastery in Nara.[12] Just one month after this event he began his journey to China. The prospect of participating in this voyage may have prompted him to formalize his priestly credentials.

For a full decade Kūkai had been reading the massive body of Buddhist sūtras and commentaries that the repositories of the Nara temples made available to him. He had examined closely the teachings of all six Buddhist schools then active in Japan, but all seemed incomplete. Tradition tells us that at one point he secluded himself for twenty days in the Great Hall at Tōdai-ji, praying to its colossal bronze image of the Great Sun Buddha. "Show me the true teaching," he begged. Exhausted from praying, he slept, and in a dream met a man who told him of a scripture called the *Dainichi-kyō*, or "Great Sun Sūtra" (Sk. *Mahāvairocana-sūtra*). A full copy of this sūtra, the man said, could be found in the Eastern Pagoda of the Kume temple, just one day's journey south from Tōdai-ji. Kūkai went at once to Kume-dera where he noticed a suspicious irregularity in the central pillar of its Eastern Stūpa. Cutting open the spot he discovered the seven volumes of the *Dainichi-kyō*.

How the *Dainichi-kyō* found its way to Japan is explained by another legend. Zenmui (Sk. Subhākarasimha, 637–735), a famous Indian Buddhist missionary to China who translated the *Dainichi-kyō* into Chinese, is said to have journeyed to Japan in the hope of spreading esoteric Buddhism there. When he discovered the Japanese were not yet ready for such a difficult teaching, Zenmui built a stūpa, deposited a copy of the *Dainichi-kyō* in one of its pillars, and returned to China. His hope was that some future Japanese spiritual genius would develop a craving for the text and be led to its hiding place.[13]

Kūkai himself writes nothing about where or how he first obtained a copy of the *Dainichi-kyō*. But he did obtain a copy, and his response upon first reading it was to call it the "Source" he had been searching for. However, the text presented difficulties. "I started reading [the *Dainichi-kyō*] only to find that I was unable to understand it; I wished to visit China" (*MW*, 27). Most especially he wished to visit China's capital of Ch'ang-an, then the center of a flowering of Esoteric Buddhism. In Ch'ang-an he hoped to find an esoteric master who could give him the necessary oral instruction on the *Dainichi-kyō* and introduce him as well to other vital esoteric texts.

So Kūkai applied to Emperor Kammu for permission to study in China, very likely specifying the *Dainichi-kyō* as his primary object of interest. Permission was granted, and the length of time he would be abroad fixed at twenty years. Twenty years would give Kūkai adequate time to absorb what the Chinese had to offer, with enough life expectancy left for him to return to Japan and pass on what he had learned. The Japanese government would finance the endeavor. That Kūkai was able to win such an appointment argues that he was by then recognized as a scholar of more than ordinary talent. Abbot Gonzō may have spoken in his behalf. Gonzō would have known better than anyone else Kūkai's mastery of Buddhist literature and skill with the Chinese language.[14] Perhaps Kūkai's uncle, as the crown prince's tutor, asked the prince to give support to the application. A third possibility is that Fujiwara Kadonomaro, the Japanese envoy who was to lead the mission to China, learned of Kūkai's linguistic abilities and desired his help. Additionally, Kūkai's special interest in *mikkyō* (Esoteric Buddhism) may have made him particularly attractive to the imperial court, for rumors were then circulating that certain esoteric Buddhist rituals carried a magical potency far greater than anything then practiced in Japan.

Another Buddhist priest-scholar also gained permission to join the journey to China. Saichō, then thirty-seven years old, was by far the most influential religious leader in Japan's new capital of Heian-kyō (Kyōto). Saichō did not plan to go to the Chinese interior capital of Ch'ang-an, however, but to the more coastal Mt. T'ien-t'ai, the primary center of Tendai Buddhism. There he hoped to study with some Chinese Buddhist scholars and obtain more accurate Tendai texts than those he presently possessed. Saichō would be in China for only a short time (eight and one-half months). His hope was that upon his return Tendai would be recognized as a distinct Buddhist sect and made the semiofficial Buddhist teaching of the imperial court.

Kūkai likely knew a good deal about Saichō. Saichō probably knew little or nothing about Kūkai, although the two may have met briefly while they were waiting to sail from Kyūshū. The two would not meet at sea or in China. In the years after China, however, their careers would come into strong conjunction and conflict.

In May 804 Kūkai's ship left Naniwa (today's Ōsaka) for a port in Kyūshū. Two months after that it sailed out into the East China Sea in the company of three other government ships. Kūkai's ship was designated ship number one, for it carried envoy Kadonomaro, the head of the Japanese mission to China. The rest of the ranking officials, along with Saichō, were in the second ship. The third ship carried scribes, accountants, and secretaries. The fourth ship's passengers included translators, shipwrights, and dock hands.[15] This dividing up of skills suggests that those in command assumed the four vessels somehow would manage to sail together and reach their destination together, a highly erroneous assumption.

TO CHINA'S CH'ANG-AN AND HUI-KUO

In earlier times the fragile Japanese ships would have headed directly across the Straits of Tsushima to Korea, a distance of around two hundred kilometers, and then worked their way along the Korean coast until they reached China. But Korean hostility now mandated a direct sail to China across eight hundred kilometers of open sea. The Japanese captains knew little of the seasonal winds they would encounter, lacked adequate maps, and were without compasses. Of the eleven missions that sailed for China during the period only one returned home without loss to its crew or cargo.[16]

Kūkai's own particular mission met with about average success. During the first day out (July 9, 804) the four ships lost sight of one another. Ship number one, Kūkai's, was overtaken by a storm and blown far south of its intended landfall near the mouth of the Yangtze, finally reaching shore only after drifting for nearly a month. The second ship, the one carrying Saichō, also was caught in storms, and remained at sea some twenty days longer than Kūkai's. Quite fortuitously, it eventually landed at Ning-po, close to Saichō's ultimate destination. The third ship, badly damaged at sea, turned back to Japan for repair, only to be wrecked the following year. The fourth ship disappeared in the East China Sea with but one survivor to tell the tale.

Kūkai's own account of the passage to China speaks of "seething waves" that "clashed against the Milky Way" and of the terrors of being driven off course.[17] Tradition relates that he prayed to the Buddha to quell the storm, and immediately the merciful Kannon Bodhisattva appeared over the waves, mildly gesturing the wind and ocean to calm. A painted representation of this Kannon, now in the possession of Kōyasan's Ryūkō-in, is one of the masterpieces of twelfth-century Japanese art. Another account says that the saving deity was the Nyoirin Kannon and that Kūkai captured its image by scratching on a piece of wood with his fingernails.[18]

When Kūkai's ship finally drifted ashore in China's Fukien province, the arrival was treated with great suspicion, for the provincial governor had never before encountered a Japanese delegation.[19] An elegant letter written by Kūkai to the governor, however, gained envoy Kadonomaro and his party a proper reception. With a second letter Kūkai obtained permission to proceed independently on the long journey to the inland capital, Ch'ang-an. Ch'ang-an, the eastern terminus of the Silk Road, was then the most cosmopolitan, as well as the most populous, city in the world, the crown jewel of T'ang civilization.[20]

Kūkai was fully equipped to appreciate Ch'ang-an's dazzling richness, but from the start his overriding interest was in its status as a center of Buddhist study and religious practice. For decades now the Chinese imperial court had supported a large sūtra translating and copying institution, with as many as one thousand specialists employed at one time. The city also was a bazaar of religious diversity, with ninety-one Buddhist temples of various persuasions, sixteen Taoist temples, at least three "foreign" churches (Nestorian Christian, Zoroastrian, and Manichaean). There was an active representation of the new Islamic religion, and very possibly a Jewish synagogue.[21] In addition, the city was China's greatest Confucianist center.

The most dynamic religious ideology by far was Esoteric Buddhism, first introduced to China early in the eighth century and now spreading widely and fashionably among members of the court. For Kūkai this was holy ground. Ch'ang-an had been the favorite residence of Shingon patriarch Zenmui. Zenmui's disciple I'hsing (J. Ichigyō; 683–727), author of an essential commentary on the *Dainichi-kyō*, also had lived and died in Ch'ang-an. The Indian Brahmin Vajrabodhi (J. Kongōchi; 671–741), eminent translator and ritualist, and Shingon's Fifth Patriarch, had lived here. Here too had resided Amoghavajra (Ch. Pu-k'ung; J. Fukūkongō; 705–74), who in middle life had returned to southern Asia to gather and bring back five hundred volumes of Sanskrit texts. Amoghavajra had instructed three Chinese emperors in the esoteric faith, initiated scores of court officials, and built at Mount Wu-t'ai China's single most famous Buddhist temple. When he died, on June 15, 774, the T'ang emperor declared three days of mourning for his court. It was this Amoghavajra, the official Sixth Shingon Patriarch, whose death date later became the agreed-upon birth date for Kōbō Daishi.

These were the dead. Many eminent masters were still living, foremost among them Amoghavajra's successor, a Chinese priest named Hui-kuo (J. Keika; 746–805). Like Amoghavajra, Hui-kuo had been a powerful influence on the court and a magnet for disciples from China and elsewhere. Unfortunately, by the time Kūkai was able to arrange a meeting with him, after five months in the capital, Hui-kuo was terminally ill. In fact he already had made his formal last testament to his followers.

The first meeting between the two took place in May 805. Here is Kūkai's account as expressed in a later report to the Japanese emperor:

> I called on the abbot [at Ch'ing-lung Temple] in the company of five or six monks from the Hsi-ming Temple. As soon as he saw me he smiled with pleasure and joyfully said, "I knew that you would come! I have waited for such a long time. What pleasure it gives me to look upon you today at last! My life is drawing to an end, and until you came there was no one to whom I could transmit the teachings. Go without delay to the altar of *abhisheka* with incense and a flower." I returned to the temple where I had been staying and got the things which were necessary for the ceremony. (*MW*, 147)

By early June, having prepared the necessary offerings and ritual instruments, Kūkai returned to Hui-kuo for the administration of the *abhisheka* (J. *kanjō*). As a key part of the ritual Kūkai, while blindfolded, was required to throw a flower onto the sacred Taizō-kai (Womb Realm) mandala. It was this mandala that had been described in the *Dainichi-kyō*. Kūkai's flower fell directly on the image of Dainichi Nyorai, the mandala's central figure. "It is wonderful," remarked the admiring Hui-kuo. Kūkai was then instructed in other rituals and meditations relating to this mandala of compassion.

By July Kūkai was ready to be initiated into the second of the two Esoteric companion mandalas, the Kongō-kai (Diamond Realm) mandala, whose central figure was Dainichi as the Buddha of Imperishable

Wisdom. Again Kūkai was blindfolded and instructed to throw the flower. To Hui-kuo's expressed amazement the flower once more fell upon Dainichi Nyorai.

In August, in the climactic initiation ritual, Kūkai was admitted to the *denpō-kanjō*, the ceremony designed to consecrate him for the Transmission of the Dharma. A third time he was blindfolded and a third time the flower fell upon Dainichi. Hui-kuo bestowed on him an epithet that conveyed this thrice-proven link with the Great Sun Buddha: *Henjō kongō*. Thus, Kūkai became an inheritor and master of Esoteric Buddhism.[22]

In demonstration of his gratitude Kūkai gave a dinner for five hundred priests, including some who directly served the T'ang emperor. More feverish training and study followed, for Hui-kuo's health continued to worsen. Artists were summoned to produce copies of the complex mandalas. More than twenty scribes were set to copying the basic Esoteric scriptures and their commentaries. The essential ceremonial instruments were collected.

With death but a few days away, Hui-ku gave Kūkai a final instruction (here as recorded by Kūkai):

When you arrived I feared I did not have enough time left to teach you everything, but now I have completed teaching you, and the work of copying the sūtras and making the images has also been finished. Hasten back to your country, offer these things to the court, and spread the teachings throughout your country to increase the happiness of the people. . . . In that way you will return thanks to the Buddha and to your teacher. That is also the way to show your devotion to your country and to your family. My disciple I-ming will carry on the teachings here. Your task is to transmit them to the Eastern Land. Do your best! Do your best! (*MW*, 149)

Hui-kuo's death came just seven months after his first meeting with Kūkai. "Once he saw me, he loved me like a son," Hui-kuo had said of his own master. Toward Kūkai he seems to have expressed a similar love. "I conferred on him mystic rituals and mudrās of both mandalas," Hui-kuo remarked. "He received them in Chinese as well as in Sanskrit without fault, just as water is poured from one jar to another."[23] Kūkai tells us that immediately after his teacher's death he went into the temple to meditate. There in the still sanctuary, with a full winter moon shining outside, the spirit of Hui-kuo appeared and spoke to him: "You and I have long been pledged to propagate the Esoteric Buddhist teachings. If I am reborn in Japan, this time I shall be your disciple" (MW, 149). When Hui-kuo's disciples gathered to decide who should compose an account of the master's life and write a formal epigraph for his monument, they selected Kūkai, a foreigner whom they had known for only a few months. "With heavy hearts we bury a jewel," Kūkai wrote. "With stricken souls we burn a magic herb. We close the doors of death forever."[24]

Stories abound concerning Kūkai's remarkable popularity in Ch'ang-an.[25] Upon giving Kūkai a string of prayer beads as a farewell gift, the eyes of the Chinese emperor reportedly fill with tears: "My intention was that you should stay here and be my teacher. But I hear your [newly enthroned] Emperor Heizei is anxiously awaiting your return, so I shall not urge you to stay."[26] The Chinese emperor also is reported to have asked Kūkai to inscribe the reception hall at the imperial palace, and to have awarded him the title of Master of the Five Skills in Calligraphy upon seeing the result.[27] Adoring Chinese are described as clinging to Kūkai's sleeve as he prepared to depart for Japan, begging him to remain with them.[28]

An especially cherished legend says that immediately before sailing (in the late summer of 806) Kūkai stood on the Chinese shore, looked in the direction of Japan, and hurled skyward a three-pronged vajra (J. sanko). As the golden instrument disappeared from view Kūkai prayed, "Go before me [to my native land] and find the appropriate place for Esoteric Buddhism."[29]

CONQUEST OF THE JAPANESE CAPITAL

Tradition tells of another great storm on the return voyage, with Kūkai again saving the ship and its passengers through intercessory prayers. On this occasion his appeal was addressed to the previously mentioned image of the "Wave-Cutting" Fudō Myō-ō that he had carved in China from a piece of wood given him by Hui-kuo. As Kūkai prayed, an apparition of the angry deity was observed walking out among the waves, hacking them down with a sword.

Soon after landing on the southern Japanese island of Kyūshū (in October 806) Kūkai sent a report of his China experience to the newly installed Emperor Heizei. This famous "memorial" opens with a brief self-introduction followed immediately by an account of his meeting with Hui-kuo. Kūkai knew his unexpected early return to Japan was in violation of instructions, but what he brought back with him surely would amaze and delight the Emperor.

> This master [Hui-kuo] granted me the privilege of receiving the Esoteric Buddhist precepts and permitted me to enter the altar of *abhisheka*. Three times I was bathed in the *abhisheka* in order to receive the mantras and once to inherit the mastership. . . . I was fortunate enough, thanks to the compassion of the great master . . . to learn the great twofold Dharma [the Womb and the Diamond Realms] and the yogic practices which use various sacred objects of concentration. This Dharma is the gist of the Buddhas and the quickest path by which to attain enlightenment. This teaching is as useful to the nation as walls are to a city, and as fertile soil is to the people. . . . In India the Tripitaka Master Subhākarasimha [that is, Zenmui] renounced his throne in order to practice it; in China the Emperor Hsüan-tsung forgot the savor of other things in the excess of his appreciation and admiration for it. . . . The Exoteric teachings were overwhelmed and paralyzed by [the Esoteric teachings], being as imperfect as a pearl of which one half is missing. (*MW*, 141)

Following this declaration of success Kūkai acknowledges the seriousness of his failure to meet the terms of his commission to China.

> Though I, Kūkai, may deserve to be punished by death because I did not arrive [at the appointed time], yet I am secretly delighted with my good luck that I am alive and that I have imported the Dharma that is difficult to obtain. I can hardly

bear the feelings of fear and joy which alternate in my heart.
(*MW*, 142)

As interpreted by Professor Hakeda, Kūkai's expression of anxiety is
not mere epistolary convention. He had reason to tremble.[30]

Following the introductory portion of the "Memorial" ("Memorial
Presenting a List of Newly Imported Sūtras and Other Items"), Kūkai
launches into an itemization of the material he had obtained. Of newly
translated sūtras he names one hundred forty-two separate documents; of
works in Sanskrit, forty-two titles; of treatises and commentaries, thirty-
two works. Of Buddhist icons he lists five mandalas and five portraits; of
ritual instruments, eighteen items; of relics from India and elsewhere,
thirteen items (including eighty grains of Shākyamuni's remains). And so
on. Along with these lists Kūkai provides a running history of Esoteric
Buddhism, an account of his own experience in China, and a commentary on the significance of the items obtained. Nearly every item is
deemed either important or essential. The documents in Sanskrit, for
example, contain sacred sounds (*shingon*) that are valid only when spoken
in that tongue. The mandalas are vital because the deeper elements of the
secret teaching cannot be expressed in writing. The various *vajra* are precious "gates" through which one may approach the Buddha's wisdom
(*MW*, 145, 146).

Kūkai's unabashed claim is that he has returned from China with the
keys to individual enlightenment and to the peace and happiness of the
nation. The emperor and court need only extend an invitation and he
will rush to Heian-kyō with his treasures. But weeks pass without a reply.
Then months. The best evidence suggests that it was three years before
Kūkai was summoned to the Japanese capital.

One biographer proposes that Kūkai's status at this time, in the eyes
of the court at least, was essentially that of a criminal. Another commentator suggests that it was the emperor's (and the court's) relationship with
Saichō, the Tendai priest who traveled to China with Kūkai, that kept
Kūkai at a distance. Emperor Kammu had instructed Saichō to "perfect
[his] understanding of Tendai and all the other schools, and come back
[from China] to establish the best form of Buddhism for this country."[31]
Saichō had returned, as planned, after less than a year, bringing with him

some 460 volumes of sacred texts of various schools, including Tendai, Pure Land, Zen, and Precept. While in China Saichō also had sought out an esoteric master and furthered his knowledge of esoteric ritual and doctrine. Additionally, he had received esoteric initiations into the Diamond Realm and Womb Realm mandalas, just as Kūkai had (although the exact nature of the rituals is unclear). Only the final *denpō-kanjō* ("consecration for the Transmission of the Dharma") had been omitted. The emperor and court promptly awarded Saichō's Tendai School status as an independent Buddhist teaching with its headquarters on Mt. Hiei, just a short distance to the northeast of Heian-kyō. Additionally, they recognized Esoteric Buddhism as being an integral part of the Tendai curriculum. In fact, Kammu was so satisfied with Saichō's mastery of the glamorous new esoteric faith that he directed him to perform an esoteric initiation for the leading clergy of the nation's major temples (*MW*, 36–37). Thus, while Kūkai was still in China receiving instructions from Hui-kuo, Saichō already was launching the esoteric revolution in Japan.[32]

Historians are uncertain how Kūkai occupied himself during his three years of virtual exile. There is some evidence that he spent a good part of the period in remote Kyūshū, living at Dazaifu's Kanzeon-ji temple.[33] Some accounts have him visiting the capital briefly, in 807, to submit through an intermediary the sūtras and commentaries he had brought from China. Another story has him re-visiting Kume-dera, the temple where he first found the baffling *Dainichi-kyō*. Kūkai is described as preaching to the monks there, telling them of the wisdom he had gained in China. Some enthusiasts compare this sermon with Shākya-muni's inaugural sermon in the deer park at Isipatana. Several accounts have Kūkai staying for a time (perhaps as much as two years) at Makino'o-san-ji in Izumi Province, the temple where he was tonsured. Many stories describe him traveling extensively about the land, performing miracles, founding temples, and depositing at various sites sacred objects brought back from China.

If Kūkai did in fact visit Kume-dera or Makino'o-san-ji, then he almost certainly would have been reunited with Gonzō, his early mentor, who was still a major figure in the Buddhist circles of Nara. One can imagine Gonzō's excitement upon learning of Kūkai's discoveries. In return Kūkai would have learned from Gonzō that the Nara circle was watching Saichō's rise in Heian-kyō with trepidation, for Saichō was openly declaring his newly established Tendai sect to be superior to all six of the Nara schools, condemning them as too theoretical and narrow. Kūkai also would have learned that Saichō was working to harmonize Tendai beliefs with the newly acquired Esoteric thought. Such information could only have caused Kūkai anguish.

On the plus side, Kūkai's long exile provided him with invaluable time for reflection and preparation. Hui-kuo may have been a profound teacher and unifier, but unlike his predecessors in the Esoteric patriarchal succession he had left nothing in writing. Thus, it fell to Kūkai to fully systematize the doctrine and practice that would become known as Shingon. When the call finally came from the capital, Kūkai was ready.

Around the middle of 809 Kūkai received an order from the imperial court to take up residence at Takaosan-ji in the mountains just beyond the northwestern suburbs of the capital. Kūkai must have been delighted. The landscape surrounding the temple was beautiful. The imperial palace was only ten kilometers from the front gate. And Takaosan-ji already had a little of the esoteric flavor, for it was here that Saichō had performed the *abhisheka* ritual at the direction of Emperor Kammu.

What brought Kūkai this assignment is not entirely clear. His uncle Atō Ōtari would not have been of any help, for Atō's former royal pupil, Prince Iyo, recently had been placed in prison under suspicion of rebellion and forced to commit suicide. Atō himself had fled to Shikoku. Another imperial event may have assisted Kūkai, however. Emperor Heizei, after only three years on the throne, had abdicated in favor of his twenty-four-year-old younger brother, Saga. Saga was an artistically talented young man whose greatest passions were Chinese classical literature, T'ang poetry, and Chinese calligraphy. He was so accomplished in the last of these that Chinese envoys were said to raise his handwritten documents to their brows and beg permission to carry samples back to China.[34] Kūkai also was becoming known as an accomplished calligrapher, poet, and literary theorist. Thus Saga, upon learning of Kūkai's interests and abilities, may have sought to bring him into the cultural orbit of the capital.

Still more intriguing is the possibility that Saichō was instrumental in the invitation. Saichō certainly would have desired to see the rare but essential esoteric materials said to be in Kūkai's possession, and to learn something of Kūkai's special training under Hui-kuo. Perhaps he wished to use Kūkai's advanced knowledge of Esoteric Buddhism to further expand those elements in Tendai.

In any event, Kūkai was now in the environs of the capital, and soon was responding to Emperor Saga's requests for poems and for samples of calligraphy in various styles, both in Chinese and in Sanskrit. Some of the calligraphic skills Kūkai had mastered in China were now being introduced to Japan for the first time, and Saga became Kūkai's eager pupil. Kūkai composed letters for the young emperor and even made him four writing brushes using methods learned in China (one brush for writing the square style, one for the semi-cursive style, one for the cursive, one for copying). He may also have manufactured Chinese-style ink sticks for Saga's use. These were not dilettantish matters, for in Japan, as in China, calligraphy was regarded as the most spiritually and intellectually profound of the arts. No other art so fully tested and manifested one's essential character.[35]

Being close to Emperor Saga meant that Kūkai had an opportunity to attract other men of power and learning. In this setting his personal charm and political astuteness began to be rewarded. Within the year the court appointed Kūkai administrative director of Nara's massive Tōdai-ji temple, national home of the Great Sun Buddha and acknowledged center of the Japanese Buddhist universe. At Tōdai-ji was the one ritual platform where the nation's priests could be ordained. The appointment likely was urged by the heads of the Nara temples, who already were seeing in Kūkai someone close to the emperor whom they could trust, in contrast to the combative Saichō. Kūkai held the post for three years, during which time he continued to develop his influence among the Nara clergy.

In his second year at Takaosan-ji Kūkai submitted a formal memorial to Emperor Saga requesting permission to initiate some of his followers in the mantra recitations documented in the texts he had brought back from China.

[These rituals] enable a king to vanquish the seven calamities, to maintain the four seasons in harmony, to protect the nation and family, and to give comfort to himself and others. . . .

Though I have received the transmission from my master, I
have been unable to perform [the rituals prescribed in these
sūtras]. For the good of the state I sincerely desire to initiate my
disciples and, beginning on the first day of next month, to perform the rituals at the Takaosanji until the dharma takes visible
effect. Also, I wish that throughout this period I might not have
to leave my residence and that I might suffer no interruption. I
may be an insignificant and inferior man, but this thought and
this wish move my heart. (*MW*, 41)

Saga acceded to the request, fully understanding that Kūkai was
giving to his own personal religious mission precedence over the cultural-
social employment the emperor habitually required of him. During one
of Kūkai's subsequent absences for meditation in the mountains Saga
sent him a wistful poem together with some warm clothes.

> This quiet monk has lived on the peak in the clouds
> For a long time.
> Here far from you, I think of the deep mountain still cold
> Even though it is Spring.
> The pines and cedars are keeping silent.
> How long have you been breathing the mist and fog?
> No recent news has come from your abode of meditation.
> The flowers are blooming and the willows are relaxing
> Here at [Heian-kyō] in the Spring.
> O Bodhisattva, do not reject this small present
> And help the giver troubled with worldly concerns.[36]

In accordance with custom, Kūkai composed in reply a poem with a
rhythm and diction modeled on Saga's.[37] The bond between Kūkai and
Saga seems to have been quite genuine, even intense. Today no other
Japanese emperor is held in such esteem at Kōyasan.

Contact between Kūkai and Saichō began shortly after Kūkai's
arrival at Takaosan-ji. Shingon historians suggest pointedly that it was
Saichō who first sought out the younger Kūkai, presumably in recognition of Kūkai's greater knowledge of Esoteric theory and practice. Tendai

historians sometimes insist the initiative went the other way. Whatever the case, contact between the two seems at the beginning to have been entirely cordial and free of ceremonial hesitation over seniority or precedence. Quite clearly, the conscientious Saichō, acknowledging his incomplete grasp of Esoteric thought, regarded access to Kūkai to be a personal blessing. "Although I have undertaken the long journey to China," he wrote to a patron, "willingly risking my life for the sake of the Dharma, I am still deficient in the way of [*Shingon-dō*]. The Master Kūkai fortunately was able to study this after reaching Ch'ang-an."[38]

Over the next several years Saichō requested the loan of some thirty sūtras and sūtra commentaries that Kūkai had brought from China. The solicitations were made humbly, in a spirit of mutual purpose, and Kūkai responded graciously. Saichō also began sending some of his better disciples to take instruction in Esoteric thought from Kūkai.

Although Saichō had received in China the introductory initiations into the Diamond Realm and Womb Realm mandalas, he had been unable to obtain copies of the mandalas themselves. Nor had he received anything more than rudimentary instruction in their ceremonial use. Therefore, near the close of 812 Saichō asked Kūkai to conduct for him the intermediate initiations into both mandalas. This Kūkai did, at first for a small group of four that included Saichō, then for a much larger group of initiates, among them several chief priests from the Nara sects, members of the nobility, some of Saichō's own disciples, and Saichō himself. In Kūkai's own written record of the initiations Saichō's name heads the list of recipients.

Saichō next requested that Kūkai initiate him into the *denpō-kanjō*, the consecration for the Transmission of the Dharma. This, the highest initiation ceremony, would qualify Saichō as a full master of Esoteric Buddhism. But the ceremony was not performed. The usual telling of the incident has Kūkai writing somewhat arrogantly to Saichō that to become eligible for such a transmission Saichō would need to enter into three years of study—that is, Saichō would need to become Kūkai's pupil for three years. Another reading of the available documents suggests that Kūkai simply was telling Saichō how long it would take to master fully the complex rituals associated with Shingon, three years being the length of time Kūkai himself had taken.[39] Although Saichō did not receive the *denpō-kanjō* transmission, he continued to send his own disciples to

Kūkai at Takaosan-ji. In the spring of 813 Kūkai conducted the *denpō-kanjō* for some of these men.

The differences between Saichō and Kūkai were now in the open. It was Saichō's belief that Tendai and Shingon were in full harmony and stood on an equal footing with one another. "The Esoteric teachings and those of Tendai permeate each other and share common ancestors," he wrote to Kūkai. "There is no distinction between the teachings of One Vehicle [the Tendai] and those of Shingon." To a disciple of his who was then studying with Kūkai, Saichō wrote: "With regard to the One Vehicle of the *Lotus* or the One Vehicle of Shingon, how can anyone claim that one is superior and the other inferior?"[40] But just such a claim lay at the heart of Kūkai's own belief and mission. Kūkai granted that there was a harmony between Esoteric teaching and Tendai teaching (and with virtually all other religious teachings as well), but this harmony he believed to be of a hierarchical order. Shingon, the True Word, because it was manifested directly by Dainichi Buddha, was the only ultimately true and comprehensive teaching, and could be transmitted only through a private communication from master to pupil. All other teachings, both Buddhist and non-Buddhist, were *exo*-teric in nature and fell away in a descending order of adequacy down to the most primitive religious awareness. In a ten-leveled system Kūkai placed Tendai near the top among Japanese religious traditions, but for him to grant to Tendai a status equal to Shingon would have been to violate all he had inherited from his master, Hui-kuo.

Predictably, in late 813, when Kūkai received a request from Saichō for the loan of the *Rishushaku-kyō*, an esoteric commentary by Amoghavajra on the *Rishu-kyō* sūtra, Kūkai refused the request. He wrote back that the text in question (which discussed the essential but easily misunderstood principle of *sokushin jōbutsu*: "attaining buddhahood in this very body") could not be studied properly without the traditional oral teaching. Saichō's independent approach, Kūkai explained, was one that would lead inevitably to a corruption of the Esoteric teachings:

> If the reception and the transmission of the teachings are not made properly, how will it be possible for future generations to discern what is correct and what is not? . . . . [The] transmission of the arcane meaning of Esoteric Buddhism does not depend

on written words. The transmission is direct, from mind to mind. Words are only paste and pebbles: if one relies solely on them, then the Ultimate is lost.[41]

Some readers of this famous letter have concluded that Kūkai was demanding that the senior Saichō become his disciple. The text is "violent in tone, unlike an ordinary letter of Daishi," remarks Professor Yamamoto.[42] But the question of discipleship (or even of deference) may not have been the primary issue. Kūkai seems to be asserting, plausibly, that if Saichō truly wishes to embrace the vision of Shingon, then he will have to accept both the fact of Shingon's primacy and the principle of private, face-to-face transmission.

Saichō, understandably, could not grant that Shingon transcended Tendai. Thus, the period of close cooperation between the two men ended. Kūkai continued to receive Saichō's disciples for instruction, but over a period of time even that arrangement soured. In 816 Saichō's closest follower, Taihan (778–858?), defected fully to Kūkai. When Saichō sent the young man a forlorn appeal to rejoin him on Mt. Hiei, Kūkai answered on Taihan's behalf, explaining that Taihan's preference for remaining at Takaosan-ji was not a matter of choosing one master over another. Taihan simply had accepted the primacy of Shingon and its direct transmission "from mind to mind."

The older priest's feelings were deeply hurt. Taihan had been both Saichō's personal favorite and his designated successor. And Taihan wasn't the only defector. Other young scholars were leaving the cold and isolation of Mt. Hiei to study Shingon with the charismatic Kūkai. Even worse, some were joining the Hosso sect in Nara. In the years between 807 and 817 only six of Saichō's twenty government-sponsored trainees chose to return to Mt. Hiei after their ordinations in Nara.[43] Saichō appeared to be losing the battle for the minds of his own disciples.

In this emergency Saichō proposed a number of organizational changes, the most revolutionary of which was a request to the court that it grant Mt. Hiei the power to perform its own ordinations. With such an arrangement Saichō could keep his followers away from hostile Nara. When the Nara clergy learned of the proposal their opposition was vigorous and bitter. The court, not wishing to involve itself in the dispute, denied Saichō's request. All the same, there were many in the capital who admired Saichō and believed Saichō's temple on Mt. Hiei was Heian-kyō's primary spiritual protector. To these people Nara's opposition seemed petty and arrogant.

Just seven days after Saichō's death, in 822 at age fifty-six, the court changed its mind and granted Mt. Hiei the requested ordination plat-form, an act that in effect made Tendai the nation's first autonomous Buddhist sect. Subsequently, the vast Mt. Hiei complex, blessed with both a strategic location and a succession of vigorous leaders, greatly strengthened its influence. In 866, just forty-four years after his death, Saichō became the first Japanese priest to be awarded by the court the posthumous title of Daishi (Dengyō Daishi).

Along with his activities as ritualist, teacher, administrator, and belle-lettrist, Kūkai produced during his years at Takaosan-ji a series of treatises that conveyed the heart of his religious thinking. Two of these productions were especially important doctrinally. The first, *Benkenmitsu nikyō ron* ("The Difference between Exoteric and Esoteric Buddhism"; c. 814), sometimes described as a "religious manifesto," is an instructional guide presented partly in the form of questions and answers. Among its primary assertions is that Shākyamuni's public sermons, although superfi-cially exoteric in nature (a concession to his spiritually ill-prepared audi-ence), contain hints of a second, secret discourse. This second discourse, which appears less disguised in the major esoteric sūtras, corresponds directly with the communication that the Central Buddha carries on con-tinuously with his own reflected selves in the great mandala. That is, it expresses the ultimate state of enlightenment.

Question: How is this possible, given that we have been taught that Dainichi, the Central Buddha, the Dharmakāya, is "formless and image-less . . . beyond verbalization and conceptualization" (*MW*, 154)? Surely, mere men and women are not capable of hearing and understanding what can be received by the highly evolved Buddhas, Bodhisattvas, and Devas of the great mandala.

Answer: Agreed, the Dharmakāya's voice cannot be heard by us at this moment, but that is because our illusions conceal from us our own true natures. Within each of us is a Buddha-seed, the true self, and this true self is present in the mandala. By means of practicing the prescribed *shingon* (Sk. *mantra*) we can attain this true self. Intrinsic to Kūkai's argu-ment is his perception that the primal "language" of ultimate reality—

that is, of the Dharma Buddha—is communicated by nature in its varied phenomenal manifestations. In short, phenomenal nature, as perceived by the enlightened mind, *is* the Dharma Buddha.[44]

The second work, *Sokushin jōbutsu gi* ("Attaining Enlightenment in This Very Existence"; c. 820), builds upon the first. Here Kūkai explains how a devotee trained in the "three mysteries" of body, speech, and mind can, without abandoning his or her present body, achieve the same meditation (*samādhi*) that is realized by the Central Buddha. That is, a person can become a Buddha without proceeding any farther in the seemingly endless cycle of birth and death.[45] Nirvāna, Enlightenment, Buddhahood, aren't conditions one achieves in death. They are achieved in life— ideally, in one's present life. Death, being illusory, makes no contribution at all.

There is a well-known story set during this period that dramatizes in miraculous fashion Kūkai's *sokushin jōbutsu* doctrine. It seems that in 813 Emperor Saga asked the head priests of Japan's various Buddhist sects to come to his quarters in the palace and there present the basic doctrines of their individual faiths. At the symposium each priest in turn explained to the emperor that while becoming a Buddha was the eventual hope of the members of his sect, the actual attainment of this goal would require a nearly infinite stretch of lifetimes. When his turn came Kūkai spoke of a shorter path, one that could be completed within a single life. "If one maintains the mind of the Buddha while searching for the Buddha's wisdom, then one can become a Buddha in this very existence."

The other priests, though respectful of Kūkai, were unanimously skeptical. In response Kūkai turned his body toward the south and began to meditate while reciting a mantra and performing the appropriate hand positions. Within moments his body took on the form of the Great Sun Buddha with divine light streaming outward in all directions. Illustrations of this famous transfiguration show the astonished emperor and audience of priests bowing down in reverence before the glare.[46]

Kūkai's years at Takaosan-ji represented a period of remarkable achievement, but he had not found at this location the optimal atmosphere either for teaching or for meditation. Callers were constantly at the gate, often carrying messages of request from court nobles and from the emperor. The thunder of sectarian politics, especially the struggle between Heian-kyō and Nara ecclesiastics, was a constant distraction. Kūkai desired a more profound sequestration both for himself and for the proper training of his disciples.

In the late spring of 816, the year following Taihan's defection from Mt. Hiei to Takaosan-ji, Kūkai submitted an intensely felt formal request to Emperor Saga. He began by observing that in India and in China mountains had long been the locales favored by students of meditation, for it was in such places that the Buddhas were most prone to preach and manifest themselves. Those who meditate in the mountains, he told the emperor, "are treasures of the nation . . . are like bridges for the people." But in today's Japan, despite an apparent flowering of Buddhism, these bridges were largely missing. The "teaching of meditation has not been transmitted, nor has a suitable place been allocated for the practice of meditation." Kūkai then made the request he had been pondering since his return from China.

> When young, I, Kūkai, often walked through mountainous areas and crossed many rivers. There is a quiet place called Kōya located two days' walk to the west from a point that is one day's walk south from Yoshino. I estimate the area to be south of Ito-no-kōri in Kinokuni. High peaks surround Kōya in all four directions; no human tracks, still less trails, are to be seen there. I should like to clear the wilderness in order to build a monastery there for the practice of meditation, for the benefit of the nation and of those who desire to discipline themselves. . . . The rise or fall of the Dharma, indeed, depends on the mind of the emperor. Whether the object is small or large, I dare not make it mine until I have been granted your permission. I earnestly wish that the empty land be granted me so that I may fulfill my humble desire. (*MW*, 47)

Permission came quickly. The letter of request to the Emperor is dated June 19, 816. The court's affirmative reply to Kūkai is dated July 8. Kūkai was then forty-three years old.

THE FOUNDING OF KŌYASAN

The following spring (of 817) Kūkai sent two disciples southward to survey the high mountain valley of Kōyasan. One of these disciples was Jichie, whom he already had appointed master of Takaosan-ji. The other disciple was Taihan, Saichō's former favorite. To these two Kūkai would entrust much of the responsibility for constructing the first buildings at Kōyasan.

On November 16 of the succeeding year Kūkai himself climbed the mountain to see what progress had been made. Likely no more than a few huts had been built at this point, but it was essential to formulate careful plans for future construction. Kōyasan was to be designed so that it represented a mandala both physically and spiritually.

In early May of the next year (819), at the height of spring on the mountain, Kūkai conducted a ceremony formally consecrating Kōyasan to its spiritual purposes. He began with an invocation to all sacred beings, starting with the Buddhas, then the divinities of the two mandalas, then the heavenly and earthly gods of Japan, then, finally, the demons who presided over the five elements of earth, water, fire, wind, and space. Every sentient as well as every non-sentient being, he said, had the capacity to become a Buddha, and it was the law of the Dharma that this should come about. "The Buddha nature and the reason of things pervade the world. They are not different. Oneself and other things are equal." He then related how Dainichi Buddha, in consideration of the meaning of this equality, had by his great compassion transmitted the previously hidden Esoteric wisdom to humankind, first passing it to Kongōsatta (Sk. Vajrasattva), and thence down the patriarchal line to Hui-kuo and to himself. Kōyasan would be a place for the teaching and propagation of this revealed Esoteric wisdom.

> May the divinities thereby be pleased and may the divinities protect. . . . May bad demons go out of the boundary of Kōyasan that extends 7[*ri*] in the four cardinal points, the intermediate directions and the upper and the lower regions. All the good gods and demons that give advantage to Esoteric Buddhism, please stay here as you like. [I ask the support of] the noble spirits of the emperors and empresses since the founda-

tion of the State of Japan as well as all the gods of heaven and earth. I would like to entreat that all the souls of the deceased persons may protect this sanctuary and thereby let my wish be fulfilled.[47]

The full consecration ceremony covered seven days and seven nights.

The location Kūkai had selected for his remote monastery was ideal. A rim of low, heavily timbered peaks circled the small valley, protecting it from the full force of mountain storms. Most of the valley floor was either level or gently sloping, ideal for the construction of monastery halls. The needed timber was immediately at hand. A stream fed by hillside springs ran the length of the valley. In all seasons water would be plentiful. "Many distant places were investigated," Kūkai said, "until at last this place was found out to be most becoming."[48]

Legend adds some colorful details to the founding of Kōyasan. One story tells of the assistance of the hunter god Kariba-myōjin and his two dogs, Shiro and Kuro.[49] The suggested time of Kūkai's encounter with the hunter god varies. Perhaps it occurred just prior to his sending the letter to Emperor Saga requesting permission to build a monastery on Kōyasan. Or it may have occurred some years before that, shortly after his return from China. In all versions Kūkai is traveling alone. As he journeys westward from Yoshino he encounters a tall man dressed in a blue hunting suit and armed with a bow. With the hunter are two dogs, one white and one black. Kūkai informs the hunter that he has been searching throughout the nation for a spiritual site suitable for meditation and the study of the Dharma. Does the hunter know of such a place?

"Mount Kōya is in the province of Ki-no-kuni," the hunter answers, pointing in that direction. "You should look there. It contains a high valley protected by surrounding mountains. For many ages this valley has been a sacred place. In the daytime a purple cloud overhangs the valley, and at night a mysterious light appears. If you wish to see Mt. Kōya, please take my two dogs with you as companions, for they know the way." With that the hunter disappears.[50]

By nightfall Kūkai and the dogs reach the south bank of the Kinokawa River, at a spot that later becomes the location of Jison-in, the temple that would serve as the primary river entry port to Kōyasan. In the morning, with the dogs still in the lead, Kūkai enters the mountain. As he is crossing the ridge above the village of Amano a royal lady appears before him dressed in a gown of blue with a golden ornament in her hair. She introduces herself as Niutsuhime-no-mikoto, the guardian deity of the surrounding mountain domain. The hunter god is her son (some versions say her husband). The goddess's primary shrine is just down the hill in Amano village.[51]

"You have permission to enter my domain," she tells Kūkai. "If you should choose to build your monastery on Mt. Kōya, my son and I will remain close by to protect the flame of the Exalted Law. We will keep our vigil until the coming of Miroku Bosatsu."[52]

Kūkai climbs farther, and just as he and the dogs reach the clouds that are hiding the highest ridge they pass through an opening in the forest and enter a beautiful valley. The valley's horizon is formed by eight peaks, like the eight petals of a sacred lotus blossom.[53]

An equally famous legend attaches to a visit Kūkai made to Kōyasan in May 819. As the workmen are felling trees to create a clearing, Kūkai walks among them trying to decide on the precise location for the monastery. The hour grows late. The sun falls below the western ridge, throwing the forest into twilight darkness. At that point Kūkai notices a bright light shining among some trees a short distance from where he is standing. Walking closer he observes a single glowing object in the crown of a three-needle pine. This object is the golden three-pronged *vajra*, or *sanko*, he had thrown skyward from China some twelve years earlier. Kūkai immediately instructs the workmen to leave the tree uncut. Henceforward it becomes known as the *Sanko-no-matsu*, or Pine Tree of the Sanko. The first monastery residence hall will be built on the north side of this pine.

A second sacred object also is found at the site of the future monastery. While digging up a stump a workman unearths a sword with an inscription only Kūkai has the skill to read. "In this place," says the inscription, "Kashō entered into eternal meditation [Nirvāna]." Kashō (Sk. Kāshyapa) is the historical Buddha who immediately preceded India's Shākyamuni. Kūkai orders that a copper container be made for the sword, and then, after performing a ground-purifying ceremony, has it returned to the earth. To the present day—or so it is supposed—the sword remains buried at the spot where it was found, beneath the Great Stūpa.[54]

Kūkai named his remote mountain monastery Kongōbu-ji, "*Vajra Peak Temple.*" The *vajra* (J. *kongō*), often translated as "diamond," represents among other things the brilliantly hard, indestructible essence of the Dharma. Thus, we have a diamond monastery at the center of a lotus formed by eight surrounding mountains: *the-diamond-in-the-lotus.*

SERVANT TO EMPEROR AND NATION

Kūkai spent a good portion of 818 and 819 supervising construction at Kōyasan, but progress was slow. Work could not be sustained through the winter months, and, since the new temple was without government sponsorship, needed money and supplies had to be obtained by making special appeals, frequently to clans in the Kii area. Meanwhile, the primary locale for training his disciples continued to be Takaosan-ji.

An equal priority with the training of monks in the Shingon faith was Kūkai's obligation to serve the emperor and the state. The two goals were intimately related. Buddhism had been embraced by the imperial court in the seventh century precisely because it promised to bring great benefit to the nation. Now in the ninth century Kūkai was offering Shingon Esoteric Buddhism as the latest and perhaps ultimate fulfillment of this pledge. A nation that lived in harmony with the Great Sun Buddha would enjoy peace and prosperity in full measure. If special emergencies arose, remedial esoteric rituals could be employed to set things right.

Thus, when an epidemic disease began to sweep the nation in 818 Emperor Saga turned to Kūkai. In response Kūkai assigned to the emperor the task of transcribing the *Heart Sutra* (*Hannya-shingyō*) while he himself presented a series of lectures on the merits of the text. Faced with this team effort the epidemic soon abated. A later account of Kūkai's intervention describes the roads of Japan as filled with men and women and children whom he had "raised from the dead."[55]

Another well-known story of Kūkai's performances as ritualist to the nation tells of a drought that threatened the area of the capital in 824. For three months no rain had fallen and fears of a general rice crop failure and subsequent famine were growing. The imperial court's traditional practice on such occasions had been to instruct the monks and nuns of the affected provinces to chant sūtras for five days in the hope of inducing rain, but this time Emperor Junna (Saga's successor) directly solicited Kūkai's help. Kūkai immediately set up an altar beside the pond in the garden at the Imperial Palace and performed a rain-inducing rite. Almost before he had finished, a steady rain began to fall, first upon the garden itself and then outward across the parched land. For three days and three nights the rain continued—one day and one night of rain for each month of the drought. In later centuries this rainfall became known as "Kōbō's rain."[56] The location of the miracle, the Shinsen-en garden near Kyōto's Nijō Castle, is a popular tourist site today.

Kūkai's job as an imperial wonder worker was a busy one. Shortly before his death he wrote that four successive emperors had appealed to him on fifty-one different occasions to prepare an altar and conduct special prayers for the benefit of the nation.[57]

There also are numerous accounts of Kūkai's practical contributions to Japanese society quite apart from his employment of esoteric ritual. The claim is made that he was the first to teach the Japanese the use of coal and petroleum and that he first discovered and publicized the health benefits of hot springs. He is said to have added to the nation's knowledge in the fields of astronomy, physics, pharmaceuticals, and metallurgy.[58] He evidently also was a skilled civil engineer. The most famous and best-documented demonstration of his engineering prowess was the rebuilding in 821 of the Mannō-no-ike, a large reservoir near his birthplace in Sanuki province of Shikoku. This reservoir, already a century old at the time, had deteriorated and finally collapsed, thereby making it virtually impossible for the rice farmers in the area to produce their primary subsistence crop. After several directors had failed to remedy the problem, the local governor wrote to the capital requesting that Kūkai be assigned to the project. The demoralized Shikoku workforce, the governor said, would not fail to respond to the leadership of a man so admired and loved. Thus Kūkai, in one of the busiest years of his life, went to Shikoku with one novice and four acolytes, set up a fire altar on an island in the pond, and spent the following summer months supervising the redesign and reconstruction of a reservoir twenty kilometers in circumference. The task was accomplished with such skill that the Mannō-no-ike operates today as one of the nation's oldest and largest irrigation reservoirs.[59]

Most of Kūkai's administrative work involved Buddhist temples. In addition to the three years as head of Tōdai-ji (in Nara) he held directorships at Atago-ji (near the capital), at Daian-ji (also a great Nara temple), at Murō-ji (west of Nara), and at Kōfuku-ji (along the route to Kōyasan). His most significant directorship was at Tō-ji temple in the capital. This assignment came in 823.

One of Emperor Kammu's strategies in founding the new capital of Heian-kyō was to free imperial authority from the influence of the powerful Buddhist temples of Nara. Kammu wished to retain the spiritual protection of the Buddhist faith, however, and for this reason encouraged the growth of Saichō's Tendai temple on Mount Hiei, which was positioned to guard the capital from the dangerous northeast direction. Within the capital city itself Kammu cautiously authorized the building of two temples to guard the city's imposing main southern entrance, the Rashōmon Gate. East of the gate was Tō-ji ("East Temple"). To the west was Sai-ji ("West Temple").

In 796, two years after the founding of the capital, construction supervisors were appointed for these east and west temples, but progress was exceedingly slow. As a consequence, in January 823, while he was still at Takaosan-ji, Kūkai received a message from Emperor Saga appointing him general director of Tō-ji. Saga was preparing to go into retirement in a few months and apparently wanted Tō-ji's lagging construction speeded up. He may also have seen in the appointment a final gift he could give to his friend. Kūkai would now have within the capital itself a temple that was ideally suited to become the headquarters of the new Shingon sect.

Kūkai immediately moved from Takaosan-ji to Tō-ji, and in a few months' time submitted to the newly enthroned Emperor Junna (r. 823–833) an outline of a course of study for students of Shingon. Emperor Junna approved the proposal, using for the first time in an official document the term *Shingon-shū* (Shingon Sect). Junna agreed that Kūkai would be permitted to keep as many as fifty monks at Tō-ji and, even more significant, to use Tō-ji exclusively for the teaching of the Shingon faith. Such exclusivity was revolutionary, for up to this time all government-sponsored temples had been open to monks of all schools. The official name given to Tō-ji was Kyō-ō-gokuku-ji—literally, "Temple of the Authorized Doctrine for the Protection of the Country."

At the time of Kūkai's takeover a Golden Hall (Kondō) already stood on Tō-ji's spacious grounds. He soon began work on a Lecture Hall (Kōdō) which he equipped internally with a large raised platform (*shumi-dan*). On this platform Kūkai placed in mandala formation twenty-one remarkable sculptures that today are world famous.[60]

Kūkai also initiated at Tō-ji a 187-foot, five-tiered pagoda, a daring technical undertaking. An old document states that in the initial construction between three and five hundred workers were required to haul a single central pillar from the mountain forests of nearby Higashi-yama.[61] Today the Tō-ji pagoda, a reconstruction dating from 1643, is both a National Treasure and Japan's tallest surviving pagoda. Its romantic silhouette observed at dusk remains Kyōto's signature image.

In 828, while continuing to expand both Tō-ji and Kōyasan, Kūkai launched one of the most innovative experiments in Japanese educational history, the Shugei-shuchi-in (literally, "synthesis providing seeds of wisdom"), a comprehensive school of arts and sciences he located a short distance to the east of Tō-ji.[62] Three aspects of the school are especially notable. First, Kūkai held that a proper setting was vital to productive learning, and so the school was placed in a pastoral area with flowing water and forest walks. Second, he installed a uniquely inclusive curriculum. Up to that time (as Kūkai made clear in his inaugural document) monastery students training for the priesthood studied only Buddhist texts while the national school students training for government service studied only non-Buddhist texts. Believing any curricular narrowness to be inhibiting to enlightenment, Kūkai designed a curriculum that included Buddhism, Confucianism, Taoism, law, logic, diplomacy, music, horsemanship, calligraphy, mathematics, grammar, medicine, art, philosophy, and astronomy. The aim was to address all the formulated knowledge of the day.

The third feature may have been the most truly innovative. Kūkai's school made no class distinctions when admitting students. Japan's national college admitted only the nobility. The private schools run by aristocratic families similarly excluded commoner children. Shugei-shuchi-in admitted children from all social classes, and most particularly the children of the poor. Tuition was free. Those who had long distances to travel were housed at no cost. Both students and teachers received free meals. Kūkai admonished his instructors to approach each student in a compassionate and evenhanded manner, never being influenced by whether a student was from an elite or an ordinary family. "'The beings in the triple world are my children,' announced the Buddha. And there is a beautiful saying of Confucius that 'all within the four seas are brothers.' Do honor to these teachings!" (*MW*, 57–58).

Arguably, only Kūkai could have succeeded in establishing such a school, or in sustaining it. Within a decade after Kūkai's death Shugei-shuchi-in was closed and its land sold to buy rice fields to support the training of priests. However, much of the spirit of Shugei-shuchi-in survives today in a Shingon college, also named Shugei-shuchi-in, that abuts the Tō-ji temple grounds. The spirit of Shugei-shuchi-in also survives in large measure at Kōyasan University and at the other schools on the mountain.

A number of well-known legends attach to Kūkai's residence at Tō-ji. Some are commonplace and trivial, such as the story that he magically straightened the great pagoda when it began to lean during construction. Some others have considerable significance. Among the latter is the legend that shortly after receiving Tō-ji from Emperor Saga Kūkai walked to nearby Mount Fushimi with an offering for the powerful rice god Inari. At the summit of the mountain Inari appeared, took the offering directly from Kūkai's hand, and said, "Together, you and I, we will protect this people."[63] From that moment forward the rice god became Tō-ji's most powerful native protector. Another version of this story has earlier incarnations of Kūkai and Inari meeting in India while attending a lecture by Shākyamuni. At that time Kūkai said to Inari, "Some day I will be born in an eastern land and will spread Buddhism there, and you will come and be the protective deity of the secret teachings." And so centuries later Inari appeared at the South Gate of Tō-ji in fulfillment of the prophecy.[64] Such stories argued that the new Shingon faith, although an importation from China and India, was not antithetical to the native gods. In fact, the native gods eagerly welcomed the opportunity to become Shingon's defenders and collaborators.[65]

A more extravagant and still better known legend concerning Kūkai's directorship of Tō-ji has him involved in a death struggle with the head priest of rival Sai-ji (West Temple). The full details of the encounter are found in the popular fourteenth-century war chronicle *The Taiheiki.*[66] It seems that Sai-ji's chief priest, a master magician named Shubin, had grown embittered at what he judged to be the emperor's open preference for Kūkai. So to punish the emperor Shubin secretly captured all the dragon gods of the universe and shut them up in a water jar. With the dragons imprisoned, not a drop of rain fell during the crucial months preceding Japan's rice planting. Called to deal with the crisis, Kūkai began praying for rain, and during his prayers discovered Shubin's plot. Although unable to undo Shubin's powerful magic, Kūkai did succeed in locating one dragon that Shubin had overlooked. That dragon, whose name was Zennyo-ryū-ō ("Good-Natured Dragon Queen"), Kūkai persuaded to come to Japan. Upon Zennyo-ryū-ō's arrival a great rain fell, the rice crop was saved, and Kūkai gained still more favor with the emperor.

Shubin's response to this turn of events was to shut himself up in the West Temple, make a three-cornered altar facing north, and summon one of the Five Bright Kings (Godai-myō-ō) from the Diamond Realm Mandala. This warrior king Shubin instructed to launch a series of arrows at Kūkai. Kūkai, secretly learning of the threat, summoned his own Bright King from the Womb Realm Mandala. So as Shubin's arrows flew over the Rashōmon Gate and began their deadly descent on Tō-ji, Kūkai's arrows rose to intercept them, dropping each one harmlessly to the earth. Realizing that Shubin would be unable to detect the failure of the arrow attack, Kūkai sent out a rumor that one of the arrows had produced a fatal wound. On hearing the sad news all Heian-kyō entered mourning. The gleeful Shubin at once began to dismantle his altar, but in that moment his magic rebounded against him. First he was struck blind. Then his nose began to gush blood. In another instant he lay dead. Subsequently, Shubin's West Temple fell into ruin, while Kūkai's East Temple grew in power and beauty. Visitors to Kyōto today will find no trace of West Temple, nor, for that matter, of the Rashōmon Gate. Tō-ji, by contrast, is one of Japan's largest and most active Buddhist temples, especially on the twenty-first day of each month, the day that memorializes Kōbō Daishi's entrance into his final meditation. On that day visitors by the tens of thousands flood through its gates to pray to Odaishi-sama and the healing Buddha, and to shop among the flea market stalls that fill the grounds.

KŪKAI'S THEORY OF THE TEN STAGES

In his earlier treatises Kūkai had been preoccupied with setting Shingon Esoteric beliefs off against the rival Buddhist schools of thinking, with particular emphasis on the contrast between esoteric and exoteric teachings. Gradually, however, he came to present Shingon more as a final stage of religious development toward which all the other faiths, including the non-Buddhist ones, were evolving. The issue now was less one of truth or falsity and more one of how far the religious mind had progressed. All earnest religious activity was to be regarded affirmatively as a manifestation of Dainichi Buddha. All ultimately served the Great Sun Buddha's compassionate desire that sentient beings attain enlightenment. This unifying theme formed the central argument of the most ambitious of Kūkai's approximately fifty religious treatises, a massive synthesis of religious thought called *Jūjū-shin-ron* ("The Ten Stages of the Development of the Mind").

The occasion of its composition was a directive issued in 830 by Emperor Junna for each of the recognized Buddhist schools to present a summary of their essential beliefs. The timing of this directive was appropriate, for Japanese Buddhism was then threatening to fracture. The six Nara schools were still viewed as a single religious cooperative, their dividing differences being largely pedantic and abstract, but the two new faiths of the capital, Tendai and Shingon, appeared to be seeking separate identities. Or at least this was true of Saichō's Tendai. Kūkai's emphasis seems to have been more integrative and less sectarian.[67] Perhaps Emperor Junna hoped the exercise would reveal an underlying harmony of belief that would reduce the potential for future disorder.

Kūkai's response to the Emperor's instruction, *The Ten Stages*, was a long and comprehensive discourse that in effect offered a schematic summation of the evolution of human religious perception.[68] In the First Stage, he argued, man was totally dominated by instinctive appetite and consequently was without ethical perceptions. Even at this primitive level, however, there was potential for growth because of the presence of the innate Buddha-mind. In Stage Two the ethical mind awakened and man discovered within himself a spontaneous desire to control his passions, perform charities, and live a human rather than a bestial life. This stage Kūkai equated with the ethical vision of Confucianism. In Stage Three, prompted by a perception of the mutability of things, man experienced a child-like hope of rebirth in the eternal peace of heaven, but the motivation was totally selfish. This stage Kūkai associated with Taoism and certain egoistic Buddhist and Indian groups that employed asceticism, good works, prayer, and magical formulas for personal gain only. In Stage Four the mind freed itself from egoistic thinking, but still accepted as real such components of the ego as perception, will, and consciousness.

In Stage Five the mind entirely overcame the ignorance that made it subject to the lures of the world. The chains of *karma* were broken and the cycle of perpetual rebirth ended. All the same, this fifth mind was inclined to grow complacent and rest, giving little thought to the torment of those who still lived in bondage. Not until Stage Six did the mind awaken to an unconditional compassion for others. Now the believer sought the salvation of all sentient beings, a sentiment that corresponded to Miroku's meditation in the Tushita Heaven and marked the transition from southern Hīnayāna ("Small Vehicle") Buddhism to northern Mahāyāna ("Large Vehicle") Buddhism. This stage Kūkai perceived in the teaching of Nara's Hossō sect. In Stage Seven the mind achieved the realization that all objects within the consciousness, including consciousness itself, were "unborn" and "void." Observer and object, birth and death, being and nonbeing, were recognized as without distinction or content. The teaching of the Sanron school of Nara expressed this level of perception.

The mind of Stage Eight recognized that matter and mind, the world of illusion, the world of enlightenment, and all other possible worlds were contained within a single thought within a single mind, but did not understand that even this knowledge could be transcended. Kūkai equated Stage Eight with the meditation of Kannon Bosatsu and the teachings of Saichō's Tendai sect. The mind of Stage Nine experienced the ultimate abandonment of a self-nature. This mind saw that there were no barriers anywhere, that all things interpenetrated all other things, that the eternal truth was everywhere present. All phenomena were empty, and because of this emptiness were unified and harmonious. This was the meditation of Fugen Bosatsu and corresponded to the teachings of Nara's Kegon sect. This ninth mind, however, did not yet fully experience the mystery of the Buddha-mind. That is, it did not know itself to be the mystical and transcendent mind of the *Dharma-kāya*, the All-Encompassing Central Buddha, Dainichi.

The Tenth and final Stage, conveyed by Shingon doctrine, was beyond verbal description, but the means to it could be acted upon.[69] The means were the adoption of the three continuous secret actions of the cosmic Dainichi: the esoteric mudrā (secret of the body), the esoteric mantra (secret of speech), and the esoteric visualization (secret of mind). Through meditation sustained by these three mysteries the practitioner came to recognize that his or her own body-mind was identical with the Dharma-Body-Mind, with Dainichi. *Samsāra* (the phenomenal world of cyclical death and rebirth) and *Nirvāna* were experienced now, in the present, as one and the same. Wisdom and Compassion were experienced as one and the same. The Secret Treasury was opened. One discovered one's true identity, and lived in that identity. None of the earlier stages needed to be despised, for each had been a necessary preparation. All early stages were contained within the final stage, just as all later stages were implicit in the first. From the very beginning the practitioner had been in full union with the Central Buddha, although oblivious to this fact.

Shortly after submitting *The Ten Stages of the Development of Mind* to the emperor, Kūkai repeated the argument in a shorter, more accessible version entitled *The Precious Key to the Secret Treasury* (*Hizō hōyaku*). This treatise again made clear that Kūkai accepted the validity of the approaches of the other Buddhist schools, regarding them as essential stages in the growth of the religious mind.[70] It also reasserted that the "secret treasury" of Shingon offered the ultimate practice.

Kūkai's *Ten Stages* and *Precious Key to the Secret Treasury* have long been regarded as brilliant achievements. Several recent Buddhist scholars, among them Kōyasan's Miyasaka Yushō, have emphasized that the two works are developmental in spirit, despite their structural comprehensiveness. Thus, the celebrated Japanese Buddhist innovators who came after Kūkai—such as Dōgen (Sōtō Zen), Hōnen (Pure Land), and Shinran (True Essence Pure Land)—may be understood to have elaborated elements already present in Kūkai's early formulation.[71]

THE "DEATH" OF KŪKAI

In 829, at age fifty-six, Kūkai was appointed director of Daian-ji, the monastery in Yamato where his early mentor Gonzō had been head priest. In the same year he was given full authority to make Takaosan-ji (renamed Jingō Kokūzō Shingon-ji, or, more informally, Jingō-ji) into an exclusively Shingon temple. He soon began adding new buildings there. Meanwhile construction at both Tō-ji and Kōyasan continued, along with a steady production of new statues, paintings, and mandalas. Shingon was attracting student monks in ever increasing numbers. Kūkai's energy and opportunities seemed boundless. Then in May 831 he became ill.

The illness clearly was serious, for it soon prompted him to request permission to resign from all official duties. He wished to go immediately to Kōyasan, he said, where he could nurse himself and, as his strength permitted, assist in the various unfinished projects on the mountain. Emperor Junna refused to accept Kūkai's resignation, arguing that Esoteric Buddhism had only just begun in the nation, that Kūkai was indispensable to a further understanding of its secret teaching. The emperor's advice was that Kūkai should lighten his load of work, but remain in the capital.[72]

So for the rest of the year Kūkai continued on at Tō-ji. From time to time he may have slipped away to a secluded hermitage in the Higashiyama hills, which supposedly he established at about this time. On the hermitage site today is the massive Shingon temple Sennyū-ji, burial place of many members of the imperial family. In the summer of the following year, 832, Kūkai finally left Tō-ji for Kōyasan. He would reside on the mountain more or less permanently for the remaining years of his life. Clearly, it was where he had chosen to die.

On August 22, 832, Kūkai conducted at Kōyasan the Offering Ceremony of Ten Thousand Lights and Flowers, a ritual that subsequently became a permanent part of the ceremonial program of the mountain. The next year he assigned the management of Jingō-ji (the former Takaosan-ji) to his disciple Shinzei (800–860) and deposited there some sacred scriptures he had copied. In the same year he selected disciple Jichie (786–847) to serve as head of Tō-ji. His younger brother, Shinga (801–879), he appointed to several positions, among them the directorship of the sūtra repository at Tō-ji. Shinzen, his nephew, he groomed to take over the management of Kōyasan.[73]

In December 834 Kūkai received from the new emperor, Nimmyō (one of Saga's sons), permission to build a Shingon chapel, to be called Shingon-in, within the compound of Hiean-kyō's imperial palace. So in the winter of 834–835 he made one last trip to the capital to inaugurate at Shingon-in a week-long ritual (January 8–14) known as the *Go-shi-chinichi-no-mishuhō* ("Imperial Rite of the Second Seven Days of the New Year"). This complex and lavish ritual, modeled after a ceremony performed at the imperial palace in China, represented the most efficacious of all esoteric devotions for the furtherance of the security of the royal family and the nation. It was a final fulfillment of Hui-kuo's directive to Kūkai that he should do all he could to bring contentment to the Japanese people.[74]

Early in 835 Kūkai solicited and received from Emperor Nimmyō state sponsorship for the training of three monks each year at Kōyasan. One of these monks would specialize in the *Dainichi-kyō* ("The Great Sun Buddha Sūtra"), another in the *Kongō-cho-kyō* ("The Diamond-Peak Sūtra"), and the third in Shingon *shōmyō* (sūtra chanting). With this sponsorship the court officially affirmed its recognition of Kongōbu-ji as a government supported and protected monastery.

According to Shingon tradition, while in the capital the previous year (in May 834) Kūkai gathered his disciples around him and said, "My life will not last much longer. Live harmoniously and preserve with care the teaching of the Buddha. I am returning to [Kōyasan] to remain there forever" (*MW*, 59). It is at about this time that his close disciple Prince Shinnyo, third son of former Emperor Heizei, is believed to have painted his portrait.

In September 834 Kūkai selected his burial place at the eastern end of Kōyasan where the stream Tamagawa flows out of a small side valley formed by three mountains. Kūkai thought this area to be the most beautiful at Kōyasan and the most conducive to meditation. Disciple Shinzei tells the end of the story:

> From the first month [of 835], he drank no water. Someone advised him to take certain herbs as the human body is readily

subject to decay, and a celestial cook came day after day and offered him nectar, but he declined even these, saying that he had no use for human food.

At midnight on the twenty-first day of the third month, Master Kūkai, lying on his right side, breathed his last. One or two of his disciples knew that he had been suffering from a carbuncle. In accordance with his will, Kūkai, clad in robes, was interred on the Eastern Peak. He was sixty-two years of age. (*MW*, 59–60)

Word of the event was carried immediately to the capital, and on March 25 Emperor Nimmyō sent a message back to Kōyasan:

I can hardly believe that the master of Shingon, the foremost teacher of Esoteric Buddhism, on whose protection the state depended, and to whose prayers animals and plants owed their prosperity, has passed away. Alas! Because of the great distance, the mournful report has arrived here too late; I regret that I cannot send my representative in time for the cremation. (*MW*, 60)

The emperor's assumption that Kūkai had been cremated was reasonable, for that Indian custom had been widely adopted by Japan's Buddhist priests. Shinzei, however, says explicitly that Kūkai's body was interred.

Other and later accounts of Kūkai's death offer further information concerning what transpired both before and after the event. We are told that starting about March 11 Kūkai recited continuously the mantra of Miroku: *Om maitareiya sowaka.* "*Om*, Lord of Compassion, hail to thee!" On March 15 he gathered his Kōyasan disciples about himself and delivered a final testament. "At first I thought I should live till I was a hundred years old and convert all the people, but now that you are all grown up there is no need for my life to be prolonged." After predicting the day of his death, he explained that there was no cause for grief, for his spirit would survive. It would come to visit his disciples daily and watch over their work.[75] "When I see that my teaching is not doing well, I will mingle with the black-robed monks to promote my teaching. This is not a matter of my own attachments but is simply to propagate the teachings and that is all."[76]

At the hour of the Tiger (4:00 a.m.) on the twenty-first day of the third month of the third year of Jōwa (835), while seated in the lotus position in his residence at Chū-in, he made the wisdom-fist *mudrā* of Dainichi Nyorai (or perhaps the *kongō-gasshō*) and closed his eyes. A great stillness came over his form. This was Kūkai's *nyūjo*, his entry into a profound final meditation.[77] After forty-nine days (some sources suggest seven days) his disciples carried him in an upright seated position to the burial place just beyond the Tamagawa stream. Many paintings have been made of this journey. In most, Kūkai is shown being carried ceremoniously in an elegant closed palanquin, although sometimes the side screen is open. In at least one painting the journey is made in darkness, with torches casting shafts of light up the trunks of the massive trees. In another illustration Kūkai is carried on an open litter, almost as if he were on a spring outing.

At the burial site his seated form was placed in a grotto. His disciples then closed up the small chamber with stones and built a modest stone monument, symbol of Dainichi, over it.[78] Later, a wooden mausoleum hall was placed over the monument.

Approximately six months after Kūkai's death his old friend Emperor Saga, now twelve years in retirement, composed a poem in Kūkai's memory.

> This high priest saw Light with the purity and clarity of ice.
> Now his boat again has passed across the ocean.
> . . . .
> Your wisdom, to whom did you transfer it before ascending to
>   the peak of clouds?
> I cling pitifully to your wonderful writings and letters.
> In Kōyasan the sound of the temple gong is heard, but there is
>   no one to translate the palm-leaf sūtras in that house of
>   incense.
> In the evening of the year the forest of meditation is leafless
>   and chilled.
> In the wintry sky a white moon shines on a tomb.
> My bridge to you is cut off forever.
> Where does your soul now guard our people?[79]

About a year after Kūkai's entombment one of his disciples, Jichie, sent a message about the master's passing to Ch'ing-lung Temple in Ch'ang-an, where Kūkai had received instruction from Hui-kuo. "We feel in our hearts as if we had swallowed fire," Jichie wrote, "and our tears gush forth like fountains. Being unable to die, we are guarding the place where he passed away" (*MW*, 6).

During the ensuing years this watchful bereavement gave way to a generally held belief that Kūkai had not died, at least not in any familiar sense. Instead, he had entered into a profound meditation for the benefit of humankind and all living creatures. This sustained *samādhi* presumably would continue until Miroku Bosatsu, the future Buddha, arrived upon the earth. Meanwhile, Kūkai's spirit was thought capable of going abroad in the nation, providing spiritual aid and a shadowy companionship to all who called upon him.

Today at Kōyasan, on October 4 of each year, a ceremony is held in the Golden Hall to pay tribute to Emperor Saga. Although Saga granted Kūkai's request to build a monastery on Kōyasan, Saga himself never visited there—unless one wishes to give credence to a story that during Saga's funeral in Heian-kyō in 842 the coffin containing the emperor's body disappeared for a brief period, flying off southward to Kōya mountain. There in the forest glen beside the Tamagawa Kūkai is said to have interrupted his meditation, come forward from his tomb, and performed the proper Shingon funeral obsequies over his imperial friend.[80]

CHAPTER FOUR

TWELVE CENTURIES ON THE MOUNTAIN

ABBOT KANGEN VISITS THE TOMB (835–921)

For the task of carrying on the management and continuing construction at Kōyasan Kūkai had selected his thirty-year-old nephew Shinzen (804–891; also known as Shinnen). Under Shinzen's direction the primary architectural feature of the Garan courtyard, the massive Daitō, was completed, along with a number of other buildings, including a hall devoted to the veneration of Kūkai. Shinzen also oversaw the development of a program in Dharma transmission for student monks. This program, called the *denpō-e*, was a practical enactment of Kūkai's wish that the mountain be devoted above all else to meditation and religious education. In 883, toward the end of his life, Shinzen submitted a formal statement to Emperor Yōzei in which he called Kōyasan a true paradise of the Buddhas, an echo of Kūkai's original petition to Emperor

Saga. Following his death at Chū-in at the age of eighty-eight Shinzen's ashes were enshrined at a spot immediately to the rear of today's Kongōbu-ji headquarters.

Overall, Kūkai was wise in his selection of his Dharma heirs, and certainly he left them many competitive advantages. They were strategically positioned in the capital. They possessed a large body of his analytical writings, as well as many of the treasures he had brought back from China. Above all they had received directly from Kūkai the required oral teachings that they could pass on to their own disciples. But the pursuit of further knowledge, especially from China, continued. In 1836, the year immediately following Kūkai's *nyūjō*, both Shinzei and Shinzen attempted to go to China, but their ship was wrecked in a storm. Two years later another pair of Shingon priests, Jōkyō (d. 866) and Engyō (799–852), made successful journeys, returning the following year. E-un (798–869) went to China in 842 and stayed for five years, returning with a large collection of esoteric materials. Twenty years after that, in 862, Shūei (809–884) and Shinnyo (?–865?), the latter Kūkai's disciple and a former Imperial Prince-Regent, traveled to China. Shūei sailed home after three years with an impressive collection of materials, after which he became head priest at Tō-ji and an active ritualist at the imperial court. Shinnyo stayed on for a time in China, then lost his life in an attempt to reach India. These trips enlarged the Shingon treasury of esoteric texts and also enhanced the prestige of Shingon leadership. But the competition was equally active. Two talented Tendai priests, Ennin (794–864; posthumously Jikaku Daishi) and Enchin (814–891; a nephew of Kūkai), also made voyages to China during these years, and upon their return were so successful in further transforming Tendai in an esoteric direction that by the close of the ninth century Tendai had risen to an even footing with Shingon in its mastery of Mikkyō.[1]

With continued internal expansion there inevitably developed certain minor divisions within the Shingon sect. One source of division was Kūkai's failure to establish any one temple as the definitive administrative headquarters for the rest. A more fundamental cause of divisiveness, one endemic to Buddhism generally, was the custom of passing on the faith by means of direct transmission from master to pupil, and then subsequently to further masters and pupils. Such transmissions invariably introduced subtle variations in both dogma and practice. Soon major new Shingon temples, such as Daikaku-ji (founded in 876), Daigo-ji (in 876), and Ninna-ji (in 887), were moving in slightly independent directions, all honoring Kūkai's teachings, but each with its own evolving special methods and loyalties. Ninna-ji became the center of a "Hirosawa" school of Shingon-shū. Daigo-ji inaugurated the "Ono" School. Over the next several centuries these two schools in turn would split into a multiplicity of subtly variant sub-schools, until by the fifteenth century there were some seventy distinguishable "styles" of Shingon.[2]

The young monks who studied for the priesthood in Shinzen's Kōyasan program were formally ordained at Tōdai-ji in Nara, after which they were required to return to Kōyasan for six more years of training. During these six years they were forbidden to leave the mountain. Later, when the Nara ordination examinations were switched to Tō-ji, an increasing number of Kōyasan's young priests chose not to return for the rigorous follow-up stint on the mountain. In an attempt to reduce these defections Kōyasan applied to the imperial court for permission to administer its own examinations. Tō-ji intervened, however, protesting that such an arrangement negated its own assumed primacy in regulating Shingon religious training. In time the court ended the wrangling by allowing each of the major Shingon temples to train and examine its own priests, thus further reducing the need for mutual cooperation.

Kōyasan, from the beginning a fragile enterprise, was no more than just holding its own when overtaken in the early tenth century by a series of damaging events. In 912 a vigorous new chief priest at Tō-ji, Kangen (853–925), asked Kōyasan's chief priest, Mukū (?–918), to return some notes written by Kūkai that earlier had been borrowed from Tō-ji. Mukū refused the request, and when the court demanded he accede to it, Mukū fled Kōyasan, taking Kūkai's precious scrolls with him. Shortly thereafter Kangen was given full authority over both Kōyasan and Daigo-ji, while retaining his post as chief priest of Tō-ji. With this expanded power Kangen quickly established Tō-ji as the undisputed head Shingon temple. Additionally, Kōyasan's cherished *denpō-e* program for training its own priests was terminated. The student monks, finding themselves no longer supported, began drifting away from the mountain. Their teachers soon followed, until by 917 Kōyasan was virtually empty of priests and monks. It seemed that Kūkai's cherished dream for the mountain monastery was being abandoned.

But in this dark hour a very salutary event occurred.

For some time the feeling had grown among Shingon priests everywhere that the state had not properly honored Kūkai's greatness. Back in 866 the court had posthumously elevated Saichō, the founder of Tendai, to a newly defined highest rank, *Hōin-daikashō-i* ("Dharma-seal Great Master"), but after more than fifty years Kūkai had not been similarly honored.[3] So in 919 Abbot Kangen (now head of Tō-ji, Kōyasan, and Daigo-ji) petitioned the court to award Kūkai its highest posthumous rank. At the same time Ex-Emperor Uda (867–931; r. 887–897), a Kūkai enthusiast who had made the capital's Ninna-ji into an influential Shingon monastery, also petitioned the court. On October 27, 921, the petitions were granted.

Shortly thereafter, in accordance with custom, imperial envoy Prince Shunnyū, together with Abbot Kangen and several other priests, made the journey to Kōyasan. While standing before Kūkai's tomb the prince read aloud the formal document of award. Henceforth Kūkai would be known as Kōbō Daishi, "Dharma-spreading Great Teacher." At the same time Abbot Kangen directed toward Kūkai a new chant of praise and trust: *Namu Daishi Henjō Kongō*. The juxtaposition of the two tributes made for a powerful occasion.

What occurred next—or at least later was reported to have occurred—was to change Kōyasan's future. Prince Shunnyū and Abbot Kangen had brought with them a "yellowish brown" monastic robe, a gift from Emperor Daigo, for a symbolic robe-changing ceremony. One account tells us that months earlier, before receiving Kangen's petition on Kūkai's behalf, Emperor Daigo himself had encountered Kūkai in a dream. In this dream Kūkai related in verse that he was still inhabiting his body on Kōyasan and that for the past eighty-four years had been traveling ceaselessly among the people of Japan to spread the teachings of the Buddha. In consequence his monk's robe had become dreadfully threadbare.

> On Mount Kōya,
> As I continue to sit in my room,
> My very sleeves in tatters,
> Beneath the darkness of moss. . . .[4]

Holding the replacement robe before him, Abbot Kangen bowed toward Kūkai's tomb. The stones that blocked the entrance were removed. We are told that upon first viewing the interior Kangen saw only a heavy mist. Five times he prostrated himself and cried out.

> Ever since I was born out of the womb of my merciful mother and allowed to become a disciple of my venerable master, I have offended none of the Buddha's Precepts. Why am I not permitted to see . . . ?

Upon this appeal the obscuring mist lifted and Kūkai's form "appeared like the moon through the rifts in the clouds." Kangen and the prince washed Kūkai's body, shaved his hair and beard, just as his disciples had done eight decades earlier, and solemnly reclothed the body with the new robe. Beads from the rosary, which had scattered about the floor of the chamber, were gathered up, restrung, and placed in Kūkai's left hand.

During these proceedings a young assisting priest named Junyū failed entirely to see Kūkai's form. In response to Junyū's torment Abbot Kangen took Junyū's hand and placed it on Kūkai's knee. The young man still saw only darkness, but from that moment forward his hand became fragrant and remained so for the rest of his life.[5]

There is another twist to the story. After the resealing of the cave Kangen was crossing back over the Tamagawa when he sensed the presence of a figure behind him. Turning about, he saw Kōbō Daishi (for that was now his name) standing at the farther end of the bridge with his hands held in a gesture of blessing. Abbot Kangen put his own hands together and bowed toward the Daishi, thanking him. Daishi answered: "Kangen, it is not for you alone that I am here, but also for every creature that possesses the Buddha nature."

Thus, Kōbō Daishi affirmed to Kangen his ongoing role as savior to the nation and to all sentient beings. He was not dead, nor was he absent in some remote heaven. He was alive in this world, and ubiquitously so. As news of the wonder spread, Kōyasan, already regarded by some as a symbolic paradise, became known as the place where the living Kōbō Daishi could be encountered directly. This new belief would play an important role in Kōyasan's eventual restoration, although not at once. First there were fires.

JŌYO, FUJIWARA MICHINAGA, AND EX-EMPEROR SHIRAKAWA (921–1129)

After Kangen's closing of the schools very little seemed to go right on the mountain. Several buildings were reconstructed and repaired with funds supplied by aristocratic supporters. Some agricultural estates were designated as sources of revenue. But the full training program for monks was not reestablished. Kōyasan existed, but not as Kūkai had envisioned. Then came a series of fires. In 933, a decade after the robe-changing at the tomb, and virtually on the eve of the celebration of Kōbō Daishi's one-hundredth year in *samādhi*, flames consumed the mausoleum structure above the place of burial. In 952 lightning struck and destroyed the worship hall that served the mausoleum. In 994 a truly great fire, also started by lightning, swept through the Garan, the main temple area.[6] After consuming the Great Stūpa the flames advanced outward in all directions, burning nearly every building of the Garan, finally spreading to the priests' residences in the *tani* to the north, south, and east. Among the more significant buildings only the Miedō survived. With the mountain now virtually uninhabitable, a decision was made to haul the surviving temple treasures down the mountain for storage at Jison-in. When this task was completed, Kōyasan was closed.[7]

For a stretch of twenty-two years the mountain remained empty. Then in 1016 a sixty-year-old itinerant priest named Jōyo (958-1047) made his first visit to Kōyasan, prompted by a vision he experienced during a seventeen-day meditation at Hase-dera.[8] This vision revealed to Jōyo that Kōyasan, although choked with weeds, was in reality the Tushita heaven of Miroku, and that his own deceased parents now awaited him there. Upon climbing the mountain Jōyo discovered Kōyasan to be desolate indeed, with most of its buildings in ruins. He proceeded to the Okunoin and lit a lamp before Kōbō Daishi's tomb. In the saint's presence he vowed to begin the work of restoration.

Gradually Jōyo recruited a group of loyal monks and started reconstructing some of the halls. He designed a fireplace (called a *tsuchimuro*) that heated temple rooms so successfully that his followers could forego the usual winter retreat to Amano and Jison-in. In Jōyo's sixth year at Kōyasan the great Fujiwara Michinaga (966–1027), for three decades the most powerful man in Japan, made a pilgrimage appearance. Michinaga's journey was prompted by his having asked a close collaborator of Jōyo's, Abbot Ningai of Ōno, if Kōyasan truly should be called the Paradise of the Buddhas. Ningai, who had lived at Kōyasan for thirty-four years, answered that the mountain was indeed the paradise "where sacred ones from all the directions dwell for ever and the Buddhas of past, present, and future stay."9 Inspired by Ningai's assurances, Michinaga, an enthusiastic devotee of Miroku, decided to see for himself.

At Kōbō Daishi's tomb Michinaga is said to have experienced the miracle of a face-to-face meeting (the saint's "head had a bluish tinge, the robe looked clean and new, and the color of the skin was remarkable").10 Immediately afterward Michinaga donated funds to rebuild both the veneration hall at the tomb and the nearby bridge over the Tamagawa. To sustain the veneration hall he donated farmland on the south bank of the Kinokawa near Jison-in. In the earth before the tomb he had several sūtras buried, among them one copied in his own hand. His prayer was that after death he himself might be reborn in Miroku's Tushita heaven.11

Inspired by Michinaga's example and by varying accounts of Kōbō Daishi's miraculous survival, other Fujiwara climbed the mountain to make their own offerings. One of Michinaga's daughters, although forbidden to enter Kōyasan proper, had her hair cut off and buried in front of the mausoleum. By the time of Jōyo's death (in 1047 at Shakamon-in, near today's Reihōkan Museum) Kōyasan had become repopulated. Many of its lost buildings had been replaced, among them Chū-in, Kōbō Daishi's home temple.12

In the Miedō today hang portraits of Kōbō Daishi's closest disciples. Also there is Jōyo's portrait, an acknowledgment of his role as the mountain's second founder. In the Lantern Hall before Kōbō Daishi's tomb stands a lamp said to be the one Jōyo lit upon first arriving at Kōyasan. Jōyo, who came to Kōyasan largely out of devotion to his deceased parents, is credited with having instituted *higan* services at the Miedō, an augury of Kōyasan's future development as one of the nation's great centers for memorializing the dead.

Starting in 1059 members of the imperial family began following
the example of the nobility and aristocracy in making pilgrimages to
Kōyasan. Prince Shōshin, the fourth son of Emperor Sanjō, was the first
to come. He later built himself a residence on the bank of the Tamagawa
just north of the bridge to the mausoleum. The most celebrated of the
imperial ascents was made in 1088 by the grandly devout Ex-Emperor
Shirakawa (1053–1129; r. 1073–1087), already described in the introduction to this book.[13] In addressing Kōbō Daishi, Shirakawa acted in
conscious imitation of the kings of India who witnessed the Buddha's
sermons on Vulture Peak. After rebuilding the Great Stūpa (in 1103),
which had burned ninety-one years earlier, Shirakawa returned to the
mountain to donate further estates for its ongoing support. Then, in
1124, accompanied by his grandson Ex-Emperor Toba, Shirakawa visited Kōyasan for a fourth time to witness the dedication ceremony for
the Garan's reconstructed eastern and western stūpas (the Tōtō and
Saitō). Shirakawa's devotion to Kōyasan was so great that some speculated he was a reincarnation of Jōyo. Today in the Tōrōdō is the *Shirakawa-tō* ("Shirakawa lamp"). Visitors are told that this lamp has been
kept burning since first lit by the ex-emperor nine hundred years ago. It
stands beside Jōyo's lamp.[14]

After the pilgrimages of Shirakawa and Toba visitors from all classes
of society began to come to Kōyasan, many of them believing that one
trip to the mountain guaranteed rebirth with Kōbō Daishi in Miroku's
Tushita Heaven.[15] It is often said that Kōyasan's true prosperity began
with the visit of Shirakawa.

KŌYA-HIJIRI, THE RISE OF PURE LAND
BUDDHISM, AND KAKUBAN (1073–1143)

In or around 1073, some twenty-five years after Jōyo's death, a sixty-
nine-year-old monk named Kyōkai (1004?–1097) left the capital district
and entered Kōyasan. Kyōkai was a *hijiri* (literally, "he who knows the
sun"), a type of ordained but unaffiliated itinerant Buddhist holy man
who traditionally specializes in asceticism, ritual healing, and retirement
to the mountains. Other hijiri had come to Kōyasan previously, some a
half-century earlier in Jōyo's time, so a number of them were on the

mountain when Kyōkai arrived. Kyōkai, however, seems to have been the first person to organize Kōyasan's hijiri into a community. By the time of his death in 1097 this community, later to be known as *Kōya-hijiri*, made up an important segment of Kōyasan's population.

The general practice of the Kōya-hijiri was to alternate periods of retreat at Kōyasan with long sojourns into the nation's villages and byways where they performed cures and narrated the legends of Kōyasan, most especially the legend of Kōbō Daishi's ongoing *samādhi* in behalf of the nation. While in the villages the hijiri collected bones and other relics of deceased loved ones, and, in return for an appropriate offering, brought the relics back to Kōyasan for burial in the earth near Daishi's tomb. They also solicited donations toward the continuing restoration of the mountain.[16]

The Kōya-hijiri potentially were a very mixed blessing, however, for the brand of Buddhism that most of them practiced and preached owed relatively little to the intricate Shingon faith, but instead was a combination of Kōbō Daishi worship and Pure Land faith in the *nembutsu*. Pure Land belief required as its sole practice the recitation of the prayer *Namu Amida Butsu* ("I take refuge in Amida Buddha"), a response to Amida Buddha's vow to save all persons who placed their trust in him, regardless of their sinfulness, ignorance, poverty, or other unpromising circumstance. At death such a person's spirit would be escorted to Amida's western "Pure Land of Utmost Bliss" (*Gokuraku Jōdo*), a paradise where eventual enlightenment was assured. According to Pure Land belief one no longer needed to live a life of asceticism or rigorous study to achieve deliverance. A simple trust in Amida's vow was sufficient. Against the charge that such a teaching was "too easy," Pure Land defenders argued that in the present degenerate age of Buddhism, known as *mappō*, anything more demanding was too difficult. For the great majority of sinners it was the *nembutsu* invocation or nothing.

As more and more residents of Kōyasan began chanting the *nembutsu* to the rhythm of fish-shaped wooden drums, the traditionalist Shingon priests and student monks became alarmed. Clearly, such a deliberate placing of Amida Buddha above Dainichi was heretical.[17] While one might find some solace in the fact that the hijiri were a notoriously ragtag bunch, usually of common birth and with dubious religious training, the fact remained that the Pure Land enthusiasm now extended far beyond the hijiri. It had become so fashionable among the nation's upper classes that some of Kōyasan's regular priests found themselves performing Amadist funeral rites, such as the Amida-*goma*, simply to retain their aristocratic patrons. Perhaps what Kōyasan needed was a skilled syncretist who could reconcile the seemingly opposed faiths of Shingon and Pure Land. Enter Kakuban.

Kakuban (1095–1143) received his early priestly training at Shingon Ninna-ji in the capital and at several temples in Nara, including Kōfuku-ji and Tōdai-ji. At age twenty he entered Kōyasan, ordered to go there by Kōbō Daishi himself, says one story, who in a dream instructed the talented young priest to revitalize the mountain and the Shingon religion. At Kōyasan Kakuban engaged in intense esoteric practice, especially the strenuous one-hundred-day *Kokūzō-gumonji-hō* used by Kōbō Daishi. That done, with the aid of ex-Emperor Toba (1103–1156) he established a new school at Kōyasan for the study of Shingon, and then, to accommodate the overflow of students, built Daidenpō-in (in 1132), where he reinstituted the *denpō-e* training in the transmission of the Dharma, the program first established by Shinzen nearly three hundred years before. Also in 1132 Kakuban built Mitsugon-in (near the present Rengejō-in), a monastery for hijiri and the practice of the *nembutsu*. It was at Mitsugon-in that he took up residence.

What Kakuban then attempted to produce, both in theory and in practice, was a synthesis of Esoteric (Mikkyō) Buddhism and Pure Land (Jōdo) Buddhism. His argument, in simplified form, was that the speech component of Kōbō Daishi's "three-secret" speech-mind-body practice included the option of the *nembutsu* invocation. Thus, a person might embrace the Amida worship of popular Pure Land faith and still remain within the fold of traditional Shingon.[18] Put another way, being reborn after death in Amida's Western Pure Land paradise was the salvational equivalent of becoming enlightened through Dainichi Budda in one's present life (Kūkai's *sokushin jōbutsu*). Esoterically, Dainichi Buddha and Amida Buddha were the same.

From the start the conservative priests of Kongōbu-ji were dubious about Kakuban's clever marriage of Shingon and Pure Land. Even more, they resented Kakuban's increasing popularity and power, one manifestation of which was that Daidenpō-in and its affiliated temples now were receiving far larger endowments than Kongōbu-ji and its affiliated temples received. When in 1134 Ex-Emperor Toba chose to appoint Kakuban chief abbot of Kongōbu-ji in addition to Daidenpō-in, even the priests of Tō-ji in the capital took alarm, interpreting the appointment as a signal that Kōyasan was about to declare its independence of Tō-ji. (Tō-ji's chief priest had been serving as head of Kongōbu-ji since Kangen's time.) Both Tō-ji and Kongōbu-ji protested to Toba, but the ex-emperor held firm.

Kakuban, now recognizing that he faced a near-mutinous opposition, quickly surrendered the directorship of both Kongōbu-ji and Daidenpō-in and retired to Mitsugon-in for a thousand-day period of contrition and meditation.[19] The emboldened opposition, however, was not content with this gesture. They still feared Kakuban's influence and desired to be rid of him altogether. As a show of strength they assembled a force of armed monks, called *sōhei*, from their outlying estates. In response, Kakuban's supporters formed their own armed militia. In 1140, in one of Kōyasan's darkest moments, the armed monks representing Kongōbu-ji attacked the temples loyal to Kakuban and set them ablaze. In all, more than eighty halls were destroyed. Kakuban, joined by around seven hundred followers, fled to the foot of the mountain, then proceeded westward along the Kinokawa River to the safety of a small branch temple in a village beneath Mt. Negoro.

At the Negoro temple (Jingū-ji) Kakuban continued to write, study, and teach, and to pray for an early return to Kōyasan. But Kōyasan did not recall him. After just three years of exile Kakuban died at Negoro, where he was buried. He was only forty-nine. He left behind a large and important body of writing, including *Amida Hishaku* (The Esoteric Explication of Amida), a succinct treatise on the nonduality of Amida and Dainichi.[20]

Following Kakuban's death many of his followers returned to Daidenpō-in on Kōyasan, and for a time the hostility with Kongōbu-ji abated. But conflict broke out again in 1168, and once more in 1175. The imperial court attempted to remove those most responsible for the strife, but the difficulties continued. Finally, in 1288, nearly a century and a half after Kakuban's exile, Daidenpō-in's chief priest, Raiyu (1216–1304), left Kōyasan for Mt. Negoro, taking his disciples with him. At Mt. Negoro this group initiated a new branch of Shingon known as *Shingi* Shingon (New Doctrine Shingon), which soon became a vigorous nationwide school in its own right. The Negoro-ji temple grew so rapidly that for a time it rivaled both Mt. Hiei and Kōyasan in size and power.[21]

Today at Kōyasan the old strife with Kakuban is largely forgotten, and Kakuban himself is ranked among the mountain's most brilliant figures. Under his brief leadership Kōyasan enlarged its material wealth and reestablished itself as a major center for Buddhist scholarship. He often is remembered as "the man who revived Shingon-shū."[22]

KIYOMORI (1150–1186)

In the latter half of the twelfth century Japan suffered through a succession of bloody conflicts of imperial succession: the Hōgen War (1156), the Heiji War (1160), and the Gempei War (1180–1185). In the last of these wars the forces of the Minamoto clan triumphed conclusively over the previously dominant Taira clan, leaving a weakened and fearful imperial court little choice but to yield political and military rule to the Minamoto leader, Minamoto Yoritomo (1147–1199). Assigned the temporary rank of *shōgun*, Yoritomo made it clear he intended to remain shōgun for life and pass the title on to his heirs, which he did.

For his administrative headquarters Yoritomo chose not the imperial capital of Heian-kyō but his own primary military base, the small eastern city of Kamakura. Life now changed for much of the nation, including its temples. The self-indulgent Heian age (794–1185) was replaced by a disciplined, warrior-dominated "feudal" period later to be designated the Kamakura era (1185–1333).

While many of the nation's most powerful Buddhist temples had been drawn into the Minamoto-Taira conflict, often to their own destruction, Kōyasan remained aloof. The sympathy of most of its priests, however, was with the Taira, in large part because the chief of the Taira clan, the arrogant and brilliant Taira no Kiyomori (1118–1181), had been one of Kōyasan's major benefactors. In legend, if not in fact, it was a prophecy Kiyomori received at Kōbō Daishi's tomb that initiated his remarkable rise to power. This prophecy also led, indirectly at least, to his subsequent fall. Here is part of Kiyomori's story as seen from the perspective of Kōyasan. Some of it is historical.

In 1149, after Kōyasan's Daitō was burned in an electrical storm, Kiyomori, then a provincial governor, provided funds for its reconstruction. Seven years later, when the project was completed, Kiyomori climbed the mountain to be present for the dedication ceremony. After praying to the Great Sun Buddha he proceeded to Kōbō Daishi's mausoleum where he encountered an apparition of the saint in the form of an elderly priest. The apparition thanked Kiyomori for the repair of "our pagoda" and urged him to attend next to "our shrine" of Itsukushima in Japan's Inland Sea. The Itsukushima Shrine, the apparition explained, was another place where the Great Sun Buddha manifested himself. If you rebuild that ruined shrine you "shall rise to high office. None will be able to keep abreast of you in your rise to glory." With this promise the apparition vanished, leaving behind only the fragrance of incense.

In response Kiyomori rebuilt the magnificent (and now world-famous) "floating" Itsukushima Shrine on the island of Miyajima.[23] Later, while staying at the shrine, Kiyomori dreamed that a youth stepped forward from the shrine's holy door, handed him a short halberd, and spoke these words: "I am a messenger from the goddess of this shrine [Benzaiten]. Keep this blade. With it you will maintain peace in both heaven and earth and thus guard the imperial family." When Kiyomori awoke he found the physical halberd beside his pillow, a certain guarantee that he would rise to the premiership. The next day, however, the goddess herself appeared to Kiyomori to deliver a word of caution: "Do you remember the [favorable] words that I caused the sage of Mount Kōya to speak to you? But if your deeds are evil, your descendants will not know prosperity."[24]

From the moment of the Itsukushima oracle Kiyomori enjoyed one triumph after another. He made Itsukushima his family shrine and prayed there to Benzaiten, asking that his daughter conceive a son whom he could declare emperor. This quickly came to pass. So godlike in power did Kiyomori become that some said he was an incarnation of the Buddha. In his success, however, he forgot Benzaiten's warning. His rule became steadily more tyrannical and cruel until even his most sympathetic advisers were appalled. Finally, in the second year of the Gempei War, Kiyomori contracted a fever of preternatural severity. Curative water was brought down from Mt. Hiei, but the sacred liquid burst into steam the moment it touched his flesh. Nothing could be done to save him. Even in his suffering, however, Kiyomori thought only of vengeance against his enemies. "When I die," he instructed those at his bedside, "do not build a temple or pagoda. Do not perform any ceremonies for me. Instead you must send an army at once to vanquish Yoritomo; you must cut off his head and hang it before my tomb."[25] These were his last words.

In conformity with the goddess Benzaiten's warning, Kiyomori's evil deeds fell as curses on his progeny. On April 25, 1185, at the bay of Dan-no-ura in the Inland Sea, his cherished grandson, child emperor Antoku, just seven years old, was carried to the bottom of the ocean in the arms of his grandmother, Kiyomori's widow. Nearly all the lords and ladies who had placed their trust in Kiyomori drowned that day. The child emperor's mother, Kiyomori's daughter, pulled from the water against her will, subsequently lived out her life in rural isolation, her head shaved, dressed as a nun.

Kōyasan possesses a major relic of this history. In order to memorialize his early prophetic meeting with the ghost of Kōbō Daishi, Kiyomori had directed an artist to produce a large painting of Shingon's Dual Mandala for placement in the mountain's Golden Hall. As he was examining the newly completed work, Kiyomori impulsively drew a knife, cut into his neck, and repainted Dainichi's jeweled crown with his own blood. This famous "blood mandala," now somewhat deteriorated, survives as one of Kōyasan's treasures.

THE KAMAKURA ERA (1185–1333)

Throughout the Gempei War and during the conflicts that preceded it, Kōyasan held frequent memorial services to placate the spirits of the thousands who had suffered violent and often humiliating deaths. Such spirits especially needed to be mourned and pacified, for otherwise their torment might cause them to seek to injure the living. These ceremonies often were conducted on a grand scale, continuing for days without interruption.[26]

Kōyasan also became a destination for many of the conflict's survivors. Veteran warriors from both sides climbed the mountain to do penance for their bloody acts, some staying on to become monks.

Bereaved servants brought their master's cremated remains for interment near Kōbō Daishi's tomb, then, with shaved heads, withdrew to temple cells to pray for the master's enlightenment in his next life. Ousted ministers and officials came to Kōyasan in voluntary exile, hoping to distance themselves from a deceiving and mutable world.

So the population of the mountain grew during this troubled period. Temple halls and residences, more than two thousand in number, extended all the way from the Great Gate at the western end of the valley to the Ichi-no-hashi bridge at the entrance to the forest cemetery. Financial support for the temple city came from a number of sources. Memorial services brought in a steady stream of fee offerings. Pilgrims and visitors left material gifts and monetary contributions. The hijiri continued their fund raising in the villages. By far the largest support, however, came from the scores of agricultural estates that had been bequeathed to the mountain by various emperors, nobles, aristocrats, and other landowners. These holdings were now quite extensive, with a particular concentration of estates in the valley of the Kinokawa and on into Nara province. With large land holdings came large difficulties, however. There was the problem of maintaining the loyalty of estate workers and stewards, especially when these people judged the mountain's imposed taxes to be oppressive.[27] Often estate boundary lines were in dispute, and even the validity of estate ownership sometimes would be challenged. Occasionally, neighboring landholders conducted encroachments or local chieftains seized estate revenues. In such circumstances Kōyasan could appeal for protection to the court in Heian-kyō or to the military government in Kamakura, but such appeals rarely brought satisfaction. Japan had become a decentralized feudal nation, and large monastery complexes such as Kōyasan, willingly or not, now functioned as feudal entities in competition with other feudal entities. To defend its interests Kōyasan was forced to establish its own trained militia.

Another problem, also in part a consequence of the mountain's continuing growth, was the increasing disharmony among its primary categories of residents. By the end of the twelfth century the conservative scholar-priests (known as *gakuryo*), who had been trained in traditional Shingon beliefs and practices and therefore saw themselves as the primary members of the community, were outnumbered by two other constituencies—the Pure Land hijiri, previously discussed, and the mountain's custodial monks (or meditation practitioners), known as *gyōnin*. The conflict between the scholar-priests and the custodial monks was especially intractable.

Unlike the scholar-priests the gyōnin did not study the mandalas and sacred texts and conduct esoteric rituals. But they did perform a number of essential services. They prepared meals, maintained the halls, acquired supplies, collected taxes, trained the militia. They also carried out the more routine religious duties, such as placing offerings of incense, food, flowers, and votive lights before the deities. The gyōnin were the worker bees, and proudly so, with a full sense of having been called to service by Kōbō Daishi. All the same, their large numbers and growing independence produced an increasingly bitter conflict with the scholar-priests.

Meanwhile Kōyasan continued to attract some of the most prominent and innovative Buddhist leaders of the Kamakura era. Hōnen (posthumously Enkō Daishi, 1133–1212), founder of the Jōdo ("Pure Land") sect, spent at least a brief time on the mountain. Shinran (1173–1263), founder of Jōdo Shinshū ("True Essence Pure Land Sect") and the first prominent Buddhist priest openly to marry and raise a family, built a hut, called Amida-in, near Chū-in. Nichiren (1222–1282), founder of the Hokke sect (Nichiren-shū), made Kōyasan an important stop in his religious education.[28]

A visitor who was especially important to the hijiri was Ippen (posthumously Enshō Daishi; 1239–1289), a mountain ascetic and founder of the Ji sect of Pure Land Buddhism. Ippen taught the hijiri the "dancing *nembutsu*," a blend of singing, dancing, and bell ringing.[29] Chōgen (1121–1206), another visiting mystic and Pure Land devotee, reestablished the Shinbessho, a remote hermitage for hijiri in the southeast precinct of the valley.[30] Today this hermitage provides an important deep woods training retreat for Kōyasan's student monks. A new leader of the Kōya-hijiri was Kakushin (1207–1298), who came to Kōyasan in 1225. A Pure Land advocate, Kakushin later traveled to China and returned a Zen master. Just before his death at age ninety Kakushin served as spiritual adviser to Kōyasan's Karukaya Dōshin, the father of Ishidōmaru, whose story we already know. Myōe (1173–1232), a learned mountain mystic who sought to protect Kegon and Shingon from Pure Land dilution, was at Kōyasan for at least one summer. The Shingon poet-monk Saigyō (1118–1190), arguably the nation's greatest composer of Japanese *waka*, was a Kamakura-era resident, arriving around 1150 and remaining off and on for the better part of thirty years.

Pilgrimages by imperial figures continued. Ex-Emperor Go-Shirakawa, a central actor in the Gempei War, climbed Kōyasan in 1169. Ex-Emperor Gotoba came in 1207. Ex-Emperor Gosaga, in 1258. Ex-Emperor Gouda climbed the mountain in 1313, and in this instance "climbed" is the proper term. He appears to have been the first emperor or ex-emperor to have declined the use of a palanquin. The spiritual efficacy of ascending the 21.5 km (13.4 mile) pilgrimage trail from Jison-in was further emphasized with the installation, in 1285, of ten-foot-tall stone markers along the entire route. These granite posts, 180 in number, were dragged up the mountain and set in place at intervals of one *chō* (109 meters), replacing the wooden markers that had been used previously. On each post was chiseled both its number in the sequence and the Sanskrit *bīja* (seed-syllable) of one of the 180 divinities of the Taizō-kai mandala. By pausing for prayer at each marker the conscientious pilgrim was able to transform the ascent into a symbolic progress through the Womb Realm Mandala. The final marker, and climax of the journey, was the image of the Great Sun Buddha seated in the Daitō.

A second series of *chō*-spaced stone markers, this time thirty-seven in number, was installed along the path that led from the Daitō to Kōbō Daishi's mausoleum in the Okunoin. The *bīja* of this second set represented the thirty-seven sacred persons of the Diamond Realm Mandala, with Kōbō Daishi himself serving as the Great Sun Buddha at the center. The entire ritualized path from Jison-in to the Daitō and the tomb became known popularly as the *Chō-ishi-michi*, or "Chō-stone-path." This path continues to be maintained today with nearly all the markers in their original positions.

Also increasing in popularity during Kamakura era was the immensely demanding 1,400-kilometer, two-month-long, eighty-eight-temple pilgrimage that circles clockwise about Kōbō Daishi's home island of Shikoku. Legend insists that Kōbō Daishi founded the Shikoku route himself in 815, the year of his forty-second birthday, as a device for warding off the ill fortune that threatens every male at that age.[31] One elaboration of the story has Kōbō Daishi sanctifying each of the eighty-eight sites with sand taken from the eight stūpas built over the Buddha's relics in India.[32]

UNDER THE ASHIKAGA SHŌGUNATE (1336–1573)

In the late spring of 1281 all Japan was alarmed by news of a second Mongol military expedition to Kyūshū, this time with a much larger force than had been employed in the first failed invasion. The new armada was estimated at four thousand ships and 140,000 warriors. As on the first occasion the government admonished all the Buddhist clergy to pray for divine protection. As its contribution Kōyasan sent sixty priests and the Nami-kiri ("Wave-cutting") Fudō to the island of Shiganoshima off the port of Hakata in Kyūshū. With an altar placed facing the sea, the priests conducted a fire offering before the Nami-kiri Fudō, beseeching him to act against the approaching enemy. The result of their endeavors—or so the event was construed—was the fabled *kamikaze* ("Divine Wind") that scattered and destroyed Kublai Khan's fleet.[33]

In 1313, with the government in Kamakura weakened politically and financially by the drawn-out Mongol threat, Emperor Go-Daigo (1288–1339) joined in a conspiracy against the shōgunate, hoping to restore the primacy of imperial rule. When this enterprise failed, Go-Daigo took refuge at Mt. Kasagi (near Nara City) and asked Kōyasan, along with other temples, to send temple warriors to fight at his side. Kōyasan, consistent with its policy of remaining aloof from such conflicts, ignored Go-Daigo's appeal. When Crown Prince Morinaga also pleaded for help for the imperial cause, Kōyasan again declined. However, when the crown prince was forced to seek refuge at Kōyasan the monks took him in and concealed him. Flagrantly ignoring Kōyasan's traditional status as a religious sanctuary, the warriors of the shōgunate abruptly entered the valley, established their headquarters in the Daitō, and conducted a temple by temple search for Morinaga. When after five or six days the search proved unproductive, they gave up and marched away. Tradition says the clever monks had hidden the crown prince in the ceiling of the Daitō directly over the heads of the searchers.

In 1333, with the Kamakura regime finally overthrown (it had lasted a century and a half), Emperor Go-Daigo regained power, but by 1336 he was forced to flee again, this time to Mt. Yoshino, a short distance up the Kinokawa from Kōyasan. At Yoshino Go-Daigo continued to proclaim himself Japan's legitimate ruler even though a new military dictatorship, the Ashikaga, had enthroned its own emperor at the palace in Kyōto.

Thus, for a time Japan had two emperors, a circumstance referred to as the period of the Northern and Southern Courts (1336–1392). During these years of almost perpetual strife, Ashikaga Takauji (1305–1358), the new shōgun, together with his "northern" emperor, Kōgan-in, made a strenuous effort to win Kōyasan's support, largely through promoting financial protections favorable to the monastery—for example, by eliminating the illegal seizure of Kōyasan's rice shipments. Takauji himself climbed Kōyasan in 1344 to extend these guarantees personally.

Entering into such protective affiliations now became a way of life at Kōyasan, both for the monastery as a whole and for its individual temples.[34] Kōyasan's Seikei-in contracted with the Ōuchi clan and Henjōkō-in with the Nambu clan. Annyō-in (near today's Kōyasan University) contracted with the Ashikaga themselves. The usual pattern of agreement required a temple to perform year-round religious services on behalf of the clan members and to provide accommodations whenever clan members and their retainers visited the mountain. In return the clans supplied the temples with political and financial support. This arrangement, known as the monastery-hostel system, gradually came to include nearly all of Kōyasan's temples. Later it evolved into the *shukubō* system we find today.

Grand pilgrimages to the mountain continued under the Ashikaga, the most ostentatious one being conducted by Takauji's grandson, Shōgun Ashikaga Yoshimitsu (1358–1408), the builder of Kyōto's Golden Pavilion. Yoshimitsu's arriving retinue is said to have extended all the way from the Daimon entrance gate down to the Kakawa temple at the foot of the mountain, a distance of some twenty kilometers. The monks set before the shōgun a display of the mountain's most sacred treasures while Shingon scholar Yūkai offered instruction on the significance of each item.[35] It was well to remind the shōgun of Kōyasan's unparalleled religious status.

In general, Kōyasan prospered during the first half of the Ashikaga rule, with a particular resurgence in the area of doctrinal study. Among the outstanding scholars of the time were Chōkaku (1340–1416) and the aforementioned Yūkai (1345–1416), both of whom attracted student monks of talent and dedication. Yūkai and his followers took an especially firm position against those whose practices contradicted the word and spirit of Kōbō Daishi's teaching. This meant campaigning against the large numbers of Kōya-hijiri who had embraced Ippen's "dancing *nem-butsu*," an opposition that resulted in nearly all the hijiri being forced off the mountain by 1413. The Kōya-hijiri did not disband altogether, however, but continued their activities in the scattered hamlets of the nation.

Another one of Yūkai's purification projects was getting rid of a marginal but persistent collection of radical esoteric teachings known as Tachikawa-ryū. Here Yūkai's goal was not mere exclusion but total eradication, for he judged Tachikawa-ryū to have turned core Shingon principles into invitations to sexual license. Kōbō Daishi's sublime doctrine of *sokushin jōbutsu* ("becoming a Buddha in one's present body"), for example, was being equated with the bliss of sexual ecstasy. Sexual intercourse was touted as a primary path toward enlightenment. Yūkai called for a complete ban on such propositions and had every discovered Tachikawa text seized and burned. The suppression of Tachikawa continued at Kōyasan and at other Shingon centers for several decades after Yūkai's death.[36]

The authority of the self-indulgent Ashikaga rulers ended finally in a protracted and disastrous war of shōgunal succession known as the Ōnin War (1467–1477). Heian-kyō was left smoldering and looted. The great Zen temples of the capital, which had flowered under the early Ashikaga, were largely destroyed and their priests scattered. The Shingon temples of Daigo-ji, Ninna-ji, and Daikaku-ju, home to major Shingon training institutions, were burned. A peasant's revolt destroyed much of Tō-ji. A few generations earlier such losses could have been repaired through the use of estate incomes, but now the temple estates were largely under the control of feudal *daimyō* who no longer responded to any central authority.

Even Kōyasan was threatened, despite its physical remoteness from the capital. At the height of the Ōnin War a pillaging army entered the mountain to seize needed food supplies from the kitchens and storehouses of the monasteries. After this event Kōyasan sent military forces down into the plains below the mountain to close off access routes and defend its agricultural estates. Clearly the monastery-hostel contracts with various daimyō no longer provided adequate protection. Kōyasan would have to protect itself. But as one of the warlords would later remark, "No matter how powerful you are, there is always someone more powerful."[37]

Kōyasan also was burdened with the renewal of internal violence. During the early period of the Ashikaga the custodial monks, or gyōnin, established their own separate temple organization and procured an independent support system of income-producing estates, an arrangement that further aggravated their simmering rivalry with the scholar monks. The event that precipitated violence between the groups was the levying of a tax against the gyōnin to finance the reconstruction of the shrine at Amano. Instead of paying the tax the gyōnin gathered allies from nearby villages and attacked the scholar monks. The ensuing struggle, which lasted for four months, reportedly left three hundred dead on the side of the scholars and seven hundred dead on the side of the gyōnin and their allies. Eleven years later, in the summer of 1464, violence erupted again. An army recruited by the scholar monks, drawn from all four counties of Kii province, entered Kōyasan through the Daimon entrance and attacked the gyōnin. The halls of three *tani* were set ablaze. Eventually, an outside mediator arranged a temporary truce, but the bitterness between the scholars and the custodial monks remained.

And again there was the scourge of fire. The most extensive conflagration in Kōyasan's twelve-hundred-year history occurred in the winter of 1521. The outbreak began at Fukuchi-in. From there, fanned by mountain winds, flames swept from temple rooftop to temple rooftop, overwhelming the monks with their bucket brigades. By the time a quenching rain started falling more than 1,300 of Kōyasan's structures had been lost, including some of its most magnificent buildings. The Daitō, the physical and spiritual heart of the monastery, once again was reduced to rubble.

In response to this crisis the still despised but irrepressible hijiri, led by Ahon and Ajun of Ippen's Ji sect, began soliciting donations toward the reconstruction of the major buildings.[38]

ODA NOBUNAGA: KŌYASAN
UNDER SIEGE (1571–1582)

In the latter half of the sixteenth century the brutal and resourceful warlord Oda Nobunaga (1534–1582) launched a series of military campaigns designed to bring the anarchic nation under his sole military

control. Others had pursued this goal, but none with Nobunaga's bold-
ness and perseverence. When by 1571 he had succeeded in subduing, or
establishing alliances with, all but a few of his most powerful competi-
tors, he turned upon an opponent his predecessors had been reluctant to
attack, the formidable Buddhist monasteries. Nobunaga's first assault was
against Saichō's Tendai temple city of Enryaku-ji on Mt. Hiei just north
of the capital.

The attack was preceded with an offer. Mt. Hiei, which had open
ties with Nobunaga's enemies, could declare itself Nobunaga's ally, in
which case certain already confiscated temple holdings would be
returned; or it could declare itself neutral, in which case Nobunaga
would exact no punishment; or it could continue to oppose him, in
which case Enryaku-ji would be destroyed. Enryaku-ji elected to treat
this offer with contempt. After all, the monastery was a sovereign sacred
community with no obligation to respond to the demands of a secular
warlord. Further, it was still the official spiritual guardian of the capital, a
function that should make it doubly immune to assault.

Nobunaga quickly ordered an army of thirty thousand men to take
positions at the foot of Mt. Hiei's eastern slope. Now alarmed, the priests
of Enryaku-ji sent him some gold and silver as a peace offering. But
Nobunaga no longer was interested in negotiation. When several of his
lieutenants expressed dismay at the prospect of attacking a holy mountain, Nobunaga reportedly defended his action as both expedient and
morally necessary. "If I do not take them away now, this great trouble
will be everlasting. Moreover, these priests violate their vows; they eat fish
and stinking vegetables, keep concubines, and never unroll the sacred
books. How can *they* be vigilant against evil, or maintain the right?"[39]

At dawn on September 30, 1571, Nobunaga's forces began advancing up the mountain. Their orders were to plunder and burn every structure, including the most sacred sites. Additionally, every soldier-monk of
Mt. Hiei, every priest, man, woman, and child was to be put to the
sword. "Surround their dens and burn them, and suffer none within
them to live!" Even the temple entry town of Sakamoto at the foot of the
mountain was to be destroyed.

Nobunaga's army followed orders. Those inhabitants of Enryaku-ji
who did not die in the flames of the temples were intercepted on the
forest paths, hacked down, and beheaded. The few who escaped into

forest thickets and ravines were searched out and shot by marksmen with muskets. Reportedly, one group of captured women and children was beheaded on direct orders from Nobunaga.

For centuries the priests and soldier monks of Enryaku-ji had been able to intimidate emperors and sway policy in the capital. Now, in a couple of days, Nobunaga had brought to completion what no one before him had dared to attempt. The number of buildings destroyed on Mt. Hiei has been put at two to three thousand, the number of people slain, both priests and laity, at three to four thousand. Nobunaga lost fifty men, counting both dead and wounded. Enryaku-ji, "Temple of the Indestructible Light of the Dharma," the burial place of Saichō, was wiped out. The temple halls burned for four days.[40]

Enryaku-ji's supporting estates were seized. To Akechi Mitsuhide, the general who had been of especial assistance in the slaughter, Nobunaga granted the prizes of Sakamoto city and Mt. Hiei itself, a fief worth 100,000 *koku* of rice.

After dismissing the last of the Ashikaga shoguns, Nobunaga next placed under siege a Buddhist enemy that was even more formidable than Mt. Hiei, the immense moat-protected Hongan-ji temple-fortress of the Jōdo-shin-shū sect at Ishiyama (today's Ōsaka). Probably no other institution of the time, either political or religious, had such a broad and zealous base of power in so many provinces. Additionally, the Ishiyama fortress could be provisioned by boat from Ōsaka Bay. Unable to subdue the fortress directly, Nobunaga took on its allies in outlying areas, and with enough success to bring about a surrender settlement in 1580 after ten years of siege. Before surrendering, the defenders set the fortress afire, determined that Nobunaga, the "enemy of the Buddhist Law," would have no opportunity to desecrate its sacred halls.[41] The Ishiyama site Nobunaga gave to another of his ace generals, Toyotomi Hideyoshi. Hideyoshi later would build there the greatest of all Japan's fortresses, Ōsaka Castle.

With both the capital and the Naniwa (Ōsaka) area secured, Nobunaga now turned his attention southward to Kii province. Already he had defeated most of his enemies there, but Kōyasan and Negoro-ji, the two most powerful surviving Buddhist centers, remained intact. Both temples on occasion had been of military assistance to Nobunaga, but he feared their expansionist ambitions might make them future enemies. He

decided to dispose of Kōyasan first, for it had given him an excellent pretext for assault.

In March 1580 Kōyasan had provided sanctuary for five retainers of
a former Nobunaga ally and now archenemy, Araki Murashige. In July
1580 Nobunaga had sent armed envoys to Kōyasan to request that the
five be surrendered for execution. From Kōyasan's point of view this
request would have been appropriate only if the retainers had been criminals, but they were not criminals. They were political enemies. Besides,
the very presence of Nobunaga's armed envoys was offensive to Kōyasan,
which claimed immunity from all external police jurisdiction. Kōyasan's
monk militia bruquely escorted Nobunaga's men off the mountain. Furious at the affront, Nobunaga sent a second group of thirty-two warrior
envoys to enforce his demand. These men had been picked carefully from
nearby Sakai and had a good knowledge of the layout of Kōyasan's temples. Thus, when their demand for the five retainers again was rejected,
they began a temple by temple search, physically abusing those monks
who protested or tried to resist. Kōyasan's response to this outrage (or so
the story goes) was to ply Nobunaga's envoys with drink, then hack them
all to death.

This violence was Nobunaga's pretext for an assault. Starting in early
September 1581 he began sending military units southward into the
valley of the Kinokawa. As the army advanced, meeting only token resistance, it burned Kōyasan-affiliated villages and took possession of estate
rice fields. The rice, already approaching ripeness, would feed the army.
After occupying the major citadels along the Kinokawa, Nobunaga's men
took up positions at each of the trailheads that led to Kōyasan.
Nobunaga's third son, Nobutaka, was put in charge of assault preparations. At the age of twenty-two Nobutaka was deemed ready for his hour
of glory.

While the military buildup was taking place Nobunaga found
another outlet for his fury at Kōyasan. He instructed his operatives to
seize all the Kōya-hijiri they could find along the nation's rural pathways.
These hijiri, lacking weapons and not knowing they were at risk, made
for easy capture. When a sufficient number had been taken prisoner they
were assembled at Heian-kyō, at Ise, and at Azuchi (the location of
Nobunaga's primary castle), then executed. The number of Kōya-hijiri
slain during this operation is placed at 1,383.[42]

Meanwhile, Kōyasan was preparing its defenses. Apart from its own affiliated villages and estates, the only possible source of outside help was the powerful Shingi Shingon complex of Negoro-ji. But Negoro-ji rejected Kōyasan's appeal for help and instead sent units of their own militia to join Nobunaga's besieging army.

The core of Kōyasan's defensive force, its army of warrior-monks, numbered around three thousand. If we can believe the paintings of the time, each warrior-monk entered battle holding a curved sword in his right hand and a string of prayer beads in his left. Around his shaved head was wrapped a white scarf that concealed the mouth and nose. Worn beneath the religious robe was a suit of light armor. Some of these *sōhei* may have been trained in the use of the musket, although in this skill they would have been far behind Nobunaga's soldiers and the monks of Negoro-ji.

To Kōyasan's army of monk-warriors was added a much larger militia made up of landholders, farmers, and villagers from the nearby affiliated estates (in theory Kōyasan then controlled some 2,063 villages), men experienced in defending their rice fields and households against external intrusion. Many of these already would have pledged loyalty and subservience to Kōyasan.[43] The written records suggest a total of thirty-six thousand defenders.[44] This army was divided into ten units. Seven units were assigned the task of guarding each of the seven trails that led to the mountain, while three units were kept in reserve. At each of the entrances was displayed a silk banner with the characters *Kon-gō-bu-ji* and the image of a tiger with glowing eyes, symbol of a determined will to resist the enemy.

While these preparations were under way, the leadership of Kōyasan sent a message to Imperial Prince Shinnō, abbot of Ninna-ji in Heian-kyō, requesting that the prince ask Emperor Ōgimachi to intercede. The emperor promptly sent a message to Nobunaga with the instruction that he end the military threat to Kōyasan. There is no evidence that Nobunaga paid the slightest heed.

In October 1581 the attack against the portals of Kōyasan began. We are told that the young men of Kōyasan who had remained at the summit now descended the mountain to risk their lives against the enemy. The older priests who were left behind bowed their heads in prayer before the flames of five goma altars.[45] During the three days the attack lasted Kōyasan reportedly lost 1,300 men, but the assault did nothing to change the basic military situation.[46] We do not know what casualties the attackers may have suffered, but clearly Nobutaka now realized he faced a determined enemy.

Manifestly, Kōyasan was more easily defended than Mt. Hiei had been. Its remote summit valley was guarded on all sides by a succession of wooded ridges and winding, steep-sided ravines, terrain in which large numbers of men could maneuver only with difficulty. Pilgrim climbers enjoyed well-marked paths to the summit, but a hostile army strung out along the same trails would be subject to constant harassment and ambush. If the army opted to advance through untracked forest it would soon become disoriented and exhausted.

Kōyasan's defenders waited for a second assault, but nothing occurred beyond a few light skirmishes. As winter approached, and Nobutaka's army remained largely inactive, Kōyasan gradually realized it was less under attack than under siege. This new circumstance caused no increase in anxiety, for the mountain's storehouses had been fully stocked as one of the preparations for battle. Additionally, some of the provisioning villages, like Amano, were still within the defensive perimeter. The snows of winter fell and melted. Spring came. In April 1582 units of Nobutaka's army attacked in the area of Mount Iimori, but again there was no significant advance.[47]

In the summer, with the desultory siege of Kōyasan continuing, Nobunaga's attention turned to the west, where a critical military engagement was in preparation. Toyotomi Hideyoshi, perhaps the ablest of Nobunaga's generals, was organizing an army to engage the forces of the powerful Mōri clan in Bitchū province. If Mōri could be defeated decisively, then the door would be opened to all of western Honshu, which in turn would give Nobunaga access to the four provinces of Shikoku and the nine provinces of Kyūshū.[48] Compared to the developing possibilities in the west, the affair of Kōyasan was insignificant.

To assure victory against Mōri, Nobunaga decided to send the armies of his allies Tokugawa Ieyasu and Akechi Mitsuhide westward to join Hideyoshi, with himself at their head. As a first preparatory step Nobunaga instructed Ieyasu, freshly returned from a victory elsewhere, to go to Sakai (immediately to the south of today's Ōsaka) and enjoy an interval of rest. Akechi Mitsuhide he instructed to go home to Tamba province to remobilize his army. Meanwhile, Nobunaga himself would make his own preparations in the capital.

In Heian-kyō, as was his custom, Nobunaga took up temporary residence at Honnō-ji, a temple located near the imperial palace. Although technically a temple, Honnō-ji physically was a fortress, protected by high walls, a moat, and watchtowers. Usually, Nobunaga surrounded his places of residence with a retinue of at least two thousand armed men, but in the friendly environs of the capital a guard of two hundred seemed sufficient. On the twentieth day of June he hosted a large tea ceremony for some fifty nobles of the court. Meanwhile, his trusted lieutenant Akechi Mitsuhide, having assembled the Tamba army, was marching with his men to the outskirts of the capital.

Early in the morning following the day of the tea party a band of Akechi's men surrounded and attacked Honnō-ji. One report says that Nobunaga had just washed his hands and face and was drying himself with a towel when Akechi's soldiers burst in upon him and shot him in the side with an arrow. Apparently Nobunaga attempted to fight back, but after suffering a further wound retreated to an inner chamber. Some say he then cut his belly, others that he set fire to the temple. Perhaps he did both. In any event Nobunaga's body was "reduced to dust and ashes" in the temple flames.[49]

Nobunaga's eldest son, Nobutada (1557–1582), rushed with his guard to Honnō-ji, but arrived too late to assist his father. Nobutada himself was then surrounded in nearby Nijō Castle, where, after resisting Akechi's soldiers for a time, he committed suicide along with ninety of his retainers. The capital secured, the traitorous Akechi now marched his army eastward to Nobunaga's castle at Azuchi, captured it, and began distributing Nobunaga's wealth to potential allies. Akechi then marched back to Heian-kyō to receive the congratulations of a thoroughly intimidated imperial court. His scheme to seize full power required just one more bold stroke. He dispatched a hard-riding emissary to negotiate with Mōri in the west.

This emissary, however, fell into Hideyoshi's hands. Upon learning of Akechi's treachery, Hideyoshi decided to risk a daring intervention. He quickly concluded a compromise peace with Mōri (while keeping Mōri ignorant of the fact that Nobunaga was dead) and rushed back toward the capital, gathering fresh troops as he went. Hideyoshi's improvised army encountered Akechi's road-weary soldiers near Yamazaki, a short distance southwest of the capital. In a battle of less than two hours' duration Akechi's army was decimated. Akechi himself, fleeing for his life, headed toward Sakamoto castle at the foot of Mt. Hiei. He never arrived. Reportedly, he was overtaken in the countryside by some peasants who killed him to obtain his splendid armor. By one account, Akechi's head was severed, presented before Nobunaga's ashes in the ruins of Honnō-ji, then sewn back onto the torso. The reconstituted body was then hung on a cross and left to rot.

This whirlwind of change in the capital altered everything at Kōyasan. On receiving news of Nobunaga's assassination the besieging army immediately broke off their encirclement, split into small units, and hurried off to find a place in the confusion of new political alignments. With the portals to Kōyasan now open, grateful villagers began climbing the mountain in celebration. The monks who had been most active in the mountain's defense were advanced in rank. The villagers who had been the most loyal were freed from paying taxes, at least for the present.

Within a year Nobunaga's third son, Nobutaka, the one who had directed the attack on Kōyasan, was dead, a suicide while seeking sanctuary in a Buddhist monastery. Nobutaka's motto during the siege of Kōyasan had been *ikken hei tenka*, "Pacify the Realm with One Sword." Now that one sword was in the grip of Toyotomi Hideyoshi.

HIDEYOSHI AND KŌYASAN'S WOOD-EATING SAINT (1582–1603)

Upon learning of Nobunaga's assassination, Tokugawa Ieyasu also had planned to gather his army to attack Akechi. But he was able to do little more than assure his own safety when news arrived that Hideyoshi already had avenged Nobunaga's death and seized the political initiative. The future belonged to Hideyoshi. Within a year Hideyoshi would turn most of his potential rivals into allies and take control of a larger portion of the nation than Nobunaga had controlled. Within four more years he would subjugate the four provinces of Shikoku. Two years after that, in 1587, he would subdue Kyūshū.

Prior to tackling Shikoku, however, Hideyoshi first looked at the province of Kii, and saw there what Nobunaga had seen before him, the troubling spectacle of two great Buddhist enclaves—Kōyasan and Negoro-ji—each powerful enough to threaten one's southern flank and block access to both the lower Kii Peninsula and Shikoku's south coast. Hideyoshi determined to end this threat quickly. Since Negoro-ji had openly backed the ambitions of Ieyasu, Hideyoshi elected to deal with it first. In the third month of 1585 he attacked Negoro-ji with an army reported at forty thousand men. Two decades earlier Negoro-ji had been able to defeat the best army a shōgun could field, but now, without allies and its strength depleted, the temple fell quickly. Within a few hours some two thousand of its *sōhei* were slain and its great armory of modern weapons captured. Most of the 2,700 sub-temples, spread over several valleys and mountainsides, were set afire. Bewildered survivors scattered into the woods and across rice fields in search of hiding places. Those priests who were caught were executed. The leaders of the two main schools of Shingi Shingon, however, priests Sen'yo and Gen'yū, slipped through Hideyoshi's encirclement. A few days later, accompanied by a number of followers, the two made their way to the presumed safety of Kōyasan.

Hideyoshi next disposed of two relatively minor annoyances in the Kii area. A short distance to the west of Negoro-ji, at Saiga (today's Wakayama City), was a small but militant twenty-six-village enclave of Jōdo-shin-shū sectarians. This confederation had earlier been an important ally of Ōsaka's Hongan-ji fortress in its resistance to Nobunaga, and more recently had supported Tokugawa Ieyasu against Hideyoshi. Now, directly confronted by Hideyoshi's massive army, the Saiga surrendered. The second minor annoyance was a small Buddhist temple complex at Kumano in extreme southern Kii. Hopelessly overmatched, Kumano also capitulated (in the fourth month of 1585).

Hideyoshi now was ready for Kōyasan. His intent was to end Kōyasan's capacity for independent military operation, but to do so without exposing his men to the dangers of a mountain campaign. Therefore, in the seventh month of 1585 he sent Kōyasan a letter inviting the monastery to give serious consideration to three suggestions. First, Kōyasan should surrender all of its far-flung estates except for that small "ancient domain" identified in the earliest documents bearing Kōbō

Daishi's handprints.[50] To fail to do so, the letter stated, would be against the spirit of Kōbō Daishi and therefore inconsistent with Kōyasan's continuance. Second, the monks of Kōyasan should stop expending energy on military preparation, for them a treacherous and morally wicked enterprise, and return to the study of the Buddhist religion. Third, Kōyasan should no longer offer sanctuary to the enemies of the government, for this was contrary to the general interests of the Japanese people. Mt. Hiei and Negoro-ji had indulged in this practice, and for that reason had been destroyed.

There was no mistaking Hideyoshi's "invitation" as anything other than an ultimatum, but for Kōyasan to accept the three propositions would amount to total surrender. The first proposition promised financial ruin. The second, by ending the *sōhei* system, would expose Kōyasan and its estates to whatever predation came their way in a land still ruled by violence. The final demand, the most dishonorable of the three, would deny Kōyasan's centuries-old right to provide sanctuary. No doubt many of Kōyasan's priests insisted that Hideyoshi's three demands be rejected outright. The gods and the Buddhas had protected the mountain before; they would do so again. But a counsel of prudence prevailed. Three monks were chosen to go to Hideyoshi's temporary headquarters at Saiga to enter into negotiations.

Fortunately for Kōyasan, among the selected monks was a former soldier, and gyōniin, named Ōgo. Ōgo already was known locally as Mokujiki Shōnin, "the Wood-Eating Saint," a name assigned to him because he abstained from rice and all other grains, limiting his diet to fruit, berries, and nuts, all of which grew on vines and trees. For all his asceticism, however, Ōgo retained the rough, frank style of a warrior. This combination of self-discipline and blunt earnestness immediately became apparent to Hideyoshi, himself a farmer's son. The two men entered into a negotiation that was less a meeting of potential victor with potential vanquished than an exchange of mutual trust.

Hideyoshi agreed that his army would not occupy the mountain, and that not a single structure of Kōyasan would be destroyed. In return, Kōyasan agreed to surrender nearly two thousand estates, approximately ninety percent of its total holdings. These holdings had rendered in annual taxes the equivalent of 173,137 *koku* of hulled rice (approximately 865,000 bushels) at a time when 10,000 *koku* was sufficient to give a feudal lord *daimyō* status. (One *koku* equaled approximately the amount of rice required to sustain one man for a year.) Kōyasan's retained estates would yield but 21,000 *koku*. But as Ōgo had anticipated, a part of what Hideyoshi took away he soon began to give back in piecemeal fashion. As a memorial for his mother, Hideyoshi granted 10,000 *koku* and 1,000 pieces of gold for the reconstruction of the Kondō. Ōgo himself was placed in charge of this project. Other grants followed, including one for the building of massive Seigan-ji, another memorial to Hideyoshi's mother.[51] Seigan-ji later become a part of the modern Kongōbu-ji headquarters temple.

Kōyasan's weapons were to be surrendered. Every sword, long or short, no matter how prized, every dagger, every bow, every spear, every musket with its balls and powder was to be brought forward to be destroyed or given over to Hideyoshi's men. This surrender of weapons proved to be but the initial step in a profounder change, for soon all the temples of the nation were disarmed. Additionally, in 1588, Hideyoshi decreed that Japan's farmers must surrender their weapons. No Japanese leader had attempted such a policy before, yet compliance was remarkably thorough, and without the need of a dragnet. Japan's history of armed temples and an armed peasantry was ended.[52]

The third of Kōyasan's concessions to Hideyoshi concerned the monks from Negoro-ji who were then enjoying Kōyasan's protection. Kōyasan conceded that these monks were indeed criminals and therefore must be expelled. Yet, as Ōgo had anticipated, the monks came to no harm. Within two years Sen'yo was given the temple of Hase-dera (in Nara prefecture), which he made the headquarters of Shingi Shingon's Buzan school. In 1600, after Hideyoshi's death, Gen'yū founded the Chishaku-in temple near the site of Hideyoshi's mausoleum in the capital, and there established Shingi Shingon's Chizan school. Hundreds of other men who had found refuge at Kōyasan, but toward whom Hideyoshi felt no animosity, were permitted to remain on the mountain. In fact, in subsequent years Hideyoshi spared the lives of many of his defeated enemies on the one condition that they shave their heads and go into exile on Kōyasan. Thus, Kōyasan escaped with a clear conscience on the most sensitive of the three concessions.

But the mountain was now a profoundly changed institution. No longer did it have its own vast estates, its own army, its own territorial jurisdiction. It existed at the mercy of an autocrat whose power stopped only where he chose to have it stop. Hideyoshi no doubt was right, however, in arguing that the old Kōyasan had accommodated itself too much to the world. Ownership of a large number of estates had given birth to many ills, among them the need to recruit bands of roughneck warrior-monks for their protection.[53]

On March 3 of the lunar calendar, 1594, nearly a decade after his negotiations with Ōgo, Hideyoshi climbed the sacred mountain with a large entourage of feudal lords, among them Tokugawa Ieyasu. The once lowly farmer's son now signed his name *Tenka*, "The Realm." All the nation, he wrote, "excepting no foot or inch of land, has entered my grasp." The strongest of the *daimyō* were now his minions: the Mōri, the Maeda, the Tokugawa, the Uesugi, even the Date in the far north. He also had become a great builder of monuments, halls, and castles. He had required sixty-two thousand laborers for the erection of a new Great Buddha in Kyōto, deliberately made two meters taller than Tōdai-ji's Great Buddha and housed in a hall one-third higher than Tōdai-ji's Daibutsuden. He had employed even larger labor battalions for the construction of his personal palace at Fushimi and for massive Ōsaka Castle with battlements thirteen kilometers in circumference. Additionally, Hideyoshi was now the nation's premier patron of the arts, with especial attention to tea and Nō.

As for further military ventures, he recently had begun a campaign to conquer Korea. He imagined that China would follow, as easily reached as "pointing to the palm of my hand." When the mood was on him even far India seemed within his grasp.[54]

It was early spring at Kōyasan. Each day of Hideyoshi's visit had its elaborate ceremonial. He attended a memorial service at Seigan-ji, built in honor of his mother. On another day he visited Daishi's tomb. On the sixth day he had a new Nō play performed, one composed especially for the occasion by his personal chronicler, scholar-poet Ōmura Yūko. Ōmura's drama, subsequently known as *Kōya-mōde*, began with an account of how Hideyoshi and his party had stopped first at Yoshino to view the cherry blossoms, then proceeded on to Kōyasan so that Hideyoshi might make solemn offerings to the departed spirit of his mother. The *shite* of the first part of the play was an elderly nun who reappears in the second part transformed into the beautiful Bodhisattva of music and dance. This transformed nun was Hideyoshi's mother, her religious elevation a consequence of her son's filial piety.[55]

In the months following Hideyoshi's visit two curious stories spread about his experience there. One story has the gods taking such offense at the self-flattery of the Nō play that they strike the stage with a bolt of lightning. Hideyoshi, startled by the reprimand, immediately stops the drama, packs up, and leaves the mountain. The other story describes Hideyoshi at the Tamagawa the night before he was scheduled to visit Kōbō Daishi's tomb. He is seeking reassurance, for someone has told him that no person with an unclean soul would be permitted to cross over the sacred stream. We can imagine the eerie scene. Two hooded figures arrive at the dark bridge. The one in the lead stops, bows in the direction of the tomb, then steps onto the first plank of the bridge. This is Abbot Ōgo. Ōgo raises his lantern, gesturing for Hideyoshi to follow. But the great warrior is unable to proceed. The sound of black water throbs in his ears. He hears the cries of the dying. He is about to turn back when he sees a ghostly companion standing at Ōgo's side. The apparition mildly gestures for Hideyoshi to come forward. The Master will receive him, no matter how drenched in blood he may be. The next morning a fully confident Hideyoshi leads a sun-splashed procession to Kōbō Daishi's mausoleum.

In any event, it is clear that Hideyoshi's 1594 visit to Kōyasan further stimulated his interest in rebuilding the halls of the mountain. In all, he was to order the reconstruction of some twenty-five buildings, among them the Daitō, for which the Kōya-hijiri also had been collecting funds. He became such a generous patron that to the present day Kongōbu-ji uses his crest as its own insignia.

But there was one dark episode, an event that many of Kōyasan's priests still think of when they think of Hideyoshi. Some years before his visit to the mountain, while preparing for the conquest of Korea, Hideyoshi had bestowed his own title of *Kompaku*, or regent, upon his nephew and adopted son, Hidetsugu. He then asked Hidetsugu to lead the Korean expedition. Although a seasoned warrior, Hidetsugu considered the venture too dangerous and declined to go. Angered and suspicious, Hideyoshi quickly found other faults in his heir, the most curious one being that Hidetsugu once had taken his wife and daughters onto the monastery grounds at Mt. Hiei (also now partly restored with Hideyoshi's help) in clear violation of the *nyōnin kinzei* prohibition.

Hideyoshi also gave credence to stories that Hidetsugu suffered from bouts of irrational violence that made him unfit for high office. When, in 1693, one of Hideyoshi's wives bore him a son, thus providing him with a natural heir, he decided to remove Hidetsugu as his successor. To achieve this goal he first openly accused Hidetsugu of treason, then ordered him to go into seclusion at Kōyasan. Obedient to the order, Hidetsugu took up residence in Seigan-ji, the temple Hideyoshi had built in honor of his mother and where Ōgo was abbot. Hidetsugu had his head shaved and placed himself under Kōyasan's protection.

But Hidetsugu's exile did not assuage Hideyoshi's fears. As long as Hidetsugu remained alive he continued to be the legal regent of the nation, with his own son enjoying precedence over Hideyoshi's son in the future succession.

In the eighth month of 1595 three of Hideyoshi's generals, each with a thousand soldiers, entered Kōyasan and surrounded Seigan-ji. They then gave Hidetsugu Hideyoshi's instruction that he commit suicide. Hidetsugu protested that he was innocent of the charges of disloyalty. Priest Ōgo attempted to intercede for Hidetsugu, but the envoys would not negotiate. Left with no option, Hidetsugu performed ceremonial *seppuku*: he sat firmly upright, parted his kimono, grasped the knife with his right hand, plunged it into the left side of his abdomen and drew it across. A young page then performed the friendly office of beheading his dying lord. Hideyoshi's emissaries ended the ceremony by beheading the page. All this took place in one of Seigan-ji's most beautiful chambers, the one with Kano Tansai's murals of the willow tree in four seasons.[56] (The room is an obligatory stop for today's visitors.)

Shortly after Hidetsugu's death, Hideyoshi had Hidetsugu's three children executed as their mothers watched. Then the mothers and their ladies in waiting, thirty-one women in all, were decapitated. The bodies of the dead were thrown into a hole, covered over, and a stone marker erected with this brief inscription: "The Mound of Beasts." Placed deepest in the hole was the body of Hidetusgu's son.[57]

In the following year, 1596, Hideyoshi had his own natural son, a child of three, declared regent. Two years after that a dying Hideyoshi summoned to his sickroom Tokugawa Ieyasu, then the nation's most ambitious and powerful feudal baron. He told Ieyasu he feared that after his death the nation once again would be rent by war. Only Ieyasu was strong enough to prevent that. "I therefore bequeath the whole country to you, and trust that you will expend all your strength in governing it. My son Hideyori is still young. I beg that you will look after him. When he is grown up, I will leave it to you to decide whether he shall be my successor or not."[58]

Ieyasu declined to accept what was in effect an obligation to keep Hideyoshi's heir in office, and when Hideyoshi died the predicted war for national dominance took place. On October 21, 1600, Ieyasu's most implacable foe, Ishida Mitsunari, together with powerful allies, sent a "western" army of Toyotomi loyalists against Ieyasu's "eastern" army in what was perhaps the single most significant civil battle in Japan's history. The encounter, with 130,000 western soldiers engaging eighty thousand eastern soldiers, took place at the mountain intervale of Sekigahara, some one hundred kilometers northeast of Kyōto (along today's Shinkansen line). Ieyasu's eastern army was a decisive victor. The western army left an estimated thirty thousand dead heaped on the field of battle. Ishida was executed and decapitated in the capital.

In 1603, the victorious Ieyasu had himself appointed shōgun by the emperor, but for a time left open what was to happen to Hideyoshi's son, about whom a large and loyal support continued to gather. That question Ieyasu answered finally in 1615 when, after a massive siege, he destroyed Hideyori's headquarters at Ōsaka castle. As the inner defenses of the fortress were collapsing, Hideyori's young wife, Senhime, who happened to be Ieyasu's own granddaughter, sent a message to her grandfather asking that Hideyori be spared. When no reply came back Hideyori committed suicide. The next year Hideyori's two children, a boy of seven and a girl of five, were beheaded in the capital. Thus fell the last members of the short-lived house of Toyotomi Hideyoshi. While alive, Hideyoshi had gone to extravagant lengths to have himself declared a god, but in death the elevation did not hold.[59] Tokugawa Ieyasu was the new hero of heroes. The Tokugawa shōgunate, begun by Ieyasu and sustained by his heirs, would impose peace on Japan for the next two hundred and fifty years.

Although a disarmed Kōyasan did not have a military role to play during the period from Sekigahara to the fall of Ōsaka castle, the monks there had a clear bias toward the pro-Toyotomi forces. Hideyoshi had been a great patron. Additional patronage had come from a number of the warlords in the Toyotomi coalition. A few years earlier, Ishida Mitsunari (1560–1600), the leader of the defeated western army at Sekigahara, had been persuaded by priest Ōgo to build a repository for Buddhist scriptures near Kōbō Daishi's tomb. After the fashion of Hideyoshi's gift of Seigan-ji, this repository was offered in honor of Ishida's mother. The repository stands in place today, although its library of 6,557 scrolls are kept in the Reihōkan museum.

Because he had allied himself with the defeated western leaders, Ōgo chose to resign as abbot and leave Kōyasan altogether after Sekigahara. His successor, Seiyo, made a trip to Ieyasu's victorious headquarters to solicit Ieyasu's recognition of his new position. Through such deferential behavior Kōyasan escaped Ieyasu's wrath, at least for the moment. Ōgo died in self-imposed exile in the fall of 1607, after which his remains were returned to Kōyasan and enshrined not far from the bridge to Kōbō Daishi's tomb. Ōgo is remembered by the monks of Kōyasan as the man whose courage and acumen permitted Kōyasan to survive and even rebuild during a period of extreme danger. Ōgo's official posthumous name is Kōzan Shōnin, but the name that has remained the most popular is "Wood-Eating Saint of Kōyasan."[60]

UNDER THE TOKUGAWA (1603–1867)

Out of the rigorous national pacification achieved by the Tokugawa shōgunate came at least one important benefit to Kōyasan, an end to the threatened seizure of estates and estate income by uncontrolled warlords and officials. So what little was left of Kōyasan's manorial empire could be enjoyed in relative security. On the negative side was Kōyasan's absorption into the administrative structure by which the Tokugawa controlled the nation. In 1609 the new government officially declared the two primary abbots of Kōyasan to be *daimyō,* or feudal lords, each with a rank consistent with an allotment of three thousand priests and 100,000 *koku* of income. Each abbot in turn was required to make an annual trip to the new shōgunal capital of Edo (today's Tōkyō) to report to the government and perform obligatory rituals of allegiance. After each had reported on the affairs of his own assembly of monasteries, the Edo bureaucracy would pass back directives. From the perspective of Edo,

Kōyasan was just another feudal principality under obligation of obedient loyalty down to the smallest detail. Such matters as the format for initiation ceremonies, the content of school curriculums, the design and wearing of priestly dress, the criteria for advancement in rank—all these were defined and regulated by the government for purposes of bureaucratic control.

Not surprisingly, such an arrangement proved antithetical to real spiritual growth. Superficially the monks of Kōyasan enjoyed something of a renaissance in Buddhist scholarship during the early Edo years, but the primary motive for this labor was Edo's declaration that henceforth scholarship would be the primary basis for ecclesiastical advancement.[61] Few priests bothered any longer to devote their energies toward sectarian innovation or leadership. Kōyasan became passively monastic.[62]

Another subtly destructive aspect of Tokugawa leadership was the requirement that every inhabitant of the nation become a temple parishioner, at least nominally. On days specially chosen for the purpose each citizen reported to his or her local Buddhist temple where such information as date of birth, occupation, marital status, and history of travel was recorded. Not to have oneself churched in this fashion constituted a civil misdemeanor. In the eyes of the public, and increasingly in the eyes of the clergy as well, the temples became bureaucratic instruments of social control. Priests became government clerks.

Under the Tokugawa administration all communication with the Asian continent, once the energizing lifeblood of Japanese Buddhism, was closed off. The construction of ships capable of long voyages was forbidden. Any unlucky foreigner (Asian, American, or European) who came ashore in Japan, whether deliberately or by accident, faced execution. Correspondingly, any Japanese who sought to return from foreign parts risked a similar fate. Even as European powers began jostling for control of the western Pacific and much of continental Asia, the Tokugawa kept Japan sealed off and aloof.

In this sternly isolated and pacified land the mystique of Kōyasan and Kōbō Daishi remained intact. When several members of the Tokugawa family renewed the old practice of establishing reciprocal relationships with particular Kōyasan temples, other provincial lords followed suit. Bone relics of the nation's most important dead continued to be carried to the mountain to be placed in granite monuments (usually five-part, pagoda-like structures called *gorintō*) built along the path to Daishi's mausoleum. Many of these monuments were constructed on a massive scale. One built by Tadanaga, son of the second Tokugawa shōgun, for his mother, took three years to complete. As before, hair and bone relics of emperors and empresses were placed in a specially designated area near Daishi's tomb. Over these imperial relics were built not the five-part *gorintō* favored by the daimyō, but rounded mounds of earth and stone after the fashion of the most ancient Buddhist practice. The trails to Kōyasan became crowded again. Edo considered pilgrimage journeys to be a safe outlet for the pent-up energies of its subjects.

Internally, Kōyasan was still tormented by the old conflict between the interests of its scholar monks and its custodial monks. In 1639, in an attempt to raise their religious status within the community, the gyōnin petitioned the abbots of the scholar monks to administer to them the *abhisheka* initiation rite. This request was refused, perhaps with some discourtesy. In retaliation 2,500 of the gyōnin cut off all communication with the scholars. A few years later, in 1643, when the rebuilt Daitō was being dedicated (it had burned yet again in 1630), a group of gyōnin insisted that they be permitted to place a tablet on the central pillar, just as the scholar monks were permitted to do. The scholars rejected the proposal. The two groups now began to appeal to the government in Edo, asking that a judgment be handed down on disputed matters. Finally in 1692, after fifty years of listening to the bickering, Edo sent a commission to Kōyasan to examine the situation firsthand. The result was radical surgery. Of the approximately 1,865 residence halls then at Kōyasan, a full 1,182 housed gyōnin. At the direction of the government all but 280 of these halls were ordered abandoned. Hundreds of gyōnin were expelled from Kōyasan. The surviving Kōya-hijiri also suffered from the surgery, with scores excluded.

During the eighteenth and early nineteenth centuries, a period of economic strain and growing external threat from the Western nations, many of the old anti-Buddhist positions took on new credibility, especially among Japan's intellectuals. Prominent among the anti-Buddhist arguments was the assertion that the threat of Western hegemony resulted directly from Japan's having adopted a decadent alien religion (Buddhism) that obscured its own indigenous spiritual roots ("Shintō"). A new term, *kokutai* ("national essence"), became shorthand for what was now envisioned as the one most important characteristic of the nation, that its imperial rulers were "holy descendants of the gods." According to the logic of *kokutai*, filial piety toward the emperor necessarily transcended all other possible relationships or duties. Only through this national fidelity could Japan recover its true nature as the "Land of the Gods," a corollary of which was that it would then again become "the chief country of the earth, providing law and order for all lands."[63] To achieve such a goal the emperor must have returned to him all those powers that had been usurped by the shōgunate. Additionally, every accretion of foreign religion that had reduced the native gods to subordinate positions must be removed. This radical nationalist argument ended with the demand that the political rule of the Tokugawa and the religious primacy of Buddhism must end.

As they watched the dramatic developments that eventually led to the return of imperial power in the Meiji Restoration the monks of Kōyasan generally felt more sympathy for the emperor's party than for the collapsing Edo shōgunate. In the last weeks of 1867, as the struggle entered its final crisis, a high-ranking servant of the emperor, Chamberlain Washio, came to Kōyasan to ask that it provide sanctuary for the young emperor, then but sixteen years old, should the anticipated revolution fail. As things turned out, no sanctuary was needed. Washio and his royalist force had no more than set up camp at the foot of Kōyasan in the village of Kamuro when a messenger from Kyōto arrived with the news that complete victory had been achieved and the shōgunate abolished.[64] On January 1, 1868, the new era received its official title, *Meiji* ("enlightened government"). A short time afterward some thirteen hundred monks from Kōyasan joined Prince Komatsu Akihito, himself a former Shingon monk, on a journey to Edo, now renamed Tōkyō ("Capital of the East"), to express their support of the restored emperor.

MEIJI PERSECUTION AND THE BUDDHIST REVIVAL (1867 TO THE PRESENT)

Once the Meiji government was firmly established in Tōkyō the pro-Shintō reformers began to impose their will. In those parts of the nation where anti-Buddhist sentiment was most concentrated the activist slogan *haibutsu kishaku* ("abolish the Buddha, destroy Shākyamuni") was given virulent application. In Mito and Satsuma hundreds of Buddhist temples were burned or transformed into government offices or private residences. Nativists hauled sacred texts out of sanctuaries and set them ablaze in the temple yards. Altar implements were melted down for their metallic value. Wooden statues of the Buddhas and Bodhisattvas were decapitated, then burned. Some energetic reformers reportedly pounded stone statues into rubble, then incorporated the debris into the walls of privies.

While a part of this activity may have been the work of overheated mobs, most of it seems to have been performed in a spirit of conscientious patriotic duty. "We students would go through town every day smashing every roadside Jizō or other Buddhist statue we could find," recalled one Nativist. "If even one [statue] were missed, it was a great disgrace to us."[65] Hundreds of Buddhist priests, their temples desecrated, were forced to reenter secular life. In response to anyone who protested these predations, the new Ministry of the People (*Mimbushō*) assigned guilt to the priests themselves.

> [Buddhist] priests who have long been bastions of decadence, ignorant of the changing times, saturated in passions of the flesh, and confused as to which road to walk, priests who have lost all semblance of a true vocation . . . are themselves responsible for the destruction of Buddhism.[66]

The priests of Kōyasan, surrounded by sympathetic communities, had little to fear from firebrands and looters, but they too suffered. Almost at once the new imperial government acted to deprive Buddhist temples of their few remaining income-producing estates. At Kōyasan this meant the loss of all but a forest fringe of some three thousand hectares (about 7,410 acres). Additionally, the nation's nobles were instructed to discontinue their sponsorship of Buddhist temples, a change that especially affected Kōyasan. The centuries-old tie between Shingon and the imperial family was cast aside. Sennyū-ji, a Shingon temple in the hills west of Tō-ji, ceased serving as the imperial family's official patron temple.[67] Royal family members no longer could become priests or nuns, and those who already had received holy orders were instructed to abandon their calling. The seven-day New Year Shingon *mishuhō* ceremony at the imperial palace—a rite designed by Kōbō Daishi specifically to protect the imperial office and the nation—was disallowed after a thousand years of observance.[68]

Henceforward, all national religious ceremonies were to be conducted in accordance with the "native" religion. Three Shintō shrines were constructed at the Tōkyō palace so that the emperor could personally lead the nation in its proper devotions. In 1869, the year after the Restoration, the emperor made a ceremonial visit to the Grand Shrine at Ise, home shrine of his sun-goddess ancestor, Amaterasu. For twelve centuries no reigning emperor had thought it appropriate or necessary to make such a visit.

Changes also began to be introduced in the highly sensitive area of funeral and memorial services. In 1866 Emperor Kōmei, the Meiji Emperor's father, had been buried at Shingon's Sennyū-ji with largely Buddhist funeral rites, but only a few years later the dead emperor's memorial ceremonies were exclusively Shintō.[69] Such Shintō intrusions were highly threatening to a Buddhist institution that previously had enjoyed nearly exclusive jurisdiction over services for the dead.

Another important Meiji religious reform was the removal of all discernible Buddhist elements from the nation's mixed "shrine-temples." At the prestigious Miwa Shrine in Nara Prefecture, for example, where a close affiliation with Shingon institutions and Shingon doctrine had existed for centuries, all Buddhist trappings were stripped away, along with eighteen hereditary positions traditionally filled by Shingon priests. The Miwa Shrine's reward for this "purification" was redesignation as an imperial shrine with a rank second only to the Ise Grand Shrines themselves.[70]

Like most Buddhist temples, both great and small, Kōyasan too was something of a "mixed" institution, a condition the government no longer would tolerate. All of Kōyasan's native gods were removed from their shrines, "liberated" from captivity as objects of Buddhist veneration. This meant that the two primary native protector gods, goddess Niu-myōjin and hunter-god Kariba-myōjin, were taken out of the Myōjin-sha in the Garan. The shrine's large Shintō gate was dismantled.[71]

Meanwhile, all Japanese citizens were instructed to re-register, this time at their local Shintō shrine instead of at their parish temple. Under

Daikyō, the new "Great Doctrine," religion and the state were to be regarded as one, bound together by a universal recognition of the emperor as ruler, supreme high Shintō priest, and beloved parent of all. Alien Buddhism had no place in this scheme. Travelers to Kōyasan told of Buddhist priests in the large cities being sent into the streets to beg for something to eat.

Faith in Buddhism, already largely eradicated in India and surviving only marginally in China, now seemed about to end in Japan. Or so many thought.

But the anti-Buddhist movement, after reaching its greatest intensity in the early 1870s, began to run into a fundamental resistance: the mass of Japanese citizens were showing little interest in altering their traditional religious loyalties. Why should they despise the kindly Jizō figure at the village crossroad simply because some politician or university scholar said it had a foreign origin? Motherly Kannon, merciful Amida Buddha, fiery Fūdō Myō-ō—these spiritual entities were enshrined in the heart. Perhaps more to the point, ordinary Japanese citizens made no distinction between Buddhist practices and Shintō practices. The religion they had embraced happily and innocently all their lives was an indiscriminate mix.[72]

Gradually, the chief Meiji leaders, many of whom from the beginning had regarded religious reform as only a secondary goal, concluded that the radical anti-Buddhist offensive was only weakening their cause, dividing the nation at a time when unity was essential. The primary enemy was not Buddhism, but the military, economic, and cultural pressure being exerted by the Western powers. To meet this external threat Japan needed to transform itself into a modern power, and as quickly as possible. That meant placating the West while vital elements of Western technology were imported and copied. As a part of its modernization program the Meiji government (in 1873) lifted its long-standing ban on Christianity, declaring that Japanese citizens henceforth would enjoy free personal choice in the area of religion, just as was the case in most Western countries. The policy of advancing "pure" Shintō as a national faith was not abandoned, however. Instead, in 1882, something called *Kokka Shintō*, or "State Shintō," was established, and defined as a "social institution" rather than as a religion.[73] Each citizen now was expected to embrace Kokka Shintō in demonstration of having accepted an assigned place in the imperial system. By 1899, when the constitution reaffirmed this technical religious freedom, obligatory State Shintō already was functioning as an effective tool of public education and social indoctrination. For the next four decades it would be employed to promote both ultranationalism and militarism.

Japanese Buddhism, now given an opportunity to revive itself, declared that it too could be of service to a nation in crisis.[74] As an act of practical patriotism, and in response to the government's call for universal literacy, many priests began offering themselves and their temple halls for the training of the young. Something called *Shin Bukkyō*, or "New Buddhism," started to emerge, a Buddhism that sought to display greater intellectual vigor and social responsibility. In the social area, Shin Bukkyō emphasized the training of physicians and nurses and the building of hospitals, schools for the blind, and institutions for the aged. In the political area, it addressed such topics as capital punishment and abortion.

As part of this intellectual offensive the New Buddhism began pointing out to the nation, and to the West, that Buddhist thought was manifestly more "scientific" than Christian thought, especially in the fields of psychology, historiography, and evolutionary theory.[75] Spokesmen for Japanese Buddhism began to enter into international religious debates, most visibly at the "World's Parliament of Religions" held in 1893 at the Columbian World's Exposition in Chicago. Among the five attending Japanese representatives was a Shingon Buddhist priest, Toki Hōryū (later to become chief abbot of Kōyasan), who explained to a largely Western audience that historical Buddhism was an evolving revelation that had come to greater and greater fullness as its followers gained in spiritual capacity. Western notions that Buddhism was characterized by idol worship, passivity, and selfishness, Toki said, were based on a failure to understand how Mahāyāna (J. *Daijō*), or the Greater Vehicle of Northern Buddhism, had superceded the relativism of Hīnayāna (J. *Shōjō*), the Lesser Vehicle of Southern Buddhism. Toki proposed that Christianity and Mahāyāna in fact had much in common, that Christianity's concepts of the Holy Spirit and the Logos were akin to his own sect's concept of *shingon*, or "True Word." Similarly, the Mahāyāna ideal of the Bodhisattva, with its emphasis upon postponing one's own deliverance for the sake of promoting the salvation of others, demonstrated that Buddhism was, like Christianity, a religion of self-sacrifice and universal love.[76]

In a few areas Kōyasan no doubt benefitted from Meiji reforms. One government intervention put a final end to Kōyasan's centuries-old internal conflict among scholar monks, custodial monks, and hijiri. The solution simply was to abolish the divisions. Henceforward everyone living on the mountain was to be identified either as a member of a religious order or as a lay person. In consequence, in 1869 the former headquarters temple of the custodial monks, Seigan-ji, was combined with the former headquarters temple of the scholar monks, Kōzan-ji, to form a single comprehensive headquarters temple. This unified temple (both parts of which had been built by Hideyoshi) was named Kongōbu-ji, the name that previously had been used to describe the mountain complex as a whole.[77]

Meiji reforms in education also stimulated changes in the training of Kōyasan's priests. After the model of Western university education, with its aggressive historical criticism, Japanese Buddhist priests began to study the classical Buddhist languages, Sanskrit and Pali, and for the first time gain an adequate grasp of Buddhism's Indian origins. Kōyasan was in the vanguard of much of this new scholarly emphasis, reenforcing its past reputation as one of the most important centers of Buddhist study and publication. Kōyasan University was established in 1926, and later the Mikkyō Bunka Kenkyūsho ("Research Institute of Esoteric Buddhist Culture"). In the latter decades of the twentieth century scholars from around the world began coming to Kōyasan to lecture and to teach, to participate in conferences, to use Kōyasan's research libraries, and to examine its collections of art. In these years Kongōbu-ji and Kōyasan University also increasingly cultivated connections with Western religious institutions, especially with the Roman Catholic Church in Italy.

And then there was the Meiji edict of 1872 outlawing the policy of excluding women from the holy mountain. This edict also announced that henceforward the monks of Kōyasan might eat meat, let their hair grow, and get married. Most of the monks were appalled by these directives (although such practices had long since been adopted by the Pure Land sects), and for years there was a general refusal to conform to any of them. Regularly scheduled "searches for women" were instituted in an attempt to keep the mountain pure. All the same, women gradually began to make an appearance in the valley, and sometimes with official sanction. In 1881 a three-day ceremony sponsored by the empress brought in so many women that a number of them had to be accommodated overnight in regular temple halls. Increasingly women, usually disguised as boys, entered the valley to work as day laborers or to gather wood, herbs, and mushrooms in the forest. As enforcement of *nyonin-kinzei* continued to slacken, women who were members of the families of monks (including some monks' wives) entered the valley for brief visits. The wives of the townspeople also came. Finally, in 1906, a year after Japan's military victory over Russia, Kongōbu-ji officially announced that women no longer were to be excluded from Kōyasan. They could come and stay on for as long as they wished. The mountain had held out against the government's 1872 edict, hit or miss, for thirty-four years.

Once family life became commonplace, schools were opened for the children and appropriate new businesses established. Some of the old ruses for importing forbidden products were abandoned. In the past, pedlars would show up periodically with such products as "white eggplant" and "used nails"—that is, hen's eggs and small dried fish. Now one could purchase openly all sorts of animal products, edible and otherwise, and also previously prohibited pungent spices and "stinking vegetables." Kōyasan remained a temple town, but increasingly a lay person could live the life of a typical Japanese there.[78]

One thing did not change. Kōyasan still was vulnerable to devastating fires. In March 1888 fire broke out on two successive days, burning in all seventy-seven monasteries and seventy lay houses. And this time there was no place to go to seek economic resources for rebuilding. At a specially convened meeting in 1891 the governing priests decided to reduce the number of active monasteries. Only one hundred and thirty would be permitted to continue. The remaining several hundred would be abandoned and destroyed.[79]

The few Western visitors who came to Kōyasan in the early decades of the twentieth century give witness to the mountain's poverty. Many of the temple halls and especially the houses of the laity were in a deteriorated condition. Several small halls in the Garan court were no more than dilapidated storage sheds. In the Okunoin the old Lantern Hall at Kōbō Daishi's tomb was slowly rotting, its interior, hidden by a grating, too dark for the eye to penetrate. As an economy, only a few score lanterns were kept burning at any one time.

In the 1930s, however, some major reconstruction was begun, not as a sign of affluence, for Japan was then in a deep economic depression, but as a gesture of religious renewal and hope. Kōyasan's present Kondō, with its elegantly understated design and decor, was completed in 1932. The Daitō, for nearly a century no more than a low mound of charred foundation stones, was gloriously rebuilt in 1937 with a frame of concrete and steel. This achievement was hailed in Buddhist circles nationwide as a major sign of Buddhist revival.

During World War II, when Kōyasan served as a military training base, no material improvements could be attempted, nor was there any significant rebuilding in the years of the American Occupation.[80] However, following the "economic miracle" of the 1950s Kōyasan was able to begin a program of new construction, much of it with an eye to serving the increasing numbers of pilgrims and tourists. An administration building was added to Kongōbu-ji, now the headquarters of a newly established national and international Kōyasan Shingon Sect.[81] In 1981 a large Teaching and Training Hall was added to Daishi Kyōkai, the center for propagation of the Shingon faith among the laity. The Reihōkan Museum of Buddhist art was expanded in 1984. The massive Daimon gate at the western entrance was renovated. A new Lantern Hall was built before Kōbō Daishi's tomb, followed a short time later by a companion hall to house the overflow of memorial lamps. Kōyasan University was largely rebuilt, as was Senshū-gakuin, the seminary for priests. A new seminary for women was completed in 1987. The sidewalks and fences in the area of the Garan, Kongōbu-ji, and the Reihōkan were upgraded, and storefronts set back along much of the valley's main east-west street so that pedestrians could walk more safely and comfortably. Near the end of the twentieth century a large two-story parking garage and bus-parking facility was erected at the entrance to the shorter path to the Okunoin. Throughout these decades many of Kōyasan's *shukūbō* temples were expanded, some to the point where they could house, feed, and bathe more than two hundred overnight guests. A large number of lay residences on the mountain, many of them notorious firetraps, were replaced. Within the Garan itself during the mid-1990s the ancient Fudō-dō was totally dismantled, repaired, and lovingly reassembled, and the central Daitō fully renovated both inside and out. The three-day celebration of the reopening of the latter was attended by more than twenty-three thousand religious and lay people attracted from all over the nation. In 2004 Kōyasan was added to the UNESCO World Heritage List as a sacred site on the ancient Kii pilgrimage route (along with Yoshino-Omine to the east and the Kumano Sanzen to the south).

Today at Kōyasan a recorded voice on the bus loudspeaker announces to arriving visitors that they are entering the "most prosperous Buddhist town in the Kinki area."[82] This description no doubt is accurate. Kōyasan enters the twenty-first century with a well-maintained, even affluent, physical appearance, and with its spiritual goals seemingly intact. It continues to be an important pilgrimage destination, a major center for religious training (of both clergy and laity), a famed repository of the nation's dead, and the venue for some of Japanese Buddhism's oldest and most significant liturgical practices. The number of visitors from overseas increases steadily (now estimated at ten thousand annually). Some of these foreign visitors are known to return to Kōyasan each year as part of their personal devotional life. One Western specialist on Japanese pilgrimages has written of Kōyasan, "If I had only a day to visit Japan, this is where I'd come. Kōyasan breathes power and beauty. It is the very best of classical Japan."[83] Kōyasan has survived.

CHAPTER FIVE

COURT OF THE CENTRAL HALLS

We are standing in bright morning sunlight at the southern entrance to Kōyasan's ancient central courtyard, the precinct known as the Danjō Garan.[1] This spacious court, built on several levels and still heavily wooded at the margins, is where the mountain's first halls of worship were erected back in Kōbō Daishi's time. None of the earliest buildings survive today, but their replacements are here, most of them constructed on the ruins of the old. The three most centrally located buildings are the Great Stūpa (Daitō) with its enthroned Great Sun Buddha, the Golden Hall (Kondō) with its complex sanctuary and hidden Ashuku Buddha, and the lovely Miedō, shrine of Kōbō Daishi's sacred portrait. In all, there are more than twenty structures in the Garan, each used for a particular religious purpose. The Garan is Kōyasan's primary ceremonial center. As a magnet for pilgrims it is second only to the Okunoin and Kōbō Daishi's tomb.

Before entering the sacred court we pause at the *temizuya* to dip water onto our hands and rinse our mouths. Most visitors no longer bother with this traditional preparation, but we find it to be an appropriate courtesy. Now purified, at least in spirit, we walk past the foundation stones of the Garan's once-imposing Middle Gate, or Chūmon. This gate, lost many generations ago, is the only major structure of the Garan still waiting to be rebuilt.[2] The path leads to granite steps that climb to the central terrace. Directly ahead is the south-facing Golden Hall, the largest building of the court. Behind the Golden Hall, and to the right, rises the Great Stūpa, or Daitō. Our exploration will start with the Great Stūpa.

THE GREAT STŪPA: DAITŌ

Given the economics of its mountain setting, the Daitō is outrageously large.[3] It also is strikingly festive in appearance, with frame and doors and outthrusting roof supports painted a brilliant orange-red. Decorative bells hang from the eaves and from the rings and descending chains of the spire. But the form of the structure is what is most striking to the Western visitor. At Buddhist temples one usually looks for a standard "pagoda," a tall stack of more-or-less identical units rising three, five, seven, or more repetitions into the air. The Daitō follows a different model, that of the Japanese esoteric *tahōtō* ("stūpa of many treasures").[4] The base unit of the structure is a large square story with a protective four-sided roof. Over this base rises a dome. From the center of the dome rises a cylinder (with surrounding balustrade) that supports a pyramidal upper roof. Finally, from the upper roof soars an ornamented spire with a small saucer-shaped dew catcher at the bottom and a "*mani* jewel" at the summit. From base story to pinnacle the sequence of geometrical forms is a cube, a sphere (the dome), a pyramid (the upper roof), a bowl or hemisphere (the dew catcher), and a jewel.[5] This sequence of five forms is interpreted as representing many things. It approximates the body of the seated Dainichi Buddha: lower torso, navel, heart, throat, and cranial protuberance. It signifies the Five Sacred Elements: Earth, Water, Fire, Wind/Air, and Space. The Sixth Element, the immaterial all-unifying Consciousness, is signified by the stūpa in its totality. The five structural units of the stūpa also represent an idealized sequence of Buddhist spiritual growth: Initial Awakening, Spiritual Practice, Enlightenment, Nirvāna, the Absolute.6 To fully comprehend the Daitō's form would be to see it as a manifestation of the material body and immaterial mind of the Cosmic Buddha. That is, it would be to attain enlightenment.

The first Daitō built on this spot was completed in 837, two years after Kōbō Daishi's entry into his final meditation. That initial structure survived for a century and a half, burning in 994. Subsequently, four more Daitō were lost to fire. The present version was completed in 1937, ninety-six years after the loss of its predecessor. It differs from all the earlier structures in that it is composed largely of reinforced concrete poured over a frame of steel girders. The hope is that it will prove impervious to both fire and earthquake. Time will tell. Certainly this morning it glows with an unflawed freshness.

We climb to the broad granite platform that serves as the pedestal for the building. The massive wooden shutter doors have been folded back from the sliding inner *shōji* doors. One of these *shōji* doors is ajar. We remove our shoes, take a small pinch of dark powder from the incense dispenser and place the powder in our left palm. After touching some incense to our lips we spread the powder over our hands and then over our bodies. Now we enter. Just inside the door a young monk is seated on the floor before a low table. We leave a coin on the table to cover the nominal entrance fee. The monk, engrossed in his reading, does not look up.

The first thing we notice about the interior is the coolness of the air and the faint odor of incense. And then the remarkable color. The air shimmers with red and gold. Colors of the womb, colors of the sun. We are standing in a forest of pillars, all painted red. The upper beams and lintels and brackets are red. At the room's center is the gold, a theatrical gathering of five seated Buddhas—the esoteric *Gobutsu* or Five Nyorai—their immense golden bodies elevated on golden lotus thrones. The centermost figure, the Great Sun Buddha (Dainichi Nyorai), is perhaps half again larger than the four Buddhas who form a circle around him. Surrounding each of the four satellite Buddhas is a further circle of four pillars, and on each of these pillars is painted the gorgeous form of a seated Bodhisattva. In all, Five Buddhas, five circles of pillars, sixteen Bodhisattvas.

We are looking into the heart of a mandala. These are the beings who sustain the cosmos. We listen for the sound of their breathing, or at least for the hum of some machinery. But the Buddhas, with half-closed eyes gazing on emptiness, are silent. The only sound we hear is the quiet chanting of a small group of pilgrims standing off in one corner.

We look more closely at the central golden Dainichi. He wears the jewelry of an Indian prince. On each of the five facets of his gold crown is a flaming *mani* jewel and a Sanskrit "seed letter" (J. *shuji*; Sk. *bīja*) that represents one of the Five Wisdom Buddhas. His blue hair is tied in a topknot that hides his protuberance of wisdom, or *ushnīsha*. Just above the blue-lotus eyes is a small light-emitting curl, the *ūrnā*, an eye of spiritual insight. His cheeks are full, his earlobes pendulous. Beneath his chin are three "folds of beauty." Except for a drapery of golden gown over his left shoulder, his upper body is bare. His shoulders are rounded and heavily fleshed (like a lion's), his arms long, his fingers slightly webbed. His body is slim-waisted and sleek. He is seated in a full lotus position, right leg placed over the left (the esoteric posture), the soles of both feet (with toes slightly webbed) resting face-up on either thigh.[7] Behind him rises an intricate and massive golden mandorla (J. *kōhai*) shaped like a lotus petal. The golden throne beneath him is a complex structure of lotus forms that proclaim the Buddha's transcendence and purity. Crushed and humbled beneath the throne is the figure of a once-powerful dragon. This dazzling image of Dainichi, beginning with his golden skin, displays all thirty-two of the traditional physical attributes of a Buddha, at least by implication.[8]

What is of greatest interest to us, however—more than the princely crown or golden skin or lotus throne—is the positioning of the Great Sun Buddha's hands. These lie relaxed in his lap, palms up, the right hand placed on the left, the two thumb-tips lightly touching. This quiet gesture is the *mudrā* of concentration (J. *jō-in*, or *Dainichi jō-in*), the one Shākyamuni assumed under the Bodhi Tree. It is understood to signify the union of thought and matter, the union of the World of the Buddha (right hand) and the World of Sentient Beings (left hand). More important for the moment, it identifies this golden Buddha as the cosmic, all-unifying Buddha who sits at the center of the generative Womb Realm Mandala (Taizō-kai), the mandala of divine Compassion and the Lotus.[9] So we now understand the placental color of the hall. It is the red of the

Womb Realm Mandala. But a glance at the four surrounding directional Buddhas tells us they are not from the Womb Realm. Rather, they are from the companion Diamond Realm Mandala (Kongō-kai), the mandala that conveys a Wisdom that is as imperishable and pure as the *kongō* or Diamond. Thus, this particular grouping of the Five Buddhas represents a fusion of the two esoteric mandalas, the Womb Realm with the Diamond Realm, together forming the comprehensive Shingon Dual Mandala. Everything is here. Nothing is missing.

The four directional Buddhas, who in appearance are almost identical to the central Buddha, do not operate independently, but are manifestations of Dainichi. Each holds his hands in a *mudrā* that proclaims a major aspect of the unifying center. As we face Dainichi, the Buddha seated at our near left is Hōshō Nyorai, the Buddha of the South.[10] With his left hand Hōshō holds a piece of cloth, a stylization of a held sleeve (the *kesa-ken-in mudrā*). This grip on the sleeve conveys his grasp of the Dharma. The right hand is extended toward us in an open-palmed "offering" gesture (the *segan-in*, or Supreme Giving *mudrā*). By this motion Hōshō expresses Dainichi's limitless charity. Hōshō offers us every good thing, but most especially the gift of Enlightenment. Appropriately, his special emblem is the wishing jewel, which his open right hand holds invisibly. Hōshō's name means "Jewel-born" or "Jewel-producing" (Sk. *Ratnasambhava*).[11] Of the Five Elements he signifies Earth. His time of day is noon. His special Wisdom is an awareness of the equal worth of all things (Sameness). He declares that the Sun Buddha's divine light falls equally on all. The perfection he teaches us is generosity. Hōshō Buddha, help us be generous to our fellow creatures.

Behind Hōshō sits Amida Nyorai, the Buddha of the West and the primary Buddha of the Pure Land sects. His name means "Infinite Light and Life" (Sk. Amitābha and Amitāyus). His *mudrā* is much like Dainichi's *jō-in mudrā*, with both hands resting in his lap, except that Amida's index fingers turn up at the first joint to touch the thumb-tips, thus forming two circles. This is an expression *par excellence* of Dainichi's love and compassion, a love that is poured out with an infinite brightness. Of the Five Elements, Amida signifies Void or Space. His time of day is sunset, appropriate for the Buddha often called upon to receive one's spirit at death. His special emblem is the lotus, emblem of purity, gentleness, and beauty. Amida's special Wisdom is Discrimination, the ability to see and prize what is unique and distinctive in every person and phenomenon. The perfection he teaches is love for all creatures. Buddha of Infinite Light, help us to love one another.

At the right front of the platform sits Fukūjōju Nyorai, the Buddha of the North. His name means "Unobstructed Success" (Sk. Amoghasiddhi). Fukūjōju is the dynamic Buddha, an embodiment of the power and energy of the universe. With his left hand he holds a stylized sleeve. His right hand, held chest high, falls open, palm up, with the middle finger flexed slightly at the second joint (a characteristic of Shingon iconography). This gesture removes all fear and teaches confidence and perseverance. Fukūjōju's element is Wind. His time of day is midnight. His emblem is the three-pronged *vajra* or the *vajra* wheel. His special Wisdom is the Wisdom to Accomplish Metamorphosis, or Merciful Activity. Thus, he is an embodiment of all the provisional devices ("skillful means"; Sk. *upāya*; J. *hōben*) that assist us along the path to final truth. A small sign placed near his throne invites us to identify Fukūjōju with Shākyamuni, the historical Buddha whose birth, life, and death were an extraordinary example of skillful means.[12] Fukūjōju, Buddha of power and perseverance, help us to be a worthy example to others.

Finally, behind Fukūjōju sits Ashuku Nyorai. Ashuku is the Buddha of the East. His left hand holds a piece of detached sleeve. His right hand hangs pendent in front of his right knee, palm turned inward, fingers pointing toward the ground. This is the well-known "earth-touching" *mudrā* (*sokuchi-in*), most often associated with Shākyamuni's request that the earth bear witness to his claim to the particular spot of ground (the Bodhi Throne or Diamond Seat [J. *kongō-za*; Sk. *vajrāsana*]) on which he sat at the time of his Awakening. Ashuku's special Wisdom is the Wisdom of the Perfect Mirror that sees all things precisely as they are, without the emotional baggage of either fear or desire. This Wisdom is disinterested, non-dual, beyond subject-object delusion. It creates no karma. It is imperturbable, immovable. Ashuku's name (Sk. Akshobhya) means "the Immovable." Ashuku's time of day is dawn. His element is fire. He is the directional Buddha most associated with Enlightenment. His special emblem is the five-pronged vajra. Kōbō Daishi, himself a holder of the five-pronged vajra, selected Ashuku as the *honzon* of the Golden Halls at both Kōyasan and Tō-ji.[13] Immovable Ashuku, relieve us of our delusions and fears. Help us remain steady along the path to Enlightenment.

Superficially, the sixteen Bodhisattvas painted on the pillars look quite alike. All are seated on lotus thrones, enclosed within white moon disks, and similarly dressed. But the skin color varies, and sometimes the facial expression. The two most important keys to identification are the *mudrā* (which sometimes includes held objects) and the position of the pillar vis-à-vis the directional Buddha whom the Bodhisattva serves.[14] All sixteen of these iconic figures, known as the Sixteen Great Bodhisattvas, come from the Diamond Realm Mandala. They are all named "Diamond" or "Adamantine" (J. *Kongō*; Sk. *vajra*) after the primary symbol of that mandala: Diamond-King, Diamond-Treasure, Diamond-Light, Diamond-Language, Diamond-Fist, and so on. We take special notice of one of these figures, Diamond-Being—in Japanese, Kongōsatta (Sk. Vajrasattva). Kongōsatta is painted on an inner pillar close to Dainichi. He holds a five-pronged *vajra* (Ashuku's emblem) in his right hand and a *vajra*-bell in his left. Although we may not have been aware of Kongōsatta, he has been in constant wait for us, for he is a projection of the Great Sun Buddha's desire for our Enlightenment. He also is an embodiment of our own inner desire to awaken to the Buddha Nature within ourselves. If we don't already feel an intense and growing kinship to the Great Sun Buddha, Kongōsatta will see to it that we soon do. This Diamond-Being also waits for us in the Golden Hall.

We step back from the central display of the Five Buddhas and look upward. On a beam high over the altar is a plaque on which are written in gold the characters *Kō-bō*, "Dharma-spreading." This plaque refers to Kōbō Daishi, supreme exemplar of achieving Buddhahood in one's present body. The calligraphy of the plaque came from the brush of Emperor Shōwa (Hirohito), who was just ten years into his long reign when this new Daitō was completed. A thread of incense rises in the stillness before the Great Sun Buddha. Votive lights flicker on the altar. A sign on the platform reads in Japanese, "Praying for Peace."

We turn toward the exterior walls of the great room. In each of its four corners are two large portraits, eight portraits in all. These are paintings of the *Hasso Daishi*, Shingon's revered Eight Patriarchs of the Propagation of Doctrine, the holy men who preserved and passed on the sacred esoteric revelation. The first of the patriarchs, Nāgārjuna (c. 150–c. 250; J. Ryūju; in Shingon, Ryūmyō), is pictured in the southwest corner.[15] To the right of Nāgārjuna is his most important disciple and second patriarch, the Indian monk Nagabodhi (fifth century to eighth century). In the northwest corner are the Indians Vajrabodhi (671–741; J. Kongōchi) and Amoghavajra (705–774; Ch. Pu-kʾung; J. Fukūkongō). In the southeast corner are patriarchs five and six, Shubhakarasimha (637–735; J. Zenmui) and the Chinese Iʾhsing (683–727; J. Ichigyō). Finally, in the northeast corner are the seventh patriarch, Hui-kuo (746–805; J. Keika), and the eighth and final patriarch, Kōbō Daishi.[16]

All the portraits, except the last, are derived from scroll paintings Kōbō Daishi brought back from China. Each patriarch is shown seated on a temple chair. Nāgārjuna holds a three-pronged *vajra*, Nagabodhi a Sanskrit sūtra, Vajrabodhi a 108-bead rosary. Amoghavajra has his hands in the "outer bonds fist," signifying his desire to be released from the bondage of the passions. Zenmui has his right index finger extended in an emphatic teaching gesture. Iʾhsing makes an "inner bonds fist," an assertion of his vow to help all sentient beings.[17] Hui-kuo is identifiable by the young temple boy who stands at his side. The painting of Kōbō Daishi is modeled after the portrait by Prince Shinnyo enshrined in the Garan's Miedō. All eight of these iconic portraits are displayed in the sanctuaries of nearly all Shingon temples. As a group they give testimony to the continuity of Shingon priestly succession. They affirm that the initial revelation of esoteric truth received by the first patriarch, Nāgārjuna, has been fully preserved and is even now being passed on without falsification.

Which brings us to the story of that first revelation received by Nāgārjuna in a mysterious "Iron Tower" in southern India, a tower not too dissimilar in structure and meaning from the Daitō we are now visiting. For seven days and seven nights Nāgārjuna circled the Tower (moving clockwise, the direction of the sun's motion), all the while confessing his sins and chanting the mantra of the Great Sun Buddha. Then, as he cast seven consecrated white pepper seeds against the Tower's sealed door, that door opened and out poured golden light and the odor of incense. Nāgārjuna had gained admission to the Great Sun Buddha's universal palace. Within sat Kongōsatta, the "Diamond-Being," who had received the full esoteric teaching from the Great Sun Buddha and had for centuries awaited Nāgārjuna's arrival. Kongōsatta placed before the

Indian philosopher the *Kongōchō-kyō* and the *Dainichi-kyō*, the source texts for Shingon's Dual Mandala. He also showed Nāgārjuna other essential texts, among them the *Hannya-rishu-kyō*, the sūtra that is the basis of the Shingon daily meditation service. As Nāgārjuna studied these documents Kongōsatta tutored him in their deepest meanings. Later, upon leaving the Tower, Nāgārjuna discovered that he could remember in unerring detail every item he had read there and every word spoken by Kongōsatta. This precious material he dutifully recorded and passed on to his successors.[18]

We step outside into the sunlight again. From the height of the Daitō's base platform we have a good view, looking to the left and right, of the nine halls that form an east-west row that extends from one end of the Garan to the other. The Daitō is at the row's center. A small, brightly painted Eastern Stūpa (Tōtō) guards the eastern end of the line and a large, beautifully weathered Western Stūpa (Saitō) guards the western end. Most of the halls in this long line function much as do side chapels in a great cathedral. The nave and primary altar of this analogous cathedral would be found in the nearby Golden Hall. Like the Daitō, the Golden Hall is kept open for visitors from morning until evening every day of the year. It is our next stop.

THE GOLDEN HALL: KONDŌ

Fire at Night

Today's Kondō, like the Daitō, is but the latest in a succession of similar buildings constructed on the same site. In all six Golden Halls have been lost to fire. The first was completed around 819, shortly after Kōbō Daishi founded the monastery. It was then known as the Kōdō, or Lecture Hall, and was where the monks heard lectures and sermons, participated in ceremonial readings of sūtras, and learned meditative practices. In time, as the monastery expanded, some of these functions were assigned to other halls, but the Golden Hall remained the primary liturgical center. Its inner sanctuary is today the largest on the mountain and the most richly furnished, with three altars, a hidden *honzon*, six visible statues, two large formal mandalas, and a fascinating and inventive mandala mural.

The Kondō that preceded this one burned in 1926, in a conflagration still recalled by some of the mountain's oldest residents. That hall, built in 1852, was an architectural jewel, with double eaves and interior pillars covered with Indian red lacquer and gold leaf. The overhead beams were carved and gilded with a profusion of angels and dragons, and each panel of the coffered ceiling was decorated with native wildflowers. On the *shumi-dan* of the inner sanctuary, hidden in the darkness of a magnificent cabinet, was a carving of Ashuku Buddha, the Buddha of the East. Three visible and bold-postured attending deities were enshrined at Ashuku's right, three more at his left.[19] These figures were believed to have been carved by Kōbō Daishi himself, or, at the very least, commissioned by him and completed in his lifetime. Their value was inexpressible. But all were lost in the fire of 1926.

At around noon on December 25 word arrived on the mountain that the Emperor Taishō (r. 1912–1926), whose health had long been in decline, was dead. For several weeks the monks had been holding nearly continuous prayer services on the emperor's behalf. Now, with the bad news they gathered in the Kondō after the evening meal to begin active mourning. It was a cold night, with snow covering the courtyard, so at the back of the sanctuary a small sunken hearth was filled with hot coals to keep the oil used for the votive lamps from freezing. The hearth's fortunate attendant was the only person in the hall with warm hands. When the memorial service concluded shortly before midnight the monks began filing out into the darkness. Normally the hearth attendant would have removed the coals at this time, but the ceremony was scheduled to recommence early the next morning, so the coals were left as they were. The oil container was placed near them, but at a careful distance. All candles and lamps were extinguished and the Golden Hall shuttered for the night.

Shortly before dawn an alarm went out that the Kondō was ablaze. Within a few minutes, all Kōyasan seemed to be running through the snow toward the Garan, each person anticipating what he would do when he got there. While the firemen doused the fire with their hoses, the monks and lay people would grab the holy statues, the rolls of scripture, the altar instruments, the mandalas, the lamps, the banners, and rush these precious objects to safety. Even a young boy could be of assistance.

But the arriving runners saw at once that none of these things could be accomplished. Those first on the scene had pulled open the doors to try to bring out some of the sacred objects, but the fire, already out of control, fed on the supply of fresh air. The rescuers were driven back. Soon the enlarging crowd could do no more than stand in an awed circle and watch in disbelief. Much of the north wall was gone already. The roof was being eaten through, its copper tiles burning with a blue flame. The Kondō's painted birds and carved dragons, liberated by the flames, seemed to be flying above the treetops of the Garan.

The firemen had brought all of their equipment to the Kondō and run the hoses down to the Lotus Pond where they smashed through a thin cover of ice. But the pumps would not work. The mechanisms were frozen. None of this made any difference, of course. Priest Yamamoto Chikyō remembers the night. He made snowballs to hurl one after another into the roaring heat.[20] Nothing was saved.

The present Kondō, which was completed in 1932, is somewhat larger than its predecessor. It is less ornate and, because of this restraint, perhaps more appealing to the modern visitor. But the mountain remains haunted by what was lost in the 1926 fire, especially the seven precious sculptures carved more than eleven centuries ago.

The Layout

The primary external visual element of today's Kondō's is its immense roof, a Japanese *irimoya* modification of the Chinese hipped roof (the hips are sliced through with end gables, producing a crisp and flaring look). The exterior walls are patterned with pillars and beams and brackets, dark chocolate-colored wood against white plaster and white *shōji* doors. On the north and south sides there are nine bays, making the hall two bays wider than its predecessor. The east and west sides are seven bays wide. A deep porch, fully sheltered by roof overhang, encircles the building. Over the south and north entry steps is a further roof extension (a *kōhei*) that protects visitors from the weather as they remove their shoes and proceed up the steps in stocking feet. Out in the court before the front entrance (on the south) is a massive lantern, corresponding to a similar lantern that stands in front of the Daitō. This lantern is crowned with a golden five-pronged *vajra*, emblem of Ashuku Buddha, the *honzon* of the hall.

We slide back one of the doors and step inside. Where the Daitō presented us with one great open room, here we find ourselves in a wide outer corridor (the *gejin* or "outer space") that surrounds a sanctuary or "inner space" (the *naijin*). A wall of black-latticed sliding doors separates the two areas. In order to get an unobstructed view of the *naijin* we go to the front center of the lattice wall where two doors have been folded back for our convenience. From this opening we can see all of the sanctuary area, a full five bays wide and four bays deep, a space nearly the size of the entire Daitō floor. In contrast to the toast-colored *tatami* of the outer corridor, the floor of the inner sanctuary is painted a mirror-smooth black that has the appearance of a calm celestial pool. On this surface rest the lotus platforms that support the major furniture of the sanctuary: eight golden pillars, three altar tables (*mitsu-dan*), fourteen altar lamps, and a long dais (*shumi-dan*) that displays the enshrined deities. At either end of the room, facing one another across the sacred space, are two giant mandalas (the Dual Mandala). From the ceiling above hang three great golden canopies (*tengai*), each positioned above one of the altar tables. These intricate canopies simulate the clouds of jewels, flowers, and incense that hover above the Buddhas in Paradise.

Dazzling as this chamber is, our attention soon comes to rest on its least ornamented object, a large closed cabinet, golden-hinged and painted black, placed at the center of the dais. Two lotus plants rise before the cabinet's sealed doors, a white lotus on the left representing the western Diamond Realm Mandala, a red lotus on the right representing the eastern Womb Realm Mandala. On the dais at either side of the cabinet are six vivid companion deities, newly carved replacements for the statues lost in the fire of 1926. Enshrined in the cabinet is Ashuku Buddha, the *honzon* of the Golden Hall. We saw Ashuku a moment ago in the Great Pagoda, where he was a subordinate directional Buddha to the central cosmic Dainichi. Here he is the supreme object of worship and attention, his holiness and power enhanced by his invisibility.[21]

Ashuku Buddha and the Sacred Six

A small sign at the *naijin* entrance says that the hidden *honzon* is "Yakushi Nyorai," the Buddha of Healing, for it is by this name that Ashuku is best known to the laity. In fact the Kondō is referred to by some people as Kōyasan's Yakushi-dō. In esoteric theory Ashuku and Yakushi are one and the same. (Yakushi has a place in the comprehensive esoteric Dual Mandala only through this identification.) The actual physical appearance of the hidden sculpture is uncertain. We know only that the combination of lotus throne, seated figure, and mandorla measures one *jo* and six *shaku* in height, about 4.5 meters (15 feet). We could guess that the sculpture has cream-colored skin, blue hair, a short neck, a thick smooth body, and wears brightly colored royal clothing, for these are elements common to several of the six visible companion figures, all of which were carved by the sculptor who did the *honzon*, Takamura Kōun (1852–1934). We wonder additionally if the sculpture's left hand holds a small medicine jar, or *kusuri-tsubo*, the usual attribute of the Buddha of Healing.[22]

But speculation about the *honzon*'s physical appearance is of little importance compared to Kūkai's reason for installing Ashuku/Yakushi Buddha here. Kūkai taught that the Healing Buddha, who cures illnesses of both the body and the spirit, also presides over *bodaishin* (Sk. *bodhicitta*), the first aspiration toward Enlightenment. "If [practitioners] do not go seeking for the remedies of the King of Medicine," Kūkai wrote, "when will they ever be able to see the Light of the Great Sun?"[23]

The name Ashuku means "the immovable." Those who seek his aid will be assisted without fail. But Ashuku does not work alone. The six visible subordinate deities on the dais together form the most robust team imaginable for imparting the principles and disciplines that lead to awakening. Kūkai received help from each during his own transformation.

At the left side of Ashuku's cabinet we find Kokūzō Bosatsu, Gōzanze Myō-ō, and Kongō-ō. On the right side are Kongōsatta, Fudō Myō-ō, and Fugen Bosatsu. We will glance quickly at each one of these holy personages.

1. Kokūzō Bosatsu (Sk. Ākāsha-garbha-bodhisattva; "Womb of the Sky" or "Treasure of Emptiness"), the Bodhisattva of Space, expresses a Wisdom and Compassion that are as boundless as the sky. He is the central figure in two of the sections of the Womb Realm Mandala. Here he is seated on a blue lotus throne, his body alabaster white. At his back is a full moon circle of midnight blue representing Wisdom.

With his left hand he displays a long-stemmed white lotus
on which rests the flaming jewel of Enlightenment. His
right hand is extended palm open in a giving gesture, with
the middle finger slightly flexed to indicate the power of the
Sword of Wisdom.[24] Kūkai's own search for enlightenment
reached its climax in the early dawn at Cape Muroto in
Shikoku when Kokūzō, appearing suddenly in the form of
the morning star, pierced his mouth.

2. To the right of the serene Kokūzō is the enraged standing
blue-black figure of Gōzanze Myō-ō (Sk. Trailokya-vijaya;
"Subduer of the Three Worlds"). Gōzanze's white fangs are
bared at us. His eight long arms gesture at us with an arsenal
of piercing and subjugating weapons.[25] With his left foot he
stomps down on the chest of the Hindu creator-god Shiva.
His right foot is raised to crush the abdomen of Pārvatī,
Shiva's consort.[26] He has four faces, each face glaring in one
of the cardinal directions, each fanged, each equipped with
an all-seeing third eye of supernatural vision.[27] His hair is
ablaze. A wall of flame rises behind him, as if the very air
were ignited by his anger. Gōzanze is the Myō-ō ("Wisdom
King") who does the specific bidding of Ashuku Buddha.
His instruction is to assist us in subduing those passions that
most inhibit our quest for enlightenment, our habitual
greed, hatred, and ignorance. He loathes our lethargy. He
roars at us to waken us from sleep.

3. To the right of Gōzanze, seated next to the cabinet of
Ashuku Buddha, is the calm, beautifully molded, golden-
bodied figure of Kongō-ō ("Diamond-king"). Kongō-ō is
one of the four instruments of Wisdom that Ashuku generates. Pink and powder blue are his dominant hues. His
wrists are crossed at his chest and his hands fisted with the
thumbs enclosed against the palms. This is the Diamond
Fist (kongō-ken-in) that simulates the diamond-hard mystical
vajra (kongō) that pulverizes all hindrances to Awakening.
The overall gesture is the "mudrā of the Victor of the Three
Worlds" (J. sankaisaishō-in). It projects the awesome strength
the practitioner will need to persist along the path.

4. Seated on a lotus throne immediately to the east of Ashuku's cabinet is Kongōsatta, (Sk. Vajrasattva; "Diamond-being"), the Lord of Mystery and Master of the Iron Tower. He is sculpted in much the manner of his colleague Kongō-ō. He sits erect, elegant, balanced, with a minimum of stylization. His skin is white (the "color of the moon"). His *mudrā* is now familiar to us: the right hand at the chest holds a five-pointed *vajra* (*goko*), the left hand at the waist holds a five-pointed *vajra* bell (*goko rei*). The five-pronged *vajra* represents the Diamond Realm Mandala. The hollow of the bell represents the Womb Realm Mandala. Kongōsatta's essence is the innate Wisdom within all beings. Sculptor Kōun has given his mouth a downward turn in indication of deep concentration and earnestness. Kongōsatta is the Bodhisattva most intimately associated with Dainichi, with Ashuku, and with ourselves. He is our aspiration to become enlightened in our present bodies.[28] Young monks entering the Golden Hall for training are instructed to imagine themselves to *be* Kongōsatta. "My body is the body of Kongōsatta, and under my every step eight-petaled lotuses are springing up."[29]

5. Seated to the right of Kongōsatta is Fudō Myō-ō (Sk. Achala-vidyā-rāja; "the Immovable One"). Fudō Myō-ō has a family resemblance to his fellow myō-ō, Gōzanze, at the other side of the dais. Both have blue-black skin and a wrathful expression, bared fangs, a surrounding wall of flames. Fudō, however, has but two arms and a single face, and is seated. His body, which is thick, earthy, is said to be the body of a servant or slave, its swarthiness a consequence of long periods of labor in the sun. Fudō's assignment from Dainichi, of whom he is a direct manifestation, is to use the upright sword in his right hand to attack our laziness and ignorance and attachment. The rope (*kensaku*) in his left hand is for binding us should we attempt to flee his ministrations. Despite his menacing appearance, Fudō is among the most beloved of the sacred beings in the Shingon pantheon. He is forever faithful. He will not let those whom he helps slip away.

6. The last figure on the dais is Fugen Bosatsu (Sk. Samantab-
hadra; "He Whose Beneficence Is Everywhere"). There is no
greater Bodhisattva than Fugen, for his ten vows as expressed
in the *Kegon* sūtra essentially define the essence of a Bodhisattva. Kūkai held that of all the Bodhisattvas he is the one
most dedicated to those who are pursuing esoteric meditation. He also is especially devoted to helping women achieve
enlightenment. In head and torso the sculpture closely
resembles Kokūzō at the other end of the dais—the same
alabaster skin, the same smooth fleshiness, the same serenity.
But here we have a far more elaborate work of esoteric art,
for this particular Fugen is the intricate and uniquely powerful Fugen-emmei ("Fugen of Long Life"), a Bodhisattva
directly linked to the health-providing Yakushi Buddha. The
Fugen-emmei's shoulders sprout twenty arms. His lotus
throne is supported by four six-tusked snow-white elephants. (A similar white elephant was the vehicle by which
Queen Māyā became pregnant with Shākyamuni.) On the
head of each elephant is one of the Four Heavenly Kings
who guard Mount Sumeru. Fugen's natural hands hold a red
lotus bud (left hand) and a three-pointed *vajra* (right hand),
evoking the Womb and Diamond Realms. The eighteen
supernumerary hands hold various attributes of spiritual and
material power—a flaming jewel, an eight-spoked wheel, a
scepter, a trident, and so on. Overall, the sculpture is a veritable arsenal of ritualized assistance and protection.[30]

So we add Fugen's manifold force to the transforming energy of the
five other sacred beings displayed on the dais. Each of these works of art
and piety inspires and comforts us. Human shapes, animal shapes, moon
shapes, lotus shapes, instruments of intimidation and control, gold and
blue and red hues, every shade of pastel. All are instruments of Ashuku,
the Buddha of the East, the direction of the rising sun and dawn of
enlightenment. With these six assistants Ashuku will coax and prod us
toward a full awareness of the Great Sun Buddha's Wisdom and Compassion—if we are willing to ask. Is this idol worship? No, it is just a skillful
device to awaken us to our own innermost nature.

An incense bowl rests on a low table near where we are standing. We bend down and carefully add a pinch of the coarse powder to the burning line. May the Buddha of the East and the Buddha of Medicine, together with his unstinting assistants, take notice of our need.

The Dual Mandala

The battery of figures on the dais gives us some sense of the complexity of the Esoteric Buddhist religious vision, but these seven holy ones are only a small part of the total revelation. The complete sacred pantheon, with its hundreds of intricately related personages and principles, is observed most vividly in the Dual Mandala.[31]

The two giant hanging scrolls that make up the Dual Mandala are positioned at either side of the inner sanctuary and directly face one another.[32] To our right, in the eastern direction, the direction of sunrise, hangs the densely populated Womb Realm Mandala (the *Taizō-kai*). Its dominant physical feature is a large central red lotus. To our left, in the western direction, the direction of the setting sun, hangs the Diamond Realm Mandala (the *Kongō-kai*). Its dominant feature is a pattern of white moon circles. Since both mandalas are articulations of cosmic Reality, both display the Great Sun Buddha at their centers. The Womb Realm Mandala images that Reality largely as it is perceived by the senses. The Diamond Realm Mandala depicts it largely as it is perceived by the mind. The union of the two perceptions, of the senses and of the mind, constitutes the experience of Awakening.

At the physical midpoint between the two scrolls, at the precise center of the Golden Hall, is a large low square altar table (*dan*) where the presiding priest sits when addressing the *honzon*. To either side of this main altar table, to the east and to the west, are two more altar tables that directly face the mandalas. Each of the three tables is similarly furnished. At each corner is a *vajra*-tipped post from which is strung a five-color, five-stranded rope that encloses the table's ceremonial space. Also at each corner is a golden vase that holds five lotus buds color-coded (red, yellow, blue/green, or black) to indicate which one of the Four Directional Buddhas is being represented. Near the table's center is a fifth vase with five white lotuses. White is Dainichi's color.[33] Placed along the four sides of the altars are small golden bowls that at the proper time receive various ceremonial ingredients (holy water, incense, fruit, rice paste, red beans, sacred leaves, and so forth). The single most important furnishing of these altar tables is the centerpiece, a small *tahōtō*-style stūpa in the case of the main table, an equivalent five-part *gorintō* tower in the case of the other two. Each of these centerpieces represents the Great Sun Buddha. Each contains a sacred text or relic of Shākyamuni.[34] Clearly, the altar tables themselves are mandalas of the Five Buddhas.

We turn again to the two hanging scrolls of the Dual Mandala.[35] They both are rich in color and design, and easily the largest of the many Dual Mandalas on display at Kōyasan. Even so, the dim light and physical distance prevent our seeing their complex detail. So in imagination let us walk out across the shining black floor of the sanctuary to take a closer look.[36]

We go first toward the east, toward the rosy glow of the Womb Realm (Sk. *Garbha-dhātu*) Mandala. In its overall layout this mandala resembles the ground plan of a royal palace, with a single large square Central Court surrounded concentrically by narrower courts. There are eleven courts in all. Each court is filled with rows of sacred figures, except for the Central Court where the four directional Buddhas and Bodhisattvas are seated in a circle formed by the red lotus. At this flower's center is the Great Sun Buddha, Dainichi. The red lotus—the color of Compassion, the rising sun, and the generative Womb—is the dominant image of the mandala.

Around the outer perimeter of the mandala is its most extensive court, the Exterior Court. Through this court pass four entrance gates, one gate in each of the primary compass directions. Arbitrarily, we enter the mandala by the gate at the top, the resplendent Eastern Gate. To either side of us here, spread along the outer perimeter, are more than two hundred divine representatives of the beings who inhabit the "three worlds"[37] and the "six transmigratory paths"—that is, all sentient beings.[38] We observe animals, ascetics, divine musicians, gods of fire and water and the other elements, lunar gods, the god of death, armored guardian gods, serpent-god kings, gods of the planets and the zodiac. All the processes and material elements of the phenomenal world are represented, as are all the saints and divinities and devils of Hinduism and, by implication, every other religion of belief and unbelief, past and present. The more than two hundred figures of the Exterior Court are oriented toward the mandala's center. They draw on the energy of the central Great Sun Buddha whose Compassion extends without interruption to the farthest margins of the universe.

We pass downward out of the Exterior Court to the next court, Monju's Court, where we find ourselves in an elaborate "gate of initiation." Here we are administered to by the Bodhisattva Monju (Sk. Manjusrī), personification of the Wisdom of Dainichi. At Monju's side are the Bodhisattvas Kannon and Fugen, and beyond them, to the left and right, ten more attendants both male and female. Monju's left hand holds a blue lotus on which rests a three-pronged *vajra* symbolizing the indestructibility of Wisdom and the intrinsic union of the Buddha and ourselves as sentient beings. Monju's right hand is flexed toward us in a teaching and wish-granting gesture. He instructs us in the practices we must cultivate if we would seek enlightenment.

We move downward again to the next court. Seated in this court's gate, another gate of initiation, is the beloved Shākyamuni Buddha, the Sage of the Shaka Clan who transcended birth and death and, therefore, acts as a model for our own aspirations. He is wearing a robe of red that conveys the intensity of the Great Sun Buddha's love. He holds his hands before his chest in a preaching gesture as he instructs us in the Dharma. At his side, assisting in this instruction, are the Bodhisattvas Kannon and Kokūzō. These three represent the "three jewels" of Buddhism: the Buddha, the Dharma, and the Sanga.

We leave the Court of Shākyamuni and move farther toward the center, to the Universal Knowledge Court located just above the Central Court. Here we encounter the "Seal of Universal Knowledge" in the form of a flaming triangle or pyramid. This is the knowledge that engenders enlightenment by burning away attachment and illusion. The triangle's secret name is *Hosshō-kongō*, "birth diamond," for it gives birth to Buddhahood. Among the many sacred figures in this court are three who are known as "Buddha Mothers," another acknowledgment of the generative power of wisdom.

We come to the glorious Central Court. The unbounded and supreme Great Sun Buddha is seated on the central seed vessel of an immense open red lotus which itself is the container of the phenomenal universe. On the lotus's eight outspreading petals are the four directional Buddhas and the four assisting Bodhisattvas who articulate the cosmic

Buddha's universal love and power. (On the northwest petal sits Miroku Bodhisattva, the Buddha of the Future so closely associated with Kōbō Daishi.) A magnificent rainbow of light shimmers around Dainichi's head. His hands are positioned in the same *mudrā* we observed in the Daitō, the *mudrā* of concentration, both hands resting palm upward in his lap, the right hand (the Diamond Realm) on top of the left hand (the Womb Realm). This union of hands establishes the nonduality of the World of the Buddhas and the World of Sentient Beings, thus asserting the credibility of our aspiration to Buddhahood. The triangle formed by the touching thumbs evokes the female sexual organ, the *yoni*, and even more explicitly the transcendental "birth diamond" that gives birth to the Buddhas. At the exterior corners of the Central Court are four vases. Each vase holds a lotus and a three-pronged *vajra*, one more confirmation of the union of the phenomenal and the transcendental. The entire cosmic system is a breeder of Buddhahood.[39]

Despite its almost numbing complexity the Womb Realm Mandala has great emotional appeal. It tells us that the central Buddha's Compassion is active behind and within our seemingly stunted daily existence. This Compassion is inexhaustible. It generates all things and redeems all things. It is what we are composed of.

We cross to the western side of the sanctuary, to the Diamond Realm Mandala (J. *Kongō-kai*; Sk. *Vajra-dhātu*). At first glance this great scroll with its multiple patterns of white moon circles (several hundred circles in all) appears to be even more daunting than its eastern companion. Much of the difficulty is removed, however, when we realize that the overall mandala is composed of nine distinct smaller mandalas and that each of these can be approached individually. Further, these nine "assemblies" (as they are called) are related to one another both structurally and thematically, and form a sequence. The dominant assembly, which serves as the energy source and primary structural model for the others, is located at the center of the mandala. This central assembly is known as the "Perfected Body Assembly" (J. *jōshinne*), for it supports those meditations that lead to "the perfection of Buddhahood in this body" (*sokushin jōbutsu*).[40]

In the innermost moon circle at the center of the Perfected Body Assembly sits the Great Sun Buddha, crowned and dressed as an Indian Prince. His *mudrā* is the Wisdom Fist, or *Chi Ken-in* (also called the

Knowledge Fist), the defining gesture of this Diamond Realm. The gesture is formed by making a special fist with the right hand, one in which the thumb is held inside against the palm and the index finger is crooked so that it touches the thumb's first joint. The left hand is then formed into a similar fist, but with the index finger extended straight out. This extended finger is then inserted upward into the right fist, where it is embraced. The two linked fists are held before the chest.

The Wisdom Fist *mudrā* is variously interpreted, but at the most general level the left fist is understood to represent the phenomenal world (the world of sentient beings) and the right fist the world of the Buddhas.[41] Just as in the case of the two-handed concentration *mudrā* of the Womb Realm Mandala, the physical contact of the fists establishes the nonduality of the two worlds and the consequent possibility of attaining Buddhahood in one's present body. The sexual implications of the Wisdom Fist are fully acknowledged.[42]

Enclosing Dainichi's moon disk is a larger disk that also encloses four female Bodhisattvas who manifest the Four Perfections of enlightenment. Farther outward in the four cardinal directions are four more large disks, each of which encloses one of the directional Buddhas (Ashuku, Hōshō, Amida, or Fukūjōju) and four companion Bodhisattvas. (We notice Kongōsatta seated between Ashuku and Dainichi.) Dainichi's energy flows outward through the Four Perfections Bodhisattvas to the Four Directional Buddhas and their satellites.

Enclosing the five large disks of the Five Buddhas is a single giant outer ring constructed of *vajras* laid end to end. This outside ring, known as the Great Vajra Disk, or Great Moon Disk, is supported by four Great Gods of the Elements (Earth, Water, Fire, and Wind/Air).[43] These four gods, in the form of star constellations, hold up the physical sky and sustain the seasons of the year. Although not visible in this two-dimensional rendering of the Perfected Body Assembly, the Great Vajra Disk also supports vertically the "Jewel Tower" stūpa found on the summit of the cosmic Mount Sumeru. Beyond the circular Great Vajra Disk is a square double border made of more *vajras* set end to end. Within this broad border are seated all the Buddhas of the present era, one thousand Buddhas in all. Of necessity these are squeezed together so tightly in the limited space that beyond the first row little more than faces are visible, but all one thousand are present.[44] Positioned among the thousand Buddhas at the eight compass points are eight Offering Bodhisattavas, each figure offering flowers or music or some other gift while gazing toward the central Great Sun Buddha.

One last exterior border remains, an approximation of the Exterior Court of the Womb Realm Mandala. Here we find some twenty Hindu *deva* protectors of the Dharma, among them the Sun, the Moon, Brahmā, Indra, and Bishamon-ten. A form of Ganesha, the formidable elephant-headed god, guards the four entrance gates in this border. Further security is provided by four tridents of wrath placed in the corners and sixteen flame-spewing *vajra* placed along the sides. Nothing is permitted to intrude on the serenity of the central assembly, nor intrude on the meditation of the practitioner who sits before it.

In all, there are forty-three moon circles in the Perfected Body Assembly. Not counting the thousand Buddhas, there are sixty-one identifiable anthropomorphic figures, each one performing an essential function in the universal system. Each figure derives its nature and power solely from Dainichi's Wisdom Fist. Here, as in the Womb Realm Mandala, Dainichi is all.

As Dainichi's energy pours out of the central Perfected Body Assembly it flows downward into the adjacent Symbolic Attributes Assembly (J. *sammaya-e*) located at the bottom of the overall nine-part Diamond Realm Mandala. This Symbolic Attributes Assembly is almost identical to the central one except that its deities are represented by traditional symbolic attributes rather than anthropomorphically. Thus, Dainichi is indicated by a stūpa, Ashuku by a five-pronged *vajra*, Hōshō by a jewel, Amida by a lotus, and Fukūjōju by crossed *vajras*. Practitioners who meditate on this assembly are instructed to focus especially on the intrinsic identity between the Buddha's compassion and the human heart.

The energy of the Great Sun next flows clockwise out of the Symbolic Attributes Assembly and into the Subtle Assembly (*misai-e*) at the bottom left corner of mandala (the southeast corner). Here the sacred figures are again pictured anthropomorphically, but each is framed by a three-pronged *vajra*. The practitioner who meditates on this assembly seeks to attain the serenity and firmness that this *vajra* signifies.

In the next assembly, the Offering Assembly (*kuyō-e*), the Bodhisattvas (here understood to be female in their essence) offer themselves to the central Buddha out of a desire that all creatures without exception achieve enlightenment. While contemplating this assembly the practitioner prays for a measure of the Bodhisattvas' spirit of ecstatic sacrifice.

The Four Mudrā Assembly (*shi-inne*), at the upper left of the overall mandala, contains only thirteen Buddhas and Bodhisattvas (depicted in a combination of anthropomorphic and sammaya forms). Because of its relative simplicity this assembly is thought to offer a more easily visualized version of the preceding four assemblies.

Simpler still is the next assembly, the Single Mudrā Assembly (*ichi-inne*), at the top center of the Diamond Realm Mandala. Here the whole pattern has been reduced (or amplified) to one large anthropomorphic Dainichi Buddha seated within a single large moon disk and surrounded by borders of leaves and flowers. Dainichi's hands make the basic Wisdom Fist, the "single *mudrā*" of the assembly's name. This Single Mudrā panel is among the most beautiful images found in esoteric Buddhist art, and consequently is reproduced often as a separate entity. When displayed alone it is known as the Highest Being Mandala. Because of the large physical size of this Dainichi figure we are able to make out for the first time a subtle but important detail in his golden crown. The crown contains small images of each of the Five Buddhas, with Dainichi at the center. In this crown image Dainichi is making the Concentration Mudrā of the Womb Realm rather than the Wisdom Fist of the Diamond Realm, thus announcing that the two realms of the Dual Mandala are inseparable and fundamentally the same.

The clockwise rotation of Dainichi's energy now enters the top right section of the Diamond Realm Mandala, the Guiding Principle Assembly (*rishu-e*). The central figure of this assembly, while in essence Dainichi, is depicted visually as Kongōsatta, the Diamond Being. In this way we are informed that the Buddha Nature lies hidden within each of us, ready to awaken the moment we aspire to enlightenment.[45] Kongōsatta is surrounded by eight Bodhisattvas, the four in the cardinal directions being the *Vajra*-Bodhisattvas who express the transformation of the common human passions of materialistic craving (*yoku*), sensual attraction (*soku*), love (*ai*), and arrogance (*man*). With the assistance of these spiritual guides one's materialistic craving is transformed into an appetite for enlightenment, carnal passion becomes the desire to embrace the *vajra* (that is, Wisdom), infatuation for particular persons becomes a compassion for all creatures, and arrogance turns into generosity and courage. We are liberated by the very emotions that originally enslaved us, just as the *Hannya-rishu-kyō* insists.

The spiral of Dainichi's energy now drops into the Gōzanze Karma Assembly (*Gōzanze-katsuma-e*) at the center right of the mandala. This assembly returns to the general structure of the original Perfected Body Assembly, but with some key differences. The figure at the assembly's center, while resembling Dainichi Buddha in all physical details, "secretly" is the wrathful Gōzanze ("Subduer of the Three Worlds"). This fact is confirmed by the appearance of the four directional Bodhisattvas: each has crossed arms in Gōzanze's "Wrathful Fist" *mudrā*. While meditating on this assembly the practitioner experiences Gōzanze's aid in overcoming the world of desire, the world of form, and the formless world. The paralyzing three poisons—desire, anger, and ignorance—are transformed into zeal for the Dharma. *Bonnō soku bodai*. "Evil passions are themselves enlightenment."[46]

The ninth and final assembly is called the Gōzanze Symbolic Attributes Assembly (*Gōzanze-sammaya-e*). Again, Gōzanze descends into the Three Worlds, but this time to transform the mind of the practitioner rather than his passions. The change in goal is indicated by the use of *sammaya* forms (sword, *vajra*, etc.) for each of the divine principles instead of anthropomorphic representation.

Here ends the clockwise vortex of Dainichi's Wisdom, a descending journey that starts with the abstract All and ends with the most human mental and physical impediments to enlightenment. Each gate to the original self has been opened. All divisions of high and low, pure and impure, ultimate and relative, near and far have been erased. The practitioner at this point may wish to begin a second contemplation of the mandala, this time starting with the last assembly (the unenlightened mind) and ascending counterclockwise toward the center (perfected Buddhahood).

The Dual Mandala is deemed a proper subject for profound study and analysis. It also is a proper object for extended meditation and veneration. The word *mandala* itself literally means to possess (*la*) the essence (*manda*).[47] Kūkai wrote to the emperor that the very sight of the Dual Mandala "may well enable one to attain Buddhahood."[48]

The Outer Space

We turn away from the inner sanctuary to look again at the broad outer space that surrounds it. In total floor area the *gejin* is more than twice the size of the inner sanctuary, a circumstance that permits large groups of priests and monks to assemble outside the sanctuary in support of ceremonies being held within. On these occasions the separating lattice doors are pulled back. The *gejin* also provides ample room, especially at the sides, for lay spectators. Thus, the entire Golden Hall can serve as a single ceremonial space, a fact reinforced by eight mural-size sacred paintings placed in the exterior corners of the hall. Pictured here are the eight Offering Bodhisattvas of the Diamond Realm Mandala, each in the act of presenting a device of adoration and celebration—flowers, perfume, dance, light. These angelic figures proclaim the hall to be in every moment a precinct of paradise.[49]

The *gejin* has one more attraction, a highly original work of religious art often unnoticed by visitors. If we enter the narrower north corridor that passes behind the inner sanctuary we discover there a four-panel mural painted by Kimura Buzan (1876–1942), the artist who did the eight Offering Bodhisattvas just mentioned. Buzan's mural is itself a mandala, but a mandala with a rare difference, for seated in the lower half of the second panel is a mortal flesh-and-blood human being, Prince Shākyamuni meditating beneath the Bodhi Tree. The prince clearly sits in a mutable world. Shriveled leaves fall about him. His garments are frayed and rotting. His face is lined with a desperate fatigue. But something marvelous is beginning to happen. An *ushnīsha* is erupting from the top of his skull. A point of light is beginning to glow on his forehead. Through narrowed eyes he looks outward (and inward) at a coalescing Great Sun Buddha at the center of the third panel. Around this Great Sun float other mandalic Buddhas and Bodhisattvas, sixteen images in all.[50] Some of the figures overlap one another, their hand gestures obscured. Three of the four Myō-ō are but fragments, a glimpsed arm or leg, a scrap of clothing, a curl of flame. But the miracle is being achieved. Dainichi's hands form the Wisdom Fist of the Diamond Realm Mandala. The four directional Buddhas drift into position.[51] The Hindu gods Indra and Brahmā assume their posts as sentinels before Dainichi's all-revealing throne. Prince Shākyamuni has awakened. He observes the primal Truth. The history of Asia is changed forever.

HALL OF THE PORTRAIT: MIEDŌ

The Miedō stands behind and to the left (west) of the Golden Hall. It is a simple yet supremely beautiful hall, a favorite of photographers who like to catch it in the early evening when its porch lanterns are turned on. The present structure, built in 1848, is low and square, 12.6 meters (forty-two feet) on a side, with a low-pitched, subtly curved pyramidal roof covered with velvety cypress (*hinoki*) bark and crowned with a large brass finial in the form of a jewel. An open porch extends along three sides. From the porch ceiling hang small copper-colored lanterns decorated with lotus petals.

Although the hall is not open to us, the exterior protective shutters have been raised, allowing us to peek inside through openings cut in the *shōji*. What we see in the dim light is a succession of portraits hung along the walls of the hall's interior corridor. Each painting shows a priest seated in formal posture with his hands held in a characteristic *mudrā*. These honored persons are Kūkai's closest disciples, plus a few others who heroically served Kōyasan in its earliest years. At the northwest corner of the corridor, holding prayer beads in his right hand and gripping his left sleeve with his left hand, is Abbot Shinzen. Shinzen, a nephew of Kūkai, was the master's immediate successor as head of Kōyasan. Beside Shinzen sits Chisen, another nephew and Kūkai's most beloved disciple. Then comes Shinzei, Kūkai's younger brother and successor at Takaosan-ji. Jichie, Kūkai's successor at Tō-ji, follows Shinzei. And so on. The last of the Miedō portraits is of Jōyo, who in the eleventh century restored a ruined Kōyasan. Before each portrait is a small table with the day's offering of fresh flowers and vegetables.

The holy of holies, of course, is Kōbō Daishi's portrait, but even if we were permitted to enter the Miedō's inner sanctuary we would be unable to see it. Only a Shingon priest with the rank of *ajari* is granted the privilege of pulling back the veil, and then only once. All the same we know what the portrait looks like, for it has been copied in meticulous detail and these copies are found everywhere.[52] The master is shown seated in a

Chinese chair, his head turned slightly to his right. With his right hand he holds a five-pronged *vajra* (J. *goko*) before his chest. Looped twice in his left hand is a string of prayer beads (J. *juzu*). The symbolism is quite specific. The five-pronged *vajra* represents the Five Wisdoms of the five Buddhas of the Diamond Realm—that is, the wisdom of the Great Sun Buddha who sits at the heart of the Kongō-kai Mandala. The prayer beads represent the Great Sun Buddha's Compassion that radiates from the Womb Realm of the Taizō-kai Mandala. The *vajra* further indicates Kōbō Daishi's status as a chief priest and the prayer beads his role as foreshadower of Miroku, the Buddha of the Future.

The origin of the precious portrait is a matter of scholarly dispute. Shingon tradition, however, assigns it to the brush of Prince Shinnyo, the third son of Emperor Heizei and one of Daishi's closest disciples. Presumably, Shinnyo painted it from life just six days prior to Kōbō Daishi's entrance into his final meditation. Daishi is said to have dotted the eyes himself, thus imbuing the material image with spiritual life. He also is thought to have told his grieving disciples that in his absence they would be able to "nourish correct thoughts" simply by contemplating the painting.[53] As a sacred possession this painting is second only to Kōbō Daishi's body at the Okunoin.

Shinnyo's own story is a curious one. In 809, at the age of ten, he was declared heir apparent to his uncle, the newly enthroned Emperor Saga, but soon was forced to abdicate the position when his father, ex-Emperor Heijō, was accused of involvement in a conspiracy to unseat Saga. So at the age of twenty-four, with the throne now forever out of reach, Shinnyo shaved his head and entered Tōdai-ji temple in Nara. Soon afterward he became a disciple of Kūkai. It was Kūkai who initiated him and gave him the name of Shinnyo ("True Thusness"). Between him and Kūkai there appears to have been great mutual respect. Reportedly, his Kōyasan residence was next door to Kūkai's.

After Kūkai's burial Shinnyo appears to have grown restless, leaving the mountain almost immediately and subsequently residing at more than a dozen different temples in the vicinities of Kyōto, Nara, and Naniwa (Ōsaka). Among Shinnyo's ambitious projects during this time was a walking trip to the most famous sites for religious meditation in western Japan. When in his mid-sixties he wrote this self-evaluation in a petition to the emperor: "For the past forty years I have kept to religious practice in the hope of attaining Enlightenment. Yet to this day I have attained nothing." He asked for permission to go to China. In the Chinese capital, however, he was unable to find a satisfactory Shingon master. He asked the Chinese government to allow him to proceed on toward India. He and his dwindling entourage arrived at the southern Chinese port of Kuang-tung (Canton), and on January 27, 865, set sail down the Chu-chiang River into the South China Sea. Beyond this nothing is known, although there is one disputed report that he was slain by a wild animal in the mountains of Laos.[54]

On one night each year, the precious anniversary night of Kōbō Daishi's entry into eternal meditation, lay visitors to Kōyasan are permitted to go inside the Miedō to kneel for a moment in the presence of the curtained portrait. The atmosphere of that night, with the Miedō illuminated by thousands of lamps and candles, will be described in a later chapter.

SHRINE OF THE MOUNTAIN GODS: MYŌJIN-SHA

We have looked at three of the four most important sacred structures of the Garan: the Great Stūpa, the Golden Hall, and the Portrait Hall. Of necessity, we will return to each of these when we discuss the ongoing ceremonial life of the mountain. A fourth important location in the Garan that every visitor should see is the Myōjin-sha, the shrine residence of Niu-myōjin, royal mistress of the mountain, and her son, Kariba-myōjin, hunter guardian of the animals of its forest. The continuing good will of these two native gods is vital. The Kōyasan enterprise operates at their sufferance.

In approaching the Myōjin-sha we take a path westward from the Kondō through a large red *torii* or "Shintō" gate that serves as the ceremonial entrance to the Garan's western woods. A heavy twisted straw rope (*shimenawa*) that hangs from the gate's lower crossbeam helps to purify our minds and bodies as we enter the holy precinct.[55] We come first to the forest-shadowed Sannō-in, "Temple of the Mountain Gods," which faces the Myōjin-sha and serves as its votive hall. From this hall's western porch we can look down into the Myōjin-sha itself. Inside the shrine's fenced enclosure are three small sacred residences (*honden*). The two at the right, both with single doors, belong to Niu-myōjin and Kariba-myōjin. The third, which was added several centuries after the first two were built, has three doors. Here the primary occupants are the spirits of Princess Kebi (brought from Tsurugi on the Sea of Japan) and her younger sister Princess Itsukushima (brought from Kiyomori's Itsukushima Shrine on Miyajima).[56]

The *honden* of Niu and Kariba, last rebuilt in 1594, are both designated Important Cultural Assets. In style they resemble the *honden* at famed Kasuga Taisha in Nara. Steep steps rise to the gable-end door, over which extends a sheltering porch roof. Prominent crossbeams (*chigi*) thrust upward from the gables, pointing toward the Plain of High Heaven. Two log-shaped beams, called *katsuogi*, lie horizontally across the ridge of the roof.[57] The residences are painted red and white. The doors and fittings are covered with gold. Keeping guard are small stone statues of Kariba-myōjin's two hunting dogs, Kuro and Shiro. Open-mouthed Kuro is voicing the Sanskrit syllable *A* while closed-mouthed Shiro is voicing the syllable *VAM*. Together they are proclaiming the sacred seed letters of Dainichi of the Womb Realm and Diamond Realm mandalas. The dogs are an emperor's gift to the shrine.

We are in heavy woods here. In fact, the forest before us extends without interruption all the way to the summit of Mount Benten. The native gods like it this way. Even when in the city native gods must have their patch of woods, the presence of the wild. At the moment we are alone before the Myōjin-sha, which is no surprise. This is not a busy place.[58] Occasionally, a guided tour sweeps in, but not to stay long. Sometimes a single visitor comes to the shrine fence to pray and leave behind a supplication written on a wooden *ema*. A number of these *ema*, most of them with images of Kariba's dogs, now hang from the shrine fence and the *ema* rack. "I want to pass the Tōkyō University entrance exam." "I want a safe delivery this time." "I want peace between my husband and our son." "I have been engaged for too long. I want to marry soon." From time to time the wooden tablets are gathered by the shrine custodian for ritual burning.

One might think that Niu and Kariba are just another pair of obscure local native gods among the nation's countless thousands, but Kōyasan's priests know better. In accordance with the esoteric *ryōbu* ("dual") system, Niu is a manifestation of Dainichi of the feminine Womb Realm and

Kariba a manifestation of Dainichi of the masculine Diamond Realm.[59] Additionally, Goddess Niu is believed to have been a direct offspring of Japan's creator gods, Izanagi and Izanami, and thus the possessor of certain special knowledge. There is a story that in the fourth century Empress Jingū obtained from Niu a sacred red soil that when rubbed on Japan's warriors and ships guaranteed victory over Korea.[60] Later, at the time of the Mongol invasion both Niu and Kariba, along with Kebi and Itsukushima, were called on to assist in the national defense.[61]

As already implied, at the local level Niu and Kariba are intimately involved in the successful functioning of the mountain. When monks grow lax in their duties the two gods become angry. As a device to mollify them, selected priests and monks gather in Sannō-in at regular intervals to display their prowess in expounding the Buddha's teaching. These sessions usually are held at night, for the native gods hear best in darkness. Niu and Kariba also observe the ceremonies held in the Kondō, their presence there indicated in the form of a large scroll painting that hangs at the left of the sanctuary dais. In that painting Niu is pictured as a Heian-era noblewoman dressed in a luxurious multilayered robe and golden headpiece. In her right hand she holds a battle fan, emblem of her authority. Beside her sits Kariba, also dressed as an aristocrat, with moustache, goatee, and tall golden *eboshi*. He holds a wooden scepter (*shaku*). At the feet of the two gods are Kariba's hunting dogs. A delicate bamboo screen covers the faces and upper torsos of the deities, shielding them from the impertinent stares of common people.[62]

The sixteenth day of each month is set aside as a time to offer special prayers to the two guardian gods. On October 16, date of the annual Myōjin Festival, a troupe of boys carries a palanquin shrine to the Myōjin-sha. Here they pick up the spirit of the male Kariba and carry him triumphantly through the streets of Kōyasan.[63] In each temple yard the boys pause, raise the golden *mikoshi* above their shoulders, and while heaving it upward again and again, shout *Wasshiyoi! wasshiyoi! wasshiyoi! How lively and powerful is our god Kariba!* From the palanquin the god takes full measure of his subjects, accepting their worship and assessing the degree to which they are living lives in accordance with Kōbō Daishi's teaching. Meanwhile, a troupe of girls is carrying the spirit of Niu-myōjin along a separate route, stopping at each temple to present the goddess to her subjects.

SOME OTHER SIGHTS OF THE GARAN

There are many other structures in the Garan, each with its own special history and function. There also are a number of "natural" places of note, such as a particular pine tree and patch of grass. Here is a limited sampling of what one might find while wandering about the court.

Poet of the Cherry Blossoms

We walk eastward from the Kondō, past the Great Stūpa, and down steps that descend from the upper terrace. To our immediate right, surrounded by a fiery display of fall maples, is the graceful Fudō-dō, the second oldest surviving structure on the mountain. The Fudō-dō was built in Gonomuro-dani in 1198 (three centuries before Columbus) and in 1910 was moved here for repair and better fire protection. We continue walking until we reach the next to last building in the eastern Garan, the tiny Sanmai-dō. This fragile and weatherbeaten "Hall of Meditation," hardly larger than a closet, draws visitors because of its association with the great twelfth-century poet Saigyō. As a young man Saigyō (1118–1190), a descendant of Fujiwara Hidesato, suddenly abandoned wife, children, and a promising military career to embrace the monkish life of a wandering poet.[64] With the adopted name of Saigyō, or "Western Journey" (his original name was Satō Norikiyo), he retreated to various mountain hermitages, and most especially to Kōyasan, which became his frequent residence for thirty years. Both while traveling and when in seclusion Saigyō composed thirty-one-syllable *tanka* (or *waka*) lyrics that made him the most celebrated literary figure of his age and a major influence on subsequent Japanese poetry. Bashō, writing half a millennium later, designated Saigyō his primary model and mentor. Approximately two thousand of Saigyō's compositions survive today.

Kōyasan tradition insists that the Sanmai-dō was the locale of much of Saigyō's meditation and composition. Perhaps the poet's residence was near here. What matters most to visitors are the two ancient cherry trees growing near the hall's steps, for Saigyō more than anyone else is credited with evoking the Japanese religion of the cherry blossom. Perhaps, just perhaps, these two trees were alive in his time.

This is my wish:
That under cover of the [cherry] blossoms
I may die in spring,
That day of the second month,
Just when the moon is full.[65]

Cherry blossoms are at their most glorious in the second lunar month when the moon is full. This particular lunar date also marks Shākya-muni's death and entry into Nirvāna. By all evidence Saigyō did die on that day, just as he had wished.

Lay cherry blossoms
Before the Buddha,
Should you wish to pray for my soul
In the world to come.[66]

In this verse Saigyō acknowledges his inability to wean himself from attachment to the earth's beauty, here represented by the blossoms. His only hope in the afterlife, therefore, is that the Buddha, upon seeing the supreme loveliness of the memorial flowers the reader offers, will sympa-thize with Saigyō's craving and forgive him.

Saigyō was preeminent among Japanese poets (of whom Kūkai him-self was a leading representative) who equated the composition of poetry with religious practice. Every poem, he said, was a fragment of the image of the Buddha.[67] When a young Shingon priest once questioned Saigyō on a doctrinal point, he reportedly replied, "First of all, train yourself in Japanese poetry. If you do not understand poetry, you will not under-stand . . . Shingon doctrine."[68] Today one finds many stone monuments around Kōyasan on which poems have been carved, each text a fragment of the image of the Buddha.

Pine of the Sanko

Directly in front of the Miedō is a small pine encircled by a sturdy two-meter-high lattice fence painted in ecclesiastical red. The fence's func-tion is to protect the enclosed pine from any impulsive visitor who

1. A weathered stone image of Kōbō Daishi found along the Chō-ishi-
michi pilgrimage trail to the summit of Kōyasan. The saint sits on a
temple chair, a five-pointed *vajra* in his right hand, a double loop of
prayer beads in his left. (All photographs are by the author.)

2. Just outside the Fudō Entrance to Kōyasan we are greeted by the priest host of the Women's Hall. Prior to the twentieth century this hall was the nearest women could approach the sacred valley.

3. Before the evening meal at Shōjōshin-in. The cuisine is *shōjin ryōri*—literally, "a diet in pursuit of enlightenment." The author and his wife are at the right.

4. The decorative wall that encloses Rengejō-in temple. Showing above the wall at the left is the temple's *hondō*. At the right is a segment of the main hall. The month is February.

5. A young Japanese family tours the central halls on a misty day. At the left is the Golden Hall (Kondō), at the right the Great Stūpa (Daitō). The white truck gives an idea of the scale of these buildings.

6. A crowd of school children sketch the Great Stūpa, the primary shrine of the Great Sun Buddha. The Stūpa, with its complex symbolic structure, is the mandalic center of Kōyasan.

7. Inside the Great Stūpa, Fukūjōju Nyorai (the Buddha of the North), embodiment of the power and energy of the universe. The gesture of his right hand removes fear and teaches confidence and perseverance.

8. Inside the Golden Hall a flame-wrapped Fudō Myō-ō offers assistance to anyone who wishes to be liberated from the bonds of sin. Fudō's throne is a geometrical representation of Mount Sumeru, the cosmic mountain at the center of the universe. At the left is Kongōsatta, at the right a twenty-armed image of Fugen Bodhisattva.

9. The slightly smaller tree inside the protective circular enclosure is a descendent of the pine in whose branches the *sanko* landed that Kōbō Daishi threw from China. Directly behind the Sanko-no-matsu is the Portrait Hall (Miedō), repository of the painting Prince Shinnyo made of Kōbō Daishi shortly before he entered his final meditation.

10. Walking on the exclusive central path of purified mats the Hōin
processes from the Daiedō to the Golden Hall where he will preside at
the annual Mandala Ceremony. In the background at the right is the
small but elegant Eastern Stūpa (Tōtō). At the center is poet Saigyō's tiny
meditation hall, in front of which two ancient cherry trees are struggling
into bloom.

11. Dressed in gray/light-blue robes, students from the women's seminary join the laity in adorning the Portrait Hall with flowers and candles prior to the lunar Shō-mieku ceremony.

12. While the chanting of the lunar Shō-mieku continues within the Portrait Hall, a senior priest steps outside onto the porch, his body silhouetted against the illuminated Great Stūpa, to address the attending crowd. "In this place and on this very night eleven centuries ago," he begins, "Odaishi-sama entered his meditation in behalf of all sentient beings." At the far right is the Sanko-no-matsu.

13. Some student monks enjoy an opportunity to relax and watch Kōbō Daishi's birthday parade. Passing at the moment is a troupe of *goeika* ladies in black kimono, singing and playing their sacred music. One student already has spotted the next group of celebrants, scores of costumed small children pulling a cart that contains an image of the holy Child himself.

14. The birthday parade ends with a series of floats. Advancing in the foreground is a menacing Tengu, a goblin-like mountain creature and important actor in several of Kōyasan's favorite legends. At the rear comes the Child Daishi kneeling on a lotus platform with hands in *gasshō*, praying to the Buddha.

15. A large *gorintō* memorial in the forest cemetery. The structure is made up of a cube (Earth), a sphere (Water), a flared triangle (Fire), an upturned hemisphere (Wind/Air), and a composite jewel (Space). On the face of each stone is carved that element's Sanskrit seed letter. The monument is an expression of the Great Sun Buddha and the entire cosmic order.

16. A Mizumuke ("water-splashing") Jizō sits with his back to the Tama-gawa, the stream that runs through the heart of the Okunoin near Kōbō Daishi's tomb. Supplicants place *toba* before the Jizō on which they have written the posthumous names of their deceased loved ones.

17. The formal pilgrim path crosses the Tamagawa and leads directly to the massive Lantern Hall, behind which is Kōbō Daishi's tomb. This day the hall is draped in ceremonial colors. Large paper lanterns display the Kongōbu-ji insignia. A procession of Kōyasan's highest ranking priests soon will be passing.

18. An outdoor fire offering (*saitō-goma*) at Hōki-in concludes with several hundred lay people being guided along the purifying path of coals and ashes. Bamboo poles at either side offer assistance in case of a loss of balance.

19. Just before the midnight inauguration of the New Year five saffron-robed monks sound the ancient Daitō bell, one purifying stroke for each of the one hundred and eight categories of sin that human beings were heir to in the preceding year.

20. This veteran *henro*, here leaving temple number 31 on the 88-temple Shikoku pilgrimage, formerly did the circuit entirely on foot. Today he is riding in an air-conditioned van with a small entourage of admirers. But that's all right. The quiet flowering of the journey still makes him feel alive and blest. At the end he will go to Kōyasan to report to Kōbō Daishi, who, in the form of the walking staff, has been his constant companion.

might wish to break off a small branch or pull out a few living needles. This tree is known as the Sanko-no-matsu, or Pine of the Sanko. It is said to be the fifth-generation descendent of the very pine in whose branches Kōbō Daishi discovered the golden three-pronged *vajra* (*sanko*) he had thrown from China. Shingon Buddhism itself is sometimes referred to as "The Light of the Pine Tree" (*Matsu-no-hikari*), so famous is that founding event.[69]

Actually, there are two pines inside the fenced enclosure. The larger tree is a two-needle pine of ordinary pedigree. The smaller pine, the one with three needles, is the descendent of the original Sanko-no-matsu. Through a system of ropes and splints the larger tree protects its companion from damaging winds. A sign asks visitors not to throw offering money inside the enclosure.

We watch a young mother with two small daughters looking about in the dirt outside the barrier. They are hoping to find a three-needle bundle that has blown down from the pine. If found, these needles likely will end up in the family *butsudan*.

Grass of the Wooden Spoon

The Pine of the Sanko is very important in the legendary history of Kōyasan. Another nearby wonder, the Grass of the Wooden Spoon, is of much less importance, but visitors find it curious and a bit amusing. On the west side of the Kondō is a small isolated area of trees and bushes and grass enclosed by a low fence. A sign explains all. Toward the end of the Heian era a Kōyasan ascetic named Johō adopted the high-minded practice of using only woven grass for clothing and only the fruit of trees for food. The supernatural powers resulting from this discipline became so great that one day Johō suddenly took off into the air, perched momentarily in a tall pine tree, then flew on to Paradise. The tree in question, thereafter known as the Tōten-no-matsu, or "Pine of the Ascent to Paradise," no longer stands, but when alive it was located inside this enclosure. At the time of Johō's ascent his most devoted disciple, a simple lad known as Shōjohō ("Little Johō"), also was snatched up to heaven. The event took place at lunch time and Little Johō, caught by surprise, dropped his wooden spoon as he accelerated into the sky. The still visible spot where the spoon fell to earth is referred to as the Shakushi-no-shiba, "Grass of the Wooden Spoon." A somewhat similar story attaches to a ancient cedar that stands just a short distance up the road from the Garan (in front of Zōfuku-in). From the crown of that tree a famous abbot who had become a *tengu* flew up to Paradise.[70]

The Sūtra Repository

Situated a short distance from the southwest corner of the Kondō is the Garan's elegant Kyōzō, or "Sūtra Repository." This small and quite beautiful pagoda-like repository was built in the mid-twelfth century by Bifukumon-in, consort of Emperor Toba, as an aid to the peaceful repose of the spirit of her deceased husband. She arranged to have placed on its shelves the complete Chinese Buddhist scripture known as the *Tripitaka* (J. *Sanzō*), each sacred scroll written in gold ink on dark blue paper.

The present Kyōzō, a reconstruction completed in 1934, is six-sided with a double roof and *sorin*. Its most curious feature is that the interior shelves that hold the precious sūtras can be rotated about the axis of the hall by pushing on long arms that extend to the outside. The traditional formula is to rotate the sūtras through three clockwise circuits or processions. The resulting spiritual benefit is said to equal what would have accrued from a complete reading of all 3,575 scrolls.[71]

It's a tempting offer. A smiling middle-aged woman in pilgrim dress has come over to help us should we decide to take on the task. And here come several school children, escaping for a few minutes from their sketch books. We all grab the Kyōzō's oar-like arms and push. The mechanism doesn't budge. An elderly man has risen from the Kondō steps and is limping our way. Fortunately, he is followed by a burly young man who is hurrying after him, perhaps his grandson. We definitely are in business now. Slowly, with much grunting from the children, the inertia of the turntable is overcome. We begin a steady march. The old man, experienced in the protocol, is counting us through each cycle. If we stop even an inch short of three complete turns, he tells us, our effort will be negated. We will reap misery instead of benefit.

At the end we grin and nod at one another. No one, not even the old man, is willing to take the matter seriously. Additionally, we suspect the Kyōzō shelves may be empty, the priceless scriptures safely stored in the Reihōkan Museum. The scriptures themselves, of course, *are* serious. They were obtained and translated at great human cost. The faithful believe them to be a literal embodiment of the Buddha. Old books say that the worms in the floorboards of sanctuaries receive *karma* boosts from merely living in close proximity to the sacred scrolls.

Bell of the Daitō

We cross to the east side of the Kondō. There, positioned directly in front of the Daitō, and in perfect balance with the Kyōzō on the west, is the Daitō-no-kane, "Bell of the Daitō." The bell's elegant low tower, constructed on a granite platform, is made up of twelve inward-canting pillars held rigid by three lines of crossbeams. Above the pillars are a succession of brackets that support an *irimoya*-style roof. The entire structure is painted a gleaming white, which gives it a striking presence against the dark background of trees.

But the bell itself is the thing. Its sound is the soul of the mountain, the "voice of the Buddha." Kōbō Daishi had wished to supervise the bell's casting himself, but illness intervened. Therefore the first casting was directed by his successor, Shinzen. Over the years Shinzen's bell has been recast three times, the present recasting having taken place four and one-half centuries ago, in 1547. On these solemn occasions, while the craftsmen slowly poured the molten metal into the mold, the assisting priests and monks chanted the *Namu Daishi* and the *Kōmyō Shingon* ("Light Mantra"), a combination that still accompanies many Shingon enterprises, both physical and spiritual. After the metal had cooled and the finish work was completed, the head craftsman struck the bell a single time to affirm the success of his work. The second ringing was delayed until after the consecration ceremony and installation in the tower.

Today's Daitō-no-kane has a soft interior throb that is quite stirring, especially when heard at a great distance through rain and darkness, or at four in the morning, the hour of Kōbō Daishi's passing into eternal meditation. The sound seems to understand the pain of millions who have climbed the mountain to mourn their dead and their own errant lives. It is a most compassionate bell. The equally famous "Six-o'clock Bell," which stands just outside the front wall of Kongōbu-ji, has a rounder, brighter sound. A local radio station begins each morning's broadcast with the ringing of the cheering, enterprising Six-o'clock Bell.

Every day at five minutes before 4:00 a.m., 1:00 p.m., 6:00 p.m, and 9:00 p.m., and ten minutes before 11:00 p.m., a young monk comes out of the back room of the Garan information office and climbs the few steps to the platform of the Daitō-no-kane. He grasps the rope that controls the wooden striking beam and slowly starts it rocking in its cradle. At the proper moment, with one firmer pull, he sends the beam against the *shōza*, the bell's lotus-flower "striking seat." The bell booms and resonates in a series of wavelike vibrations. The monk counts out five units of time as the striking beam rocks back and forth, then pulls it again against the *shōza*. The vibrations of the first stroke have just died away when the second is sounded. After five more rocking intervals, the third stroke. And so on.[72]

The number of times the Daitō bell is struck is a curious matter. At 4:00 a.m., 1:00 p.m., 6:00 p.m., and 9:00 p.m. it is sounded eighteen times. At 11:00 p.m. the number of strokes is doubled to thirty-six. Therefore each day the Daitō bell is sounded a total of 108 times. Most commentaries point out that 108 is the number of *karma* bonds or *bonnō* ("evil passions"; Sk. *kleśa*) that pollute the human mind and body.[73] Thus, as we listen to each stroke we are reminded of our enslavement and of the Buddha's desire to liberate us.

This solemn but purifying message is heard most eloquently just before midnight on New Year's eve. At precisely 11:30 p.m. five young monks in saffron robes leave the warmth of the information office and mount the bell platform. One monk starts the striking beam rocking while the other monks stand to the side, waiting their turn. *DONG-ung-ung-ung. DONG-ung-ung-ung.* As the slow-paced strokes continue, the listeners who have gathered for the event walk about the Garan court, gaze up at the icy stars, warm their hands before one of several bonfires, dip *sake* from a large, newly opened keg, and reflect on the year past and the year to come. On and on the bell tolls. Bad *karma* is being replaced with good. Life and hope are being renewed. Elsewhere in the nation, from northernmost Hokkaido to the southernmost tip of Kyūshū, other temple bells are ringing the same 108 times. This is the *Joya-no-kane*, the "watch night bell" of the New Year.[74]

The physical Daitō-no-kane is an alloy of copper and zinc and approximately two meters in diameter. It is decorated with several of the traditional elements of Buddhist temple bells, the most conspicuous of which is the *chi-no-machi*, or "town of breasts," a pattern of nipples in four divisions that covers much of the upper quarter of the bell. These nipples (bells play a feminine role in esoteric symbolism) are presumed to have a subtle influence on the sound. In a small temple bell the nipples may total as few as thirty-six (four groups of three-by-three), a precise third of the sacred 108. But in large bells 108 nipples is the standard. The mathematics of dividing 108 into four symmetrical divisions is daunting. In fact it is impossible. The usual solution in modern bells is to place twenty-five nipples in a five-by-five pattern in each of the four quarters of the bell, then add two extra nipples in each of the four dividing borders. The Japanese Buddhist "Peace Bell" at Manhattan's United Nations Headquarters is such a bell. But the Garan's Daitō bell follows an older model, probably one chosen by Shinzen, or perhaps even by Kōbō Daishi. Each of its four quarters has twenty-eight nipples, for a grand total of 112. In the super-symbolic world of Shingon the four extra nipples stand for the four directional Buddhas. The comprehensive fifth Buddha, the central Great Sun Buddha, is represented by the totality of the bell itself.[75] This is but another way of stating that the womb-shaped Daitō-no-kane corresponds to the Dainichi Buddha of the Womb Realm who sits a short distance away at the center of the Daitō. The bell's corrective and nurturing voice is the voice of that life-giving Buddha.

The Lotus Pond

> Meditate on a lotus flower; be aware that your intrinsic
> nature is also pure!
>   —Kūkai[76]

Every large Buddhist temple, even one in the mountains, must have a lotus pond (*hasu-ike*). Kōyasan has several, but the primary one, and the oldest, is located at the southeast corner of the Garan directly beneath the embankment that rises to the main terrace. From the porches of the Kondō, the Daitō, and the Fudō-dō one can look down through a screen of trees to its cloud-reflecting surface. A Chinese-orange bridge extends from the pond's eastern shore to a shrine island at the center. This island houses Zennyo-ryū-ō, the "Good-Natured Dragon Queen" who assisted Kōbō Daishi in his rainmaking miracle at the capital's imperial garden pond in 824. A nearby sign notes that Zennyo-ryū-ō did not live in this pond in Kōbō Daishi's day, but came later and was induced to stay.

As for the lotus flowers, they are no longer in bloom. But back in August they were beautiful beyond imagining, simultaneously lush and delicate, white lotuses on the north side of the bridge, red lotuses on the south. Their sturdy stems drove upward out of muddy darkness to spread immense leaves in the sun, sometimes thrusting two, three, or more feet above the surface. Buddhists imagine much of paradise to be covered with such ponds and such flowers. In fact some have used the other-worldly beauty of the lotus as an argument for the existence of Paradise.

The lotus also is a teacher. That it evolves effortlessly from the putrescence of mud is a metaphor for humankind's innate purity and a demonstration of the redemptive power of the Sun. If you slice through a lotus stem you will discover the eight-spoked Wheel of the Law. The eight petals of the flower image the eight compass directions, the solar disk, the Eightfold Path of Self-Conquest, and the Womb Realm's assembly of Buddhas and Bodhisattvas. It is a symbol of self-existence.[77] In Buddhist iconography every Buddha and every Bodhisattva is supported by a lotus throne. In sum, the lotus tells us that we live even now in Paradise, nurtured by Light.

But this is a difficult teaching. Life appears to be so fleeting.

A hundred lotus flowers bloom in the sunlight. No two are alike. A grandmother and her small grandson walk onto the bridge. The boy sees an orange and black carp just beneath the surface and stops for a moment to watch. The carp drops from sight into the murky broth. The sun too is moving. The grandmother tilts her fragile parasol against it. Summer insects sing shrilly on the shrine island, racing against the cold nights to come.

CHAPTER SIX

THREE MOUNTAIN INSTITUTIONS

KONGŌBU-JI: HEADQUARTERS TEMPLE
OF KŌYASAN SHINGON-SHŪ

To reach historic Kongōbu-ji we walk eastward out of the Garan along
the beautiful Jabara Path, and in minutes stand before the great temple's
main southern entrance, the *Omote-mon*, also known as the *Sanmon*, or
Mountain Gate.[1] Large paper lanterns at either side of the gate display
the temple's two famous crests: a clockwise rotating "three-comma" pattern (the *mitsu-domoe*) and a stylized design of pawlonia leaves and flowers (the *kiri-no-gomon*). Both insignia are derived from the *mon* of warlord Toyotomi Hideyoshi, the original builder of the temple.

As we pass through the Omote-mon we face immediately the full
facade of Kongōbu-ji's immense main hall with its high, complex roof
covered with cypress bark. On the two highest roof ridges sit large
wooden tubs (called *karasu-tobi*, "crows-flying"), in former times used for

extinguishing roof fires. The stone pathway before us leads directly to the formal *tara-to* entry with its imperial chrysanthemum crest, but we would need to be members of the imperial family or priests transporting some supremely sacred object (such as Kōbō Daishi's robe) to use this portal. The next entry on the right, the *genkan*, or "main entry," is guarded by a carved whiskered dragon. It also is above our station. And so is the third entry, despite its open *shōji* doors, for only priests' *geta* are scattered about the steps. So we come at last to the entry for visitors at the far eastern end of the hall. Here we find a room lined with open cubbies for our shoes and other belongings. At the room's center is a large box filled to overflowing with hundreds of pairs of slippers.

In the first room of the main hall is an information office where we pay a nominal entrance fee and examine some purchasable books and religious items. New since our last trip is a volume of scholarly articles in English published by Kōyasan University's Research Institute of Esoteric Buddhist Culture. Off on a side table are several free publications, among them copies of *Kōyasan Kyōhō* ("Kōyasan Newsletter"), an illustrated twice-monthly bulletin featuring short articles.[2] There also are some English-language bulletins called *Kōyasan*, co-published by Kongōbu-ji and the Shingon Mission of Hawaii. Additionally, and most interesting of all, we find the latest issue of a Kongōbu-ji Japanese-language series entitled *Jinken Keihatsu Shirīzu* ("Enlightening Human Rights"). This is a polemical publication governed by such slogans as *mamorō jinken* ("protect human rights") and *nakusō sabetsu* ("abolish discrimination"). Its articles often are quite radical by Japanese standards.

We pass into the next area, the *chumon*, a formal entryway to the interior rooms of the great hall. On display here are an outsized flower arrangement and a cross-section of a five-hundred-year-old Japanese cedar tree (*sugi*) removed from the forest at the Okunoin. Kōyasan is greatly admired for its groves of *sugi*, Japan's largest conifer.

We pause in front of the *ōhiroma* (big room), the main hall's largest, longest, and most active ceremonial room. Among the rituals observed in the *ōhirama* are celebrations of Shākyamuni's birthday and entry into *Nirvāṇa* and the annual inauguration of Kōbō Daishi's ceremonial successor, the *hōin*. The paintings on the room's inner doors—images of delicate bamboo and feeding cranes against a background of gold foil—are in the orthodox Kanō *wakan* ("Japanese-Chinese") style. The foil brightens the room with light reflected in off the white surface of the front court.

At the western end of the *ōhiroma*—in direct line with the formal *tara-to* entry—is a large *butsuma*, or Buddha alcove. The *honzon* on its *shumi-dan* is a golden Sanskrit letter *A*, embodiment of Dainichi of the Womb Realm. On either side of the *A* stand memorial tablets of emperors and other celebrated dead. Before the alcove is a low incense table and carpet for kneeling.

We come to the Ume-no-ma, or Plum Room, with *fusuma* painted by Kanō Tan'yu (1601–1674), thought by many to be the supreme artist of the Kanō school. The gnarled limb of an ancient plum angles upward toward the right. It is crossed by a downflowing wintry stream. From a tree branch a bird gazes quietly toward the west. Both sky and earth are covered with gold foil.

Next is the Yanagi-no-ma, or Willow Room, named for its *fusuma* paintings by Kanō Tansai. This is the one notorious room in Kongōbu-ji, for here Toyotomi Hideyoshi's adopted son, Regent Hidetsugu, was forced to commit *seppuku*, as described in an earlier chapter. We imagine Hidetsugu sitting before us on the *tatami*, gazing at Tansai's delicate snow-laden willow as he releases his blood. His page quickly steps forward to provide the final stroke.

We have arrived at the western end of the great hall. Down the corridor to our right is a porch that looks out on a small pond and grassy glade with a backdrop of forest. Several of our fellow visitors have paused to sit here and enjoy the quiet scene. Nearby is the *oku-shoin*, or inner drawing room. In former years this room was a resting place for nobility. On its doors are monochrome drawings by Unkoku Tōeki (1591–1644), son of the founder of the Unkoku school.

At the rear of the main hall are several more rooms. One is the westward-facing Jōdan-no-ma, or Higher Platform Room. This gorgeous chamber, covered floor to ceiling in gold foil, was designed as a private room for visiting emperors. In its *tokonoma* hangs a large scroll portrait of Kōbō Daishi. In a second alcove are the staggered shelves called *chigaidana*, a common element in *shōin*-style decor.

Farther along the rear hallway is the Tsuchimuro, located at the back of the Ōhiroma. This chamber is used to accommodate monks and visiting laity who wish to listen in on ceremonies taking place in the larger Ōhiroma. The Tsuchimuro has a sunken hearth at its center. In winter this hearth is a source of much-needed heat, especially during the long night of chanting that commemorates Shākyamuni's entry into Nirvāna. Above the hearth is a small sculpture of fiery-red Aizen Myō-ō. A scroll painting of Aizen, said to be a copy of one done by Kōbō Daishi, hangs on the chamber's back wall. Aizen Myō-ō was the personal deity of Abbot Shinzen, Kōbō Daishi's immediate successor at Kōyasan.[3]

Finally, we come to an immense barn-like kitchen with high smoke-blackened ceiling, large storage lofts, and a stove with rice cauldrons big enough to boil rice for two thousand guests. Recently designated a "Prefectural Treasure," this old kitchen is still used for preparing food for certain religious ceremonies—for example, the *mochi* for the New Year.

We return to the western end of the main hall and exit along a covered walkway that passes through an ancient wall. This wall separates the precinct of former Seigan-ji from the precinct of former Kōzan-ji, the two temples that were fused to form Kongōbu-ji. For a period prior to the 1930s the Kōzan-ji precinct housed Kōyasan's middle school and an ecclesiastical college. Now it is the location of six new temple halls of varying sizes and functions, plus the nation's largest garden of sand and stone.

The walkway takes us first to the Betsuden ("hall for resting"), a large building with an encircling exterior corridor and eight interconnecting interior rooms. The *fusuma* doors of the eastern rooms feature marvelously detailed monochrome drawings of scenes from Kōbō Daishi's life: (room 1) the three ships of the Japanese embassy to China leaving Ōsaka Bay; (room 2) the Japanese entourage pausing outside the Shunmei-mon of the Chinese capital; (room 3) Kōbō Daishi cutting a branch from a willow tree as he says farewell to his Chinese friends; (room 4) Kariba Myōjin's two hunting dogs searching for the site of the future Kongōbu-ji. The far different *fusuma-e* of the western rooms are impressionistic renderings of the flowers of the four seasons: chrysanthemums, cherry blossoms, irises and water lilies, and maples. Once a year, on Kōbō Daishi's birthday, nearly all the partitions of the Betsuden are removed and the entire building turned into exhibition space for a spectacular show of flower arrangements.

We pass from the south corridor of the Betsuden to a still larger building, the Shin-Betsuden ("new hall for resting"). The central room here measures a full 169 *tatami* and can seat well over one hundred visitors. A smiling woman approaches us as we enter and invites us to sit on one of the ribbons of red carpeting. She disappears for a moment, then returns with a cup of green tea and two sweets for each of us. The tea is warm rather than hot, as is the custom. The sweets are round sugar candies, one red, one white (the defining colors of the Dual Mandala; also the national colors). One piece is embossed with the Kongōbu-ji "three-comma" insignia, the other with the pawlonia flower insignia.

The visual focus of the resting room is a painting of Kōbō Daishi flanked by the Dual Mandala. The Womb Realm Mandala is on the right, as always, the Diamond Realm Mandala on the left. These particular renderings of the mandalas show each sacred personage as a Sanskrit "seed" letter (Sk. *bīja*; J. *shuji*) rather than anthropomorphically.[4] Dainichi of the Womb Realm, for example, is the letter *A*, the first syllable of the Sanskrit alphabet and source of all sounds. Dainichi of the Diamond Realm is the letter *Vam*, the last syllable of the alphabet and the consummation of all sounds.

At the rear of the room, directly opposite the Dual Mandala and portrait of Kōbō Daishi, is one of Kongōbu-ji's most prized new art treasures, a 1985 painting of Monju Bodhisattva (Sk. *Manjushrī*). The painting is by Goryū Hayashi, best known for his portraits of Kabuki actors. Monju, the great Bodhisattva of Wisdom, sits on a lion, a wand-like sword in his right hand, the text of the *Prajñā-pāramitā-sūtra* resting on a lotus in his left hand. His hair is dressed with five knobs, a *bīja* letter above each knob identifying each of the five Buddhas. The iconography of the painting is conventional, but the execution is all flamboyant color and motion. The petals of Monju's throne are soft and sensual. The lion mount is more a ferocious flower than a flesh and blood animal. The aureole of light that surrounds the Bodhisattva spills to the right and left, a spiritual waterfall shedding blessings everywhere.

From the corridor that links the Betsuden and the Shin-Betsuden we get a view westward across the front of Kongōbu-ji's famed rock garden, the Ban-ryū-tei, "Garden of the Guardian Dragons." From this side angle, however, the garden is more puzzling than striking, its remarkable stones forming an intriguing but apparently incoherent combination of textures and forms. The proper place for viewing is the front porch of the Okuden ("inner hall") that sits at the garden's center. But the Okuden is off-limits to visitors—except on June 15, Kōbō Daishi's birthday.

So let us imagine for a moment that it is Kōbō Daishi's birthday, a day when a number of Kōyasan's forbidden places are open to all. In the first room of the Okuden we would find women in pastel summer *kimono* quietly preparing tea, measuring the green powder into individual bowls, adding hot water with wooden dippers, then whisking the tea to a heavy green froth. One of the women gestures for us to sit with the others on the *tatami*. After a moment she returns, smiles, kneels, bows low, and places a bowl of tea before us. We take up the bowl, examine its subtle beauty, then drink. This is a very informal sort of tea ceremony. Just a few doors away a more formal one is taking place. That ceremony begins in the Shin-shoin ("new sitting room"), then proceeds to a small tea house, the *Chashitsu-shinmatsu-an*, "Tea House of the True Pine," a classic unadorned tea chamber with an air of cultivated poverty known as *wabi*. The *-an* in the name means "hermitage." We can join in that ceremony if we wish, and are invited to do so, but we are not suitably dressed (a dark suit and *kimono* would be appropriate).

We step out onto the Okuden's front porch. The immense stone garden spreads before us and around us to either side. It is composed of 2,340-square meters of raked white sand carefully punctuated by one hundred and forty stones. No two stones are alike in shape, color, or texture. Some are quite massive. All were brought from Kōbō Daishi's home island of Shikoku. From this vantage point we can see the garden's simulation of two giant dragons, long rough bodies partially lost in the cloud of sand, protectively surrounding the spot where we stand. At the garden's edge is a border of dark trees.

Kongōbu-ji is a major ceremonial center, social venue, art gallery, and historical museum. But its most essential function is administrative, for it is the headquarters temple of the one hundred sub-temples on the mountain and the nearly four thousand affiliated Kōyasan Shingon-shū temples spread across the nation and beyond. The instruments of management—the bureaucratic personnel, the records, the computers—are in an office building, the Shūmusho, located at the northeast corner of the precinct. The two-story, steel-and-concrete Shūmusho has several exterior elements of Buddhist architecture, but inside it is all business. No mandalas, no incense, no golden canopies or decorated doors, just large glass windows, banks of fluorescent lights, and scores of desks.

The second floor is largely one great room organized according to departmental assignments: the equipment section, the accounting department, the forestry department, the travel arrangements department, the Daishi Kyōkai section, and so on. Some sixty desks, with accompanying computers and files, pack the room. The women are dressed in white and blue, the men in white shirts and dark pants. Only a few priests are in the room. In all, Kongōbu-ji employs around seventy people—thirty laymen, twenty laywomen, and twenty priests. Many of the employees live on the mountain, but many also commute daily by train or automobile.

All of Kōyasan's financial affairs are monitored at the Shūmusho. Income derives largely from the leasing of property, from forest holdings, from religious offerings, from annual contributions made by individual temples and temple members. The outflow is largely for salaries, for educational programs, for travel, for major repairs and new construction. The long stretch of boom years is now over in Japan. Times are growing harder. But Kongōbu-ji's Chief of General Affairs is not discouraged. In fact he thinks the recent financial difficulties may be salutary. The mission of the mountain has always been "to pass on what has been inherited from the past," and that work does not require great wealth. Wealth often proves to be a distraction.

Perhaps Kongōbu-ji's single most important task is to maintain close communication with the Kōyasan Shingon temples in the nation, for these temples are the primary means by which Kōbō Daishi's teaching is spread to the wider public. A major ally in this endeavor is an educational institution known as Daishi Kyōkai ("Daishi Mission," or "Daishi Educational Center"). A number of Kongōbu-ji's employees work at Daishi Kyōkai, the headquarters of which is just a five-minute walk from the Omote-mon gate.

DAISHI KYŌKAI HONBU:
HEADQUARTERS OF THE DAISHI MISSION

The east-facing gate to the court of Daishi Kyōkai Honbu makes a grand statement: broad granite steps and broad entrance walk flanked by outsized granite lanterns and pillars. Straight ahead is the Lecture Hall, the Dai Kōdō. This hall, built in 1915, has the largest seating capacity of any of Kōyasan's halls of worship. Behind it is a second worship hall, the much smaller Jukaidō ("Hall for Administering the Precepts"). The Jukaidō was built in 1931. To the left of the Dai Kōdō is Daishi Kyōkai's modern Kyōka Kenshu Dōjō, or "Hall for Teaching and Training." This handsome two-story hall, one of Kōyasan's largest buildings, was finished in 1981. The dates of construction of the three halls define the period of Daishi Kyōkai's most rapid growth.

The Daishi Kyōkai organization was first established around the time of World War I with the intention of providing the nation's scattered Shingon lay associations with an administrative umbrella. These lay groups, called *Daishi-kō*, had begun forming a few decades earlier in response to the Meiji government's anti-Buddhist policies. Each kō would meet on the twenty-first of the month (the day of Kōbō Daishi's entry into *nyūjō*) to worship and study, to sing, to dance, and to share testimonials. Often money was collected, mostly for use in support of pilgrimages. At the present time there are some seven hundred Daishi-kō in direct affiliation with Kōyasan's Daishi Kyōkai. Their membership is the recognized bedrock of Japanese faith in Kōbō Daishi.[5] They are not the only ones who use the services of Daishi Kyōkai, however. Anyone who is curious about Kōyasan and Shingon is invited to come here.

A prominent feature of Daishi Kyōkai's front court is a large white granite shrine with a stone sculpture of Chigo Daishi, Kōbō Daishi as a small child. To the right of this sculpture, and integral to it, is a broad granite stele on which are carved in simple phonetic *hiragana* the forty-seven syllables of the "Iroha-uta," a Buddhist poem popularly attributed to Kōbō Daishi. The poem speaks of a mountain journey beyond the attachments of an evanescent world.

What is especially remarkable about the "Iroha-uta" ("A-B-C Song") is that it employs each of the forty-seven Japanese syllabic characters just once. No phonetic character is missing and none are repeated. Thus, to learn to write the poem is to learn to write the complete Japanese phonetic alphabet. For centuries all Japanese dictionaries and reference works were alphabetized according to this poem's sequence of syllables. Tradition holds that Kōbō Daishi also invented the simple *hiragana* system itself, thus giving to millions of illiterate Japanese, especially the women and the children, a first opportunity to read and write.[6]

Kyōka Kenshu Dōjō: Hall of Education and Training

Four decorative elements in the spacious, brightly lit entry to the Kyōka Kenshu Dōjō immediately identify some specific purposes of the hall. Overhead is a framed picture with the boldly brushed characters for *MAN-DA-RA*. Against the main wall is a flower arrangement. At either side of the flower arrangement are portraits of Kongō-ka, the patron Bodhisattva of sacred music, and Kongō-bu, the patron Bodhisattva of sacred dance. Calligraphy, flower arrangement, sacred song, sacred dance—four important skills of religious worship that are taught at the Daishi Kyōkai complex.

An information office is on the right. The monks on duty offer to show us about or sell us one of the religious articles on display. Most of the purchasable scroll paintings are of Kōbō Daishi, Fudō Myō-ō, or Dainichi Buddha, and thus suitable for placing in a family *Butsudan* or *tokonoma*. One scroll depicts a golden Sanskrit syllable *A* resting on a lotus throne within a white moon disk. This image is used in the meditation practice known as *A-ji-kan*, a Shingon parallel to Zen meditation. Also on sale are a variety of *wagesa*. All *kō* members and serious Shingon practitioners own a *wagesa*, a narrow surplice worn about the neck when meditating, copying a sūtra, or performing sacred music. The office also stocks a number of videotapes, both documentary and instructional, and selected books and pamphlets, a few in English. Among the latter is a small English-language manual of Shingon prayers and ceremonies titled *Shingon Buddhist Service Book*.[7] This source contains most of the prayers one hears at Kōyasan.

We inquire about upcoming training courses (all given in Japanese). One choice is a basic three-day introductory program that focuses on meditation, sūtra copying, sacred music, and the study of selected aspects of Kōbō Daishi's teaching. If we wish to bring our children with us, Daishi Kyōkai offers a couple of three-day options for them. For the younger children there is a course that focuses on singing, rudimentary meditation, and the playing of musical instruments in front of an image of Chigo Daishi. For ages nine through fifteen the course emphasizes sūtra reading, cleaning the grounds of a temple, and personal discipline.

Those who wish training in *A-ji-kan* may enroll in a basic four-step course. Step one, "Entering the Gate," provides instruction in the theory and history of the Sanskrit letter *A*. Step two, "Advanced Breathing Practice," helps the practitioner "feel the Buddha" in the sound of the letter. Step three, "Moon Ring Practice," visualizes the Buddha in the light of the Moon Ring that surrounds the letter. Step Four integrates all of the elements that help the practitioner "return to the palace of the eternal syllable *A*"—that is, become identified with Dainichi Buddha.[8] Two likely locations for *A-ji-kan* training are the Kyōka Kenshū Dōjō and a specially built A-ji-kan Dōjō at the rear of the sand and rock garden at Kongōbu-ji. Many Shingon believers practice *A-ji-kan* meditation regularly.

Other courses include training in *goeika*, a choral chanting of sacred songs to the accompaniment of hand bells. Daishi Kyōkai is the national headquarters for approximately 1,500 groups that study this art. It also is headquarters for some fifty branches of Kōyasan Shūkyō-buyō Kai, an association for religious dance. For several days in May each year members of the *goeika* and *shūkyō-buyō* societies come to Kōyasan to perform before the Buddhas and compete for prizes. These are not casual arts. *Goeika*, for example, with twenty-one differentiated levels of skill, can be studied for years.

The most intense program offered by Daishi Kyōkai is an eleven-day course called Kyōkai Kyōshi Kōshukai. This program teaches several techniques of Shingon Mikkyō ritual and methods for spreading the faith. Enrollment is selective, many of the participants already being leaders of Daishi-kō. Instruction proceeds relentlessly through all eleven days: rise at 5:00 a.m., attend a morning sūtra service, eat breakfast, attend four hours of lecture and ritual practice, eat lunch, attend a full afternoon of lecture and ritual practice, eat dinner, bathe, attend more lectures, study privately until the lights go out at 9:30 p.m. Students report feeling overwhelmed at times by the demanding nature of the material, but also exhilarated. They prize especially the training in *kaji kitō*, esoteric rituals of healing that draw on the Buddha's power and grace to alleviate physical and mental illness. Faith healing? Magic? Yes indeed, but not necessarily in the usual Western sense.[9]

Beyond the front office is a rest area with vending machines, bulletin boards, pamphlet racks, and glass cabinets displaying more items for sale. At the moment a large TV screen is showing an animated life of Kōbō Daishi entitled "Odaishi-sama," a production financed by Kongōbu-ji for use in the religious education of children. This film is for sale. Other available videotapes include instructional films on such topics as esoteric flower arrangement (*Mikkyō-no-hana*) and documentaries about various Shingon charities. Also in the videotape library are two feature-length motion pictures on the life of Kōbō Daishi—*Kūkai* (Tōei, 1984) and *Mandara* (Towa, 1991). The former film, which stars several of Japan's most respected actors, is especially powerful. In the pamphlet rack are copies of *Kōyasan Shakai Fukushi* ("Kōyasan Social Welfare"), *Fureai* ("Touching Each Other"), and *Aimaito* ("Eye-Mate"), publications about such topics as the care of incapacitated elderly, aid to victims of earthquakes and volcanic eruptions, and the training of guide dogs for the blind. All these programs are promoted by Daishi Kyōkai.

On the second floor of the Kyōka Kenshū Dōjō are two large training rooms. The smaller of the two, known as the Koko-dō ("Small Lecture Room"), is seventy-two *tatami* mats in size. The larger one, the Chūkō-dō ("Middle Lecture Room"), is one hundred and eight *tatami*. Around the walls of both rooms are storage lockers and closets where *zabuton* and ritual tables are kept, along with *futon* and other bedding materials. When taking courses the students both study and sleep in these halls. Elsewhere in the building are bathing, laundry, and dining facilities.

Between the two large training rooms is a smaller third room, the Shakyō-shitsu ("Sūtra-copying Room"), devoted to one of Buddhism's most traditional and popular religious practices. A lone visitor with an hour to spare may use this room, or an organized group of as many as thirty. The practitioner sits on a *zabuton* before a low writing table.[10] When a copy of a sacred text is finished it is carried to the west end of the room and prayerfully placed before an image of Kōbō Daishi.

Shakyō, sometimes referred to as "written Zen meditation," is a solemn devotion with a set protocol.[11]

1. Wash your hands and rinse your mouth.
2. Light incense to purify the room.
3. With your hands held together in *gasshō* make three bows, reciting a mantra with each bow.
4. Say the following prayer: "I am about to write the *Hannya-shingyō*. If possible, may each word and each sentence reach the world of the Buddha."
5. Make the ink to be used (by rubbing a block of dried India ink in water on an inkstone) while reciting *Namu Daishi Henjō Kongō*.
6. Carefully and prayerfully write each character of the sūtra.
7. Read each character solemnly and without haste.
8. When the reading is finished, recite with especial earnestness *Namu Daishi Henjō Kongō* seven times.
9. Say a prayer to the Buddha, or to Kōbō Daishi, asking for the benefit being sought. End with this sentiment: "I have performed this devotion not only for my own benefit but also to help everyone follow the Buddhist path."
10. With hands held in *gasshō* make three concluding bows.

The almost universal preference for the *Hannya-shingyō*, or "Heart Sutra," is based on several considerations. First, the brevity of the text makes it practical to copy. Second, most Japanese Buddhists know it by heart, having recited it since childhood. Finally, and most important, the profundity of the *Hannya-shingyō* makes it especially appropriate for reflection, its central doctrine of "emptiness" or "void" (Sk. *shūnyatā*; J. *kū*) being an important element in the evolution of esoteric Buddhist thought. Kōbō Daishi wrote extravagantly of the sūtra's virtues: "Such [is] the nature of [this] sūtra, if anyone recites or holds fast to it, explains or respects it, he will be relieved from his suffering and granted bliss. If he practices the teachings and meditates upon them, he will attain enlightenment and develop supernatural powers."[12]

Only the most devoted, however, are able to write all two hundred sixty-two Chinese characters from memory, so each semitransparent copy sheet supplied by Daishi Kyōkai is accompanied by an underlying second sheet on which the full text is printed.

Dai Kōdō, the Great Lecture Hall

Entry to Daishi Kyōkai's grand Great Lecture Hall, the Dai Kōdō, is made from the front court, although one also may enter from the Kyōka Kenshu Dōjō. The interior of the Dai Kōdō is rather startling in size—two hundred and twenty *tatami*. As already mentioned, this is the largest indoor worship space at Kōyasan. The elevated altar at the western end of the room also is among the mountain's most dazzling and ornate. On either side of the altar large golden canopies cascade from ceiling to floor. Directly overhead a third canopy hangs from an escutcheon shaped like a golden lotus. Because the altar area is elevated and unscreened it is easily seen from any point in the room. At the center of the dais sits a statue of Kōbō Daishi, the *honzon* of the hall. He is in the familiar pose of Shin-nyo's painting, a string of beads in the left hand, a five-pronged *vajra* in the right. To the right and left of this *honzon* are Fudō Myō-ō and Aizen Myō-ō, two tough disciplinarians. The primary function of the Dai Kōdō as a training venue is clear.

Since the Dai Kōdō is a center for "Daishi worship," painted scenes from Kōbō Daishi's life have been hung along the walls above the transoms, twenty-five scenes in all. The narrative begins with Daishi's conception in Shikoku and ends with his entrance into *nyūjō*.

The Dai Kōdō is put to many uses—lectures, training sessions, musical recitals, religious dances, large public rituals. Of all these events the observance of Kōbō Daishi's birthday is the most important. Early in the morning of June 15 hundreds of chanting priests and monks and students gather on this floor, with hundreds of laity kneeling around the periphery, all honoring the precious newborn child. Even though no special event is scheduled for today, the day of our visit, the Dai Kōdō is still busy. At the moment a large *kō* from Okayama is lining up before the altar to have their photograph taken.

Jukaidō: Hall for Administering the Precepts

The small Jukaidō is tucked in behind the much larger Dai Kōdō. This is where one of Shingon's most fundamental ceremonies for lay believers is held, the solemn pledge to observe the Ten Precepts of Mahāyāna Buddhism.[13] These precepts, sometimes referred to as the "Buddhist Ten Commandments," are deemed to be universal moral laws implicit in the nature of the universe. Since we have read enough about them to be convinced of their great value, we ask the monks at the information office of the Kyōka Kenshu Dōjō to admit us to the ceremony.[14]

The Jukaidō is completely dark inside except for two dim candles that burn before a portrait of Kōbō Daishi. We seat ourselves on the *tatami* facing the portrait. The young monk who accompanied us to the hall leads us in the chanting of several mantra, including the *Namu Daishi Henjō Kongō*. Soon a senior priest arrives and steps inside the altar area. He makes a series of preparatory gestures, his body a black silhouette against the candlelight. We concentrate as intently as we can as, item by item, he leads us in the recitation and acceptance of each precept. The first three precepts relate to the body, the next four to speech, the final three to mind—Body, Speech, and Mind, the mystical trinity by which one becomes identified with the Great Sun Buddha. Each precept has a positive and a negative application.

1. I will not kill. *I will show compassion toward all sentient beings.*
2. I will not steal. *I will pursue lofty conduct.*
3. I will not commit adultery. *I will be pure in my sexual behavior.*
4. I will not lie. *I will be honest and trustworthy in my speech.*
5. I will not exaggerate. *I will use appropriate and judicious language.*
6. I will not slander. *I will speak respectfully of others.*
7. I will not be duplicitous or equivocating. *I will be forthright.*
8. I will not be greedy. *I will be generous and content.*
9. I will not be angry. *I will be forbearing.*
10. I will not hold false views. *I will be unbiased and just.*

The brief ceremony is over. We move from the darkness of the Jukaidō out into the dazzling sunlight. The whole experience has been quite abrupt. We trust we have made our vows worthily. "Unless one observes all these precepts," Kūkai warned, "one's eye of wisdom will be dark. Knowing this, protect them as you would protect your life."[15]

Each of us is carrying an *o-fuda* sealed with a broad red seal, across which is written *Bosatsu-kai-chō*: "Sign of the Bodhisattva Precepts." This is heady stuff. The Ten Precepts may be no more than enlightened common sense, a distillation of almost universally accepted conduct, but their observance will not be easy. We have pledged to become vegetarians. We must sort that out. And pledged to avoid exaggeration—an exceedingly subtle notion. And not to hold false views—surely a project for several lifetimes.[16] The senior priest is walking beside us, chatting amiably, enjoying the novelty of having foreigners in his group.

Kechien-kanjō: *An Initiation Ceremony for the Laity*

The single most important formal initiation ritual open to the Shingon laity is the *Kechien-kanjō*, or "Bond-establishing Sprinkling of the Head." This Dharma-entry gate (*hōmon*) instills in its recipient a full awareness of being truly a child of Dainichi Buddha. Faulty habits and past errors are washed away, clearing the path toward Buddhahood.

The ceremony is held twice each year, for three days in early May and three days in early October.[17] The venue is not Daishi Kyōkai, but the inner sanctuary of the Golden Hall in the Garan. The administering priests are the highest-ranking clergy of the mountain. Nothing is skimped.

Immediately prior to the ceremony the lay participants gather in a large tent erected near the east entrance to the Golden Hall. There a priest explains to them that the *Kechien-kanjō* for laity derives its structure from the *abhisheka* ritual Hui-kuo administered to Kūkai in 805 and that Kūkai later administered to Saichō, to Gonzō, and to his Shingon disciples.[18] The ceremony also mimics an ancient Indian ceremony of royal succession, where the heir to the throne was seated at the center of a diagram drawn in the shape of the kingdom (think *mandala*) while the old king sprinkled his head with water taken from the "four seas." In this way the son's claim to the throne was legitimated. The son also received the special knowledge needed to rule wisely. In parallel fashion the modern layperson is made a royal heir to the wisdom and divinity of Dainichi Buddha.

After a period of devotional prayer, the *Kechien-kanjō* initiates enter the Golden Hall, where they gather in the darkened corridor in front of the curtained-off inner sanctuary. A priest instructs them in the formation of the *fugen-sammaya-in*, made by pressing both palms together and interlocking all but the two middle fingers, which are left extended. A sprig of *shikimi* (Japanese star anise, *illicium religiosum*; also pronounced *shikibi*) is inserted between the extended fingers. A blindfold is placed over the initiate's eyes and secured at the back of the head. In darkness the initiate forms a mental picture of Dainichi Buddha seated at the center of the mandala. To this visualization is added the repeated chanting of the phrase *On sammaya satoban. On*: I empty myself. *Sammaya*: I enter a state of oneness. *Satoban*: I unite with the Buddha.[19]

The Three Mysteries of Body, Speech, and Mind—*mudrā, mantra*, and visualization—are sustained as the initiate is guided forward through a progression of blindfolded turns and pauses until all sense of direction and location is lost. One knows only that somewhere in this darkness Dainichi waits at the heart of a mandala. The chant throbs on and on. The two extended fingers grasp the sacred flower ever more firmly. Kōbō Daishi describes the coming experience as "the Buddha entering me and I entering the Buddha."[20]

A touch at the elbow. The time has arrived. The *shikimi* is released into the darkness. A voice whispers the name of the sacred being upon whom the flower has landed. *"Dainichi Nyorai!"*[21] The blindfold is removed. One gets a glimpse of the mandala table and the *shikimi* as it is whisked off into a folded white paper.

With hands in *gasshō* one is led before the chief master and seated. A five-sided golden crown is placed on one's head, the same crown that Dainichi Buddha wears. The gorgeously robed presiding priest takes up his wand, dips it into a vessel, and sprinkles one's head with water. A five-pronged *vajra* is placed in the cradle of one's hands, raised to the forehead, replaced at right angles, then again brought to the forehead. An assisting priest holds up a mirror. There, in the trembling reflection of the glass, an otherwise familiar face is wearing the royal crown of the Great Sun Buddha.

The ceremony is over. The new child of the Buddha walks in a half-trance past a row of witnesses starting with the sacred beings on the *shumi-dan*, past the cabinet of Ashuku Buddha, past Kongōsatta, Fudō

Myō-ō and Fugen Bosatsu, past the portraits of the eight Shingon patriarchs, then the scroll paintings of the twelve Indian divas. Each diva in
turn is offered a pinch of incense and asked for help and protection. A
prayer to Nit-ten, holder of the sun, to Gat-ten, holder of the moon, to
Bon-ten (Brahmā) and Taishaku-ten (Indra), to Ka-ten, diva of fire, to
Emma-ten, judge of the dead. All you divine beings, help me. At the exit
door of the Golden Hall a monk makes a brief congratulatory speech and
stamps the carried blindfold with Dainichi's red Sanskrit *A*. Then out
into the spring rain and the Buddha path.

REIHŌKAN: MUSEUM OF SACRED TREASURES

> In every production of the brush, the chisel, or metal
> The vital force of the universe is made manifest,
> . . . .
> And in this way every man is called to the knowledge
> Of his own glorious nature even in his present physical being.
> —Kūkai

Kōbō Daishi has been called the "father" (and also the "mother") of
Japanese culture, and, perhaps most especially, of Japanese religious art.
He declared that sacred art was itself an avenue to enlightenment, that
the manufacture of artistic representations was essential to the full understanding, communication, and practice of the deepest teachings. This
perception was sustained by his successors. So it is not surprising that
Shingon temples—most famously Kōyasan, Tō-ji, and Daigō-ji—are
among Japan's greatest repositories of Buddhist art.

Prior to the building of the Reihōkan Museum in 1921 Kōyasan's
religious treasures were spread widely among the various sub-temples,
with the greatest concentration at Kongōbu-ji. At each temple the most
prized possessions usually were the *honzon* in the *hondō* sanctuary and a
few items displayed on other temple altars. These sculptures and paintings typically stood at a distance from the viewer and were poorly illuminated or even hidden. Their function was to attract veneration and supplication, not aesthetic examination. Valued items that were not on
display or used liturgically were locked away in protective earth-walled
storage houses called *kura*. Temple visitors who asked to see such objects

sometimes were accommodated, but this practice was costly. Scroll manuscripts and scroll paintings, for example, were especially vulnerable, gaining new creases and losing elements of detail with each unrolling.

When Japan opened to Western travelers in the nineteenth century a number of foreign visitors came to Kōyasan to see its famed treasures. For these displays a temple room would be closed to traffic and selected objects brought out for inspection. If a scroll was especially large it would be rolled out flat on the *tatami*. Such temple cooperation earned good will and a certain amount of income, but the fees were not fixed and often visitors were motivated to keep offerings modest in order to protect those who followed.[22] The greatest income potential lay in outright sale. In the decades that followed the Meiji disestablishment of Buddhism, when many of the nation's temples became destitute, some of Kōyasan's artistic possessions entered the collections of museums in Tōkyō, Kyōto, and Nara, or slipped into the hands of art dealers and private collectors both domestic and foreign. Not all sales were made openly, and even today old stories circulate about falsified inventories and temple halls set ablaze in order to destroy evidence of clandestine sales.

Near the end of the nineteenth century (in 1897) the government moved to deal with the increasing problem of outflowing cultural assets by passing the Preservation of Ancient Shrines and Temples Law (*Koshaji Hozon Hō*). This action was followed in 1929 by the Preservation of National Treasures Law (*Kokuhō Hozon Hō*), which further documented and mandated protection for the nation's most prized works of art. A third bill, the Law for the Protection of Cultural Assets (*Bunkazai Hogo Hō*), passed in 1950 and revised in 1954 and 1975, refined further the methods of identification, retention, and preservation.[23]

Kōyasan's Reihōkan ("Museum of Sacred Treasures") was constructed in 1921 in a wooded area just a few minutes walk to the southwest of Daishi Kyōkai. Into its protective halls soon passed hundreds, and eventually thousands, of items gathered from the temples of the mountain. The first museum building was made up of two connected halls designed vaguely to resemble the eleventh-century Phoenix Hall of Byōdo-in in Uji, an architectural affirmation of sacred contents. In 1984, as one of the major projects honoring the 1,150th anniversary of Kōbō Daishi's entering *nyūjō*, a large addition was constructed on the east side of the Reihōkan complex. This stand-alone new building provided visual balance to the museum's design and approximately doubled the size of the display area. It also gave the museum a fireproof structure with modern lighting and full temperature and humidity control. Even today the older buildings are not air-conditioned and can be heated only marginally. For illumination they depend largely on natural light admitted through high transom windows.

At the detached admissions office we exchange our shoes for slippers, leave our surplus baggage in a locker, buy our tickets and receive a brochure. From here sheltered walkways lead to each of the three museum buildings. The brochure suggests starting with the new hall.

Perfectly framed by the entrance door to the first room, the sculpture room, is an immense late-Heian statue of Amida Nyorai contributed to the museum by Jizō-in. This Amida is so large that a portion of the room's ceiling has been raised to accommodate it. Immediately to the right of the Amida are several other large statues. The rest of the room features a raised dais that extends along three walls. On this dais are placed a remarkably diverse array of statues. We recognize three Dainichi, a Yakushi, an Amida Triad, a Fudō Myō-ō, an Aizen Myō-ō, a Jizō, two of the four Heavenly Kings, a Nyoirin Kannon, and several other figures.[24] Five of these sculptures have been designated National Treasures or Important Cultural Assets. All are beautifully illuminated, with no protective glass to impede our view.

The next room, square and high-walled, is devoted to large hanging scroll paintings. We seat ourselves on the central bench and look about. One painting, a National Treasure from Fumon-in, is a portrait of Kōbō Daishi's early mentor, Gonzō. The priest's vigorous expression and emphatic gesture suggest he was a forceful teacher. Next to Gonzō hangs a portrait of Zennyo-ryū-ō, the rain dragon enshrined at the Garan's Lotus Pond. Although a female dragon, Zennyo-ryū-ō is presented here as a male government official dressed in a Chinese robe and wearing a crown. The dragon nature is revealed only by a discrete few inches of scaly tail that protrude from beneath the robe. This painting also is a National Treasure.[25]

By far the largest painting in the room is the museum's glorious *Amida-shōjū-raigō,* "Descent of Amida to Welcome the Spirit of a Believer."[26] Many art historians declare this to be the greatest of all Pure Land paintings. Against a background of misty mountains Amida

Buddha and entourage are shown descending earthward on a carpet of cloud. Amida's hands, one raised, one lowered, are in the "pinch" gesture he employs when consoling and gathering in the dying. Kneeling just ahead of Amida, and physically much smaller, are his two primary heavenly deputies, Seishi Bodhisattva and Kannon Bodhisattva. Seishi presses his hands together in greeting. Kannon holds out a lotus throne on which the spirit of the dying believer will be gathered. Among the joyous figures at Amida's side are the Bodhisattvas of music, flowers, incense, and banners. Also present is the philosopher-priest Nāgārjuna, first patriarch of Shingon and the traditional founder of the Pure Land sect.

At the center of the third room are a number of large glass cases for manuscripts, scroll paintings, and liturgical instruments. Among the manuscripts is a request written by Toyotomi Hideyoshi concerning the construction of a memorial for his mother. There is an illuminated sūtra scroll in gold and silver ink on dark blue paper that is another National Treasure. Occasionally we find here a text written by Kūkai himself, but not today. Against the outside wall of the room are further display areas for sculptures and other vertical objects, and here we find Unkei's remarkably lifelike and appealing carvings of Fudō Myō-ō's eight boy attendants, the Hachi-dai-dōji. All eight figures are National Treasures.

We go now to the original hall of the Reihōkan, the one completed in 1921. Just inside its entrance door are paintings of the Dual Mandala. Most of the first room is taken up with a special exhibition of paintings of the Twelve Indian Divas (the *Juni-ten*). These exotic Divas are among esoteric Buddhism's most popular artistic subjects.

From the scroll room we pass into the Reihōkan's western wing, a room of miscellaneous treasures. The most remarkable items on display here are several portable shrines, miniature wonders of intricate carving, painting, and metal work. One of the "pillow" shrines, a National Treasure formerly kept in the Miedō, is believed to have been brought back from T'ang China by Kōbō Daishi. It is only nine inches high and made entirely of wood, yet contains a Shākyamuni surrounded by two Bodhisattvas, ten *arhats*, twelve mid-range divinities, four servants, six lions, and twelve assorted guardians, musicians, and demons.[27]

The final room of the Reihōkan is a high-ceilinged sculpture hall with a full range of sacred figures set in alcoves. The most admired sculptures here are Kaikei's twelfth-century rendering of the Four Heavenly

Kings. They guard the room's four corners. Dominating the scene is a noble Dainichi Buddha who sits in the central alcove of the north wall, an eight-spoked wheel of the sun radiating behind him. Seated on lower thrones at either side of Dainichi are Amida Buddha and Shākyamuni. Above this triad is a plaque with the golden characters *Hō-kō-kaku*: "Radiating Light." The description is appropriate. Dainichi is the universal illumination. Amida's Sanskrit name, *Amitābha*, means Infinite Light. And Shākyamuni, according to the *Mahāparinirvāna Sūtra*, at the moment of his Enlightenment and again upon his entrance into Nirvāna gave off a radiance that filled the universe.

CHAPTER SEVEN

THE TEMPLE TOWN

It is time to relax and do some shopping. And to choose a place for lunch.

Temples that receive large numbers of visitors, especially those located in the remote countryside, usually have a cluster of commercial enterprises just outside their front gates. In these *mon-zen-machi*—"towns before the gate"—visitors can purchase meals, souvenirs, devotional materials, clothing, medicines, and various other needed goods and services. Often, overnight accommodations are available. Kōyasan has a somewhat different arrangement, a *ji-nai-machi*, or "town within the temple." Outside Kōyasan's front Daimon gate is nothing but a wilderness of steep and uninhabited mountainside. But inside the gate, mixed in among the austere and beautiful temples, is a thriving town.

We begin our examination of Kōyasan's *ji-nai-machi* at the locale of its greatest concentration, a busy street crossing about one hundred meters east of Kongōbu-ji. At this intersection are a modern drugstore, a

noodle restaurant, a large souvenir and gift shop, and the main office of
the Kōyasan Tourist Association. Within the first block in each direction
are a dozen more shops, several more restaurants, two banks, a post
office, a fire station, three bus stops, a public restroom, and, enclosed
behind high walls, eight serene *shukubō* temples.

We start with the souvenir and gift shop on the southeast corner, the
Juzu-ya Shirobei. This establishment is one of Kōyasan's largest and
oldest, dating back more than eleven generations. Juzu-ya means "prayer
bead shop," but many other items are for sale here, including small Buddhist statues, altar cloths, *ihai* tablets for the dead, floor bells for prayer,
incense, pilgrim staffs. One can buy a family *butsudan* along with scroll
images suitable for each of the shrine's three compartments.[1] A customer
also may purchase the three utensils needed for performing shrine devotions: a candle holder, an incense burner, and a flower vase. The shop
offers many nonreligious items as well, especially ones that make suitable
gifts to take home to friends and relatives. Traditional Japanese sweets are
popular, or a box of Japanese writing paper. Several display counters are
filled with informal souvenir items such as chopsticks, rice scoops,
change purses, walking sticks, ear picks, key chains, and backscratchers
(called *mago-no-te*, "hand of a grandchild"), nearly all with the name
Kōyasan stamped on them. A more upscale gift might be a wooden
Kokeshi doll or, for good luck, a carved image of Daruma (Sk. Bodhid-
harma), the semilegendary founder of Zen Buddhism.

Kōyasan has no busier shop than the Juzu-ya Shirobei. In summer
the tourist buses sometimes park directly out front, blocking traffic in the
westbound lane while passengers rush in to make last-minute purchases.
No one honks. No police appear. Everyone understands.

We have entered the Juzu-ya Shirobei with the intension of purchasing a string of prayer beads. There are thousands to choose from. The
long counters in the middle of the store display the less expensive sets.
Mid-range *juzu* hang from the rear wall. The most costly are inside glass
cases. The number of beads in a string depends somewhat on the
intended use and the Buddhist sect to which one belongs. Members of
the Pure Land Sect, for example, use strings with only twenty-six beads.
The standard Shingon *juzu*, which is based on a set Kōbō Daishi brought
back from China, has 108 beads.[2] The beads are made of glass, crystal,
semiprecious stones, or wood. The color of the tassels varies, with an

option of white, red, purple, pale green, and brown. Student monks carry *juzu* with white tassels.

We pick out several sets and run the beads through our fingers. The sandalwood beads are especially appealing, with a velvety feel and a subtle sweet-tangy odor. We rub the beads together with a scrubbing motion. This action, known as "rubbing away the passions," is said to relieve the pressure of the 108 karma bonds. *Juzu* are grasped one way when being "rubbed," another way when counting prayers, a third way when held in simple reverence. There is a special etiquette for folding and placing the beads before a Buddha, or when storing them away. When counting, one does not make a complete circuit of the string. One starts at an oversized bead known as an *oyadama* (Mother Bead), counts ahead for fifty-four beads to the second Mother Bead, then reverses direction, counting back to the starting point. It is irreverent to leap over a Mother Bead, for that bead represents either Dainichi of the Womb Realm or Dainichi of the Diamond Realm. Each half string is further divided into sequences of seven, fourteen, and thirty-three beads by the interposition of small marker beads. To keep track of large prayer counts, which can extend into the hundreds of thousands in some devotions, one repositions special recorder beads attached to the ends of the four tassels.

With a sandalwood set beautifully boxed and wrapped, we exit the Juzu-ya Shirobei and walk eastward past the post office. Postal service did not come to Kōyasan until 1872. Prior to that date the mail was back-packed up the Fudō-zaka three times each day from Kamiya village. The fire station across from the post office wasn't built until 1980, prior to which time Kōyasan had no professionally trained firemen.[3] We pass the Hanabishi, one of the more expensive restaurants in town. Among Hanabishi's special offerings is a "Garan" *bentō*, served in lacquered boxes. Another is the "*Sanko-zen*," a vegetarian lunch named after Kōbō Daishi's three-pronged *vajra*. Actually, although the Hanabishi advertises itself as serving "Kōyasan cuisine," few of its meals are strictly vegetarian.[4] A near neighbor of the Hanabishi is an old pharmacy named Tora-ya ("Tiger Shop"). The Tora-ya has been at its present location for one hundred and fifty years. We step inside and purchase a small box of the shop's best-selling item, *Daishi-darani-jō* ("Daishi's Mystic Sustaining Pills"), an ancient remedy for stomach ailments based on a formula Kōbō Daishi is thought to have learned in China.[5]

At the eastern end of the block is the Kasakuni ("Pilgrim-hat Country") *manjū* shop. Large characters on the storefront declare its primary
claim to fame: "Original Home of the Miroku Stone" (*Miroku-ishi
Honpo*). The product referred to is the dark-toasted *manjū* pastry we were
served on our arrival at Rengejō-in, a pastry designed to resemble the
sacred "Miroku Stone" near Kōbō Daishi's mausoleum. According to
prophecy this stone is where Miroku, the next Buddha, will make his
inaugural appearance on earth. *Manjū*, a popular sweet, is made of sweetened bean paste covered with toasted rice dough.

The shop owner's college-age son waits on us. We choose an assort-
ment of products linked, by name at least, with Buddhist religious
themes: three Miroku-no-ishi ("Stone of Miroku"), three Sanko-matsu
("*Vajra*-pine"), three Hijiri-yōkan, and three Kagami-ishi. The Sanko-
matsu uses a combination of brown bean paste and green cookie to represent the trunk, branches, and needles of the Garan's sacred pine. The
Hijiri-yōkan is a special jellied bean paste formerly eaten by the Kōya-
hijiri (made according to "a secret document" owned by Kongōbu-ji).
The Kagami-ishi is a delicate mirror-shaped *manjū* associated with the
goddess Kisshōten, a Buddhist patron of beauty and good fortune.[6]

We turn right at the next streetcorner and proceed to the Hamada-
ya, the most famous of Kōyasan's several manufacturers of *tōfu* products.
The first floor of the store is devoted to the manufacturing and sales area.
The Hamada family lives upstairs. The Hamada-ya's particular specialization is *goma-dōfu*, a food historically so basic to the diet of the monks
that it is said to be "another name for Kōyasan." Two other popular *tōfu*
products are *momengoshi-dōfu* ("cotton-cloth *tōfu*"), named for the wrapping that is used in draining the water, and *hirosu*, the waffle-tasting
patty of *tōfu*, carrot, burdock, and seaweed we had at breakfast.

Like most of the other manufacturing establishments at Kōyasan,
Hamada-ya sells the bulk of its production to Kōyasan's temples. But
walk-in customers are welcome. We buy a box of *hirosu*. Just outside
Hamada-ya's front door is a small garden where we pause for a moment
to drink the spring water that is used in the manufacture of the *tōfu*. On
the summit of the wooded hill that rises behind the shop is a shrine to
Benzaiten, goddess of the flowing spring. Some visitors come to the
Hamada-ya just for the water, filling up several plastic bottles and leaving
an offering.

Seeing all this food reminds us of our need for lunch, so we reverse our direction, return to the intersection where we began, then continue along the main street for another half block to the Maruman restaurant. Our preference for the Maruman is based in part on our having found warm shelter there on many cold and windy winter days. We also are fond of the Maruman noodle broth. In all seasons we order the same lunch, a bowl of *kitsune-soba*, a combination of buckwheat noodles (*soba*) and deep-fried *tōfu* served in a hot broth. *Kitsune*, which means "fox," refers to the fried *tōfu*, by tradition the fox's favorite food.

We often find conversation companions at the Maruman, and, sure enough, today we are joined by a young couple we've only exchanged glances with before. They both are students at Kōyasan University, which is located just one block from here. The young woman is in her junior year, majoring in General Buddhism and English. Two years ago she transferred from a small Christian women's college, having decided "Kōdai" would better serve her personal religious interests. Her hometown friends tease her, she says. They insist a Buddhist school must be terribly boring and conclude she is looking for a young priest to marry. "It's not all Buddhism here," she tells us. "In many ways Kōyasan is like any other college town."

Her male companion expects to enter Kōyasan's seminary for priests after he graduates from Kōdai next year. His father is the head priest of a Kōyasan temple, and he is the only son. It always has been assumed that he will become a priest. Right now, however, he just wants to get away. Perhaps he will visit England or America. He confesses that England sounds more attractive to him because of all he has read about violence in America. And would I please answer a question on another subject? The pope wrote recently that Buddhism was atheistic and taught its followers to be indifferent to the world. Is that my own personal view? I tell him that the pope was expressing an understanding that remains quite common in the West. Many Westerners think there's only one kind of Buddhism. And what about the Westerners who say that Buddhism is polytheistic? he asks. I don't believe Shingon is polytheistic, I say. Both he and the young woman nod in agreement. Our encounter has cheered them up.

As we leave the Maruman we ask the proprietor about the small prayer bracelet he always wears around his wrist. He holds it up to the light so we can see the tiny image of Kōbō Daishi encased in its Mother Bead. He says he never removes the bracelet, not even when bathing, out of gratitude to Odaishi-sama for providing him with a means for making a living. As we pass through the door he calls out to us a familiar "*Matta yama ni!*" Please come to the mountain again!

A short distance beyond the Maruman is the Izui *sake* store, which has sold *sake* on the mountain for more than three centuries. We think it may be Kōyasan's oldest surviving business. Displayed inside the door is a sign in Japanese designed to put customers at their ease. "Kōyasan strictly forbad the drinking of liquor, but Kōbō Daishi relented because of the severe cold, permitting priests to drink one cup of *sake*." A featured brand of the shop is *Reijō Kōyasan Hannya-tō*, which translates to something like "Warm Wisdom Water of Holy Kōyasan." We purchase a six-sided bottle with a drawing of Kōbō Daishi in pilgrim dress on the front. Beside St. Kōbō is Kariba-myōjin's white dog Shiro. On the back of the bottle is the full text of the *Hannya-shingyō*, just to reenforce the religious theme. An accompanying leaflet explains that the manufacturer, the Hatsuzakura Company, sent kegs of *sake* on horseback to Kōyasan for many generations, and that Kōbō Daishi's own mother brewed *sake* for him each year at harvest time "to help her son's health."[7] "With the first sip [of our *sake*] you will hear the wind through Kōya's trees. With the second you will float free of all care and worry. With the third sip you will feel that you are regaining your youth."

Near the Izui *sake* shop is Kōyasan's leading antique store, Nishiri and Company. We've come to like everything about Nishiri and Company, especially its proprietor, Nishimoto Fumio. On our first visit to Kōyasan he made us tea and told us about the store, about his own history, and about Kōyasan's history as well. On our second visit he showed us a small ceramic statue of Yakushi, the Buddha of Medicine, made affordable because it had once been broken, repaired, and then broken again. This Yakushi is now one of our most prized possessions.

We visit Mr. Nishimoto frequently, and unfailingly on Kōbō Daishi's birthday. For the birthday parade he provides us with sidewalk chairs and keeps up a running commentary as the marchers and dancers go by. Mr. Nishimoto was born on Kōyasan in 1920. His grandfather and grandmother came to the mountain early in the twentieth century, at about the time it was first opened to women. In those days, he says, women were a rarity and therefore were treated with unusual respect. His grandfather made wood products for household use, bringing the wood up the mountain on horseback or in wagons pulled by oxen. His father started the antique business. Young Nishimoto attended Kōyasan's grammar school, but since the middle school back then was restricted to boys training for the priesthood, he went down the mountain to Kōyaguchi (on the Kinokawa) for grades seven through eleven. His personal dream was to escape from the mountain altogether. The opportunity came when he attended a foreign language college in Ōsaka and studied German, English, French, and Chinese. Afterward he found employment with an international company that required him to travel to the United States and Europe.

In 1961, when he was forty-one, he returned to Kōyasan to take over his father's antique business. This change was difficult, for after so much time in the outside world Kōyasan seemed narrow and suffocating. But he has adjusted. He now loves recalling the mountain of his childhood, when the roads were unpaved and the winter snow much deeper than at present. His personal temple is Takamuro-in, located a short distance from the store. His grandparents, parents, and one sister are buried in the forest cemetery near Kōbō Daishi's tomb. Two or three hundred other relatives are buried there also, seven generations in all. He lives in the rear of the store. Each year in June Mr. Nishimoto goes to Europe for two weeks—usually to Germany, Switzerland, and the Netherlands—to purchase Japanese antiques (mostly wooden Buddhas) and bring them home again.

CHAPTER EIGHT

EDUCATING A SHINGON PRIEST

THE STUDENT YEARS

The typical priest at Kōyasan today most likely grew up as an eldest son in a temple family. And the family temple itself may have been located at Kōyasan. If that was the case, then he would have attended the mountain's own kindergarten, elementary, and middle schools along with other temple and town children, both boys and girls. For high school he may have been sent away (no doubt his personal preference), but just as likely he would have been enrolled at Kōyasan's three-year Buddhist high school. There he again would have been surrounded by the products of temple families, although now many of his fellow students would be from places other than Kōyasan. And only about one in five would have been female.[1]

For the four years of college our representative priest may have attended either a Buddhist or a secular institution. Kōyasan's own

Buddhist university, Kōyasan Daigaku, would have been one option, although, again, getting away from the mountain most likely was the student's personal preference. At "Kōdai" the choice of majors would be Chinese philosophy, Western European philosophy, Japanese history, Japanese literature, English and American literature, sociology, social welfare, general Buddhism, and Esoteric Buddhism. All of these majors would be supplemented with a general education program, a course in the theory of religion, and two foreign languages (English plus a choice of German, French, Chinese, or Sanskrit).[2]

The next step following the university experience would be enrollment in a seminary for Buddhist priests.[3] By this time our representative candidate, as a temple son, already would have been given *shukke-tokudo*, perhaps receiving it as early as the age of six. *Shukke-tokudo* involves, among other things, the shaving of the head and donning of a black robe, the adoption of a Buddhist name, the taking of refuge in the Three Jewels of Buddhism (the Buddha, the Dharma, and the Sangha), and the reception of the first Dharma teaching. With these actions the son symbolically leaves his family, becomes his father's disciple, and embarks on the path laid out by the Buddha. Most importantly, he establishes himself, with further study and qualifications, as the hereditary spiritual heir of the home temple.

Of course, the priest father might not elect to serve as his son's spiritual master, in which case another senior priest in the father's lineage would be chosen. In either circumstance the duty of the master, known as the *shisō*, is to instruct his disciple, the *deshi*, in religious conduct and to act as a spiritual and intellectual model. The relationship would be registered at the Kongōbu-ji headquarters prior to entering the seminary. In the ideal, the *shisō-deshi* bond is deeper than any blood kinship and continues for life.

Our future priest now enters Kōyasan's seminary for men, Senshū-gakuin ("Specialization School"), more formally known as Hōju-in. There he will undergo an intensive three-semester program of doctrinal study and ritual practice. If female, the candidate will enter Nisō-gakuin, Kōyasan's new seminary for women, formally known as Nisō Shudō-in.[4] The all-male Senshū-gakuin is a sequestered temple complex located directly off the northwest corner of the Garan. Some eighty men are enrolled in its program each April, approximately ten of whom will drop out or be excluded somewhere along the way. The women students at Nisō-gakuin, which is located south of the Garan in Minami-dani, number around a dozen, with three or four expected to withdraw.

The year of training at Senshū-gakuin is divided into three equal sessions or semesters. Among the major topics studied are the theory and history of Shingon, basic Sanskrit, sutra-copying (*shakyō*), Buddhist liturgical chanting (*shōmyō*), methods for teaching the Dharma, selected ritual procedures, and various meditations, climaxing with the Letter *A* Meditation (*A-ji-kan*). The students also study Buddhist painting, flower arrangement, and tea ceremony. In addition there are the usual domestic disciplines of monastery life, such as preparing meals and baths and cleaning the temple buildings and grounds.

The program for the middle one-hundred-day session known as *shido kegyō* ("Fourfold Preparatory Enlightenment Practice") is notoriously severe. Where earlier the students had enjoyed one hour off on Wednesdays and two hours off on Sundays, now all opportunity for ease and rest are removed. Each day begins at 3:00 a.m. "Noontime" is at 8:00 a.m. "Evening" begins at three in the afternoon. The *shido kegyō* program is subdivided as follows: training in the Wisdom Principle Sūtra (*Hannya-rishu-kyō*), one week; in the Five-Point Protection (*Goshinbo*), one week; in the Eighteen Stage Practice (*Jūhachidō*), four weeks; in the Diamond Realm (*Kongō-kai*), three weeks; in the Womb Realm (*Taizō-kai*), three weeks; and in the Fire Offering (*goma*; Sk. *homa*), three weeks. Each studied ritual is performed three times daily (at 4:00 a.m., 9:00 a.m., and 2:00 p.m.), a task that may require up to sixteen hours of sustained concentration.[5]

Nearly every graduate of Senshū-gakuin has a war story to tell about the physical and emotional strains of *shido kegyō*. "I found time to eat only one meal each day. I lost twenty pounds." "I was so overwhelmed by lack of sleep I sneaked off to take a nap between each session. Otherwise I could not have kept going." "They said we could go to the bathroom during practice if it was absolutely necessary, but before returning to the *dōjō* you had to pour cold water over your body 108 times for purification." "The *dōjō* was never heated. *Goma* practice was the only time you got your hands warm." "Sitting *zazen* for hours caused the worst pain I have ever experienced. I so pitied the few foreigners." The shared misery, however, produced an invaluable bonding. "We all formed some great friendships. That was the best part."

Prior to *shido kegyō* the students attend an important Ten Precepts (*Jukai*) ceremony conducted at Entsūritsu-ji, a monastery retreat located deep in the forest just beyond the southeast rim of the valley. This retreat temple, usually referred to as the *shinbessho* ("temple set apart for religious practice"), was founded in the twelfth century and reestablished in the seventeenth.[6] At its entrance path is an ancient stone sign: "No Garlic, Wine, or Women May Enter." Today women students do enter to join the male students for the three day *Jukai* ceremony, but they are present only during the daylight hours.

Visitors to Kōyasan often see the priests-in-training marching in platoon formation, saffron surplices blowing, hurrying from one prayer station to the next.[7] Each day's prayer circuit begins with a sequence of chants before the Daimon (Great Gate) at the head of the valley. The group then moves successively to the site of the Garan's long lost Chūmon Gate, to the Kondō (Golden Hall), the Kyōzō (sūtra repository), the Myōjin-sha (shrine of the mountain gods), the Saitō (Western Stūpa), the Kujaku-dō (hall of the Peacock King), the Juntei-dō (hall of the Juntei Kannon), the Miedō (repository of Kōbō Daishi's sacred portrait), and the Kondō-ura (rear of the Kondō). Kondō-ura is the tenth stop. The group next faces westward toward the Benzaiten Shrine on the summit of Benten-dake. Then follow prayers before the Great Stūpa. After this they descend from the upper terrace, face southward, and chant toward the Kakkai-sha shrine near the valley's southern rim. Then, in clockwise succession, they pray to the Fudō-dō, the Aizen-dō, and the Daie-dō (hall of Amida Buddha). After paying tribute to the Sanmai-dō (Saigyō's meditation hall), they turn northward to pray toward the Yugitō stūpa on Lion's Hill above Chū-in temple. At the extreme eastern edge of the Garan they stop at the Tō-tō (Eastern Stūpa) and pray to the Dainichi there. Then, facing south-south-east, they launch a prayer to the fire god Kōjin on the summit of Mt. Kōjin-ga-take, a full ten kilometers away (or, alternatively, to the Kōjin shrine at nearby Kongōbu-ji).[8] Finally, as they hurry out of the Garan and down the Jabara Path, they make a brief leftward bow toward a hidden object in the forest. Deep in the woods, obscured behind a curtain of green, is the burial place of

Chisen, the beloved disciple and nephew who preceded Kūkai in death by ten years.[9]

Senshū-gakuin students also occasionally journey outside the borders of Kōyasan. One hike takes them into the mountainous region to the south known as *oku-Kōya* ("inner Kōyasan"), where they visit the summit shrine of the god Kōjin.[10] Another journey takes them to the foothill village of Kudoyama on the Kinokawa, where they perform *shōmyō* at a memorial *samurai* festival at Sanada-an, the former residence of the heroic Sanada clan. Dressed in formal black robes and white *kesa*, the students crowd into the Sanada sanctuary (Zenmyōshō-in), perform their chant as festival-goers listen appreciatively at the open windows, then vanish down a side pathway on their way back to the mountain.

A third off-mountain experience is of an entirely different nature. Each student is required to assume for a time the role of a pilgrim monk with begging bowl in hand. In this way they establish a spiritual link with the traveling monks of earlier generations, including Kōbō Daishi himself. The setting for this experience may vary, but sometimes (especially for the women) it is the full eighty-eight temple pilgrimage on Shikoku, which is traveled by bus over a period of about two weeks. The rules for begging are strict. No offering (*settai*) may be actively solicited. When a donation of money or food is received, no gratitude is expressed. Gift-giving is primarily for the benefit of the giver. All food offerings must be eaten, even if the food contains an animal product. To fail to eat the offered food would negate the giver's generosity.

Shortly after the successful completion of *shido kegyō*, and before the third semester of study, the trainees of Senshū-gakuin and Nisō-gakuin receive the *denpō-kanjō*, the formal "Dharma-transmission" initiation into the full esoteric priesthood. Those students who do not attend Senshū-gakuin or Nisō-gakuin, but choose instead one of the alternative programs of training offered at Kōyasan—at Kōyasan University or at Entsūritsu-ji (*shinbessho*), or privately at a temple *dōjō*—may gain admission to the *denpō-kanjō*, but only after an examination. Has the student absorbed the essential historical and doctrinal information? Have the complex ritual practices been learned? Is there evidence of a proper disposition and maturity? Has a sustaining spiritual bond been formed between the candidate and Kōbō Daishi? Often, as many as half of these candidates do not receive the *denpō-kanjō*, at least not immediately.

The *denpō-kanjō* ceremony itself follows the form used by Hui-kuo when he initiated Kūkai in Ch'ang-an. The blindfolded candidate has a sprig of *shikimi* placed between his (or her) extended middle fingers, then is guided into the sanctuary where a special mandala has been placed on an initiation altar. Still unsighted, the candidate drops the *shikimi* onto the mandala, a gesture that establishes a Dharma-relationship between the candidate and the cosmic Dainichi Nyorai at the mandala's center. Water representing the Five Wisdoms is sprinkled on the candidate's head, a re-enactment of the initiation Nāgārjuna received in the Iron Tower.[11] With this initiation, the candidate is declared a Shingon priest, an *ajari* ("holy teacher"; Sk. *āchārya*).

ADVANCING IN RANK

Seminary attendance and ordination do not end the need for training, for at this stage our young Kōyasan priest knows only a small fraction of the practices of Shingon tradition (in all, there are said to be more than two hundred and fifty advanced practices). He likely will apply for the *kangakue* study of Kūkai's works, a program that includes ceremonial commentary in classical Chinese. If this training goes well he will proceed to an advanced rank of *ajari*, at which time he will be admitted into the presence of Kōbō Daishi's portrait in the inner sanctuary of the Miedō. At some point he will have "entered" a Kōyasan temple—perhaps his own family temple—in a *nyū-ji* ceremony, formally becoming one of that temple's lineage holders. With the *gakushū-kanjō* ritual ("Dharma-learning initiation"), he will receive the title of *dai-ajari* (Great Master) and may accept disciples on his own authority.

Still far off is appointment to Kōyasan's highest ecclesiastical position. The climb toward Hōin-daikashō, or Dharma-seal Great Master, usually begins around age fifty when a priest with the rank of *dai-ajari* is invited to serve as one of the two priests who devote a year to the veneration of the mountain's native guardian gods. This remarkable year opens with the guardian gods (Nyū-myōjin, Kariba-myōjin, Princess Kebi, and Princess Itsukushima) being brought to the priest's home temple where they are installed on the private altar of the temple *butsuma*. Since the native gods cannot be housed in an area polluted by death, any *ihai* or ashes that are present on the altar are removed. The installation, known as the "Honorable Seeing-off and Welcoming of the Ryūgi and Seigi Gods" (Rissei-ryō-myōjin-no-hōsōgei), is a great occasion for the honored priest and his temple.

Promptly at ten o'clock on the morning of lunar September 3 a two-man procession arrives at the temple gate and proceeds along a specially prepared path bordered with purifying *sugi* branches.[12] In the lead is a young priest, white-masked, white-gloved, white-robed, a formal fan tucked at his throat. This priest carries an incense burner to purify the air through which the second priest moves. The second priest, who was host to the mountain gods the preceding year, carries two objects hidden beneath white silk wrappings. One of these objects is a small container that holds articles especially precious to the Myōjin. The other is a scroll that represents the Myōjin themselves. The older priest enters the temple's banner-draped main hall and proceeds to the area of the *ōhiroma* immediately in front of the *butsuma* alcove. There he kneels at a low table and delivers to his successor the precious items—first the container, then the sacred scroll. The receiving priest retires into the *butsuma* and, after closing the sanctuary doors behind him, installs the scroll on the altar. This scroll is kept veiled throughout the operation and will remain veiled the entire year.

From an adjoining hallway, a crowd of excited temple friends and visitors has been watching in silence. Finally, the new host priest reemerges from his *butsuma* sanctuary. The Hōin and other gathered priests step forward to congratulate him. The transference ceremony is over. Together the priest participants withdraw to an adjacent room for a meal of celebration.

Thus, the sacred year begins. Every morning for the next twelve months the new host priest (whose informal title now is *tōban*, "being on duty") will rise at four a.m. to prepare food offerings and conduct prayer services before the holy visitors in the *butsuma*. For the year he will not officiate at, or even attend, a funeral. Should his wife or mother or one of his children die the funeral would have to be held at another temple and without his attendance. He will eat no meat or animal product for the year. Although a married man he will live celibate. For the year he will not leave the mountain.[13]

Approximately eight months into this year, on lunar May 3, the hosting priest will participate in an all-night ceremony at Sannō-in known as the *Sannō-in Rissei,* or "Ceremonial Debate at the Temple of the Mountain Gods." For this stylized debate the host priest, seated regally on an elevated throne beneath a red canopy, assumes the role of Answerer (*Ryūgi*). Directly behind him sits the previous year's hosting priest, who assumes the role of Commentator (*Seigi*). In the course of the night five questions are presented to Ryūgi, and these he answers one by one in a loud, melodious voice. Out in the forest darkness the mountain gods listen and are reassured that the quality of priestly knowledge and devotion truly remains high at Kōyasan.[14]

During the next year, the Ryūgi priest will supervise Kōyasan's *Gakue* ("Learning Society") in a question and answer ritual informally called the *Saru-biki-mondō,* or "monkey-pulling question and answer."[15] On lunar June 9 and 10 of some subsequent year he will act as *gakutō* ("learning head") in the *Uchi-dangi* ("Private Discussion") ceremony held at Kongōbu-ji, another examination of doctrinal matters. Finally, he will serve as *gakutō* in the *Mi Saishō-kō* ritual held at Sannō-in on lunar June 10 and 11. This last ceremony, which at one time was performed at the imperial palace, is designed to promote the health of the emperor and the well-being of the state. Like the Sannō-in Rissei, however, it is specifically dedicated to the mountain gods of Kōyasan.[16]

After completing all of the above assignments our priest will be advanced to the rank of *jōgō.* Formerly, he was addressed as *inge-san.* Now he will be addressed as *jōgō-san,* or "upper fellow." He will add black *geta* and a black silk scarf to his ordinary dress. At major ceremonial events he will don red shoes and a resplendent brocaded robe with red, silver, and gold strings. As *jōgō* he is a member of the ecclesiastical elite, a sort of Kōyasan cardinal. Only one more upward step is possible. Once each year one of the *jōgō* is selected to serve as *Hōin,* the ceremonial surrogate for Kōbō Daishi and the wearer of Kōbō Daishi's robe. Hōin is the highest priestly office on the mountain. The honor usually comes, if it comes at all, when a priest is in his seventies.

The *Hōin-tenne-shiki,* or installation ceremony of a Hōin, takes place in the *ōhiroma* of Kongōbu-ji on some "auspicious day" between February 22 and March 15. The principal priests of Kōyasan seat themselves in four lines that run the length of the long room. Several hundred chairs are placed in the exposed front corridor to accommodate the invited guests, who arrive in black suits and formal *kimono*, but remain without overcoats despite the bitter cold.[17]

The new Hōin, dressed in a red robe, enters the *ōhiroma* from the rear and walks slowly down the rows of fellow priests to his designated place at the *kami-za*, or "high seat." Three representatives of the Kōyasan headquarters come forward to place three offering stands before him. Two of the stands hold *o-fuda*. The third holds rice heaped up in the shape of a mountain. On this mountain lies a piece of seaweed (*mokombu*) cut in the shape of a coin. The priest who is scheduled to become the following year's Hōin, using a pair of oversized *hashi*, places some rice on the seaweed and passes the gift to the new Hōin. The Hōin receives the gift on a piece of Japanese paper, which he then folds and inserts inside his gown. The rice represents the productivity of the land, the seaweed the productivity of the sea. Three sprigs of pine that have been inserted into the rice mountain represent longevity. The welfare of Kōyasan is directly dependent on the continuing health of the natural world. As the ceremony closes all the senior priests come forward to kneel before their new spiritual leader. The freshly installed Hōin then leaves the hall through Kongōbu-ji's *tara-to* entry. Outside, he steps into the black and red *kago* that will be his ceremonial mode of transportation for the coming year.[18] At the year's end he will receive the title of *zengan*, after which he is free of all further official duties, but may, if he wishes, continue to be an active priest.

CHAPTER NINE

A PILGRIMAGE THROUGH
THE FOREST CEMETERY

In the view of many Japanese visitors, the greatest single enterprise of Kōyasan, exceeding even the training of priests and laity and the constant conduct of ceremonial events, is its function as a repository and memori-alizer of the nation's dead. Memorial activities are performed daily at individual temples, but the primary center of the mountain's commit-ment to remembrance is the "Inner Temple" (Okunoin) at the eastern end of the valley. That is where Kōbō Daishi's tomb is located. It is where the ashes of the dead are deposited and where most pilgrimages to the mountain reach their climax. Leading into the heart of the Okunoin, and an integral part of it, is Kōyasan's world-famous forest cemetery, two kilo-meters in length and containing more that two hundred thousand tree-shaded memorials. It is a fascinating and beautiful place. It is where we are going now.

FIRST BRIDGE TO THE MIDDLE BRIDGE

From the center of the valley's "downtown" to the beginning of the forest cemetery is a walk of about twenty minutes. Upon reaching the cemetery entrance we wash our hands and rinse our mouths at the *temizuya*, then bow solemnly before the Ichi-no-hashi, or "First Bridge." The final segment of the pilgrim path lies before us.

We count the bridge's planks as we cross. There are thirty-six planks in all, one for each of the sacred figures who surround Dainichi Buddha in the central assembly of the Diamond Realm Mandala. Underneath us flows the Ōdogawa, or "Imperial Domain River." The stream begins as a spring on the lower slope of Mount Benten and runs the length of the valley.

We quickly survey the wooded cemetery ahead. In all directions, up slope and down, are thousands of stone memorials, some large, some small, many obscured beneath multiple layers of lichen and moss. Most of the monuments take the form of a *gorintō* ("five-ring tower"), a structure made of five separately carved stones set atop one another. The square base stone signifies the element Earth. Above that is a globular stone for Water. Next is a flared triangular stone, Fire. Then a hemispherical stone, Air or Wind. Finally, a jewel-shaped stone, Space. The sixth of the Six Great Elements, the immaterial integrating Consciousness, or Sacred Wisdom, is represented by the *gorintō* monument as a whole. All the diverse phenomena of the universe are the products of these Six Elements (the *rokudai*). Each *gorintō* signifies the Dharma Body and the Dharma Mind of the Great Sun Buddha.[1]

Some monuments do not follow the form of the traditional *gorintō*. Some of these are quite unique in design. Just beyond the bridge on the left, soaring up against the dark forest background, is a white cylinder framed by white flame-shaped wings. The cylinder's surface is covered with hundreds of hands in bas-relief, each hand reaching upward. At the cylinder's base is a small mausoleum faced with blue tile. We join two elderly men who are standing before this mausoleum examining its brass name plate: *O-dōki-no-sakura*. "Honorable Cherry Blossoms of the Same Season." The men perhaps are remembering the lyrics of a proud but poignant song from their youth.

You and I are cherry blossoms of the same season . . .
Because we are now in full bloom everyone
knows that soon we must fall.
Let us fall beautifully for our country.

Beside the plaque are three familiar emblems—an airplane propeller, an anchor, a single white cherry blossom. This mausoleum and its cylindrical tower were erected in honor of the Japanese Navy fliers of World War II, most specifically for the young men who were drafted in December 1943, the fourteenth training class. Those youths, many of them destined to become "*kamikaze*" fliers, referred to themselves as "cherry blossoms" in acknowledgment of an expected early death. Some wore a cherry blossom insignia on their flying uniforms.

The upward-reaching hands on the tower express the presence of the Thousand-handed Kannon (Senju Kannon), the compassionate Bodhisattva who hears the calls of the dead, even the dead who call from ocean graves. The flames that surround the tower are the purifying action of Fudō Myō-ō, the deity who first meets the dead in the afterlife.

A short distance beyond the bridge, to the right, is a side path. We go down this side path until we come to another unique monument (located where the path first angles sharply to the left), a large nine-foot-tall rectangular granite stele being carried on the back of a Chinese stone tortoise. The entablature of the stele features two dragons holding a *mani* jewel. Between the dragons, as the primary object of their protection, is an unmistakable Christian cross. What we have here is one of the cemetery's greatest surprises, a precise copy of the famed "Nestorian Stone" that was erected near the Chinese capital of Ch'ang-an in 781—just twenty-three years prior to Kōbō Daishi's visit there. This stele, discovered in 1625 by Jesuit missionaries to China, provided Western historians with evidence that Nestorian Christianity, the so-called "Luminous Religion," had penetrated China much earlier than formerly supposed. For Victorian Englishwoman Elizabeth Anna Gordon (1851–1925), Christian author and enthusiastic student of Mahāyāna Buddhism, the text carved on the stone (duplicated in Syriac and Chinese) provided evidence that Kōbō Daishi had encountered and adopted elements of the Christian faith while in China. In 1911, with the full cooperation of Kōyasan's clergy, Mrs. Gordon had this "most valuable historical monument in the World" copied and installed in the forest cemetery.

When Mrs. Gordon died fourteen years later in Kyōto, her cremated remains were divided according to her instructions. One portion was buried at Chang-an-sa monastery on Diamond Mountain in Korea, her way of celebrating Korea's role in introducing Buddhism to Japan. The other half was buried here on Japan's Diamond Mountain (Kongōbu), next to the Nestorian Stone. We notice that her grave is marked by a granite globe on which has been carved the Sanskrit letter *A*, a representation, in Mrs. Gordon's mind, both of the "Great Illumination" that is Dainichi Buddha and the "Light of the World" that is Jesus Christ. All the major world religions, she had come to believe, taught a similar faith.[2]

We retrace our steps, returning to the main path. Once well launched along the ancient pilgrimage route we quickly discover the full atmosphere of the cemetery—the hilly terrain, the damp, woodsy scent, the intricate complexity of thousands of lichen-covered monuments erected beneath a canopy of tall cedars and cypresses. The larger memorials are fixed on heavy granite foundations that make them at least partially secure against the effects of forest growth and seasonal change. Some plots are additionally equipped with granite fences, elaborate stone lanterns, and receptacles for flowers and other offerings. But by far the most numerous memorials are small single-stone *gorintō* that appear to have no clearly designated spot of ground on which to stand. Such stones, often crudely carved, are scattered along the edges of the paths, in among the roots and hollows of trees, tucked beneath bushes. If one climbs up into the woods above the pilgrimage route, beyond rows of the official plots, these free-floating miniature memorials are discovered lying about by the hundreds, slowly sinking beneath the forest debris. Such anonymous stones, with no identifiable family connections, are categorized as *muen-tō*, literally "no relation *stūpas*." The dead spirits they represent are *muen-botoke*, "no relation Buddhas."[3] These dead are not entirely forgotten, however, at least not at Kōyasan. Each year hundreds of the *muen-tō* are brushed off, set upright, and clothed with colorful bibs.[4] Some have become objects of special devotion, as we discover at the top of the first rise along the pilgrimage trail.

To our right, up on the side of an embankment, is an informal little shrine made from an ordinary unpainted wooden box laid on its side. Inside the box someone has placed two anonymous single-stone *gorintō* and a tiny golden statue of Kōbō Daishi. The two *muen-tō* probably were memorials for children, or at least that is how they are now treated. Identical red bibs with white trim have been tied about their "necks." Such bibs are presumed to provide warmth and comfort for a child in the other world. At the front of the box are a single candleholder, two plastic flower containers, and the remnants of several bouquets. Melted wax darkens the box floor. This anonymous, makeshift shrine attracts many visitors. More than a thousand coins rest in the offering basket. Each coin (mostly one yen pieces) represents a personal prayer, however casually delivered. Perhaps one day a custodian from the Okunoin headquarters will come by and collect the money.

A short distance farther along the path, on the left, are three large standing figures of Jizō Bodhisattva. All are ebony black. Although at first glance the three appear to be identical, we soon note that the figure at the left wears a cowl and has narrower shoulders and more delicate facial features. This Jizō clearly is female. In fact she closely resembles the Virgin Mary, even with her Buddhist attributes of elongated ears, three fat folds at the neck, and a light-emitting curl of hair in the middle of her forehead. What is most striking about this statue, however—and the other two statues as well—is that it is holding in its left hand the figure of a golden human fetus. The fetus is enclosed in a circular golden womb and is anatomically quite complete, with tiny golden arms and legs, closed eyes, locked nostrils, rudimentary ears, and umbilical cord. The message seems to be that the unborn human, just like the *mani* jewel that a Jizō traditionally displays, is an expression of the Buddha's progenitive love, and therefore supremely sacred.

A pamphlet found in a nearby box provides further information about the shrine. The three statues, known as the San-hei Mizuko Jizō Bosatsu, offer consolation to aborted and miscarried fetuses (called *mizuko*, or "water babies"). The statue at the left, informally known as "Maria-sama," is the "Jizō of Peace." Her task is to calm the frightened spirit of the lost child. The statue in the middle is the "Jizō of Relief." He removes the child's sorrow at being cheated of birth. The figure at the

right is the "Jizō of Equality." He informs the world that the fetus possesses rights equal to those of the already born. Inside the three statues
are ten thousand copies of the *Hannya-shingyō* along with seals from the
thirty-three temples of the Kannon pilgrimage of Western Japan and the
eighty-eight temples of the Shikoku Kōbō Daishi pilgrimage. Any
passerby who suffers from guilt, or fear, in connection with an aborted
child is encouraged to contact a particular Buddhist organization in
Ōsaka. A spirit-appeasing ceremony for the dead child (*mizuko kuyō*) will
be arranged. A fee is involved.[5]

About four hundred meters from the First Bridge, on the right side
of the pilgrim path, is the oldest dated tombstone in the cemetery. It just
may be the oldest dated *gorintō* in the nation. A faint inscription tells us
that the monument was installed in 997 in remembrance of Tada Mit-
sunaka (912–997). Tada, better known to historians as Minamoto Mit-
sunaka, was the founder of the powerful Minamoto (Genji) clan that
established the Kamakura shōgunate. No Japanese visitor will want to
miss this stone, partly because of its great age and partly because of its
association with the grand and romantic history of the Genji.

Twenty-five paces beyond the Tada monument, on the left, is a
small shrine containing a seated Jizō. We might as well take notice of
this little figure for he is taking careful notice of us. This is the Kazutori
("Number-counting") Jizō. His assignment is to keep careful track of all
visitors who enter and exit along the pilgrimage path. To assure this
Jizō's protective blessing we drop a small contribution into the collection
basket (*saisen bako*).

We stride along for another fifty paces through the forest of trees
and monuments, and stop at an innocuous foot-high boulder known as
the *Koshi-kake-ishi*, or "sit-on-chair-stone." On this quite ordinary object
Kōbō Daishi is said to have sat and rested whenever he walked through
the forest to the Tamagawa. Since it would be presumptuous for today's
weary pilgrim to sit where Kōbō Daishi sat, the Hashimoto Rotary Club
has placed two large benches nearby. Also available is a trash basket in
case someone has brought a picnic lunch.

At about thirty-five paces beyond Daishi's Seat a narrow side trail
leads uphill to the left. This trail's final destination, visible from the main
path through the trees and monuments, is a small red-painted memorial

hall for the great warlord Uesugi Kenshin (1530–1578). The wooden structure is heavily decorated with flower and animal designs, and is registered as an Important Cultural Asset. Any evocation of Uesugi Kenshin quickens the pulse of male Japanese. A paragon of warriors, Kenshin arranged to fight as many brilliant battles as possible, but never stooped to vulgar or devious tactics. His rival of choice was a warlord of equal majesty and brilliance named Takeda Shingen (1521–1573). On five occasions over the space of twelve years the two met on the same battlefield to test their strategic skills, with neither achieving a decisive victory. The men were too well matched and perhaps too filled with mutual esteem to force their game to any absolute conclusion. Kenshin died suddenly at the age of forty-eight while preparing to battle against the brutal Oda Nobunaga. Upon receiving news of his rival's death Takeda Shingen is said to have wept openly.

As chance (or calculation) would have it, Uesugi Kenshin's mausoleum on the hillside faces in the direction of Takeda Shingen's own stone memorial, which is located on a large platform near Daishi's Seat. A combat enthusiast might observe that Kenshin enjoys the advantage of higher ground while Shingen's memorial has better access to water. Looks like another draw.[6]

About eighty paces beyond the side trail to Kenshin's shrine is another side path that extends off to the right. Thirty meters up this path is a memorial to a third powerful warlord, Date Masamune (1567–1636). Near the memorial's entrance is a statue of Kōbō Daishi mounted on a high pillar. Date, known to his enemies as "the One-Eyed Dragon" (he lost an eye in childhood), was the dominant northern *daimyō* during the same period of civil struggle that involved Uesugi Kenshin and Takeda Shingen. At various times Date served as a key ally to both Hideyoshi and Ieyasu. But Date was more than just a redoubtable warlord. His interests included Nō drama, calligraphy, the art of incense, and general patronage of artists and scholars. He even was a diplomat and international figure of note, sending personal embassies to the king of Spain and to the pope.

Surrounding Date's massive central *gorintō* are twenty smaller *gorintō*, and it is largely for these twenty that we have stopped here. Date died at age seventy of natural causes. There was nothing exceptional about his death. Yet his closest twenty retainers felt compelled to perform *seppuku* as a final gesture of loyalty. From a traditional Buddhist perspective their suicides only increased the prospect of an unfavorable afterlife. Nevertheless, here they are, giving witness to the high calling of the samurai code, their ashes resting beside a portion of their lord's ashes.

Back on the main path, and just a few paces beyond the entrance to the Date memorial is a memorial to a somewhat different type of courage. A woman, sculpted life-size, holds a small child in her arms as a second child clutches at her garments. She wears inexpensive *mompe* pants and cheap straw *zori* instead of *geta*. This sculpture, known as the "Mother and Children Monument," pays tribute to the hundreds of thousands of hard-pressed Japanese women who kept the nation's children alive during World War II and in the years of severe deprivation that followed. Because of her resourcefulness and determination a generation was saved.

About 120 paces beyond the "Mother and Children Monument" is a side path on the right that leads to the *gorintō* of Oda Nobunaga's assassin, the notorious Akechi Mitsuhide (d. 1582). The sign that directs us to the site includes a dramatic touch: Akechi's name written in blood red characters. The many visitors who come here seem about evenly split in their attitude. Half come to heap scorn on Akechi for his treachery. The other half come to honor him for ridding the nation of a bloody tyrant and saving Kōyasan from possible destruction. But all reflect with wonder at the *gorintō*'s signal feature: the spherical Water stone is split and the cube-shaped Earth stone is fractured on three sides. All the old *gorintō* of the cemetery suffer from some minor erosion, but the actual splitting of stones is virtually unknown. A Kōyasan legend explains what happened here. Shortly after its erection Akechi's monument was struck by lightning and shattered. Replacement stones were installed immediately, but these too were struck and broken. So it was concluded that any further attempt at repair would be fruitless.

A group of visitors has joined us at the memorial. A slender, well-dressed gentleman holds up a small bouquet of flowers, then after a moment of silence places the bouquet in one of the two flower holders. The second holder already contains flowers. The offering basket here is piled with coins. Akechi is not forgotten.

Opposite the entrance path to Akechi's *gorintō* is a memorial built in honor of the legendary Kabuki actor Ichikawa Danjūrō I (1660–1704). This monument is easily identified by the Ichikawa *mon* chiseled at its center, a stylization of three nested boxes. Danjūrō I was the founder of Japan's greatest acting family. Even today, three centuries after his death, his fame remains undimmed. Among Danjūrō's innovations was an aggressive, super-masculine manner of acting known as *aragoto* ("bombast"), a style often used to depict such historical figures as the just-observed Akechi Mitsuhide and the super-warrior Kumagai Naozane. The signature moment in an *aragoto* performance occurs when the actor strikes a supremely dramatic *mie* ("pose"), fixes the audience with a furious stare (crossed eyes are appropriate), and pumps wave after wave of demented energy into the theater. "*Matte imashita!*" someone shouts ("That's what I've been waiting for!"). There also may be shouts of "*Naritaya!*", a reference to the Ichikawa family temple, the famed Shingon Narita Fudō (Shinshō-ji) near Tōkyō.[7] A popular belief holds that the "Danjūrō stare" is modeled on Fudō Myō-ō's own angry visage (including crossed eyes) and consequently has the power to cure certain enervating diseases, most especially male impotence. *Matte imashita!*

Two hundred meters farther along the pilgrimage path brings us to the Naka-no-hashi, or Middle Bridge. Here, in accordance with pious custom, we pause again to bow eastward in the direction of Kōbō Daishi's tomb.

THE MIDDLE BRIDGE

Historically, the area around the Middle Bridge has been one of the cemetery's most sacred locations. For centuries visitors came here to get healing water, taking it from the narrow brook or from a nearby well. At one time miracle-producing cherry trees also grew in the area, the product of shoots said to have been taken from the cherry trees at the tomb of Emperor Saga in the capital. These trees miraculously assumed the pain of sufferers who prayed to them.

The compassion of Saga's trees is now replaced by the Asekaki ("Perspiring") Jizō located on the eastern side of the bridge. We alert this Jizō to our presence by shaking the bell rope that hangs in front of his shrine. We tell him of our burden of pain and sin. Should we find him bathed in perspiration tomorrow morning that would be a sure indication that he has assumed our suffering.[8]

Near the Jizō's shrine is a dug well understood to have prophetic powers. If upon looking down into the well shaft we observe only a blurred reflection, then we can expect an early death. If, on the contrary, the water's surface is calm and our reflection clear we can expect many more years of health. We wait our turn, then look into the hole, careful not to dislodge any forest debris that rests on the sill. The reflection is brilliantly clear—in fact, our head is circled with a halo of cloud and sky. This well is the Sugata-mi-no-ido, or "Mirror Well." Kōbō Daishi is supposed to have been the first to discover its powers. (There are at least two other famous wells at Kōyasan, one associated with the annual preparation of Kōbō Daishi's new robe, the other with a poignant love story involving a nun and a Kōyasan priest.[9])

We proceed along the pilgrim path. On our right is a monument to the Japanese, Australian, and Malaysian soldiers who died in North Borneo during World War II. The three national flags hang in remembrance from a single pole. At the top of the next rise we leave the path briefly, climbing two short flights of steps that lead to the right. There we find one of the cemetery's quietest and most beautifully shaded precincts. Giant red-barked *sugi* and flat-needled *hinoki* close out the sky overhead. In this enclosure is the Mitsugon-dō, or "Hall of the Paradise of Dainichi." This is Kōyasan's memorial to Kakuban (1095–1144), the famed teacher and chief priest who was driven from Kōyasan. Posthumously, Kakuban became the founding patriarch of the Shingi-Shingon sect. Before the shrine are a rack for votive candles and a screened cage for food offerings. Several candles are burning now, having been lit by one of the parties walking ahead of us. There also are fresh flowers. We ring the shrine bell, bow, and light our own candle. Kakuban's bones are not here at the Mitsugon-dō. They are some thirty kilometers distant in his mausoleum at Negoro-ji. Very likely, Kakuban, who yearned to return to Kōyasan, would have preferred this location over the other one.

Eighty paces on from the Mitsugon-dō, at the left side of the path, are two large rectangular stele that honor the warriors "of both sides" who died during Hideyoshi's invasions of Korea between 1592 and

1598. None of the presumed goals of the invasions—to intimidate the Chinese, to open Korea and China to trade, to make Hideyoshi a great figure on the Asian continent—were achieved. On his deathbed a remorseful Hideyoshi begged that his soldiers be brought home. "Let not the spirits of the hundred thousand troops I have sent to Korea become disembodied in a foreign land!"[10] The older of the two stele, known as the Kōrai-jin Tekimikata Kuyō hi ("Memorial Stone for the Dead of Both Sides in the Korean War"), was erected immediately after the war by a Satsuma warlord, Shimazu Yoshihiro (1535–1619), "to the end that those who fell in the Korean War, foe and friend alike, may be gathered everyone into the way which leads to Buddhahood." The second stele, obviously much newer, presents a translation into English of the text of the older one. The second stele was erected in 1908 by a Shimazu descendent, Shimazu Tadashige, who wished to make twentieth-century English-speaking visitors aware of the benevolence the Japanese always had felt toward foreign peoples. This was a timely issue, for Korea had just been made a Japanese protectorate in the wake of Japan's triumph over Russia. The English translation, still legible beneath a covering of lichen and moss, says that upward of eighty thousand foes and more than three thousand Japanese warriors died "by arrow and by sword" during the battles of 1597.

Ninety paces farther along the path, on the right, is a modern echo of the Shimazu memorial. Once again, thousands of Japanese soldiers have died in a foreign land, this time in Burma during World War II. The memorial, in the form of a Burmese stūpa, sits a short distance back from the path and rises well above the surrounding monuments. Its cubical base is surmounted by a dome. Above the dome is a ringed spire crowned by a lotus and jewel. Seated in the pagoda is a Burmese-style Shākyamuni, his golden right hand "touching the earth." For Japanese visitors this memorial carries great emotional power, for it contains the bones of Japanese soldiers retrieved from Burma by Ueda Tenzui, a Shingon priest and Kōyasan University professor. Ueda, himself once a teacher in Burma, returned to that country in 1956 to pray for the dead and to bring home what remains he could find. Each year a service is held at the Burmese stūpa for all who died in that theater, whether Japanese, Burmese, English, Indian, or Chinese. In attendance are representatives of the bereaved families and a few surviving comrades.[11]

We go on for 125 more paces to where a broad stone side path
enters from the right. We take this side path, for the moment leaving the
pilgrimage route. After walking through a wooded area used primarily for
the burial of members of temple families, we exit from the forest altogether and enter a great open rectangular field of monuments.[12] This is a
new section of the cemetery that was not fully opened until after World
War II. Some of its monuments are quite recent, among them a twenty-
foot-tall granite *irei-tō* built to console the spirits of the six thousand and
more who died in the 1995 Kobe earthquake.

Conspicuously absent from this new section are the massive *gorintō*
monuments of the sort erected in the old forest by the great feudal warlords of the past. Instead, we find an abundance of equally ambitious
"secular" monuments memorializing the deceased executives and employees of some of Japan's most successful postwar companies and corpora-
tions. Nissan Motors, Matsushita Electric, Ezaki Glico, Kubota Steel. But
in a remarkable duplication of present and past, the number of corpora-
tion monuments in the new cemetery corresponds almost exactly to the
number of *daimyō* monuments built in the old cemetery—108 and 110,
respectively.[13]

A pronounced visual feature of the layout of the new cemetery is a
wide ceremonial approach (called a *sandō*) that leads directly to an imposing vermilion and white memorial hall set back against a wooded hillside.
This hall is the Eireiden, or "Hall of Heroic Spirits." It was constructed
in 1952 as Kōyasan's first major memorial for the Japanese soldiers,
sailors, and airmen who died in World War II. The Buddha it enshrines
is Amida, the Buddha most widely associated with the redemption of the
dead, especially outside Shingon. Unlike Tōkyō's famous and controversial Yasukuni Jinja, Kōyasan's Eireiden has escaped the charge that it
serves to glorify the military and celebrate imperial authority.[14] The
bridge that leads to the Eireiden is called the Heiwa-bashi, or "Bridge of
Peace." Standing before the shrine at this moment are some twenty elderly Japanese men and women, a gathering of survivors. A young monk is
leading them in a rapid sing-song recitation of the *Hannya-shingyō*.

Immediately to the south of the Eireiden is a much newer shrine
(completed in 1996) that has a greater potential for provoking contro-
versy. Dedicated to the "Shōwa era martyrs," it gives specific succor to the
spirits of the nearly one thousand Japanese military, almost all of them

officers, who were condemned as war criminals by various Allied tribunals following World War II. For decades the status of these dishonored dead was largely excluded from public discussion, even though popular belief held that neglect of the dead exposed the living to the action of angry *goryō* (unhappy dead spirits seeking revenge). Fifty years passed without a memorial being built.

This new "martyrs" memorial is handsomely done, complete with trees, shrubs, a granite entrance walkway, a gleaming *gorintō*, a statue of Kōbō Daishi as pilgrim, and a series of signs and stele informing the visitor of the nature of the place. At the shrine entrance is a multicolored map of the major theaters of the war—China, the Philippines, Malaya, Burma, Borneo, the Dutch East Indies, New Guinea, the Solomon Islands—together with the locations of Allied military prisons. A second sign board displays a chart with the name of each prison, the number of Japanese military executed at each, the number of deaths by disease, by accident, by *seppuku*, and by unknown causes.[15] Within the shrine's forecourt are several black stele with the names of the enshrined dead carved in gold characters. This admonition appears on a prominent granite pillar: *Shōwa Era Martyrs and Those Who Died in Prison, Comfort Their Spirits.*

The dedication of the shrine took place on the morning of April 29, 1996, a national holiday now known as "Greenery Day," but which earlier had been used for the observance of *Tenchōsetsu*, the ceremonial birthday of the Shōwa Emperor, Hirohito. The Kōyasan clergy were present in full ritual attire. The several hundred laity wore black, both the men and the women. No military uniforms or military insignia were visible. The Kōyasan University band played the *Kimigayo* ("Sovereign Reigns"). The national flag, the *Hinomaru*, was presented. A large wreath was placed before the shrine's central *gorintō*. A priest read a tribute. While other priests chanted, Kōyasan's highest administrative officer, the Kanchō, conducted a memorial ceremony before a portable altar. A *joruri* reciter intoned a poem with *shamisen* (three-string lute) accompaniment. The poem, entitled *Senpan-no-uta* ("Poem of a War Criminal"), was written by a Japanese officer just prior to his execution in Canton. *"I committed crimes, but only to protect my family, my country, my Emperor. Why must I alone accept the blame? Why should only those who did the fighting be blamed? Given these circumstances, I am not ready to die."* An elderly

veteran went to the microphone and, with his voice breaking, cried out
in sorrow to the thousand dead.[16]

ON TO THE THIRD BRIDGE

After returning to the pilgrimage path we come almost immediately to a
side trail that climbs up the slope to the left. Seventy paces along this
path, backed up against the hillside, rises the cemetery's largest *gorintō*,
popularly known as the *Ichi-no-hi* ("Number One Gravestone"). This five-
sectioned tower is twenty-eight feet high, with a foundation twelve feet on
a side. The memorial's formal name is *Gorintō-no-Suruga-dainagon*,
"Monument of Chief Councilor of State and Lord of Suruga." The chief
councilor in question was Tokugawa Tadanaga (1605–1633), and he built
the monument for the spiritual benefit of his mother. He himself was a
grandson of Ieyasu, the first Tokugawa shōgun. His father was the second
shōgun and his older brother the third. With such connections came great
power, and also risk. Shortly after the construction of the monument
Tadanaga was charged with plotting against his brother, was banished,
then required to commit *seppuku*. He died at age twenty-eight.

There is a well-known woodblock illustration of the Ichi-no-hi's
cubical Earth stone being carried up the mountain. Seventy-two laborers
are shown supporting the weight of the single stone while five others
walk ahead and alongside to guide them. On top of the stone rides a sev-
enty-eighth laborer who calls out the rhythm of the march as he waves a
purification wand and the banner of Suruga province. This remarkable
gorintō took three years to construct.[17]

Our next stop is another Jizō about forty paces farther along the pilgrimage path. He is impossible to miss. His stone face, round as the
moon, is brightly rouged—lips, cheeks, eyelids. The result of this attention is a glowing, clownish appearance. On this particular afternoon
someone has dressed him in a blue rain cape, a gingham hat, and a bright
red bib. On the ground before this "Rouged Jizō" is a collection of new
gifts, among them a rattle, a coloring book, and a box containing a dress-
up doll. We ask a fellow pilgrim who has just added another gift what she
can tell us about this remarkable figure. She says she knows nothing, but
believes the Jizō cares deeply for all the world's children.

Close by is an equally conspicuous sculpture: two chubby stone Jizō standing together on a lotus throne. The older Jizō wraps a comforting arm around the younger and with his free hand holds up a *mani* jewel. The hands of the younger are pressed together in *gasshō*. The two look quite drowsy and unafraid. The sculpture, known as the *Nakayoshi Jizō* ("Bosom-friend Jizō"), was new in 1990, but already has grown dark with moss and lichen. Such is the way of the forest.

Almost directly across the path from the two children is a large water-smoothed boulder on which a *haiku* has been carved. The *haiku* was written by the great Bashō (1644–1694), a devotee of Kōyasan's monk-poet Saigyō. In the poem Bashō tells us that he once heard the call of a pheasant and the sound reminded him of his dead father and mother.[18]

About 150 paces farther on, at the left side of the path, are two stone mausoleum halls surrounded by a single stone fence. The one on the right, which is slightly larger, enshrines Tokugawa Ieyasu's second son, Hideyasu (1574–1607). Hideyasu took the name of Matsudaira and through his sons founded the eight branches of the mighty Matsudaira clan of Echizen. The mausoleum at the left enshrines Hideyasu's mother. Both buildings reward close examination. By looking carefully we can make out twenty-seven Buddha figures carved on the walls of each. Stone *torii* serve as the entrance gates, a familiar architectural juxtaposition of "Shintō" and Buddhist elements.

The main path forks left and right a short distance beyond the Matsudaira Mausoleums. The right fork leads directly toward a cluster of large halls that serve the Okunoin. We choose the left fork, thus keeping to the formal pilgrimage trail.

Twenty-five more paces bring us to a set of stone steps that lead up the hillside on the left. At the top of the steps is a leveled opening in the woods and a modest memorial for supreme warlord Toyotomi Hideyoshi (1546–1598), "the greatest man in the history of Japan."[19] Here also are *gorintō* for Hideyoshi's mother, for his councilor of state, and for the councilor's wife. This Kōyasan memorial is in remarkable contrast to the massive constructions in the capital that were intended to persuade the nation that Hideyoshi was a god.

Another 150 paces brings us to our first view of the bridge over the Tamagawa, the "Jewel River." We descend to the bank of the holy stream. Straight ahead of us, across the bridge, is the final stretch of pathway. It ends in a flight of steps that climb to the Lantern Hall where homage is paid continuously to Kōbō Daishi. The saint's mausoleum is immediately beyond that hall. Groups of fellow visitors are sweeping past us now, crossing the bridge to say their prayers to Odaishi-sama. We will cross shortly, but first will look at some of the halls and activities on this side of the water. We are in the heart of Kōyasan's Inner Temple, the Okunoin.

CHAPTER TEN

THE INNER TEMPLE AND
KŌBŌ DAISHI'S MAUSOLEUM

THE HALLS BEFORE THE TAMAGAWA

Immediately to the right of the bridge, lined up with their backs to the flowing Tamagawa, are fourteen statues of bronze and stone. These statues, which have expanded in number through the centuries, are popularly known as the "Mizumuke [Water-splashing] Jizō." Not all in fact are Jizō. From left to right, there are two standing Jizō, three seated Jizō, a seated Dainichi, a standing Fudō Myō-ō, four standing Jizō, a seated Jizō, and two standing Sho-Kannon. Visitors take their pick. At the present moment a half-dozen pilgrims are standing before the statues and prayerfully splashing them with dippers of water drawn from the stream. The water flows off the statues and over memorial tablets. The tablets, called *tōba* (or *sotōba*), are thin slats of wood cut in the profile of a *gorintō*. On each has been written the posthumous name (*komyō*) of a deceased

217

person. The water of the sacred Tamagawa provides the dead spirit with purification and comfort.

If we wish, we can purchase a *tōba* a the nearby Gomadō ("Hall of the Fire Offering"), where the clerk is glad to help with its preparation. Instead of writing the name of some deceased person a visitor may choose to submit a personal supplication, such as a wish to have a child or to enjoy a peaceful death. We watch as a young man and young woman, both dressed in black, purchase two *tōba* at the Gomadō. They are asking a number of questions, as if uncertain of the procedure. Or perhaps they are just anxious not to commit an error that will make their appeal ineffectual. Finally, they walk to the row of statues and carefully place both *tōba* before a Sho-Kannon. As the man watches, the young woman lifts the dipper and slowly pours water over the *tōba* and over the feet of the Bodhisattva. The fresh ink on the *tōba* immediately begins to blur.

An elderly woman and a teenage boy companion are distributing about a dozen *tōba* between Dainichi Buddha and one of the seated Jizō. After splashing the two statues they go to the beginning of the line and proceed to splash all the other twelve statues in turn.

A young mother is helping her son with Down Syndrome manage a dipper. He directs all his attention at Fudō Myō-ō, splashing that strange fierce face over and over again. Finally the mother leads him to the bridge and across toward Kōbō Daishi's tomb. Later in the day, after most of the visitors have left the Okunoin area, a priest and some custodial workers will gather up the hundreds of wet *tōba* from in front of the Mizumuke Jizō and burn them ritually.

The Gomadō is a building of moderate size, about ten meters wide and twelve meters deep. Its front doors are pulled back, making visible two side-by-side sanctuaries. On the *shumi-dan* of the left sanctuary is an especially handsome Fudō Myō-ō carved from some fine-grained golden wood. This sculpture is relatively new, a replacement for a Fudō of the Fujiwara period now in the Reihōkan museum. The main figure in the righthand sanctuary is an ancient image of Kōbō Daishi. Tradition says this murky sculpture, blackened by centuries of votive fires, is a self-portrait carved by Kōbō Daishi at age forty-two. The story is that he made the statue after completing a journey around Shikoku Island, the purpose of which was to exorcize the ill fortune that threatens every male at age forty-two.[1] For centuries Japanese men have been urged to follow

Kōbō Daishi's example, either by walking the eighty-eight temple Shikoku pilgrimage or, more conveniently, by coming to Kōyasan to pray to this dark statue.

To the right of the Gomadō is the much larger Gokusho, or "Offering Hall." Both buildings face a public plaza. The Gokusho, with a frontage of some twenty meters, serves several functions. The central room of the hall (closed to the public) is used by priests for assembling and robing prior to ritual processions across the Tamagawa to the Lantern Hall. The Gokusho's enclosed garden court also is used for assembly purposes. At the rear of the building is a long corridor that crosses the Tamagawa to a residential hall for the monks of the Okunoin. On the Gomadō side of the Gokusho is an office where financial accounting takes place. Near this office is a small kitchen used in the preparation of Kōbō Daishi's two daily meals. It is these meals and the other offerings prepared in the hall that give it its name. Close by the kitchen entrance is a small shrine occupied by *Ajima Jizō*, the "Taste-testing Jizō." This small Jizō, like a food taster for a monarch, tests all meals before they are taken to Kōbō Daishi.

The front of the Gokusho, the side that faces the plaza, is divided into three sections. The two end sections are taken up with large counters where at the moment eight clerks are selling books, *o-fuda*, *tōba*, *oizuru* (white pilgrim's smocks), and other religious supplies. The main occupation of these men, however, is providing visitors, especially those on pilgrimage, with temple seals. These seals (*nōkyō*) are entered either in a small album (*nōkyō-chō*) with accordion-folding pages or on a long scroll (*kakejiku*) with specially designated positions for each entry.[2] We have brought our own *nōkyō-chō* and now ask one of the clerks to enter the seal for Okunoin. He rapidly inks three stamps with red ink and applies them to the indicated page, then dips his calligraphy brush in black ink and with a series of flourishes produces three vertical lines of text. The completed seal is quite handsome and mysterious. At its center is a large red Sanskrit *VAM* for Dainichi of the Diamond Realm.

In the middle of the facade of the Gokusho is a shrine that houses three familiar esoteric divinities, all now hidden from view in their respective cabinets. Inside the cabinet at the left is the goddess Benzaiten, whom we discussed earlier. On the right is the great warrior Bishamonten, guardian of the northern flank of the cosmic Mount Sumeru and special protector of the Dharma. The Dharma is represented by a small stūpa Bishamon-ten holds in his left hand.[3] Hidden in the center cabinet, and the featured deity of this trio, is Daikoku-ten, literally "Great Black God." Daikoku-ten is the primary Buddhist deity of the Japanese home, the "black" in his name possibly a consequence of his habitual position above a sooty hearth. Daikoku-ten promises security and abundance. The central structural pillar of a well-made Japanese house is known as the *Daikoku-bashira*, or "Daikoku pillar." A Japanese husband who greatly esteems his wife's resourcefulness refers to her as the *uchi-no-Daikoku-samma*, or "honorable Daikoku of the house." The three gods enshrined here—Benzaiten, Bishamon-ten, and Daikoku-ten—also are prominent members of the famed Seven Lucky Gods (*Shichi-fuku-jin*) whose arrival is awaited at the New Year.[4] Each of the three was championed by Kōbō Daishi, or so tradition insists.

The forest cemetery comes right up to the edge of the plaza. Not far from the Offering Hall are two memorials we should take note of. One is a small mausoleum that contains the remains of Ōgo Shōnin (1536–1608), also known to us as Mokujiki Shōnin, "the Wood-Eating Saint." We remember that it was Ōgo's negotiating skills that saved Kōyasan from destruction at the hands of Hideyoshi. Near Ōgo's memorial is one dedicated to Lord Asano Naganori and his forty-seven loyal retainers, the primary actors in Japan's most famous revenge drama. The difficulty began when young and impulsive Lord Asano (1667–1701), while visiting the shōgun's palace in Edo, drew his sword against another visitor, Lord Kira, a man who had openly taunted and humiliated him. Since the drawing of weapons was forbidden in the palace the shōgun was compelled to impose the maximum penalty. He instructed that Asano's lands be confiscated, his family name declared extinct, and Asano himself forced to commit *seppuku*. With their lord dead, and no successor to follow, Asano's retainers were reduced to the despised status of *rōnin*, or masterless samurai. Despite this circumstance, however, the retainers remained loyal to their dead lord and secretly plotted revenge against Kira. After spending two years lulling Kira into a state of inattention, the forty-seven suddenly stormed Kira's manor, lopped off his head, and carried the bloody trophy to Sengaku-ji temple where they placed it before Asano's grave. As violators of the public peace they too now were ordered to commit *seppuku*. News of the attack on Kira and the deaths of the *rōnin* electrified an admiring Japanese citizenry. All forty-seven were acclaimed *gishi*, "men of rectitude."[5] After nearly three centuries their fame continues almost unabated.

A small crowd has gathered at the *rōnin* memorial, drawn largely, we think, by the fact of our being Westerners. An elderly man asks if we have seen where the *rōnin* are buried side by side at Sengaku-ji in Tōkyō? We say that we have. Have we also attended a performance of the Kabuki play *Kanadehon chūshingura*?[6] We tell him we hope to do that at the first opportunity. "It is the best thing we have," he says.

It is time now to cross the Tamagawa. As we walk back through the public plaza we find that a group of *goeika* ladies has assembled in the shade of an open-fronted tent and is just beginning a concert. Each lady holds a small bell in her left hand which she sometimes shakes and sometimes strikes with a small mallet. Each also has the use of a second bell that rests on the table before her. Their hand movements are remarkably synchronized. So is their singing. When we stop to listen, the ladies smile at us, happy that someone in the milling crowd is taking notice of the sacred music:

> *On top of Mount Kōya*
> *[Sealed] behind a rock*
> *Kōbō Daishi is still there.*

A sign beside their tent says the concert is dedicated to the safety of all travelers who have come to visit Kōbō Daishi this day.

THE JEWEL RIVER AND THE MIROKU STONE

The bridge over the Tamagawa is named *Mimyō-no-hashi*, or "Bridge of the Sanctuary." A notice in both Japanese and English lists five prohibitions for those who wish to cross. "Don't wear a *yukata*. Don't smoke or eat. Don't do an impure act. Don't take photographs. Don't use a microphone." In earlier centuries it was appropriate to perform a purification ritual in the flowing stream before attempting to cross. Emperor Shirakawa did so in 1088, and Toyotomi Hideyoshi, who had ample reason to tremble, may have done so in 1594. At various times during the year one will see groups of nearly naked student monks or perhaps members of a Shingon *kō* seated in the water below the bridge performing a *mizu-gyō*, or "water austerity." Each winter the newspapers unfailingly print a photograph of monks crouching up to their chests in the sacred stream, slabs of ice floating nearby, vapor pouring from their shaved heads and chanting mouths.

At the moment a guide is standing in the middle of the bridge and delivering his standard speech to a group of Japanese pilgrims. "We are now going to leave the present world," he says. "We are entering the world of the future. But don't worry, we will soon return. Please remember not to pound on the bridge with your sticks, for each of the thirty-six planks represents a Buddha." With that warning the group moves on.

At the bridge threshold we bow in the direction of Kōbō Daishi's mausoleum, now so close. In theory, the great saint might come forward to meet us here and escort us across, but this rarely occurs at midday with so many people about. We pause in the middle of the bridge to look upstream. Suspended in the purifying flow are hundreds of small *tōba* memorials for *mizuko*. Many of the *tōba* have floral offerings tied to them. Day and night, the water comforts these bewildered early dead.

The Tamagawa descends from three low mountains, known as the sacred *Sanzan*, that enclose the Okunoin area. To the east is Mani-san, named for the jewel of satisfaction that symbolizes the Buddha's compassion. Enshrined on its summit is the jewel-holding Nyoirin Kannon, one of the most beautiful of Buddhist images. The mountain to the north is Yōryū-san, or "Willow Mountain," where the Yōryū Kannon is enshrined. This Kannon, who is the Bodhisattva of medicine, displays a willow branch known for its medicinal properties. The mountain to the west, Tenjiku-san ("Axis Mountain"), is named after the world's cosmic central mountain, Mount Sumeru. The sacred being enshrined on its summit is the Buddha of the Future, Miroku Bosatsu. In the saddles of the three mountains are shrines to En-no-Gyōja and Kōbō Daishi, esoteric Buddhism's supreme mountain saints. A traverse of the Sanzan ridge is one of Kōyasan's popular day hikes. From that height the climber can see nothing of the halls of the Okunoin, for they are hidden beneath tall trees. However, when the wind is right the air may carry a faint odor of incense.

We cross the bridge. The path points directly toward the Lantern Hall, while the areas to either side remain crowded with trees and monuments. Well off to the left, largely hidden from view, is a small gated bridge that recrosses the Tamagawa to a fenced-off precinct that is forbidden to us. In that precinct are the burial mounds of nine Japanese emperors, their consorts, and selected family members. As we proceed up the path we notice a group of people gathered a short distance off to the left. They are looking attentively at a small elevated wooden cage, on the floor of which is a black stone about the size of a human head. Two men, probably a father and son, are now taking turns trying their luck with the stone. The idea is to make a wish, then reach one arm through an opening in the cage, grasp the stone, and lift it to a higher platform in the cage, thus affirming that the wish will come true. The endeavor takes some strength, for the stone is very dense and quite slippery. The son fails and shakes his head. The father succeeds on his third try, and receives nods of congratulation.

This dense black stone is the Miroku-no-ishi, or "Miroku Stone," that is the model for the bean paste confection referred to earlier. When and how it first arrived at Kōyasan is unclear. Mrs. Gordon was told that Kōbō Daishi threw it to Kōyasan from China.[7] A better-known story has Kōbō Daishi lowering it on a lotus thread from Miroku's Tushita paradise (J. *Tosotsu-no-naiin*).[8] Either of these two suggestions jibes with the likelihood that the stone is a meteorite (like the sacred black stone of the Mother Goddess Cybele at Pessinus in Turkey or the Black Stone in the Kaaba at Mecca, said to have been given to Abraham by the archangel Gabriel). A third tradition, largely of the sixteenth century, suggests that Kōyasan's Miroku Stone formerly marked the grave of Kōbō Daishi's mother, a plausible notion since Lady Tamayori herself was thought by some to be a manifestation of Miroku.[9] The most striking of the traditions associated with the stone is the prophecy, already mentioned, that when Miroku finally does appear on earth as the new Buddha he will position himself upon the stone to deliver his inaugural sermon. So it must be kept in a public place. Meanwhile, as we have observed, it is being employed as a humble *omo-karu-ishi* (literally, "heavy-light-stone"), a common instrument of rock divination.[10]

We proceed to the flight of steps that climbs to the terrace of the Lantern Hall and Kōbō Daishi's Mausoleum.

THE TŌRŌDŌ: LANTERN HALL

Tradition relates that immediately following Kōbō Daishi's forest burial in 835 his closest disciples built a shelter before his tomb and began to hold regular devotions there. That first shelter was expanded from time to time until in the year 1023, Fujiwara Michinaga, after a visit to the tomb, financed the construction of a large veneration hall. Apparently, it was at this time that devotional lamps, symbolic of the eternal Great Sun Buddha, began to be placed in the hall. Head priest Jōyo contributed such a lamp. Not long afterward, in 1088, Emperor Shirakawa gave one. As the custom of donating lamps continued, the hall, which previously had been referred to simply as a *haiden*, or oratory, was renamed the *Manrōdō*, or "Hall of Myriad Lamps." Today *Tōrōdō* ("Lantern Hall") is the name commonly used.

Michinaga's hall was replaced several times. The present Lantern Hall, constructed in 1964, it is one of Kōyasan's most beautiful large structures. Externally, it is distinguished by a great sweep of roof and multiple rows of lanterns that hang from the eaves on all sides. Lanterns especially are the dominant feature of the interior.[11] Most of them hang overhead, row on row. Some lanterns are stacked vertically, forming veritable lantern walls. Visitors to the previous Tōrōdō complained of its dark and gloomy interior, an ironic condition for a lantern hall, but at that time it was considered too costly to try to keep more than a few dozen lanterns burning at any one time. In the present hall nearly all the lanterns are electrified. They burn day and night with a soft, low-wattage glow.

The Tōrōdō's interior layout is designed to accommodate both a steady flow of visitors and an almost constant ceremonial activity. A wide public area at the front of the interior room has a scuff-proof floor so that visitors need not remove their shoes when purchasing religious services from the monk-clerks or when observing rituals taking place in the sanctuary. A low barrier separates this public space from the sanctuary space, but visitors who wish to do so may step beyond the barrier (sans shoes) and sit on *tatami* virtually within the sanctuary itself.

The sanctuary space is divided into three discrete sections, with stacked floor-to-ceiling lanterns providing the walls of separation. In the left section (to the west) is a *goma* altar with fire-red Aizen Myō-ō as its *honzon*. In the right section is another fire ceremony altar, this one with

Fudō Myō-ō as its *honzon*. The middle section, which is much the largest, has a long dais, or *shumi-dan*, against its back wall, but no visible *honzon* or *honzon* cabinet. Instead, there is a central window that opens directly on the precinct of Kōbō Daishi's mausoleum, for Kōbō Daishi himself is the *honzon* of the Lantern Hall. Two fully equipped altar tables, arranged one behind the other, face the mausoleum. A wooden tablet above the altar is inscribed with the golden characters *Kō-bō*, just as in the Garan's Great Stūpa.

Every visitor notices the three oil lamps that rest conspicuously on the dais. One of these lamps, known as the *Jikiō-tō* ("Lamp of the Repeater of Prayers"), is said to be the one priest Jōyo lit for his mother in 1016. A second perpetual lamp, the *Shirakawa-tō*, was lit by Ex-Emperor Shirakawa at the time of his fourth pilgrimage in 1103.[12] The third lamp, "The Poor Woman's Lamp," is by far the most famous of the three. It was presented to Kōbō Daishi many centuries ago (some say in Jōyo's time) by a destitute young woman named Oteru ("Shining") who sold her hair to a wig maker to obtain money for the purchase. The lamp was offered as a memorial for Oteru's beloved foster parents. Its dedication came on the same day as the dedication of some ten thousand lamps contributed by a wealthy farmer. When the farmer saw the meagerness of Oteru's contribution he immediately cried out, "Why is this ugly candle allowed to desecrate my grand display?" At that moment a powerful wind blew in from the direction of the mausoleum and in an instant extinguished all ten thousand of the rich man's lights. Only Oteru's modest lamp continued to burn. "It appears that religion lies not in power or money, but in true feelings," observed the head priest. "Mr. Yabusaka, you are a sincere man, but you also are rich. After all, your sacrifice was not so great."

Oteru's lamp has never been allowed to go out. As for Oteru herself, she afterward took up residence in a small nunnery, Keijitsu-an, in Amano village at the foot of the mountain. There she spent her life praying to Kōbō Daishi and honoring the memory of her parents.[13]

On this busy weekend afternoon, customers are lined up four and five deep before the monk-clerks at the Tōrōdō's counters. A sign lists the various available services and the donation required for each. We watch one man hand a clerk a fifty thousand yen donation (around five hundred dollars) together with a package of ashes wrapped in red, orange, and purple brocade. The monk takes the package of ashes and places it before the altar. A woman gives another monk a package, this one much smaller and wrapped in white and gold brocade. The two packages, along with several others, will be blessed in a special Tōrōdō ceremony, then deposited in the Nōkotsudō, a small ossuary building that stands near Kōbō Daishi's tomb.

We are keeping an eye out for a man we met on Shikoku Island two weeks ago. He is a Japanese-American widower from Sacramento who was making the eighty-eight temple Shikoku pilgrimage while carrying his wife's ashes. Early in their marriage they had visited Kōyasan and often talked afterward about returning to Japan to do the Shikoku pilgrimage together. So they did return, except that the wife was carried in a small box hung about her husband's neck. The man told us he planned to surrender the ashes at Kōyasan's Tōrōdō on today's date. We agreed to watch for one another.

A middle-aged man and younger woman, both wearing white *henro* smocks and carrying pilgrim staffs, have just entered the Tōrōdō. For a moment we think we recognize our friend from Sacramento. Certainly the smile is the same, and the dyed, thinning hair is the same. As for the companion, she easily could be one of the young women we saw on the pilgrimage bus the man was riding. We wave tentatively and start forward. Perhaps our bereaved pilgrim has found himself a new wife. But we are wrong. They are total strangers to us. They stand together just inside the door, hesitating, apparently discussing whether or not they are going to surrender their walking staffs (*kongō-zue*). Custom dictates that they should. "We Two, Pilgrims Together" is the slogan of the pilgrimage, the second person of the "two" being Kōbō Daishi's spirit as represented by the staff. That spirit now has returned to Kōyasan. The decision made, they place their staffs with the others that have accumulated near the door, then get into line at one of the counters. We see that their pilgrim smocks are stained from the long Shikoku journey.[14] When their turn comes they hand the monk clerk a rolled-up *kakejiku*. The monk takes the *kakejiku* into the sanctuary and unrolls it for everyone to see. All eighty-eight temple seals are clearly visible. This is a proud moment. The scroll will be returned to them as soon as a priest has conducted a blessing ceremony over it.

Many of those in line are asking that a holy lantern (*sei-tō-rō*) be lit for the benefit of a deceased loved one, or for some other benefit. A three-day lighting requires a donation of one thousand yen (about ten dollars). A full year costs fifty thousand yen. Memorial lanterns, which come in two sizes, also may be purchased outright. The larger one costs one million yen. The purchaser's name, address, and supplication are inscribed on the lantern, which then is hung in the Tōrōdō or in the Tōrōdō annex.[15] Its "flame" (a small electric light) will burn perpetually as an emblem of Dainichi's universal illumination.

We ourselves now go to the counter on the left side of the Tōrōdō. Here we select a *soe-goma-gi* ("attached-*goma*-stick"), a small wooden stick on which we ask the monk to help us write a *kigan*, or supplication. The stick will be burned before either Aizen Myō-ō or Fudō Myō-ō at tomorrow morning's *goma* (fire offering). We also buy a *goma-ofuda*, a flat, slightly tapered wood tablet partially wrapped with paper. This tablet will be placed on the *goma* altar for a certain number of services, then mailed to our home address.

Below the Tōrōdō's main floor is a basement level known as the "crypt of remembrance." Few casual visitors go there, so it is rarely crowded. The stairs are located outside on the Tōrōdō's eastern porch. The first thing we encounter as we descend the stairs are painted images of the Six Jizō (*Roku Jizō*), traditional comforters of the dead and important figures in every Shingon cemetery.[16] Fresh flower offerings have been placed in front of each painting. A few steps forward and we are surrounded by memorials to the dead themselves, crowded row upon row, shelf upon shelf, from floor to ceiling. Each dead spirit is represented by a small metal image of a seated Kōbō Daishi. There are many thousands of these images, distinguishable from one another only by a small plate that identifies each by name and number in a sequential numbering system. All this efficiency is a bit chilling, especially when compared to the warmth of the crowded upstairs room with its flood of visitors and ceremonial activity and glowing lamps and golden altars.

But today the crypt of remembrance is not entirely empty of life. We hear the sound of chanting and move toward it. At the rear of the crypt, the side nearest to Kōbō Daishi's tomb, is a small, brightly lit open space. Here we find a group of middle-aged and elderly people kneeling before a shrine built against the wall. The shrine obviously is dedicated to Kōbō Daishi, for at its front are huge replicas of a five-pointed *vajra* and a string of *juzu* beads. At the back, framed against the wall, is what at first looks like a painted rendering of glowing fog, but after a moment we discover in the haze the familiar features of Shinnyo's portrait of Kōbō Daishi. The misty quality of the painting may be an accidental trick of the light, or perhaps the artist deliberately intended to remind us of Abbot Kangen's initial inability to make out the form of Kōbō Daishi seated in his tomb. In any event, the painting is a reminder that Kōbō Daishi's burial chamber is directly ahead of us here. Presumably, he sits facing us (that is, southward), separated from us by a precisely measurable distance of earth. Many visitors to this shrine believe the painting to have been mounted on the surface of a sealed door, behind which is a tunnel that goes directly to the burial chamber. We might ask a senior priest about this matter, but suspect no clear answer would be forthcoming. Generally speaking, such details about the Gobyō are kept private.

As the worshipers continue to chant, they go forward one by one to rub the oversized *vajra* and beads, then apply the absorbed energy to whatever parts of their bodies are most in need of help. The oldest member of the group vigorously rubs his shoulders and knees. When the chanters are finished they signal to us to take their place, then bow in farewell.

But another visitor has already arrived, a ruggedly built man with several weeks' growth of beard. We have met him before, have even exchanged letters with him. Once a month he travels from extreme western Honshu (Yamaguchi Prefecture), where he serves as a priest in an esoteric Buddhist mountain sect. We watch him now as he pulls his priest's robe from the pack he carries, puts the robe on over his rough clothes, then settles on the floor before the shrine. He has brought with him a thick stack of wooden *tōba* given him by his parishioners. He will spend the next several hours holding up each *tōba* in turn, praying to Kōbō Daishi to assist with its petition. Afterward, he will go to the Tamagawa and place the entire stack of *tōba* at the feet of the water-splashed Fudō Myō-ō. The sect he represents is not Shingon, but its followers revere Kōbō Daishi and consider Kōyasan an entrance to paradise.

We leave the crypt. It is time for the tomb.

THE GOBYŌ: KŌBŌ DAISHI'S MAUSOLEUM

We circle the wide porch to the rear of the Lantern Hall. Between the back wall of the Lantern Hall and the fence before the mausoleum is a long corridor that is now filled with visitors. The scented air vibrates with their rapid chanting of the *Namu Daishi* mantra and the *Hannya-shingyō*. A few visitors also are chanting the mantra of Miroku Bodhisattva, asking that he receive them into the Tushita paradise where they will be with Kōbō Daishi.[17] *Om maitareiya sowaka.* Most have lit a votive candle and a bundle of incense sticks.

A *kō* from Ōsaka known as the "Yanagi" group is chanting in prayer at the left of the mausoleum area. They have brought offerings of food, flowers, *sake*, and *tōba*, and have placed them on display. This group comes to the Gobyō once each month.

We purchase our own bundle of three incense sticks, light them, and place them in one of the incense urns. The three sticks represent the Three Treasures of Buddha, Dharma, and Sangha, or perhaps the Three Mysteries of Body, Speech, and Mind. Or perhaps sometimes three incense sticks are just three incense sticks. We maneuver forward until we are standing directly opposite the open *hira-karamon* gate to the Gobyō's inner precinct. This is the only spot that offers an unimpeded view of the elegant three-bay wooden mausoleum set back among the trees. The mausoleum faces due south, as do all the most important halls of Kōyasan. It is constructed of unpainted velvet-smooth cypress and has a cypress-bark roof. Except for a crowning brass *mani* jewel it is without decorative carving or insignia. Between us and the mausoleum are a low wooden fence, then a wide border of white pebbles (the *saniwa*, or sacred garden), then a higher wooden inner fence, and finally an entrance path covered with white pebbles. The border of pebbles also is known as the "Emperor's Lawn," for that is where ex-Emperor Shirakawa knelt.

We are uncertain what is inside the mausoleum hall. Some visitors imagine that Kōbō Daishi sits there in a deep trance, and that when a new robe is brought to him at the annual robe-changing ceremony the presiding priest enters the mausoleum door to dress a physical body.[18] Some say the mausoleum hall contains a modest *gorintō* set at ground level, with Kōbō Daishi's chamber directly underneath (five meters deep according to one testimony). Most ancient accounts of the burial describe his being placed in a grotto or cave, the entrance to which is then sealed with stones. Such an arrangement is difficult to visualize today, for the area around the mausoleum has been reconstructed over the centuries and is now quite level.[19]

The mausoleum is not the only structure within the precinct's inner fence. Immediately to the right of the mausoleum hall, almost hidden now by rhododendron bushes, are two small shrines. One shrine houses Kariba-myōjin, the guardian god of the mountain who assisted Kōbō Daishi in the building of Kongōbu-ji. The other houses Shirahige Inari, the harvest god who assisted him in building Tō-ji in the capital.[20]

To the left (west) of the mausoleum, well outside the precinct fence, is an octagonal ossuary building known as the Nōkotsudō, or "Hall for the Interment of Remains."[21] At intervals of between six months and a year the accumulated human ashes in the Nōkotsudō's charnel chamber are removed, cremated a second time to reduce their volume, then carried to a final resting place on a sacred mound behind the mausoleum. This mound is known as the *O-yama*. Normally only a portion of a deceased person's cremated remains are deposited in the Nōkotsudō—perhaps no more than the *nodobotoke*, or "throat Buddha" bone (so named because it looks somewhat like a seated Buddha). If the body is not cremated, a lock of hair may be deposited in the Nōkotsudō. Generally speaking, it is understood that a deceased person's "spirit" may be present simultaneously in a number of different locations and be represented by a number of different forms—the whole body, a portion of ashes, a bone, a lock of hair, a carved memorial stone, or a piece of wood or paper on which the posthumous name has been written.

To the right (east) of the mausoleum precinct, in spacial balance with the Nōkotsudō, is a Kyōzō, or storehouse for Buddhist scriptures. The Okunoin's present Kyōzō was built in 1599 by the feudal warlord Ishida Mitsunari (1560–1600), who also placed there the full 6,557 scrolls of the Chinese Buddhist canon known as the Tripitaka (J. *Sanzō*). Such a collection was considered the spiritual equivalent of a major relic of the Buddha's body. Today the Kyōzō's ancient shelves are empty, Ishida's scrolls having been removed to the Reihōkan for safe keeping. The Gobyō still has its necessary collection of scripture, however. In the eleventh century Fujiwara Michinaga buried a large body of sacred texts near the tomb, much of it written with his own brush. Those scrolls remain undisturbed, safely sealed in watertight boxes, awaiting the arrival of Miroku, when they are expected to burst forth from the earth.[22]

RECORD OF A NIGHT'S VIGIL AT THE GOBYŌ

Nightlong vigils once were commonplace in Japanese Buddhism. Pilgrim temples had special vigil halls called *tsuya-dō* where *henro* could spend an entire night in worship and supplication. Sometimes during the hours of darkness the watcher would receive a visitor who announced the granting of the requested miracle (*reigen*). For those who spent nights at the Okunoin's Gobyō the visitor was Kōbō Daishi.

One late April afternoon, encouraged by a favorable weather forecast, I decided to make my own all-night vigil at the Gobyō. I invite the reader to share that experience with me.

By four o'clock the crowds of visitors before the mausoleum and in the Lantern Hall had begun to thin. People were heading off to their hot baths and temple meals. At the stroke of five the monks at the counters of the Lantern Hall closed their stations, slipped into *geta*, and went clicking away toward their quarters behind the Gokusho. Only one monk remained behind. He took a seat in a corner of the sanctuary and began chanting a sacred text that lay open before him. At six o'clock the doors were locked with the chanting monk inside.

At that point I strolled back across the Mimyō-no-hashi. Already the electric lanterns along the pilgrim's path were glowing. The Gokusho and the Gomadō were both shut tight for the night. I checked the front door of the Rest Hall (the Gokyūkeisho), then went around to its back door. It too was locked. I had counted on finding shelter there should the night turn stormy or painfully cold. At least the public lavatory behind the Gomadō was open, as always. I took a cotton undershirt, a second sweater, and a pair of long johns from my backpack and put them on. The air was cooling rapidly, but with my windbreaker zipped to the chin I expected to be quite cozy.

As I re-crossed the bridge I noticed a crisp half moon directly overhead. The sky was going to be full of stars. Along the back wall of the Tōrōdō is a long padded bench that directly faces the mausoleum. That is where I began my vigil. Twenty or thirty candles still flickered in the candle racks. A hundred threads of incense continued to rise from the incense bowls. But otherwise I was alone. In front of me the mausoleum slowly faded in the darkness. In a short while it would disappear altogether. Only the white pebbles of the Emperor's lawn would glow in the moonlight.

7:20: Two visitors arrive, an old man and an old woman. They leave a food offering, drop money in the offering box, light candles, pray. They are very methodical. The woman has a tremor. They lean against one another. They hold their hands in gasshō. *I move down the bench into the deeper shadows, not wanting to be conspicuous.*

7:25: Three women arrive. They say good evening to me, so I am not invisible. They light about fifty sticks of incense and distribute them among all the incense urns. Clouds of incense hang like fog around the amber-colored memorial lamps under the Tōrōdō eaves. The women recite the Hannya-shingyō *three times—a vigorous staccato singsong. They add several* Namu Daishi *at the end. They leave, talking very loudly as they go. Warding off ghosts?*

7:40: Her arrival unnoticed, I become aware of a lone figure standing in front of the Gobyō gate. She does not speak. Makes no gesture. When I look up again she is gone. I did not see or hear her go. Perhaps it was a man.

7:42: Someone is at the Nōkotsudō. I hear the bell ringing at the door of the charnel chamber. The bell rings on and on.

The persistent bell ringers turn out to be two men who sit down beside me on the bench. They toss off their shoes and sit cross-legged the way they would for a conversation over *sake* and squid. But there is no conversation. They light no candles or incense. Very likely their thoughts are on the ashes in the Nōkotsudō.

7:55: A single Buddhist priest. After directing prayers to the Gobyō he directs prayers to the neighboring shrines of Kariba-myōjin and the Shirahige Inari. He is the first person I've seen do that. Kōyasan's priests are required to visit the Gobyō at least once each month. Perhaps this is his monthly visit. His manner is professional and efficient.

8:15: More people have come. Thirty-two candles are burning.

At around eight-thirty I light my own first candle, praying that its light might bless someone in my family who is in need. Many people are coming and going now. It must be the post-dinner rush. I no longer try to keep count of them.

9:00: I've decided I like the idea of ashes mingling in the Nōkotsudō. And then being cremated again and taken to the O-yama. The processes of the universe involve mingling and rendering everything that dies. So get used to it.

A Japanese colleague tells of coming to Kōyasan with a friend who brought with him a package of ashes for ceremonial disposal. However, after looking at the Tōrōdō's price list the friend decided to dispose of the ashes in his own way. When no one was looking he simply poured them out at the base of a large tree that grows near the Gobyō enclosure.

9:30: I'm eating the meager supper I brought in my backpack. So as not to violate the sanctity of the Gobyō I first re-crossed the Tamagawa. I am sitting near the mausoleum of priest Ōgo, the "wood-eating saint."

10:00: Back at the Gobyō. I hear the clacking of hyōshigi. *The night watchman is approaching. The clacking reaches the Tōrōdō steps, then begins to circle the building. The watchman is making certain that any lurking spirits have ample time to move out of his way. I take off my hat before he arrives. I know it is discourteous to Odaishi-sama to wear a hat, but am feeling the need of more protection against the cold.*

10:15: Twelve henro in white Shikoku pilgrim dress. They light candles, incense, and pray in unison. They begin circling the Tōrōdō, walking swiftly, clockwise, the bells at their waists jingling as they go. Actually some move more swiftly than others. They make no attempt to stay together. Each henro pauses for prayer when passing the entrance gate. The energy of their presence

*is very pleasing. I don't want them to leave. They keep up their devotion for
more than thirty minutes.*

Just before midnight another group of nine arrives at the Gobyō and
begins parading back and forth between the Gobyō gate and the
hyakudo-ishi ("one hundred times stone") next to the sūtra repository. I
lose accurate count of the times they pass me, but when they leave, after
about twenty minutes, they are well short of one hundred trips. So apparently one hundred repetitions isn't always required, not even when one is
dealing with a "one hundred times stone."

*12:35: Four women and one man, ages about forty to seventy. They are
doing the* Namu Daishi *and* Hannya-shingyō, *but in a complex, highly
lyrical manner. They are in motion all the time, sweeping back and forth
from the Nōkotsudō to the Kyōzō, almost dancing, their blended voices rising
and falling in pitch. Wonderful to watch and listen to, in a dark forest in the
dead of night.*

1:00: The beginning of ushi-mitsu-doki, *the "hour of the ox." The gods
and the spirits of the dead are most active now, until three o'clock. The
Tōrōdō cat has arrived. She walks slowly past me and curls up next to the hot
charcoal box used to ignite incense sticks. I've seen her before. She is snow
white without a single visible dark hair. I've read that a white fox once lived
in a burrow beneath one of the trees of the Gobyō. If a temple animal eats the
food you offer, that is a good sign, but I have no food.*[23] *Twenty-seven flickering candles. A cold wind has started to blow.*

The white cat and I are watching the Emperor's Lawn, looking for
signs of Kōbō Daishi. Here is a narrative written by a returning veteran
of the Pacific War.[24] The year is 1946.

> I survived the war as a soldier, so I came to Kōyasan to give
> thanks. At eleven o'clock at night I suddenly wanted to go to
> the Okunoin. I went with caution because I was wearing *geta*. It
> was very dark. I became frightened when I heard a bird singing
> among the old cedar trees. The stone Buddhas on both sides
> looked mysterious, very different than in the daytime. When I

went past Naka-no-hashi and passed the memorial for Bashō I saw a very large man wearing a soldier's uniform walking in front of me. Since I was lonely I asked him what time it was in a loud voice, but he didn't answer me, and walked away quickly. I wanted to catch up with him and say a prayer together, but he had disappeared in the darkness. I felt awkward, but went to the Gobyō and gave thanks for my safe return. As I re-crossed the bridge of the Gobyō I felt that someone was behind me. I turned around and saw the big man in uniform standing facing me, doing the *gasshō*. Then I thought, Odaishi-sama has just returned from the battlefield himself. I started weeping. I realized how fully Odaishi-sama, too, had shared the suffering of the war.

The cold now is downright painful. I begin to circle the Tōrōdō to get my blood flowing. On each circuit I pause before the Gobyō gate, praying for the dead of the mountain and for both the living and the dead in all other places. My emotions are unraveling a little. The cat has left me. But the human visitors have not left me. They continue to arrive in the darkness.

2:40: I am rarely alone now, never for more than a minute or two. The present group, after the usual Hannya-shingyō *and* Namu Daishi, *suddenly breaks into the* Nembutsu. *This is strange. Perhaps I will hear the Nichiren* Namu Myōho Renge-kyō *before the night is over. Mrs. Gordon probably prayed the Lord's Prayer here.*

3:00: The hour of the ox has concluded. I am shaking with cold. I will hike out of the cemetery by the short route to the vending machines at the Naka-no-hashi entrance. Perhaps I can find something hot to drink.

I buy a can of hot "milk-tea" and a can of hot "Cocoa-shake." *It'll be captivate with relish.* That's the English language advertisement on the Cocoa-shake. I buy two more cans and slide them into my windbreaker pockets to use as hand-warmers. I hurry back through the new section of the cemetery, less cold now but feeling guilty at having left my post at the Gobyō. When I reach the Gokusho I see lights burning inside the

Gokusho kitchen. It is 3:30. The central door to the Gomadō is open. A bird is singing. As I cross the dark bridge over the Tamagawa I make out a ghostly monk up ahead of me. He is carrying a tray of offerings. The morning routine is beginning already. Kōbō Daishi soon will want his breakfast. I have a sense that my vigil has been abruptly cut short.

At the Tōrōdō another bird is singing. The song is so loud and gorgeous I wonder at first if it is coming through a loudspeaker. Then I see the bird itself up among the glowing lanterns above the Tōrōdō's front porch. The small body trembles with each burst of song. The bird sees a dawn somewhere that I cannot yet see. But at the Gobyō things are as before, with a small group of visitors peering into the dark woods and chanting. I resume my vigil.

4:00: The night watchman has arrived, but without the hyōshigi. *He vigorously applies a stiff broom to the racks of candle holders, knocking off the accumulated drippings of the previous day and night. To be watchman and custodian of a place such as this is an enviable calling.*[25]

4:30: Birdsong is pouring in from all directions. A group of ten women in rhythmic prayer. But now a voice suddenly cries out in a loud, heartbroken wail.

I am sitting with my eyes closed, my mind drifting, when I hear the wrenching cry. One of the women in front of me is sinking to her knees, sobbing. Another woman stands over her, shouting down at her, clapping her hands, demanding obedience. The remaining women have made a circle about their fallen comrade and are continuing their chant. The leader keeps barking out a single command. Is this an exorcism? The afflicted woman is now lying face down on the pavement, trembling. When at last she is pulled to her feet her legs are wobbly. The women lead her off slowly into the darkness, away from the Gobyō.

Twenty minutes later I go around to the front of the Tōrōdō to see if its doors have been opened. The troubled woman is sitting on a lower step of the porch, her friends still gathered around her. She is sobbing softly, but seems calm otherwise.

I conclude that visitors have great freedom at the Gobyō, especially at night. Inside the temples and halls of Kōyasan the rituals proceed on precise schedules and in accordance with fixed designs. But the Gobyō belongs to the faithful. They come when they wish and do as they wish, in accordance with their own wisdom and need. A Kōyasan scholar said to me, "The Daitō is the center of Esoteric Buddhism in Japan, but the Gobyō is the center of popular faith."[26]

The sky is growing bright. Morning has come. My mind still lingers over the sensations of darkness, however. At 5:30 I recross the Tamagawa. Visitors in pilgrim dress are arriving in the plaza. Most of these have stayed the night in one of the temples, but are skipping the temple breakfast in order to meet with Kōbō Daishi. They pray at the *Mizumuke Jizō*, then pass over the bridge. The door to the kitchen at the Gokusho is partially open now. Inside, a young monk with a white mask drawn across his mouth and nose is preparing Daishi's breakfast. The white kitchen cabinets, tile walls, and stainless steel counter suggest almost surgical cleanliness. Daishi's meals must be fresh and perfectly cooked. They also must be varied. The second meal of the day sometimes includes such items as spaghetti and a mild curry rice, dishes Kūkai could not possibly have known in his own lifetime.

A second young monk arrives at the Gokusho to light incense at the shrine of the Taste-testing Jizō just outside the kitchen. The breakfast, now fully prepared (with the soup and rice kept in warm containers for later serving), is placed before the Jizō. When the testing is concluded the two monks lift the box by its rails and, joined by a third, older priest, march off toward the bridge. At the bridge entrance they pause, genuflect, then move on, the older priest leading, clacking a pair of *hyōshigi*. A dozen or so early visitors have fallen in behind them. Just then we hear the six o'clock bell ringing from the residential quarters of the Okunoin, its harsh crescendo announcing the upcoming *Rishu-zammai-hōyō* service in the Tōrōdō.

The three men carry the breakfast box into the Tōrōdō and up to the window that opens on the mausoleum. There they lay out the offering on the dais: the tea, the warm rice, the warm *miso* soup, the *tōfu*, the vegetables. The older priest seats himself at the larger of the two *dan*. I find a place on the *tatami*, sliding as close as possible to one of two kerosene heaters. I am still cold from the night's vigil. A troupe of saffron-robed young monks rush into the sanctuary, bow quickly, and take their positions at either side of the *dan*. The *Rishu-zammai-hōyō* begins.

My body is warming. The bird has begun to sing once more from under the porch roof. I close my eyes, my thoughts drifting with the sounds of birdsong and the familiar chant. For a moment I dream I am outside in the darkness again, facing the mausoleum.

Zen-zai. Zen-zai. Zen-zai. The service is over. The presiding priest and the two assisting monks go forward to remove the dishes of Odaishi-sama's breakfast.[27] I am thoroughly warm now, and too comfortable to attempt to rise from the floor. A *goma* offering will soon be made in one of the two side chapels.[28] I decide to stay where I am.

THE MORNING FIRE OFFERING

This morning's *goma* priest is tall and youthful, with a freshly shaved head. He makes three prostrations to the fire altar of Fudō Myō-ō, then seats himself.[29] Except for the recessed iron bowl at its center, the *goma* altar, or *goma-dan*, is similar to a conventional Shingon altar. The bowl will serve as a hearth for the fire. Directly overhead, enclosed within a decorative canopy, is a chimney that will draw off most of the smoke and flying sparks.

The priest glances about, quickly taking stock of the paraphernalia he will need to perform the offering. Before him on the *goma-dan* are several *vajra* and ladles, an incense burner, a container of sesame oil, and a row of cups that contain perfumed water, powdered incense, leaves of *shikimi*, rice, and a mix of five cereal grains. On a side table at his left are a hand-held incense burner and containers of mustard seed, medicinal herbs, broken bits of *shikimi*, and several kinds of incense. To his right are a bell, a basket of *shikimi* leaves, a pair of tongs, a fan, a cup of white sesame seeds, a cup of incense, and a bundle of kindling. Also on his right is a stack of hundreds of wooden *soe-goma-gi*. At the proper time these sticks, each bearing someone's petition to the Buddha, will be fed into the fire.

The priest lights the candles and some incense, then rubs his beads together. He prays to the Buddha for the wisdom and power needed to make the offering worthily. He visualizes a wall of flame rising up to protect himself and the precious altar from any opposing disturbance. Actually there isn't much physical activity to observe at this point, and several of my fellow watchers, losing interest, have slipped away. I lean forward, fighting against sleepiness, trying to match the intense concentration of the priest. He continues his visualizations, including one in which the hearth becomes Dainichi's mouth. From this divine mouth flows the fire of the Great Sun Buddha's Wisdom.

The priest becomes more outwardly active. He opens a bundle of kindling and with the tongs arranges eleven pieces, representing the delusions of conduct and perception, in a designated pattern. He takes a stick of sap wood, ignites it in the righthand candle flame, and places it under the kindling.[30] A tongue of smoky flame appears. He fans the flame three times, purifies it three times with perfumed water, then waves the three-pronged *vajra* before it three times. The wisdom of the flame begins to consume the delusion of the firewood. In imagination, the enlarging flame evolves into a triangular fire *cakra* that expands to encompass the altar and priest, then grows to an infinite size, its heat permeating the entire phenomenal world.

A cluster of *shikimi* leaves is tossed onto the burning kindling, followed by perfumed water and three pinches of incense. More offerings follow. Sticks of wood, rice, the five cereal grains (representing greed, anger, folly, arrogance, and doubt), flowers, ball incense, *sankō* incense. The offerings sizzle and crackle and give off unexpected aromas that we can smell even out on the *tatami*. Sesame oil flares up in great bursts of flame and the heat sweeps out over us watchers. Each ingredient is an offering to the Buddhas, the Bodhisattvas, and all the holy beings of the mandala. And a prayer for liberation.

> *Most sincerely do I offer up*
> *the marvelous pūjā offering of the Goma.*
> *I desire that the Buddha*
> *may in his compassion accept*
> *and protect his disciple,*
> *and may final enlightenment be perfected in me.*

The priest perceives the Sanskrit syllable *KAN*, the seed syllable of Fudō Myō-ō, glowing brightly in the hearth. The *KAN* changes into Fudō's flaming sword. The sword evolves into flame-wrapped Fudō himself. The priest opens a bundle of 108 sticks. One by one he places these corrupting passions in Fudō's holy flame. Each passion in turn is transformed into its beneficial counterpart.

The priest's movements grow more and more animated. Some of the sticks he submits calmly, but others he tosses with vehemence. One stick bounces away from the hearth. He drags it back. All must become ashes. The flame rises to a height of six feet or more. Sparks fly up into the shadows of the ceiling. A second priest enters the sanctuary and together the two men build a cross-hatched stack of *soe-goma-gi*, perhaps a hundred sticks or more. The stack quickly dissolves into smoke and flame. They build a second stack and it too is enveloped in flame. Then a third and a fourth stack. The moment one stack collapses a new one is constructed on the glowing ashes of its predecessor. Each flaming petition reaches Dainichi. The priest's hands and face are getting scorched. His eyes ache. But each moment he advances a little further along the path toward Buddhahood.

The last stack of *soe-goma-gi* has turned to ashes. The ceremony grows quiet. Fudō Myō-ō fades from the hearth. Perhaps the priest imagines him returning to the golden cabinet above the altar. Now the priest is repeating, in reverse order, the ceremony's opening *mantra* and *mudrā*. He strikes the closing bell, rubs his beads together, rises from his seat, and makes three prostrations. The gathering of watchers begins to disperse. There will be no concluding "fire walk," as in the much rarer outdoor *goma*.[31] My face is hot. I am wide awake.

CHAPTER ELEVEN

KŌBŌ DAISHI'S
BIRTHDAY CELEBRATION

Each morning's Rishu-zammai-hōyō and *goma* ceremonies, and the daily round of prayers to the mountain gods and before Kōbō Daishi's tomb, provide steady nourishment for the spiritual life of the Kōyasan community. In addition, there are grand spiritual banquets that take place at intervals fixed by the calendar: Kōbō Daishi's birthday (June 15), Kōbō Daishi's *nyūjō* (solar March 21 and lunar March 21), Shākyamuni's birthday (April 8), Shākyamuni's death day (February 15), and the national festival honoring the ancestral dead, Bon (August 13–15). Nearly all of Kōyasan's priests and monks participate in these occasional ceremonies. Lay visitors also attend, sometimes by the thousands. Many visitors return year after year.

We begin with the ceremony that offers the most fun and excitement, the Daishi Nativity Ceremony, or *Daishi-tanjō-e*, held on June 15. This event also is known as the *Aoba-matsuri*, or "Green Leaves Festival."

The rice paddies along the Kinokawa are fully planted by now. The flowering orchard trees of the lower mountain have germinated. Up on the mountain the intricate temple gardens have entered their most beautiful period.

The party begins on the evening of the fourteenth. We have barely finished our post-dinner bath when the sound of street music starts floating in through the open windows. Quickly, we cinch the belts of our *yukata* and shuffle out through the temple gate. A procession of illuminated floats is slowly moving up the street through the twilight, a swaying tree of glowing lanterns leading the way. The first float in the parade carries an internally lit upright mandala pushed by a team of Kōyasan Boy Scouts. On one side of the display is a simplified version of the Diamond Realm, on the other side a version of the Womb Realm. But notice, scattered among the painted mandala images are the cartooned faces of children. And more than that, Shākyamuni is wearing a Cub Scout cap and Dainichi sports a handlebar moustache and an Indiana Jones fedora. What should we make of such playfulness? The float answers with its cheering slogan, *Itsu-mo-genki.* "Always healthy."

Actually, the first float is a bit amateurish in construction, but the second one is remarkable. An immense purple-robed, giant-nosed Tengu lurches toward us, eyes and body glowing. He stretches out menacingly with one arm, threatening each onlooker as he passes. Some twenty young men are maneuvering the creature while a dozen small children dance in its wake. These children have nothing to fear. All of Kōyasan's forest Tengu are sworn friends of Kōbō Daishi.

Behind the Tengu comes a smaller float, an illuminated tribute to Kōbō Daishi's exercise in popular Buddhist philosophy and phonetic script, the "Iroha-uta." The children who are pulling this float have written and recited the poem in school.

The final float celebrates the birthday boy himself in the form of a towering internally illuminated image of Chigo Daishi. The red-gowned sacred child is kneeling on a lotus flower, hands pressed tightly together, as he prays to the Buddha.

The procession reaches the gate of the last temple on the street. There it turns round and heads back toward the center of town, its destination the parking lot in front of Kongōbu-ji. We fall in with the children and the *dani* residents, following the glowing light of the child

Daishi. Someone hands us a balloon. The Kongōbu-ji parking lot will be filled with stalls selling food and toys and souvenirs.

We awaken the next morning to the sound of rain. The flowers below the window are dripping. The shoulder of Mount Benten is miserably swallowed in mist. As we rinse our faces and brush our teeth in the washing area we all agree that the rain is no surprise, for we are in the middle of the *baiu* season. All the same, it is necessary that there be some sunshine for the parade. Odaishi-sama always sees to that. We sit through the six-o'clock sūtra reading, hurry through breakfast, then walk in a downpour to the Great Lecture Hall at Daishi Kyōkai. The hall already is packed to the doors, but we manage to squeeze through and crouch near a side wall. At the center of the gathering are rows of chanting priests and monks. The seminary students of Senshū-gakuin are wearing their black robes and white *kesa*. The women seminarians are in robes of gray. The boys of the Buddhist high school are in their dark quasi-military uniforms, the girls in blue and white sailor outfits. Most of the laity hold strings of beads and wear *wagesa* about their necks. The chanting is quite wonderful, full-voiced and confident.

When the ceremony ends, the fidgety high school students immediately scramble toward the doors, but most of the priests and student-monks and a good many of the laity stay behind, lining up quietly on the red and white runner that leads to the altar. Up on the elevated altar, as *honzon*, is the usual life-size image of the adult Kōbō Daishi. But on this one day, placed directly in front of the *honzon*, is a carving of the Child Daishi kneeling in prayer. This Chigo Daishi soon will be put in a *mikoshi* and carried the length of the town to the Ichi-no-hashi bridge. From there he will lead the noontime parade back up the main street to Kongōbu-ji.

At the center of the dais, also for this one day, is a six-inch-tall figure of a newborn infant. The infant stands in a bowl of fragrant hydrangea tea beneath a bower of chrysanthemums and *sugi* branches. The line of worshipers is now moving slowly toward this bower. When our turn comes we will take up one of the dippers and pour sweetened tea over the infant body. All day long visitors will be entering the Dai Kōdō to perform this tribute.

By the time we leave the Dai Kōdō the rain has diminished to a drizzle. The air is filled with the fragrance of wet forest. It is just ten o'clock, so we have time to attend the open house at Kongōbu-ji. We enter through the visitor's door (but without an admission charge this day) and hurry down the long front corridor, past special exhibitions of scroll paintings and student calligraphy, to the Betsuden. There we find all eight rooms devoted to flower arrangements sponsored by Kadō, Kōyasan's school of *ikebana*. Many of the arrangements this year present difficult aesthetic puzzles. Some are restrained, most are extravagant. Only a few could be construed as religious offerings, but apparently that is not their function—except for the largest display, a massive floral simulation of the Taizō-kai Mandala. In the end we award our private Best-in-Show to a quiet clustering of white and purple flowers set among pine branches.

There remains time for an abbreviated tea ceremony and for sitting on the porch of the Okuden, gazing out into the garden of sand and stone. The last lingering mist is lifting from the valley's circling ridges. Suddenly the sun comes out in full brightness. It is going to be a splendid day for a parade.

At twelve-thirty we are seated in front of Nishiri & Co. on Main Street. Mr. Nishimoto is at our side, ready to provide running commentary. And right on time, here come the marchers! At the front, as always, is a flute and drum corps made up of Kōyasan's elementary school children. As they troop past they sing the "Aoba Matsuri Song."

> *A thousand years ago,*
> *in the season of young leaves,*
> *there was a violet-colored cloud in the sky. . . .*

Next come the Boy Scouts, practiced marchers, carrying the national flag and an Aoba Matsuri banner. They are followed by two adult dew sweepers in traditional brown coats and green pants. The sweepers drag and tap their metal *konbō*, preparing the way before the *mikoshi* of Chigo Daishi, warning all low-lying creatures to escape from under the royal cart's wheels.

The cart does not arrive at once, however. First, we have a large troupe of black-gowned *goeika* ladies, sixty or seventy in all, singing and chiming a hymn to the sacred child. Then two long rows of very small children with their mothers (the mothers in inconspicuous black, like the puppet masters in Bunraku). Each child is wearing a royal golden headpiece and an open-sleeved floral blouse with a purple skirt. On their fore-heads are two black painted dots, the "eyes of the Buddha." Each is hold-ing a lotus flower in one hand as the other hand grips a multicolored cord that passes back through the line of marchers.

As the last child passes we can see that the cord is attached to the cart that carries the *mikoshi* of Chigo Daishi. Marching along protectively at the corners of this cart are the armored Four Heavenly Kings, the heroic Shitennō. Happy birthday, Precious Child!

Following the *mikoshi*, dressed alternately in green and yellow, is the parade's first group of dancers, students from the town's high school. The girl dancers arrive first, swaying gracefully to the rhythmic "Daishi Ondo." The high school boys follow, moving awkwardly but with spirit. We count sixty-eight student dancers. The infectious "Daishi Ondo" fades away and the pounding rhythm of drums takes over. Eighteen high school boys in checkerboard *happi* are pulling a heavy *taikō* float. Boom, boom, *boom.* Boom, boom, *boom.* The five standing drummers, all trained athletes, are dressed in red and black. Riding on the float with them is a single young woman in white kimono, the Princess of the Drums.

The rhythm of the "Daishi Ondo" returns and with it twenty-six young women in pale lavender *kimono* and billowing blouses with butter-fly designs. Their bodies weave and tilt and dip as their flower-holding hands gesture skyward, then earthward. All things in nature conspire to make these young women beautiful. Across the street from us a gathering of student monks watches in slack-jawed awe. No longer do they face a vow of celibacy.

The next dancing group also is made up of women, but of a genera-tion or two older than the butterfly girls. They wear simple pilgrim white with blue head scarves and red *wagesa.* Their dancing is soberly devo-tional. Immediately behind them comes a much less formal group, some eighty bareheaded men and women in blue checkerboard *happi* display-ing the Kongōbu-ji *mon.* These dancers exude exuberance and fun. The crowd applauds them as they pass.

A second sacred wagon is moving our way. Seated at the corners of the wagon platform are four young women wearing the red and white costume of shrine maidens. On each dark head is a golden *eboshi.* At intervals they toss paper lotus blossoms and the crowd surges into the street to pick them up. These are the Green Leaves Maidens.[1] They are

the court for a garlanded little boy who peeps out at us from behind
purple drapery. We salute him with a wave. He is the designated living
Child Daishi, the child known as Mao, or "True Fish." Today is the greatest day of his young life.

Another dancing group comes by, some thirty young women in
yellow and green *kimono* with billowing transparent sleeves and heads
adorned with flowers. With waving fans they sweep through the motions
of their dance. They are like leaves and flowers bending in the wind.
Behind them comes a dancing group of eighty men and women dressed
in Kongōbu-ji's purple and white. These are the *chōnaikai*, or "neighbors," and we recognize the faces of many of them. Behind the dancing
neighbors comes an immense herd of Kōyasan University students, both
male and female, all wearing *happi* with a red Sanskrit *YU* on their backs.
The *YU* is Kōbō Daishi's sacred syllable. Some of the women students
dance beautifully. A few of the men have elected to wear football uniforms under their *happi*. These are members of Kōyasan's notorious football "Ravens."[2]

The parade is now approaching its close. Three of the smaller floats
from last night's street procession pass by, and with them one new float, a
model of the huge Japanese black beetle known as the *Genji*. This beetle
float is a reminder of an ongoing environmental campaign at Kōyasan,
the slogan of which is "make Kōyasan again a *Genji-no-mori*"—that is,
make it a forest habitat that supports the Genji, a sensitive ecological
bellweather.[3]

The final dancing group is huge, more than one hundred women
dressed in white gowns and golden sashes. These women are from
Shikoku and are easily the most striking dancers of all. The crowd mur-
murs with delight. At the very end come the two largest floats from the
night before—the giant Tengu and the Child Daishi. The parade is over.

The crowd disperses, some heading for home, some heading for the
Kongōbu-ji parking lot where two of the dance groups will give a reprise
performance before Kōyasan's Kanchō and Hōin. Two popular professional *enka* singers, Makimura Mieko and Tenkoken Mangetsu, also will
perform there from a temporary stage. We have learned already that
Tenkoken is going to introduce a new ballad entitled "Kūkai." The lyrics
will thank Kūkai for continuing to serve us by sustaining his life on
Mount Kōya.

The *Daishi-tanjō-e* is a great event. Nearly everyone, from the very young to the very old, participates in one fashion or another. But it is not the year's most sacred event. That would be the commemoration of Kōbō Daishi's *nyūjō*.

CHAPTER TWELVE

CELEBRATING KŌBŌ DAISHI'S *NYŪJŌ* AND THE "CHANGING OF THE ROBE"

PREPARING THE NEW ROBE AT HŌKI-IN

Although modest in size and set well back from any frequented road, ancient Hōki-in is a temple the serious Kōyasan pilgrim needs to locate and visit. Just beyond its main hall, at the end of the entrance path, is a freestanding chapel about the size of a one-car garage. Two attractions draw us to this simple, dirt-floored structure. One is a small shrine that displays a painting, known as the *Go-nyūjō-daishi*, that purports to show how Kūkai appeared to Abbot Kangen in 921 when Kangen opened the tomb to present Kūkai with his posthumous title.[1] By that time Kūkai had sustained his meditation for eighty-six years. The painting portrays the saint as sitting firmly upright, eyes closed, skin fresh and normal looking, hair grown to shoulder length. Although the hands are hidden beneath a frayed robe they appear to be forming the Knowledge Fist of

Dainichi, or perhaps the *kongō-gasshō*, a *mudrā* of adoration in which the ends of the fingers are interlaced.[2] A misty light glows behind Kūkai's head. The poor condition of the robe is important, for a part of Abbot Kangen's mission was to bring Kūkai a new garment.

The matter of the robe brings us to the second object of veneration in the chapel, a dug well known as the *Okoromo-no-i*, or "Well of the Robe."[3] Each year "spiritual water" drawn from this well is used to set the dye in the silk cloth used to fashion Kōbō Daishi's new robe.[4]

The yearly presentation of the robe takes place at the Tōrōdō on solar March 21, the solar date of Kōbō Daishi's entry into his final meditation. Four days prior to that date the robe is purified at Hōki-in in a ritual known as the *Gyoi-kaji*, or "Precious-Clothes Invocation." Visitors are not admitted to the sanctuary where the purification takes place, but with special permission one may watch from an adjacent room through a bamboo screen. In the dimness beyond the screen one can make out a number of Kōyasan's highest-ranking priests, among them the Hōin. Above the sanctuary's *shumi-dan* are three paintings. The one at the left portrays Abbot Kangen with his young disciple Junyū. The middle painting is a copy of the Shinnyo portrait of Kōbō Daishi in the Miedō. The painting at the right is a depiction of Abbot Kangen and his entourage kneeling before the figure of Kōbō Daishi in his cave. On the floor before the altar is a box that contains the new robe together with some other necessary garments and accessories: a kimono for wearing under the robe, a change of underclothes, an *obi* (waistband), a *kesa*, a scarf, a fan, a pair of socks, a pair of wooden shoes, a set of *juzu* beads. The solemn Precious-Clothes Invocation takes about one hour, after which the participating priests share a lunch in Hōki-in's main hall.

When we attended the ceremony one of the participating priests gave us the memento he himself had received, a folded sheet of white paper enclosing two small squares of dark brownish-red silk cloth. These pieces of cloth were cut from material left over after the making of the robe. Tradition assigns to them the power to cure any physical or spiritual illness.

THE SOLAR *SHŌ-MIEKU*

March 21 has arrived, the solar anniversary of Kōbō Daishi's *nyūjō*. At seven o'clock in the morning a procession leaves Hōki-in carrying the trunk containing the sacred clothes. At Kongōbu-ji the trunk's contents are inspected, after which the head priest of Hōki-in receives a formal receipt. The trunk is then transported in an expanded procession to the Ichi-no-hashi bridge and then the length of the forest cemetery path to the Tōrōdō. There it is placed in the central sanctuary.

Meanwhile, the Hōin and the highest-ranking clergy have assembled in the Okunoin's Gokusho to put on their vestments. Precisely at nine o'clock they emerge in single file from the Gokusho garden gate. Leading the procession are two dew-sweepers in black boat-shaped hats and green *yama*-decorated tights, clanking their alarm staffs in rhythmic march, opening the way through the crowd of onlookers. The Hōin, who will preside at the ceremony, follows at the rear, walking beneath a large red umbrella held by attendants. The *goeika* ladies serenade the procession as it crosses the bridge over the Tamagawa.

The Tōrōdō already is packed with worshipers, all aware of the trunk of precious clothes that rests before the dais. The Hōin takes his place at the primary *dan*. The assembled priests begin to chant the *Rishu-kyō*, at intervals rising to their feet to process clockwise about the altar. When the ceremony ends, two monks wearing white masks close the lid of the trunk, cover it with red and gold brocade, and remove it from the sanctuary. Porters are waiting outside on the porch. They start off immediately toward the Garan where the clothes will be placed before Kōbō Daishi's portrait in the Miedō. The new robe and accessories will remain in the Miedō for 360 days—that is, until the following March 16, the eve of the next Precious-Clothes Invocation at Hōki-in.

The Tōrōdō ceremony is known as the *Gyoi-hōken*, or "Precious-Clothes Presentation." This presentation and the earlier invocation at Hōki-in (the *Gyoi-kaji*) together constitute the *Shō-mieku* of the solar calendar. *Shō-mieku* may be translated as "The Exact Day Ceremony of the Sacred Portrait," *mie* being a specific reference to the Shinnyo painting. *Mie* might also be understood to refer to the actual presence of Kōbō Daishi at both the Miedō and the mausoleum. The solar *Shō-mieku* places special emphasis on the mausoleum. The lunar *Shō-mieku*, held on lunar March 21, comes several weeks later. It will put greater emphasis on the Miedō.

It is important to note that the "presented" robe was positioned no closer to Kōbō Daishi's mausoleum than the sanctuary of the Tōrōdō.

Contrary to popular belief the tomb is not opened. Apparently, there was a time, and not so long ago, when the priests at the Tōrōdō displayed for foreign visitors a robe described as "worn during the previous year by Kōbō Daishi." Its frayed and soiled hem was offered as evidence that the saint still occasionally interrupted his meditation to visit the villages and byways of the nation. Today's prevailing tradition is that Abbot Kangen, after his visit to the tomb in 921, ordered that it be sealed and not opened again.[5] This latter tradition is not intended to undermine the belief that Kōbō Daishi continues to make appearances at Kōyasan and elsewhere.

THE LUNAR *SHŌ-MIEKU*

The lunar Shō-mieku takes place on the twenty-first day of the third lunar month, and therefore follows the solar Shō-mieku by some three to six weeks. In the course of these weeks the effects of early spring have greatly altered the appearance of the lower mountain. The orchards of the foothills are in full bloom, most especially the warm pink peach (*momo*) and the yellow-white pear (*nashi*). The flooded rice terraces are shimmering mirrors, waiting for planting. Up on Kōyasan the temple gardens have come alive, although snow is still a possibility. The *uguisu* are singing in the forest.

Just as in the case of the solar Shō-mieku, the lunar Shō-mieku is preceded by an invocation over a special gift for Kōbō Daishi. At ten a.m. on lunar March 17 the Hōin and a group of priests gather at Sambō-in temple for the *Tsuma-muki-no-sake-kaji*, "Invocation of the Nail-Peeled Sake."[6] This ceremony derives from the previously mentioned story that Kōbō Daishi's mother, while residing at Jison-in, prepared *sake* for him by husking the rice grains with her fingernails. Each year, in remembrance and imitation of this devotion, a special *sake* is prepared using water from the Tamagawa.

The Evening Ceremony

The primary lunar Shō-mieku celebration begins the evening prior to the twenty-first day of the third lunar month (lunar days begin with nightfall) and concludes with ceremonies on the following morning and after-noon. As we walk toward the Garan though growing darkness we find both sides of the Jabara Path already decked with flowers and burning candles. At the *temizuya* an attendant hands us a bundle of flowers and candles that we can distribute ourselves. The Eastern Stūpa's doors are wide open. Inside, the three enshrined deities are illuminated with flood-lights. The doors of the Sanmaidō, Daiedō, and Aizendō also are open and their interiors illuminated. Tonight nearly every barrier in the Garan has been opened so that all the enshrined deities can participate fully in the Shō-mieku events.

We climb to the Garan's upper terrace. The steps of the Daitō base platform are covered with rows of burning lanterns. So is the north porch of the Kondō. The Miedō, which is the ceremonial focus for this night, is surrounded by garlands of flowers and long trays filled with burning candles. Two large stages have been erected in the court area next to the Miedō, and here, illuminated by elevated braziers, a group of dancers and an assembly of *goeika* ladies have already begun offering their sacred arts. The shutters of the Miedō are open. The *shōji* doors have been pushed aside. Within the hall we see rows of seated priests. Beyond the priests, in darkness too deep to penetrate, the new robe rests before Kōbō Daishi's portrait.

At 7:45 a long column of seminary students from Senshū-gakuin and Nisō-gakuin arrives. They pass silently through the crowd, circle to the rear of the Miedō, and disappear into the hall. Soon we hear their chanting added to that of the priests. A little later a senior priest steps out onto the Miedō porch, microphone in hand. *In this place and on this very night eleven centuries ago,* he says, *Odaishi-sama began his long meditation in behalf of all sentient beings. We must do our best to imagine the events of that wonderful night. And let us reflect upon Abbot Kangen's visit to the tomb eighty-six years later. It was this visit that affirmed that Odaishi-sama truly remained alive, that he was continuing his work in behalf of the Japanese people. He continues to work for us today. He never fails. We thank him for his great teaching and for all he has contributed to our nation and to our individual lives. Tonight's ceremony of ten thousand lights and ten thousand flowers expresses our love and gratitude.*

The chanting within the Miedō continues for a time, then stops abruptly. The Hōin comes out onto the porch and is helped down into his *kago*. Most of the priests exit from the Miedō, followed by the seminary students. Then an invitation goes out to the waiting crowd. All lay people who wish to do so may enter the Miedō to pay their respects to Odaishi-sama. We find a place in the rapidly expanding line. When we finally reach the Miedō steps we remove our shoes and climb to the porch. There a monk hands us a souvenir paper lotus petal and directs us to circle the porch to the left. The petal has a lotus-bearing angel on one side and a brief history of this night on the other. At the rear of the porch a second monk offers us powdered incense with which to purify our hands and bodies. We pass through a door and are inside the Miedō. We move slowly past the individual portraits of Kōbō Daishi's disciples displayed in the outer corridor. They are but an arm's length away. Abbot Shinzen is easily recognized. Chisen, beloved by Daishi, is next to Shinzen. In front of each portrait is a table heaped with offerings. All the early disciples are being honored on this night.

As we reach the entrance to the inner sanctuary we kneel beside the others there. Directly before us is an altar table furnished like all the other ritual altars of the mountain. In the darkness beyond the altar we can just make out the folds of a partially drawn curtain. Perhaps we are looking directly at Shinnyo's portrait, but all we see is blackness. The two women kneeling in front of us are holding their hands out toward the darkness as if warming them before a fire.

We would like to remain longer, but must make room for those still waiting behind us. We hobble forward on our knees to add incense to the incense bowl, then rise and step outside onto the Miedō's front porch. It is snowing! The dark air is filled with the slowly falling flakes. Already the courtyard is covered with white.

As we step away from the Miedō we observe custodians emptying hot coals from the braziers and extinguishing the last of the lanterns. Other workers are rearranging the outdoor stages for tomorrow's ceremony. Up on the Daitō's base platform a small group of visitors has gathered to chant the *Hannya-shingyō* to the still-illuminated Dainichi Buddha. His massive head and shimmering golden body glow through the screen of snow.

Later, back at Rengejō-in, we find it difficult to sleep, so we put on our slippers and go out onto the temple porch. The snow is continuing to fall over the front garden. We put on our street shoes, slip out though the small night door in the front gate, and enter the street. We hear chanting. In front of the stūpa at Nan-in, where the *shari* of Shākyamuni is enshrined, the group of worshipers we saw earlier at the Daitō is again chanting the *Hannya-shingyō*. Perhaps they are going to spend the rest of the snow-filled night this way, processing slowly from sacred hall to sacred hall, like a band of carolers.

The Morning and Afternoon Ceremonies

Lunar March 21 began last evening. Now, at eight o'clock the next morning, the Hōin and twenty-plus high-ranking priests have gathered in the Gokusho at the Okunoin, just as they did for the earlier solar Shō-mieku. Again they walk in procession across the Mimyō-no-hashi bridge to the sanctuary of the Tōrōdō. There they celebrate the *Rishu-kyō* while protective fires burn at both *goma* altars. Afterward, the Hōin is transported back to Kongōbu-ji by a team of eight black-robed *kago* bearers. Inside Kongōbu-ji he removes his bright red Hōin's robe and dresses for the first time in Kōbō Daishi's brownish-red robe.[7] For the liturgical purposes of the day he has become Kōbō Daishi.

Promptly at noon the Hōin comes out of Kongōbu-ji and seats himself on a *koshi*, the type of litter that was used to carry the meditating Kōbō Daishi to his tomb burial at the Okunoin. The *koshi*, its curtains raised, moves in procession out of the Kongōbu-ji gate, up the Jabara Path, and into the Garan. The eight litter bearers now are dressed in white, just as were the disciples of old. The rows of spectators along the way bow as the litter passes. It is as if Kōbō Daishi has returned.

At the steps of the Miedō the Hōin leaves the *koshi* and enters the hall. The senior priests, already gathered inside, have been waiting for him. The student nuns and monks, about eighty in number, have been waiting outside at the west of the Miedō. The chanting begins.

The sun is out now. The snow of last night is forgotten. A spring wind blows the banners and curtains of the Miedō. Inside, we see the silhouette of the Hōin before the altar, surrounded by his priests just as Kōbō Daishi had been.

As the chanting continues inside, outside on the red-carpeted stage the first of two sacred activities begins, the preparation of tea. This year's tea master is Sen Sōshitsu (b. 1923), Grand Master of the Urasenke school of tea in Kyōto. A tall grey-haired man with regal bearing, Sen Sōshitsu is a direct descendant of famed Sen no Rikyū (1522–1591), tea officer to Oda Nobunaga and Toyotomi Hideyoshi. Today's Sen is without rival as the world's most esteemed living tea master. In fact, many in the audience are here primarily to witness his skill. They crowd close enough to see the small pale-blue gingko *mon* on the chest and sleeves of his black *haori*.

The tea stand and utensils—kettle, water container, brazier, bowls—are a quiet muted black and brown. With unhurried precision the master, seated on a reed mat, moves through each stage of preparation. When finished, he rises and carries the bowl of thick tea up the ramp that connects the stage to the Miedō. There he bows and presents his offering to a priest who takes the bowl inside to place before Kōbō Daishi. The tea master returns to the center of the stage, prepares a second bowl, this time of a thinner tea, and delivers it in the same manner to the Miedō. The master now leaves the stage altogether and walks, unaccompanied, northward out of the Garan, a closed fan in his right hand, a double loop of *juzu* beads in his left. Behind him several male assistants quietly clear the stage of the tea furniture.

Now the flowers. This year's flower master is Gomi Suihō, head of Kōyasan's *ikebana* school, Kadō Kōyasan.[8] Gomi-sensei is dressed in a gold-colored silk robe and a tall black *eboshi* headgear. Unlike Sen Sōshitsu, Gomi-sensei wears a white mask across his mouth and nose. Assisting him closely at the low table is another grand master of ikebana dressed in red-and-gold silk. Also at his side is a woman in a traditional sewn-sleeve black kimono. Eight other women kneel at the edge of the stage, four in black, four (the unmarried women) in open-sleeved white blouses and red skirts. Slowly, deliberately, the stems of seven pale yellow chrysanthemum flowers are cut to different lengths and placed in a preformulated vertical design.

The flower master rises and carries the offering to the porch of the Miedō. There, he kneels. A priest receives the offering and takes it into the sanctuary. The master rises and retreats, moving slowly and solemnly, like a character exiting from a Nō drama. The furniture of the flower ritual is removed from the stage.

Meanwhile, within the Miedō the chanting, the bells, and the clockwise processionals continue. Finally, a group of senior priests emerges from the hall carrying golden platters heaped with fresh cherry blossoms and paper lotus petals. Three times the priests process around the margin of the stage tossing blossoms and petals over the heads of the crowd. On each paper lotus is a picture of *gokuraku*, the Buddhist paradise. The priests reenter the Miedō, then come out again to shower us with more flowers of paradise.

The ceremony ends at around three p.m. The Hōin comes forward onto the Miedō porch and again seats himself on the *koshi*. The watchers bow toward the figure in brownish-red silk as the *koshi* is carried away. Once again, Kōbō Daishi has received our gifts and gratitude. His living presence has been affirmed. Thus ends the most sacred day of the year at Kōyasan.[9]

ADDENDUM: RITUALS OF SHĀKYAMUNI'S BIRTH AND DEATH

Kōyasan also observes the dates of Shākyamuni's birth and death, although these ceremonies receive less public attention. The traditional birth date for Shākyamuni is April 8, the day the ancient Indians believed to be the optimal time for entering this world. It is presumed to be the birth date for all Buddhas, past and future.[10] The celebration, known as the *Busshō-e*, begins at nine a.m. in Kongōbu-ji's *ōhirama*. A scroll painting of Shākyamuni's nativity is hung at the western end of the long room and before it is placed a bower of green branches and flowers (the *hanamidera*).[11] Within the bower stands a small image of the infant Shaka. At the close of the ceremony all the participants, plus many of the observers who have been watching from a side room, come forward to pour sweetened hydrangea tea over the infant. Later the *hanamidera* and infant are placed in the front corridor of Kongōbu-ji, where for the rest of the day visitors will come to offer the same liquid tribute. Traditionally, the first lay group to attend to the infant is made up of the town's kindergarten children.

The observance of Shākyamuni's death day—known as the *Nehan-e*, or "Ritual on the Occasion of the Buddha's Entering Nirvāna"—begins in Kongōbu-ji's *ōhiroma* at eleven p.m. on February 14 and ends at noon the following day. This all-night ceremony offers visitors a supreme opportunity to listen to Shingon liturgical chanting (*shōmyō*).[12] One is advised to bring warm winter clothing and arrive early for a steaming bowl of *tōfu* and noodles prepared by the Temple Women's Society. The *honzon* for the *Nehan-e* is a large scroll painting of the Buddha's death scene, which can be examined closely after the ceremony has concluded.[13] Again, Kōyasan's kindergarten children come by to pay their tribute. They gaze in wonder at the images of solemn deities and heartbroken animals. A priest explains to them the significance of the large man with the golden skin who appears to be sleeping at the center of the scroll. Afterward, he gives each child a piece of *manjū*.

CHAPTER THIRTEEN

ANNUAL RITUALS FOR THE DEAD

BON: MID-SUMMER VISITATION OF THE DEAD

The Bon festival, which reaches its national climax on August 15, is Japan's supreme occasion for gathering the family together and attending to the needs of ancestral spirits.[1] The ideal arrangement is for the scattered family members to assemble at the primary ancestral farmhouse, visit the family graves, invite the dead spirits to join in the festival activities, reminisce about old times, and end with eating and dancing. Bon is a time of relaxation and rejuvenation, with all routine work set aside. Estimates of the number of Japanese families who participate in some kind of Bon observance run as high as 90 percent. *Jigoku no kama mo yasumi*: "Even hell's boiling kettle is on holiday."

Among the first preparations for Bon at Kōyasan is the cleaning of the Okunoin forest cemetery. The grave plots are carefully raked and swept, the fallen needles and branches gathered into great piles and either

259

carted off or burned. Particular attention is paid to the free-floating anonymous stone *gorintō* that are scattered alongside the pilgrimage paths. Devoted women tie hundreds of brightly colored bibs around the necks of these memorials as a gesture of love and remembrance. A forgotten grave, it is said, is more than a failure of compassion. It is a planted seed of evil.

But housecleaning and remembrance are only the beginning. The essence of Bon is the gathering together of the living and the dead.

Shōryō-mukai: *Inviting the Spirits of the Dead*

From the first of August to August 15 the spirits of the deceased are believed to be free to leave their shadowy realm and rejoin the living. These spirits may be shy, however, or somewhat bewildered. Some likely harbor resentment at the circumstances of their deaths, or believe they have been neglected posthumously by family, friends, and clergy. A heartfelt invitation must be extended to all.

It is August 9, early in the afternoon. We are accompanying the head priest of Rengejō-in and four assisting temple monks as they perform a cemetery mission known as *Shōryō-mukai*—"Inviting the Spirits of the Dead." We are not physically visiting every grave in the forest and surrounding cemeteries, for that is impossible. But what we are able to do is visit a selection of memorials, especially of the recent dead with ties to Rengejō-in, including the grave of the father of the head priest. Before each of these monuments we observe the same protocol. While two monks light a candle, burn incense, and lay down an offering of *Kōya-maki* and five vegetables (rice, carrot, *daikon*, cucumber, and eggplant), the head priest and the two other monks recite the *Hannya-shingyō* and *Namu Daishi*. Each spirit is invited to join us when we return to Rengejō-in at the end of the day. Among the last stops of the afternoon is the stone of an arbitrarily chosen *muen-botoke*. We ask this unknown spirit to serve as stand-in for the cemetery's myriad anonymous and forgotten dead.

The sun has already set by the time we finally cross the Tamagawa to the Nōkotsudō in the vicinity of Kōbō Daishi's tomb. Before the charnel house the head priest addresses the tens of thousands of spirits whose ashes have been deposited there through the centuries. He then calls to the dead everywhere, to the dead of all nations and times. All of you, everyone who may still be wandering in the dark, come to receive the comfort of our temple ceremonies.

The one task left is to obtain *seika*, or "holy fire." Throughout our walk two of the monks have been carrying unlit lanterns. These they now take into the Tōrōdō and light from the flame of the Poor Woman's Lamp. This flame embodies both the spirit of Kōbō Daishi's eternal life and the compassion the Poor Woman felt for her deceased parents. We return now along the rapidly darkening pilgrim's path, moving swiftly toward Rengejō-in, carrying the holy fire. As we walk we are surrounded by a cloud of invisible guests.

Upon reaching Rengejō-in one of the monks uses the Poor Woman's flame to light the O-Kiriko-dōrō, or "faceted lantern," that hangs above the doorway of the *hondō*. This light becomes the welcoming beacon for the arriving spirits. We then enter the dark sanctuary and light a candle on the *shōryō-dana*, the shelf for the spirits of the dead. This shelf is crowded now with rows of *ihai*, including the *ihai* of members of the temple family. But there is room for all. Everyone, come.

Beloved Spirits of the Dead, we are honored to have you as our guests. May any torments you still suffer be eased. May your path to eternal peace be swift.

In addition to the ceremonies held at the individual temples, each morning from August 7 through August 13 a special *Fudangyō* ("continuous sūtra reading") takes place in the Golden Hall to assist the dead in their journey. On these occasions all three sanctuary *dan* are employed. At the *Fudangyō* in 1994 a scroll painting of the female rain dragon Zennyu-ryū-ō was placed before the main altar, for that year a severe summer drought was threatening the nation's rice harvest. As the living prayed for the dead, the dead and the living together prayed for rain. Bon is a communal enterprise.

Mandō-kuyō-e: *Memorial Ceremony of Ten Thousand Lights*

In most parts of Japan the Bon festival ends on August 15 with an elaborate sending-off ceremony for the dead. At Kōyasan this *Mandō-kuyō-e* takes place two days earlier.[2] During the morning of August 13 each temple sends a lit lantern to the Okunoin cemetery. Visiting spirits make their way back to their grave sites by following this lantern. And there they wait for the Memorial Ceremony of Ten Thousand Lights, which begins with the coming of darkness. The primary locale of the Mandō-kuyō-e is the Lantern Hall before Kōbō Daishi's tomb—or at least that is where the priests assemble. In reality the entire two-kilometer pilgrimage route through the forest becomes a single ceremonial stage. Lay participants number many thousands and the memorial candles they place at selected graves number well beyond one hundred thousand. The sides of the pilgrimage path become two long channels of light that lead from the first bridge all the way to the porch of the Tōrōdō. *Mandō* in *mandō-kuyō-e* literally means "ten thousand lights," but the real meaning is that the lights are beyond counting.

At Rengejō-in the evening meal has been moved up to five o'clock so that we will be able to reach the Ichi-no-hashi bridge in time for the start of the great illumination at six. But the meal is late. Like most of the other *shukubō* this day, Rengejō-in is so crowded with guests that the monks and kitchen staff are overwhelmed. Finally, at ten minutes after six we head out the temple gate to catch a bus. Fortunately, the Nankai buses, ever alert to Kōyasan's needs, are running tonight at five-minute intervals.

When we reach the Ichi-no-hashi we see that both sides of the path are already ablaze with light. A young woman hands us a bundle of unlit candles, then a single candle with a living flame. This flame, she assures us, was drawn from the Poor Woman's Lamp. We try to push on quickly, still hoping to catch some of the Tōrōdō ceremony, but the pathway ahead is too crowded. We can manage no more than a slow shuffle. And actually this is no great matter. On such a night every flame is its own complete memorial observance. We light our first candle and place it before a stone vaguely shaped like a Jizō—for someone's child lost years ago. Several dozen candles are already burning there. In fact, hardly a foot of space along either side of the path is without its cluster of candles. In certain places, before a favored Jizō or *muen-botoke*, the candles glow in clusters of a hundred or more. The atmosphere of the crowd is strangely exuberant. Everyone seems to be smiling, especially the children.

A few drops of rain.

We continue to shuffle along. We place more candles at carefully chosen locations. There are so many memorial stones we would like to honor, but we must keep some candles in reserve for later use. The rain is more steady now, the first rain in weeks. We remember the prayer for rain at the morning's *Fudangyō* service.

Here and there, deep in the woods, isolated candles flicker in the darkness. Obviously, a number of people have left the path to search out particular stones. So we ourselves head away downhill through the darkness, advancing by dead reckoning among the trees and invisible monuments. We find Mrs. Gordon's grave. As anticipated, she has received no candles tonight. We light one for her. Next door, at the Nestorian Stone, three candles are burning. On our way back toward the pilgrimage path we locate the side-by-side *gorintō* of warrior Kumagai and the beautiful young man he killed, Atsumori. Despite their obscure location this pair already has received a tribute of more than twenty candles.[3]

After thirty more minutes of slow movement we reach Akechi Mitsuhide's memorial. The traitor-assassin is doing well tonight. There are a dozen still-burning candles and another fifty either burned down or sputtered out in the rain. At the Middle Bridge we come upon the greatest glow so far. The "Sweating Jizō" is surrounded by a great carpet of candlelight. At the top of the next rise we turn into the shrine of priest Kakuban and add two candles to the several already burning there. As we move closer to the Tamagawa the crowd becomes still more compact. Amazingly, no one appears to be discouraged by the rain. The younger children delight in having an excuse to light and relight the sputtering candles.

The poet Bashō's memorial is surrounded with a ring of light, as is the "rouged Jizō." We go up the bank in darkness to Toyotomi Hideyoshi's memorial. We count a total of forty-four candles, a few of them still burning. Only three of our own candles are still unused. One we place at the grave of Ōgo Shōnin, the "wood-eating saint." He has attracted little attention, for most visitors know nothing about his contribution. Across the path from Ōgo a whole bonfire is burning before Lord Asano and the Forty-Seven Loyal Rōnin.

We reach the bridge across the Tamagawa. The view ahead is rather dismal. Instead of two great streams of light pouring down from the porch of the Tōrōdō, we see only a few scattered patches of guttering flames. It is now impossible to keep anything burning for more than a few seconds. As we approach the Tōrōdō steps, moving against the flow of the exiting crowd, we see some gowned priests leaving by a side entrance. Their day began at four this morning. It is now nine in the evening. The myriad dead are well on their way back to the shadow world. The festival of Bon is over.

After re-crossing the Tamagawa we take a right turn and climb up a dark path looking for Oda Nobunaga, that most notorious of Kōyasan's historical enemies. Even the generous Jesuits condemned him, though they preferred him to the Shingon priests, whom they believed to be devil worshipers. In the darkness we see no candles. We feel along the wet surface of the gravel, in the shallow pools of water. We find one fallen candle. And another. In all we locate eight partially burned candles. In Nobunaga's offering basket, soaked with rain, stuck together, are some business cards. We peel the cards apart in order to count them. Nine cards. Bon is for everyone. Even if Nobunaga is in hell it will only be a temporary address. The compassion of the Great Sun Buddha wills that all should be saved.

We head out of the cemetery by the short route, aiming for the Okunoin-mae bus stop. We pause just once, at poet Yosano Akiko's monument.[4] There are no candles here, so we stick our remaining two in the wet ground, making no attempt to light them. The rain continues. This has been a glorious night. The dead spirits are at peace. The nation's families have been reunited. The drought has ended.

HIGAN-E: CEREMONY OF THE OTHER SHORE

The spring and fall equinoxes (March 21 and September 23), both national holidays (*Shumbun-no-hi* and *Shūbun-no-hi*), also are times when the Japanese citizenry travel into the countryside to care for ancestral graves. In late March the orchards, fields, and rice paddies (still unplowed) glow with new grass. By late September the rice already has started to come into golden ripeness and the field embankments are blooming with *higanbana*, the brilliantly red "equinox flower." The two holidays are wonderful times to be out of the city.

For the week of each equinox the nation's Buddhist temples hold special ceremonies known as *Higan-e. Higan* means, literally, "the other shore," a reference to the shore of paradise that lies across the river of death. These ceremonies help the dead spirits make the difficult passage.

On the actual day of each equinox a steady flow of visitors pours into Kōyasan's several cemeteries to tend the graves and pray at the halls of the Okunoin.

Two of the fall events are of special interest. One is *Dosha-kaji*, or "Blessing of Sacred Sand," a complex ceremony that takes place in the Kondō at nine a.m. on the day of the equinox. Over a portion of passive sand the participating priests repeatedly chant the transforming *Kōmyō-shingon*, "Mantra of Light":

> *On abokya beirosha nō maka bodara mani handoma jimbara harabaritaya un.*
> [Om Unfailing Dainichi, the great symbol, jewel, lotus, and light, evolve! Hūm.][5]

As the chant proceeds the sand begins to glow until each grain is transformed into a radiant Sanskrit syllable. Such sand can be used to redeem the dead. One need only sprinkle a handful over a corpse or grave or gravestone. Priest-mystic Myōe Kōben (1173–1232), designer of the *Dosha-kaji* ritual used at Kōyasan, explains that such a redemption is not illogical, but is instead a consequence of good karma. Even if the deceased person failed "to cultivate the slightest good, and [has] fallen into the Avīci Hell . . . [the] sin will dissipate spontaneously, and the deceased will attain birth in the Land of Bliss." Playing an important role in this event is the compassion of the person who administers the sand. Ultimately, of course, the sand's effect is a manifestation of the universal, boundless compassion of the Buddha.[6]

Another interesting event at Kōyasan is the sometime scheduling of Takigi Nō ("Torchlight" Nō) on the eve of the day of the fall equinox. The performance takes place at night on a stage temporarily erected in the Garan courtyard between the Miedō and the Kondō. The traditional Nō backdrop of a painted sacred pine is provided in this instance by an actual living tree, Kōyasan's own Sanko-no-matsu. In 1995 the plays chosen were Zeami's *Tōru*, Kan'ami's *Kayoi Komachi*, and Zeami's *Matsukaze*, all three telling of an encounter between a traveling Buddhist priest and a tormented dead spirit. In the first play, the dead spirit of Prince Tōru cannot overcome its continuing attachment to the remembered luxuries of a princely life. In the second play, Komachi, in life the greatest beauty of the Heian age, now in death cannot rid herself of remorse at having mistreated her most faithful suitor. In the third play, the fisher-girl Matzukaze retains in death the passion she had felt for an aristocratic lover who abandoned her. In each of the three cases the tormented ghost protagonist begs assistance from a sympathetic priest.[7] *In your kindness give me comfort!*

The intoning of poetry of spiritual remorse before Kōbō Daishi's sacred pine, from a stage lit by torches, and at such a significant time of year, makes for powerful drama. Each narrative ends with the traveling priest providing comfort for the anguished spirit in the name of the compassionate Buddha.

And what do all these devices for ministering to the dead add up to? For one thing they help to establish, and to sustain, a bond (*en*) of love and loyalty between the living and the dead. Death need not be a severance. It can be an occasion for continued devotion and mutual assistance. Additionally, memorial activities, especially those sponsored by the temple and administered by a priest, help cleanse the dead spirit of its anguish and sin, transforming it into a spirit at peace (*nigimitama*)—that is, into a Buddha.

CHAPTER FOURTEEN

LEAVING THE HOLY MOUNTAIN

Through fading twilight, with loaded backpacks, we walk up the familiar exit road past the glowing soft drink and coffee machines, past Mr. Iwatsubō's sweet-smelling wood products shop, past the Kinrin-tō stūpa and Rengejō-in, and on out the forest gate at the Fudō Entrance. We make a final farewell bow to the great bronze Jizō sitting hunched and silent in the early dark. The Women's Hall is closed. Reverend Nakata locked its doors several hours ago. On this our last night we have decided not to take a bus to the summit cable car station. Instead, we will descend the upper mountain on foot, by moonlight, along the Fudō-zakka trail.

Ten minutes of steep descent through dark woods brings us to the sound of falling water and the chapel of the Purification Fudō. This is where climbers are urged to shed their sins before continuing on toward the Fudō Entrance.[1] We step up onto the chapel porch and put an eye to the hole in the door. A soft votive light is burning inside beside the fierce deity. Hundreds of thousands of foot travelers have paused here

since young Ishidōmaru spent a lonely night on the chapel porch in the thirteenth century.

Behind the chapel, invisible in the darkness, is a cave dug deep into the mountainside, a mysterious tunnel with a partially collapsed entrance and ceiling. The abandoned hole is an unnerving place to enter, even by daylight. As to its function, one suggestion is that groups of mountain ascetics once locked themselves temporarily in its black womb to pray for a spiritual rebirth. But there are other theories. So we are leaving Kōyasan with this and many other mysteries unsolved.

We continue on. Immediately below the Fudō chapel the path crosses a small bridge over a stream. At this spot the dark forest suddenly opens up to early stars and the glow of a moon rising over the ridge across the ravine. Below us the stream drops off into space.[2] From a little farther down the trail we look back to see the cascading water transformed into an almost vertical ribbon of silver in the moonlight.

Fifteen more minutes and the lights of Gokuraku-bashi Station appear below. The Fudō-zakka passes beneath the cable car track, then descends to the bank of the Fudō-gawa. We cross the "Bridge to Paradise" where we bow a last farewell to the two Jizō that stand guard at either end of the span.

One year ago, at early dusk, a lone pilgrim overtook us on this bridge, an old man with sun-blackened face and soiled pilgrim clothes. He had just completed the full Shikoku pilgrimage, doing it all on foot, starting from Kōyasan and then returning, perhaps sixteen hundred kilometers in all, never entering a car or train or bus, although he did use the ferry when crossing between Wakayamakō and Komatsushima. He boarded the train with us, his first acceptance of land transportation in months, and together we rode all the way to Ōsaka. The old man said he had not once been ill or felt lonely or unhappy during the pilgrimage. He said he often had been unhappy before, and tapped his forehead by way of explanation. The other train passengers looked at us intently from time to time, puzzled to see two Americans taking such interest in a disheveled old man with scraggly beard and matted white hair. Only as we neared Ōsaka did the man tell us about a strange event that had occurred during his pilgrimage. Kōbō Daishi had come to his pallet one night. The saint had placed a warm hand on his head and pressed down with considerable pressure. Several minutes passed with the hand gripping him in this way. Then Odaishi-sama whispered, "You can see your daughter now." The old man had not seen his daughter for more than forty years. As we parted at Namba Station the man gave us a metal medallion with an image of Kōbō Daishi on one side. On the other side was the Sanskrit letter *A* representing the Great Sun Buddha. We tried to give him a small amount of money, as *settai*, but he refused. He was no longer on pilgrimage, he said.

We knock on the office window at Gokuraku-bashi Station. The attendant rouses slowly and comes to the window to sell us tickets. Foot travelers rarely show up at this hour. When the descending cable car arrives it empties out fewer than a dozen passengers. We glance up at the moonlit flank of Kōyasan. The mountain air feels good in our lungs. Ōsaka will be hot. It will smell of restaurant kitchens.

The warning bell clangs. We step aboard the train and begin our twisting descent. Kōyasan slides away behind us. A few passengers get on at Kudoyama and at Hashimoto. More get on at Kawachi-Nagano. By the time we reach the outskirts of Ōsaka the train, now expanded to eight cars, is nearly full. The platform of Namba Station is bright with noise and movement.

At we start down the broad main stairway we see mounted above us a large billboard photograph of Kōyasan's Miedō. The Miedō porch lanterns are shining softly through an early evening mist. The Pine of the Sanko is at the left side of the picture.

We descend more stairs, down and down, until we reach the level of the Midosuji subway, the track that burrows north and south beneath central Ōsaka. Even at this hour the platform is so crowded that only a few of us are able to find seats on the arriving train. The rest of us stand pressed together, simulating sleep, patiently swaying with the motion of the car.

NOTES

I have made frequent use, usually without citation, of several basic sources: Hisao Inagaki, *A Dictionary of Japanese Buddhist Terms*, 3rd edition, with supplement (Kyoto: Nagata Bunshodo, 1988); *Japanese-English Buddhist Dictionary*, revised edition (Tokyo: Daitō Shuppansha, 1991); *Kenkyusha's New Japanese-English Dictionary*, Koh Masuda, editor in chief, 4th edition (Tokyo: Kenkyusha, 1974); E. Papinot, *Historical and Geographical Dictionary of Japan* (Rutland, VT: Charles E. Tuttle, 1972); and Kodansha's *Japan: An Illustrated Encyclopedia* (Tokyo: Kodansha, 1993).

INTRODUCTION

1. Quoted material is adapted from Hiroshi Kitagawa and Bruce T. Tsuchida, trans. *The Tale of the Heike* [Heike Monogatari] (Tokyo: University of Tokyo Press, 1975), 638–41.

2. *Shingon*, a translation of the Sanskrit *mantra* ("words of truth"), is the name Kōbō Daishi gave to his esoteric Buddhist sect (Shingon-shū). When rendered with the proper posture and visualization, the sacred "words of truth" provide access to the divine light that frees one from illusion.

CHAPTER 1. GOING TO THE MOUNTAIN

1. An esoteric Buddhist addition to Japan's creation myth has Izanami and Izanagi initiating their procreative activity at a spot where the ocean floor was marked by the two characters *Dai-nichi* (Great Sun). Another early esoteric theory held that the sun goddess Amaterasu herself was a cognate of the Great Sun Buddha.

2. The older priest, whose religious name was Karukaya, was unwilling to violate the holy vow he had made on entering Kōyasan, a pledge to reject forever the attachments of his earlier life. The whole Karukaya narrative, full of heartbreak and high thinking, supported the general public notion that Kōyasan was an otherworldly Buddhist cloud land to which sorrowing people escaped, never to return. The Karukaya-dō shrine at the summit of Kōyasan, which is much larger than the Kamuro shrine, features three carvings of Jizō Bodhisattva, a Buddhist protector of children and the dead. The three images, designated the *Oyako-Jizō*, or "Parents-and-Child Jizō," are presumed to have been carved by young Ishidōmaru and his father. The small Kamuro village shrine has its own treasures to show to visitors, among them a jewel-like stone (obtained by Ishidōmaru's grandfather from a Jizō statue) that bestows fertility, a bamboo walking staff that burst into bloom when Ishidōmaru thrust it into the earth to mark his mother's grave, and a remarkable mummified "mermaid" (*ningyo-no-miira*) used by the mother as an object of devotion. There are well-known Nō and Bunraku versions of the story, entitled, respectively, *Karukaya* and *Karukaya-dōshin tsukushi no iezuto*. A prose version is Tokutomi Ganryū's *Karukaya Dōshin to Ishidōmaru*, for sale at Kōyasan's Karukaya-dō. For an account of the mermaid, see Iwahashi Tetsuya, *Ningyo-kō: Kamuro Karukaya-dō-no-hihō* (Mermaid study: a hidden treasure of Kamuro Karukaya-dō) (Kamuro: Karukaya-dō Hozon-kai, 1992). For a recent scholarly take on the narrative's significance, see Susan Matisoff, "Barred from Paradise? Mount Kōya and the Karukaya Legend," in *Engendering Faith: Women and Buddhism in Premodern Japan*, ed. Barbara Ruch (Ann Arbor: Center for Japanese Studies, University of Michigan, 2002), 463–500.

3. The venue of the demon dance is the courtyard of the local Shingon temple (Jizō-ji) and its adjacent shrine (Shiide Itsukushima Jinja). Jizō-ji's head priest commutes daily to his primary employment on Kōyasan.

4. The Kōya Line reached Mikkaichichō (halfway between Ōsaka and Kōyasan) in 1897, Hashimoto (on the north shore of the Kinogawa) in 1915, Kudoyama in 1924, and Gokuraku-bashi Station in 1929. The cable car from Gokuraku-bashi Station to the summit Kōyasan Station was opened thirteen months later, on June 6, 1930. That day was declared a holiday at Kōyasan, with all local children receiving free rides. Nankai's founder is buried on the mountain. Twice each year representatives of the company hold ceremonies at the Great Stūpa to give thanks to Dainichi Buddha for the success of the railroad and to pray for the future safety of company employees and passengers.

5. As an alternative to the bus one may take a taxi. Taxis follow a different and somewhat longer route, entering Kōyasan by the Daimon, or Great Gate, at the western end of the valley. The altitude of Kōyasan's valley is around 2,800 feet (850 meters).

6. This particular statue, the largest outdoor figure at Kōyasan, was placed outside the Fudō Entrance by an Edo woman some two hundred fifty years ago. The woman's name was Yokoyama Take, so the statue is known informally as the "O-take Jizō."

7. There are tales of men (because they were "endowed with good karma") quite suddenly abandoning wives and children in favor of the contemplative life, not even bothering to say goodbye lest their flight be hindered. Ishidōmaru's father, Karukaya, was such a person. The Kōyasan holy man credited with bringing Emperor Shirakawa to the faith was another. This man, overtaken on the road by a desperate and weeping daughter, thrust her aside with the cry, "Get away, I won't be hindered by you." He then pulled out his sword and slashed off his hair. The daughter later became a nun, joining others like herself at the foot of Kōyasan. There she sewed and laundered her father's garments. See Marian Ury, translator, "Recluses and Eccentric Monks: Tales from the *Hosshin-shū* by Kamo no Chōmei," *Monumenta Nipponica* 27, no. 2 (1972): 163–66.

8. This dramatic rescue appears often in painted illustrations of Kōbō Daishi's life. Today pilgrim climbers along the Chō-ishi-michi pilgrimage trail will find (near marker number 54) the purported "Push-Up Rock" (*oshiage ishi*) with a dimly visible imprint of Kōbō Daishi's hand. Nearby is a small stream called "Tear Brook," said to have been started by Her Ladyship's tears. The barrier rocks themselves are a full ten kilometers from the trail's beginning at Jison-in, but still more than five kilometers short of the western Daimon entrance to Kōyasan. One early version of Lady Tamayori's attempt to approach Kōyasan has her emphasizing to her son that at age eighty-three she is altogether free of the defiling blood that formerly made her ritually impure. When she attempts to step over his *kesa*, however, a drop of menstrual fluid falls upon the cloth and the desecrated garment bursts into flames. For a general discussion of *nyonin-kinzei kekkai*, with particular application to Kōyasan, see Bernard Faure, *The Power of Denial: Buddhism, Purity, and Gender* (Princeton and Oxford: Princeton University Press, 2003), 219–49. Also see Matisoff, "Barred from Paradise?", which includes a discussion of Lady Tamayori and a reproduction of an old illustration of the burning *kesa* incident. The primary Shingon interest in Lady Tamayori is not related to *nyonin-kinzei*, however. Lady Tamayori is the focus of an active cult at Jison-in (in Kudoyama), where she is perceived to be a female foreshadowing of Miroku, the Buddha of the Future. Her body is believed to be buried directly beneath Jison-in's Miroku hall. (The name *Jison* is a reference to Miroku.) Women visitors pray to Lady Tamayori concerning "female" matters, most especially assistance with conception, child birth, and breastfeeding. They purchase simulated breasts made of silk stuffed with cotton, which are labeled and hung at the shrine. Lady Tamayori's primary statue bears a striking

resemblance to the Christian Virgin Mary. Outside in the temple yard is a wide-spreading tree of great age said to symbolize the perfect mutual devotion between Kōyasan's founder and his mother. In the end, then, there were no hard feelings between the two. In fact, Kōbō Daishi is said to have made the following appeal to Kōyasan head priest Jōyo in a dream: "Rather than worship me ten times, pray nine times to my mother." Here is one more curious story about Kōyasan and female "impurity." We are told that near the end of the tenth century the great Fujiwara Michinaga sent the dead body of his two-year-old daughter to Kōyasan in the hope that its priests could restore the body to life. This the priests were able to do (the daughter later became an empress), but the holy men did not permit the girl's body to pass into Kōyasan proper. They came outside the gate to perform the cure. As ashes she would have been admitted, but not as a female corpse. See Robert E. Morrell, *Sand and Pebbles* (Shasekishū): *The Tales of Mujū Ichien, A Voice for Pluralism in Kamakura Buddhism* (Albany: State University of New York Press, 1985), 252.

9. The desire of Japanese women to gain access to Kōyasan's teachings, rituals, and monastic life prompted the establishment of a species of Shingon temple known as Nyonin Kōya, or "Kōya for Women." Among the more famous Nyonin Kōya were Murō-ji in Nara Prefecture, Amanozan Kongō-ji in Ōsaka Prefecture, Ōkubo-ji on Shikoku Island, Amada-ji at Kumano in southern Kii, the Shingon complex at Amano at the foot of Kōyasan, and the already mentioned Jison-in in the village of Kudoyama. The vitality and fame of some of these Kōya for Women did much to expand further the cult of Kōbō Daishi. For an account of Murō-ji's emergence as a Kōya for Women see Sherry D. Fowler, *Murōji: Rearranging Art and History at a Japanese Buddhist Temple* (Honolulu: University of Hawai'i Press, 2005), 64–74.

10. The valley immediately adjacent to Kōyasan on the north, popularly known as Uguisu-dani ("Valley/Neighborhood of the Nightingale"), is thought to have served as a residence for some of Kōyasan's secretly kept wives and lovers. Certain obscure paths through Kōyasan's perimeter forest are still pointed out to visitors as routes once used for clandestine meetings.

11. Several of the mountain's married priests have told us they are acutely conscious of having to balance two lives. In one life they are "householders." They love their wives and their children, and are responsible for them. In the other life they shave their heads, put on sacred garments, and approach the altars in the spirit of the Bodhisattva ideal. In this second life they are disciples of Kōbō Daishi, servants of the Dharma, and children of Dainichi. There is a tension between the two lives, but ideally each life serves the other. For a thorough discussion of the complex matter of priestly celibacy in modern Japan see

Richard M. Jaffe, *Neither Monk Nor Layman: Clerical Marriage in Modern Japanese Buddhism* (Princeton and Oxford: Princeton University Press, 2001).

12. Two paper lanterns hang above En's statue in the Nyonindō. Each has the inscription *Jimben Bosatsu*, "Bodhisattva of Supernatural Powers," a title awarded to En (b. 634) by the Imperial Court in an attempt to make up for the court's having exiled him for sorcery some eleven centuries earlier. The Japanese esoteric mountain religion known as Shugendō, whose followers are called *yamabushi* (literally, "those who lie down in the mountains"), regard En as their founder and model. The largest Shugendō center in Japan is in the area of Ōmine-san, a mountain ridge to the east of Kōyasan. Many Shugendō temples are affiliated with Shingon, and several of Kōyasan's temples today have Shugendō connections. Another shrine to En-no-Gyōja is located on a ridge of Mount Mani that overlooks Kōbō Daishi's mausoleum. For a general discussion of En's relationship to his mother and the Shugendō practice of excluding women from sacred mountains, see Miyake Hitoshi, *Shugendō: Essays on the Structure of Japanese Folk Religion* (Ann Arbor: Center for Japanese Studies, University of Michigan, 2001), 117, 143–58. For some popular stories about En, see Jan Vandercammen, *A Legendary Guide of Osaka* (Osaka: Osaka Shunjūsha, 1995), 31–34.

13. For an account of the evolution of Benzaiten imagery and worship in India, China, and Japan, see Catherine Ludvik, "From Sarasvatī to Benzaiten" (PhD diss., University of Toronto, 2001).

14. The beads presumably remain there under the protection of a *tengu* (a mythic creature, part human, part bird) that lives in the top of a giant cedar. Legend has Kōbō Daishi hiding sacred objects at many other locations in Japan—most famously a wish-fulfilling jewel buried on Mount Murō, the location of Murō-ji temple. See Fowler, *Murō-ji*, 21–27.

15. Important as Benten/Benzaiten is to Kōyasan, she is much more important to a Japanese "new religion" known as Benten-shū, founded in 1934 at a village Shingon temple not far from Kōyasan. The belief of Benten-shū is that the central position in the cosmic drama is held by the goddess Benten rather than by the "male" Great Sun Buddha. This revelation was received in a vision experienced by the sect's founder, Omori Kiyoko (1909–1967), a Kōyasan-trained faith healer whose husband was himself a Kōyasan-trained priest. In her vision Kiyoko followed a swimming white snake that led her into the presence of the supreme goddess. Kiyoko is regarded as an avatar of Benten, her husband an incarnation of Kōbō Daishi. Benten-shū has published two books in English on the sect's history and beliefs: Omori Jisho, *Doctrine of Water: An Introduction and Guide to Bentenshu Faith*, trans. Satoshi Tatsumi (Ibaraki

City, Osaka: Bentenshu Kyomuka, 1971), and Yamaoka Sohachi, chief editor, *The Water for the Thirsty: The Life of Lady Chiben Who Lives in Love* (Tokyo: Dainichi Publishing Co., 1982). The sect's primary headquarters are at Gojō, a short distance up the Kinokawa from Kamuro, and at Ibaraki City, near Ōsaka. Benten-shū became fully independent of Shingon-shū in 1953. Among the many watery places in Japan famous for ancient Benten worship are the islands of Enoshima (near Kamakura), Miyajima (near Hiroshima), and Chikubishima (in Lake Biwa in central Honshu, a lake shaped like the instrument Benzaiten plays). Kōbō Daishi is thought to have trained at Miyajima. He also trained at or near the location of the important Benten shrine of Tenkawa Benzaiten on the Tenno River, a site that is a two-day walk eastward from Kōyasan along the Kōya-Ōmine pilgrimage trail. In the early seventeenth-century Nō play *Chikubishima*, when a woman visitor's presence on the sacred island is challenged by an offended court official, the official is informed by an old local boatman that the island's primary resident deity, Benzaiten, is an "incarnation of eternal enlightenment" who most especially invites women to make pilgrimages there. The lowly woman (a mere fisherman's assistant) is then revealed to be the resplendent Shining Goddess herself. In a parallel transformation the old boatman becomes the Dragon God or snake divinity of the lake, a further manifestation of Benzaiten. For a fuller account of the drama, see Andrew M. Watsky, *Chikubushima: Deploying the Sacred Arts in Momoyama Japan* (Seattle and London: University of Washington Press, 2004), 236–38.

16. The full Japanese name for the man-snake is *Byaku-ja-gyō-uga-benzai-in-ryū-ō*, which translates to something like "White-snake-shape Uga Benzai Dragon-king." Prior to his association with the river goddess the native Uga-jin was primarily a *kami* of harvest. Small shrines to this white snake are found throughout Japan, most especially in secluded watery mountain grottoes. According to folk belief a snake's flickering tongue controls lightning and the coming of rain.

17. For a description of this sculpture see Soeda Ryūshō and Miyatake Mineo, *Odaishi-sama wa Ikiteiru* (Tokyo: Linden, 1996), 43. Legend says the sculpture originally was enshrined on Mount Benten. Today it is in the possession of Kōyasan's Hōki-in, where it is a major object of worship.

18. Ariyoshi Sawako, *The River Ki* (Kinokawa), trans. Mildred Tahara (Tokyo, New York, and San Francisco: Kodansha International, 1980). First published in 1959.

19. Lyrics by Arai Shōhei. Melody by Suzuki Jun. Recorded by singer Tagawa Toshimi.

20. Akuno Shizuka apparently was still alive in 1994, living in Wakayama City near the mouth of the Kinokawa.

21. Kosugi's full story is found in Takano Shunme, *Nyonindō no Yurai* (The origin of Nyonindō), Kongōbu-ji, 1981. Like the tale of Ishidōmaru and Karukaya, it is a classic Kōyasan drama. Here are a few more details. When Kosugi was a young woman her father, falsely thinking her to have been wilfully disobedient, slashed off the fingers of both her hands and left her on a snowy mountainside to die. Following a near-miraculous survival (she was nursed through the winter by bears) she married a daimyō's son to whom she had been affianced before her maiming. After Kosugi gave birth to a healthy boy her conniving stepmother tricked her into believing that her husband secretly found her repugnant and wished both her and the baby dead. Overwhelmed with fear for the child's safety, Kosugi fled Echigo. During a stop at Zenkō-ji temple in Nagano she heard some nuns discussing a distant paradise known as Kōyasan. "In Kamiya on the slopes of Kōyasan lives an old man named Zembei," one of them said. "I'm told that Zembei never turns away a sorrowing woman who comes to him for assistance." Kosugi decided to take her baby to Kōyasan. When the malnourished infant died in a mountain storm Kosugi buried the body, saving only the baby's hair and soft underclothes, which she placed against her still tender breasts. Upon reaching snowy Kamiya village (near today's Goku-raku-bashi Station) she found Zembei waiting for her. "I will climb to Kōyasan in the morning," Zembei told her, "and place your baby's hair in the Nōkosudō near the tomb of Kōbō Daishi. Odaishi-sama will comfort his spirit and lead him to paradise." Kosugi asked if she might accompany him. "From the time of its founding," Zembei explained, "no woman has been permitted to pass through the gates of Kōyasan. Not even Odaishi-sama's own mother was permitted to do so, and she was a woman to whom the Buddha appeared." Zembei agreed, however, that Kosugi might climb with him as far as the Fudō Entrance. When they reached this gate Kosugi thanked Zembei and gave him the silk cloth in which the baby's hair had been tied and the pouch containing the birth gift of gold. "When spring comes," she said, "use this gold to build a hut at the place where we now stand. It will be a shelter for women like me who follow Kōbō Daishi's footsteps. It will give these women an opportunity to rest and pray. Perhaps someone will prepare a cup of tea for them here and listen to their stories with sympathy." A few years later Kosugi—now with shaved head and dressed in white—returned to the Fudō Entrance to pour tea for pilgrim women.

CHAPTER 2. STAYING AT A *SHUKUBŌ* TEMPLE

1. For a listing of the temples in each of the nine *tani*, see David Gardiner, trans., *Koyasan*, a guide book (Kōyasan: Kongōbu-ji, 1992), 72–73.

2. The Kōyasan mausoleum is not to be confused with the far grander Tokugawa Mausoleum north of Tōkyō at Nikkō. Both, however, were intended to be places of worship, for shortly after his death Ieyasu was declared by imperial decree to be the Tōshō Daigongen, "Great Avatar Illuminating the East," a manifestation of the Buddha as Healer.

3. If we pronounce the *hrīh* aloud we will be taking a step toward our awakening, for the four constituent parts of the sound form a *mantra* that destroys delusion. See Adrian Snodgrass, *The Matrix and Diamond World Mandala in Shingon Buddhism* (New Delhi: International Academy of Indian Culture and Aditya Prakashan, 1988; reprint 1997), 54.

4. For many years Seichō had put off entering the religious life in order to support his parents. Once they were both dead he immediately quit his job as a chef in Tōkyō and came to Kōyasan.

5. The rectangular *tatami* mat, approximately three feet by six feet in size, has a 2.4-inch-thick straw base with a covering of tightly woven rush. The mats are easy on the feet, the body, and the eye, and have an appealing grassy odor. *Tatami no ue ni shinu* ("dying on *tatami*") is a commonly expressed desire of Japan's elderly, for it means dying at home in familiar surroundings rather than in the sterile environment of a hospital. On this important and intensely felt subject see Susan Orpett Long, "Becoming a Cucumber: Culture, Nature, and the Good Death in Japan and the United States," *Journal of Japanese Studies* 29, no. 1 (Winter 2003): 55–56.

6. This modest garden was designed by Iwata Hannojo, who also designed the immense sand and stone garden at Kongōbu-ji, which will be visited later.

7. *Shukubō* accommodations at Buddhist temples in Japan vary considerably in both price and quality. In 2006 the basic Kōyasan charge per guest for one night with dinner and breakfast was 9,500 yen (around eighty-five dollars), with the option of paying more, up to 15,000 yen. The extra money assures extra dinner dishes and the most beautiful available room, usually one directly off the inner temple garden. The higher price also provides a few extra souvenir items. At Kōyasan we found little incentive to pay more than the minimum.

8. Dan Furuya, *Kōyasan: sanjō toshi* (Ōsaka: Nambā Shuppan, 1983), 122.

9. The expanded translation of *itadaki-masu* is adapted from Hanayama Shōyū et al., eds., *Understanding Japanese Buddhism* (Tokyo: Japan Buddhist Federation, 1978), 106, 142.

10. *Fu* came from China in the fifteenth century and was added to the cuisine of tea by the tea master Sen no Rikyū. A small shop in a side lane of Gono-

muro-dani, the Fu-zen, has provided the temples of Kōyasan with *nama-fu* ("fresh *fu*") for more than one hundred and seventy years.

11. The *o-furo* is friendliest out on the Shikoku pilgrimage where fellow nude bathers will ask your age, shake your hand, and smile and nod as if establishing a lifelong bond. Sometimes a bather, emboldened by *sake*, will insist upon providing a shoulder massage, a real blessing if you've spent the day lugging a backpack. At Kōyasan the *o-furo* is rarely so informal.

12. This translation of Kōbō Daishi's poem is taken from Yoshito S. Hakeda, *Kūkai: Major Works, Translated, with an Account of His Life and a Study of His Thought* (New York: Columbia University Press, 1972), 100. The distinctive *bup-pō-sō* call is made by the *Konohazuku*, a type of owl, and not (as popularly believed) by the Broad-billed Roller erroneously named the *Buppōsō*. Although the *Konohazuku* is now almost extinct, Rev. Takagi Shingen, ex-president of Kōyasan University, reports having heard one sing at the Kōjin shrine near the summit of Kōjin-ga-take, not far from Kōyasan. See Ueda Akinari, *Ugetsu Monogatari*, trans. and ed. Leon Zolbrod (Tokyo: Charles E. Tuttle, 1977), 235–36 n. 304, and Yamashina Yoshimaro, *Birds in Japan: A Field Guide* (Tokyo: Tokyo News Service, 1961), 126.

13. An *ihai* is a memorial tablet on which is written the *kaimyō*, or Dharma name, of the deceased. This *kaimyō*, validated by the transmitted authority of the eight Shingon patriarchs, is awarded at the time a person receives the Buddhist precepts. Or, as seems most often to be the case today, it is assigned posthumously. Above the written *kaimyō* appears the Sanskrit letter *A*, emblem of Dainichi Buddha, into whose life the spirit of the deceased is now incorporated. If the deceased is very young, a Sanskrit *Ka* may be substituted for the *A*. The *Ka* represents Jizō Bodhisattva, the special comforter of those who die in infancy. On the back of each tablet is written the regular name of the deceased, the date of death, and the age at death. Each *ihai* stands on a golden lotus throne. See Arai Yūsei, *Shingon Esoteric Buddhism: A Handbook for Followers*, trans. George Tanabe, Seichō Asahi, and Shoken (Ana) Harada; ed. Eijun (Bill) Eidson (Kōyasan and Fresno: Kōyasan Shingon Mission, 1997), 107–108. Many of the *ihai* on the temple shelves were first kept on home family altars until the completion of the last required memorial service (usually in the thirty-third year).

14. In Buddhism generally, and perhaps especially in Shingon, meditation and ritual worship are not thought of as separate religious practices. Even the large-scale communal Shingon rituals described in this book have strong meditative components. The link is most clear in such private rituals as the *goma* (fire offering), *a-ji-kan* (letter *A* meditation), and *shakyō* (sūtra copying). Religious

chant (*shōmyō*), religious song (*goeika*), religious dance, flower arrangement, and the practice of tea also are viewed as meditative arts. Physical movement is no impediment to meditation. Climbing the pilgrim path to Kōyasan from Jison-in (the *chō-ishi-michi* trail) is simultaneously a ritual, a meditation, and a long mountain hike.

15. The *Hannya-rishu-kyō* exists in several versions. The one employed in the Shingon service is a translation into Chinese by the eighth-century Shingon patriarch Amoghavajra (705–774). Its Sanskrit title is the *Adhyardhashatikā-prajñā-pāramitā-sūtra* (or the *Prajñā-pāramitā-naya-shatapanchashatikā*). The Chinese title is the *Ta-lo-chin-kang-pu-k'ung-chen-shih-san-mo-yeh-ching*, usually abbreviated to *Li-ch'ü-ching*. The full formal Japanese name is the *Tairaku-kongō-fukū-shinjitsu-samaya-kyō*, which typically is abbreviated to *Hannya-rishu-kyō*, or simply *Rishu-kyō*. An appropriate English rendering of this shortened title would be "Wisdom Principle Sūtra." At least three English translations and commentaries are available: (1) Thomas Wayne Gelfman, "The *Rishukyō* and Its Influence on Kūkai: The Identity of the Sentient Being with the Buddha" (PhD diss., University of Wisconsin-Madison, 1979); (2) Taisen Miyata, trans. and annotator, *The Way of Great Enjoyment: Mahā-sukha-vajra-amogha-samaya-sūtra (Prajñā-pāramitā-naya)* (Sacramento: Northern California Koyasan Temple, 1989); (3) Ian Astley-Kristensen, *The Rishukyō* (Tring, UK: Institute of Buddhist Studies, 1991). I draw especially on Astley-Kristensen for my summary. Kūkai wrote an important, and radical, interpretation of the sūtra. For a discussion of Kūkai's formulation see Ryūichi Abé, *The Weaving of Mantra: Kūkai and the Construction of Esoteric Buddhist Discourse* (New York: Columbia University Press, 1999). Also see Shiba Rotaro, *Kukai the Universal: Scenes from His Life* (Kūkai no Fūkei), trans. Takemoto Akiko (New York: ICG Muse, 2003), 66–67, 240–42.

16. Astley-Kristensen, *The Rishukyō*, 163.

17. This partial "translation" of the "Light Mantra" is largely irrelevant, for, like nearly all esoteric mantra, it transcends rational understanding. The Sanskrit version of the mantra is written in Roman letters as *Om amogha-vairocana mahamudrā mani-padma-jvala pravarttaya hūm*. The Japanese recitation is *On abokya beirosha nō maka bodara mani handoma jimbara harabaritaya un*.

18. The presiding priest typically offers a brief message or sermon after the sūtra reading. Some temples give a tour of the sanctuary with special emphasis on the history and significance of selected sculptures and paintings, perhaps pausing a moment to identify the *ihai* of some famous person.

19. Since our last visit he has become principal of the Kōyasan Senior High School.

CHAPTER 3. THE LIFE AND LEGEND
OF KŌBŌ DAISHI (KŪKAI)

1. After Kōbō Daishi's death Chū-in became the residence of his successor, Shinzen, and Kōyasan's headquarters temple.

2. This is not the actual physical room where Kōbō Daishi's *nyūjō* began, of course. That room was lost to fire, as were a succession of replacements.

3. The statue is substantially fire damaged. When efforts were made to assure its future survival by placing it in the care of Kōyasan's Reihōkan museum, Ryūkō-in prevented this action by declaring it to be the temple *honzon.*

4. As George J. Tanabe Jr. remarks, "Take away the philosophy and Mount Kōya will still thrive, but remove its legends and the monastery will lose its call to the people." George J. Tanabe Jr., "The Founding of Mount Kōya and Kūkai's Eternal Meditation," in *Religions of Japan in Practice,* ed. George J. Tanabe Jr. (Princeton: Princeton University Press, 1999), 356. For a detailed English-language life of Kūkai "as a historical person," see Hakeda, *Kūkai: Major Works,* 13–60. For a brief but judicious separating out of the historical and legendary elements in the life, see chapter 11, "Master and Saviour," in Joseph M. Kitagawa, *On Understanding Japanese Religion* (Princeton: Princeton University Press, 1987), 182–202. Both of these studies include evaluations of the available biographical materials. Shiba Rotaro's informal "psychological" life has been published in English as *Kukai the Universal.* A 1934 compilation of Japanese-language biographies of Kūkai written prior to 1868 (*Kōbō Daishi Zenshū*) lists ninety-three works in 194 volumes. Shiba Rotaro estimates that a comparable mass of Kūkai biography has been published since 1868.

5. One Shikoku story has Kōbō Daishi's mother becoming pregnant after dreaming that a golden fish had entered her womb.

6. Today a statue of the seven-year-old Kūkai stands at the proposed jumping-off spot. Safety chains have been installed along the final stretch of trail.

7. Presumably the monk was Abbot Gonzō of Nara's Daian-ji, Kūkai's first important religious mentor. For a traditional account of Gonzō's sustained importance to Kūkai, see Ikeda Genta, *Kōbō Daishi Takahatsu no shi: Gonzō Daitoku* (Nara City: Nanto Daian-ji, 1977).

8. Hakeda, *Kūkai: Major Works,* 102. Most subsequent references to this source will be entered in the text using the abbreviation *MW.*

9. Professor Hakeda describes the *Sangō shīki* as "an epoch-making work in the history of Japanese literature and thought." Hakeda, *Kūkai: Major Works,*

24–25. Although comparing the "three teachings" was a common exercise in Chinese and Japanese intellectual circles at the time, Kūkai's performance was uniquely inventive and "sumptuous" (it includes references to some two hundred Chinese and Japanese literary documents). See Shiba, *Kukai the Universal*, 28–29. An original draft in Kūkai's own hand, a "National Treasure," is one of Kongōbu-ji's most valued possessions.

10. Biographer Shiba speculates that Kūkai's strong sexual appetite may have led him to believe he might be ill-suited for the priesthood. Thus, his delay in seeking ordination until just before the trip to China. Sexual urges also might explain in part Kūkai's special enthusiasm for the *Dainichi-kyō* and *Hannya-rishu-kyō*, sūtras that celebrate the presence of the passions. Or so it has been argued. See Shiba, *Kukai the Universal*, 82–83.

11. Hakeda, *Kūkai: Major Works,*121–122. "One who subsisted on half a grain a day" is an allusion to Shākyamuni, the supreme model for Buddhist mendicants.

12. Yamamoto Chikyō, *History of Mantrayana in Japan* (New Delhi: International Academy of Indian Culture, 1987), 23.

13. The device of concealing sacred scriptures or magical objects for later discovery by a uniquely endowed individual is common in Asian religious history and legend. At the Kume-dera temple today is a small stūpa said to be a duplicate of the one built by Zenmui. In the temple's Daishi-dō are statues of Zenmui and Kōbō Daishi seated side by side in equal honor. Some claim that Kōbō Daishi used Zemmui's Kume-dera stūpa as a model for the Great Stūpa at Kōyasan. See Kōno Seikō and F. M. Trautz, trans., *Der Grosse Stūpa auf dem Kōyasan* (Kōyasan:1934), 10.

14. One theory has a youthful Kūkai gaining skill in modern Chinese language (and technology) through encounters with Chinese technicians who were mining and refining various minerals in Japan's mountains. See Shiba, *Kukai the Universal*, 316 n. 2.

15. John Stevens, *The Marathon Monks of Mount Hiei* (Boston: Shambala, 1988), 19.

16. Ibid., 18.

17. Quoted by Alan G. Grapard, "Patriarchs of Heian Buddhism: Kūkai and Saichō," in *Great Historical Figures of Japan*, ed. Murakami Hyoe and Thomas J. Harper (Tokyo: Japan Culture Institute, 1978), 40.

18. A giant copy of this image in clay is the primary object of worship at hilltop Oka-dera temple in Nara Prefecture. Japanese travelers sometimes wear pictures of this Kannon about their necks to ward off danger at sea. See Mark MacWilliams, "Living Icons: *Reizō* Myths of the Saikoku Kannon Pilgrimage," *Monumenta Nipponica* 59, no. 1 (Spring 2004): 60.

19. A large Buddhist memorial hall named the Kūkai-Daishi Kinen-dō has been built near the beach where Kūkai landed. Its dedication in 1994 was attended by some three thousand people, including fifty-two Shingon priests and twenty lay members of Kōyasan Shingon-shū. See Kongōbu-ji, *Kōyasan,* bulletin no. 9: 1–4.

20. Ch'ang-an already had served as a physical model for six previous Japanese capitals and was then being used as a model for the construction of Emperor Kammu's new Heian-kyō.

21. Yamamoto, *History,* 29.

22. For an account of the method and significance of Kōbō Daishi's initiation under Hui-kuo, see Ryūichi Abé, *Weaving of Mantra,* 127–49.

23. Yamamoto, *History,* 31, 33, 107.

24. For an English translation of a portion of Kūkai's lament, together with commentary, see Konishi Jin'ichi, *The Early Middle Ages,* trans. Aileen Gatten, vol. 2 of *A History of Japanese Literature,* ed. Earl Miner (Princeton: Princeton University Press, 1986), 42–43.

25. Kūkai remains popular in modern Xi-an (formerly Ch'ang-an) partly because his fame draws affluent Japanese pilgrims and tourists to the city's splendidly rebuilt Ch'ing-lung (Qing Long), Hui-kuo's old temple. In the temple's beautiful new *hondō* statues of Kūkai and Hui-kuo sit side by side, pupil and master enshrined as examples of peaceful Chinese-Japanese cooperation. The eastern precinct of the temple is dominated by a pagoda-like stone and brick memorial to Kūkai constructed in 1982 and financed by Xi-an City and Japan's four Shikoku prefectures. The temple administration and staff are all secular government employees, so the general atmosphere is not particularly religious. During our visit in 1994 members of a Red Army platoon drilled back and forth across the lawn in front of the *hondō,* advancing and retreating on knees and elbows as they "fired" unloaded rifles. Government-influenced regional guidebooks make a point of Kūkai's scholarly interest in Chinese culture, mentioning his *Bumkyō hifu ron* (on the theory and phonology of T'ang poetry), his pioneering Chinese dictionary, and his works on Chinese calligraphy. Kūkai's indebtedness to Chinese Buddhism is largely ignored. See *Handbook for Xi'an* (Shaanxi Travel and Tourism Press, 1988), 276–78. Nevertheless, several students from China have studied at Kōyasan in recent years, their stated intention being to reintroduce Buddhism at home. See *Kōyasan,* bulletin no. 6 (1990), 4.

26. Abe Zentei, *The Life of Kōbō Daishi* (Osaka: Bukkyosha, 1936), 10.

27. This event is often pictured erroneously and grotesquely in illustrated narratives of Kōbō Daishi's life. The seated Kōbō Daishi is shown grasping five inked calligraphy brushes—one in each hand, two with the toes of his feet, one

with his teeth—and writing simultaneously five different lines in five different styles.

28. Abe Zentei, *Life of Kōbō Daishi*, 10. Perhaps the Chinese were prescient. The Chinese disciple whom Hui-kuo officially appointed to succeed himself soon died, and Esoteric Buddhism fell into decline. Within a few decades of Kūkai's departure all forms of Chinese Buddhism underwent a brutal suppression. In the year 845 alone some 4,500 Buddhist monasteries and 40,000 temples were destroyed and more than a quarter million monks and nuns driven from the religious life. There are, however, scholars who challenge the notion that the influence of Esoteric Buddhism all but disappeared in China. See Charles D. Orzech, "Seeing Chen-yen Buddhism: Traditional Scholarship and the Vajrayāna in China," *History of Religions* 29 (1989): 87–114.

29. Reportedly the *sanko* landed in a pine tree at the site of the future Kōyasan. The priests of Shōryū-ji temple in Shikoku will tell you that Kūkai also threw a *dokko* (a single-pointed *vajra*) while in China. This *dokko* landed in a pine tree at the site of the future Shōryū-ji.

30. *MW*, 142 n. 7. Kūkai's early return (after just two years instead of twenty) was made possible because of the unscheduled arrival in China in 806 of a special Japanese mission sent in response to news of the T'ang emperor's death. Had Kūkai not obtained a ride back with this mission he might well have died in China, for the next Japanese mission, after much delay, did not return from China until four years after Kūkai's final illness at Kōyasan. Kūkai's decision to return early presumably was motivated largely by his desire to introduce Esoteric Buddhism to Japan as quickly as possible. He also may have exhausted his funds. The collecting of materials had been costly, and there were other expenses—the lavish banquet for five hundred priests, for example.

31. Quoted by Stevens, *Marathon Monks*, 18.

32. However, the death of Emperor Kammu in 805, followed by the less supportive rule of Emperor Heizei, slowed Saichō's progress. For an account of Saichō's experience in China and his labor to advance Tendai upon his return to Japan, see Paul Groner, *Saichō: The Establishment of the Japanese Tendai School* (Berkeley: Berkeley Buddhist Studies Series, 1984), 38–87.

33. The priests at Kanzeon-ji assured us that this was the case.

34. Ueda Akinari, *Tales of the Spring Rain*, trans. Barry Jackman (Tokyo: Japan Foundation, 1975), 11.

35. For a discussion of Kūkai's calligraphy, see Shiba, *Kukai the Universal*, 256–67. Sonada Kōyū describes the art of Kūkai's brush as having "the resonance of the vast ocean." Sonada Kōyū, "Kūkai," in *Shapers of Japanese Buddhism*, trans. Gaynor Sekimori; ed. Yusen Kashiwahara and Kōyū Sonoda, 39–51 (Tokyo: Kōsei Publishing Company, 1994), 47.

36. Beatrice Lane Suzuki, *Impressions of Mahayana Buddhism* (Kyoto: Eastern Buddhist Society, 1940), 122.

37. For a translation and evaluation of several of Kūkai's poems about the attractions of the hermit life, see Paul Rouzer, "Early Buddhist Kanshi: Court, Country, and Kūkai," *Monumenta Nipponica* 59, no. 4 (Winter 2004): 446–59.

38. Stanley Weinstein, "The Beginnings of Esoteric Buddhism in Japan: The Neglected Tendai Tradition," *Journal of Asian Studies* 34, no. 1 (Nov. 1974): 186.

39. Ibid., 186–89.

40. Ibid.

41. Quoted by Grapard, "Patriarchs," 44.

42. Yamamoto, *History*, 45. For a balanced recent discussion of the Kūkai-Saichō relationship, see David L. Gardiner, "Transmission Problems: The Reproduction of Scripture and Kūkai's 'Opening' of an Esoteric Tradition," *Japanese Religions* 18, no. 1 (Jan. 2003): 5–68. In this article Gardiner also discusses Kūkai's "campaign" in 815 (through the wide dissemination of his *Kan'ensho* and accompanying esoteric texts) to make himself publicly known as Japan's primary transmitter of the new esoteric teaching. Also see Groner, *Saichō*, 77–87, and Shiba, *Kukai the Universal*, 240–55, for discussions of the exchange of letters between Kūkai and Saichō and the defection of Saichō's disciple Taihan.

43. Daigan and Alicia Matsunaga, *Foundation of Japanese Buddhism*, vol. 1 (Los Angeles and Tokyo: Buddhist Books International, 1974), 148.

44. Kūkai's comments on the various forms and mystical properties of language are found in two other works written during this period, *The Meanings of Sound, Word, and Reality* (*Shōji jissō gi*; 817 or 818) and *The Meanings of the Word Hūm* (*Ungi gi*; 817 or 818). For two translations of these texts together with introductory commentary see Hakeda, *Kūkai: Major Works* and Rolf W. Giebel, and Dale A. Todaro, trans., *Shingon Texts* (by Kūkai and Kakuban) (Berkeley: Numata Center for Buddhist Translation and Research, 2004). Kūkai also wrote while at Takaosan-ji *The Secret Treasure-house of the Mirrors of Poetry* (819) and *The Essentials of Poetry and Prose* (820), works that reflected his belletristic interests, especially in the areas of phonetics and the theory of poetry. Additionally, he was thinking through the basic arguments of what was to become his single greatest work, an examination of humankind's capacity for religious growth entitled *The Ten Stages of the Development of Mind* (830).

45. Shingon identifies three categories, or stages, of becoming a Buddha in one's present body (the *sanshu no sokushin jōbutsu*). First there is "intrinsic embodiment" (*rigu-jōbutsu*), the understanding that the self, the Buddha, mind and matter, the Six Great Elements, and all sentient and non-sentient beings form an inseparable and harmonious unity. Second, there is "transference of

power and response" (*kaji-jōbutsu*), a spiritual calming and healing achieved through one's surrender to the absolute compassion of the Buddha. The mechanisms of this transfer are the three mystic practices (the *sanmitsu*) of body, speech, and mind, of which the Shingon *A-ji-kan* meditation is a prime example. Third, there is "manifest attainment" (*kentoku-jōbutsu*), a full realization of the wisdom and compassion of Buddhahood, which is manifested primarily in the desire to assist all other sentient beings toward a state of enlightenment. See Oda Ryuko, *Kaji: Empowerment and Healing in Esoteric Buddhism* (Tokyo: Kinkeizan Shinjo-in Mitsumonkai Publishing, 1992), 44–45. Practically speaking, some people may not have the capacity to achieve Buddhahood in their present life, but the outlook remains optimistic. There is no reason for passivity or despair. The next rebirth may provide a better opportunity.

46. See Arai Yūsei, author, and Nakajima Kimi, illustrator, *Odaishi-sama: A Pictorial History of the Life of Kobo Daishi* (Kōyasan: Kōyasan Shuppansha, 1973), image 11. Also see Reihōkan Museum, *Kōyasan-no-nyorai-zō* (Figures of Nyorai [Tathāgata] at Kōyasan), Special Exhibition No. 17 of the Grand Treasure at Kōyasan (Kōyasan: Reihōkan, 1996), plate 60.

47. Yamamoto, *History*, 51–53.

48. Ibid., 53. One of the "many distant places" Kūkai considered seems to have been in the area of Mt. Futatabi immediately north of today's Kobe city. The priests at Dairyū-ji, a Shingon temple near the summit of the mountain, told us that Kūkai rejected the location because of Futatabi-san's insufficient water supply. Kūkai did, however, twice perform ascetic practices there—once prior to his trip to China, once after—thus the mountain's name, "Two Times." The primary trail to Mt. Futatabi is called the "Daishi Path." See Makoto Tanabe and Kris K. Shibuya, *An Exploration of Historic Kobe* (Kobe: Shimbun Shoin, 1985), 47–48.

49. Kariba-myōjin (God of the Hunting Field) also is known as Kōya-myōjin (God of Kōya) and as the Dog-Keeper of Nanzan (South Mountain).

50. Abe Zentei, *Life of Kōbō Daishi*, 14–15. The founder of Buddhism in Korea similarly was led to the site of his future monastery by two dogs.

51. Kūkai is believed to have built a shrine residence for Kariba-myōjin in Amano adjacent to goddess Niu's. In the Kamakura period the goddesses Kebi and Itsukushima (Benzaiten) also were enshrined there.

52. In another telling of the story Goddess Niu makes a poignant appeal to Kūkai: "At one time I was guilty of the sin of taking human life, and came here for refuge. What I pray is that you will take away my sin." Richard Ponsonby-Fane, *Studies in Shinto and Shrines* (Kyoto: Ponsonby Memorial Society, 1962), 272.

53. Sacred geography is a standard part of an esoteric temple's setting, especially when located in the mountains. Makino'o-san-ji, where Kūkai was tonsured, is said to be surrounded by a lotus display of eight mountain peaks. Murō-ji temple claims to be surrounded by nine peaks, one for each assembly of the Diamond Mandala, and eight valleys, one for each petal of the Womb Mandala.

54. Abe Zentei, *Life of Kōbō Daishi*, 16; also Elizabeth Anna Gordon, *The Lotus Gospel*, 2nd ed. (Tokyo: Waseda University, 1920), 201. In a carefully labeled drawing of Kōyasan this sword is shown resting directly beneath the Great Stūpa. Its hilt, which lies to the west, is associated with the Kongō-kai, or Diamond Realm. The eastward pointing blade is associated with the Taizō-kai, or Womb Realm. Thus the sword symbolically unites the two primary aspects of the Cosmic Buddha, Wisdom and Compassion. The drawing is reproduced inside the back cover of Nagasaka Yoshimitsu, *Junrei Kōyasan* (Shichosha, 1990).

55. Arthur Lloyd, *Creed of Half Japan: Historical Sketches of Japanese Buddhism* (London: Smith, Elder, 1911), 252. Another somewhat similar story tells us that as early as 808 Emperor Heizei, Saga's predecessor, summoned Kūkai to the capital in the hope that he had discovered in China a formula for ending a plague that was devastating the region. Kūkai proceeded to climb a mountain to the northeast of Heian-kyō and build there a great bonfire in the shape of the character *dai* ("great"). Almost at once the plague abated. The burning of a *dai* on the side of Mount Daimonji remains one of Kyōto's most famous annual events. See Gouverneur Mosher, *Kyoto: A Contemplative Guide* (Rutland, VT: Tuttle, 1964), 126, 271.

56. For a scholarly treatment of the rain-making story at Shinsen-en, see Brian D. Ruppert, "Buddhist Rainmaking in Early Japan: The Dragon King and the Ritual Careers of Esoteric Monks," *History of Religions* 42, no. 2 (Nov. 2002): 143–74. Today during periods of severe drought villages in the Kōyasan area send representatives up the mountain to purchase specially blest "sacred fire" to bring back for use in local rainmaking ceremonies. The borrowed fire is said to maintain its rain-producing potency for a week. Geoffrey Bownas, *Japanese Rainmaking, and Other Folk Practices* (London: Allen and Unwin, 1963), 113–15, 120.

57. Arai and Nakajima, *Odaishi-sama*, text for image no. 20.

58. One tradition has Kūkai's trip to China being financed in part by Shugendō mountain monks, the agreement being that upon his return he would share with them whatever information he gained about Chinese metallurgical skills. Subsequently (according to this story) Kōyasan itself became a center of technical instruction. Near the close of World War II the Japanese government reportedly scrutinized several ancient documents in an attempt to learn the

location of copper and mercury deposits believed to be known only to Kūkai and the mountain monks. See Takagi Toshio, *Mikkyō no hon*, Books Esoterica, vol. 1 (Tōkyō: Takagi Toshio, 1992), 34–35.

59. Hakeda, *Kūkai: Major Works*, 52–53. Among Kūkai's other practical assignments was the directorship of a shipbuilding yard at Ōwada, Settsu province (near today's Kobe).

60. Fourteen of the twenty-one original statues survive today, each a designated National Treasure. According to Tō-ji's own publicity all were "carved by Kōbō Daishi."

61. Hakeda, *Kūkai: Major Works*, 56; Yamamoto, *History*, 64.

62. Yamamoto, *History*, 66–70.

63. Lloyd, *Creed of Half Japan*, 254. Some historians have speculated that Kūkai himself founded the Inari shrine at Mount Fushimi, which later expanded nationwide to become the largest shrine system in Japan, with between thirty-two and forty-five thousand shrines, not counting the hundreds of thousands (if not millions) of private household Inari shrines.

64. Karen A. Smyers, *The Fox and the Jewel* (Honolulu: University of Hawai'i Press, 1999), 17.

65. Many sacred texts of medieval Shintō are attributed to Kūkai. There also is a legend that Kūkai was the first to carve Shintō gods in human form, among them a rendering of the god Hachiman (originally Emperor Ōjin). One story has the grateful Hachiman reciprocating by carving for Kūkai a self-portrait in which Hachiman represents himself as a Buddhist priest—that is, as Kūkai. Ryūichi Abé, *Weaving of Mantra*, 452.

66. Helen Craig McCullough, trans., *The Taiheiki: A Chronicle of Medieval Japan* (Rutland, VT, and Tokyo: Charles Tuttle, 1979), 374–79. For a version of the rainmaking competition in which Shubin (or Shūen) is not a villain, see Fowler, *Murōji*, 46–47.

67. Ryūichi Abé emphasizes the "nonsectarian manner in which [Kūkai] organized his nascent Shingon School, which enabled the school to transcend the boundary between the ancient Buddhist establishment of Nara and the new Buddhist community centered in Kyoto." The goal was a "new orthodoxy" that would be "an amalgamation of the esoteric and exoteric schools." *Weaving of Mantra*, 376.

68. *The Ten Stages* has been variously described as an analysis in depth of human consciousness, as a detailed outline of the various schools of Buddhism, as a compendium of Eastern thought, as an explanation of the process of enlightenment, and as an expression of the ultimate philosophy of the mandala (that is, the absolute equality of the phenomenal and the transcendent realms, of the self and the Buddha). See Okamura Keishin, "Kūkai's Philosophy as a Man-

dala," *The Eastern Buddhist*, New Series 18, no. 2: 19–34. For a discussion of the ten stage system in the context of Kūkai's philosophy of language see Paul O. Ingram, "The Power of Truth Words: Kūkai's Philosophy of Language and Hermeneutical Theory," *Pacific World*, New Series, no. 7 (Fall 1991): 14–25.

69. The overall ten stages may be subdivided into pre-Buddhist (1–3), Hīnayāna (4–5), Mahāyāna (6–9), and Vajrayāna (10). Kūkai is assumed to have found inspiration for this hierarchical system in the first chapter of the *Dainichi-kyō*. See Giebel and Todaro, *Shingon Texts*, 11.

70. Mikkyō scholar David L. Gardiner has written suggestively that "there is no doubt that from one perspective Kūkai sees all Buddhist teachings, indeed even all religions, as emanating from the Dharmakāya itself." David L. Gardiner, "Kūkai's View of Exoteric Buddhism in *Benkenmitsu nikyōron*," *Mikkyō Bunka Kenkyūsho Kiyō* [Bulletin of the Research Institute of Esoteric Buddhist Culture] 5 (March 1992): 198.

71. Miyasaka Yūshō, *Ningen no shujusō: Hizō hōyaku* (Various aspects of man: the precious key to the secret treasury) (Tokyo: Tsukuma Shobō, 1967), 263.

72. Bruno Petzold, "Japanese Buddhism: A Characterization, Part 6 (Kōbō Daishi)," in *Mikkyō: Kōbō Daishi Kūkai and Shingon Buddhism*. Special Issue (October 1990) of *Mikkyō Bunka Kenkyūsho Kiyō* [Bulletin of the Research Institute of Esoteric Buddhist Culture], (Kōyasan University), 75.

73. Yamamoto, *History*, 74.

74. For a description and analysis of the *Go-shichinichi-no-mishuhō* (usually shortened to *Mishuhō*) see Brian D. Ruppert, *Jewel in the Ashes: Buddha Relics and Power in Early Medieval Japan* (Cambridge and London: Harvard University Press, 2000), 102–35, and Ryūichi Abé, *Weaving of Mantra*, 344–57.

75. Abe Zentei, *Life of Kōbō Daishi*, 28–29.

76. Quoted by George J. Tanabe Jr., "Founding of Mount Kōya," 358.

77. There are Shingon priests today who believe Kūkai's final trance-like state, while extraordinary, was nevertheless "natural" and capable of duplication. Head priest Miyatake Mineo of Kōyasan's Hōki-in suggests it was an action Kūkai carefully trained for throughout his life. As a child he practiced *shashin-no-higan*, a prayerful wish to sacrifice one's life on behalf of others, as depicted in the story of his leap from a cliff near his boyhood home. The next step, pursued during early manhood, was *metsujin-no-jō*, a training during which one surrenders utterly to the expectation of death. Miyatake relates how on three occasions in his own life he himself reached a state similar to Kūkai's *nyūjō*, entering a depth of meditation where both the pulse and the breathing stop. Miyatake warns the reader, however, that the practice can seriously injure one's health. He also notes that *nyūjō* does not, of itself, constitute the condition of *sokushin*

jōbutsu, or "bodily Buddhahood," the highest goal of Shingon practice. See Soeda and Miyatake, *Odaishi-sama wa Ikiteriru*, 20–24. Shākyamuni's death is thought to have been quite different from Kūkai's *nyūjō*, although one of Shākyamuni's disciples, Anuruddha, described the master as having entered voluntarily into a deep meditation. See H. W. Schumann, *The Historical Buddha*, trans. from the German by M. O'C. Walshe (London, New York, etc.: Arkana, 1989), 250.

78. The above summary of the death and entombment of Kūkai is a composite of several popular sources, all of which vary in some details. For a translation of an early account, dated 968, see George J. Tanabe Jr., "Founding of Mount Kōya," 354–59. Tanabe observes that the most salient legends associated with Kūkai did not have their origins in the piety of peasants and farmers, but were supplied and propagated by educated scholar priests. Some historians assert that contemporary documents indicate the cremation of Kūkai's body immediately after his death. See, for example, Shimode Sekiyo in Kazuo Kasahara, ed., *A History of Japanese Religion*, trans. Paul McCarthy and Gaynor Sekimori (Tokyo: Kosei, 2001), 111.

79. Poem adapted from Petzold, "Japanese Buddhism," 79.

80. Ex-Emperor Uda (r. 889–897; d. 931) was somewhat similarly honored. When he climbed Kōyasan in the year 900 to receive initiation into the priesthood, Kōbō Daishi is said to have appeared at the altar to serve as the officiating priest.

CHAPTER 4: TWELVE CENTURIES ON THE MOUNTAIN

1. The argument is sometimes made that Saichō's personal failure to master Esoteric Buddhism and produce a fully integrated Tendai doctrine actually worked to Tendai's long-term advantage, for it forced Saichō's successors to continue the process of doctrinal development. "In contrast, the Shingon School with its more complete doctrinal system often seemed to languish after Kūkai's time." Groner, *Saichō*, 304–306.

2. Yamasaki Taikō, *Shingon: Japanese Esoteric Buddhism*, trans. and adapted by Richard and Cynthia Peterson; ed. Yasuyoshi Morimoto and David Kidd (Boston and London: Shambhala, 1988), 38.

3. Also in 866, the year Saichō received the title of Daishi (Dengyō Daishi), his second successor at Mt. Hiei, Ennin (794–864), only two years dead, received the same honor, becoming Jikaku Daishi. Kūkai did have one ear-

lier posthumous recognition. When Shinzei, after nine years at Tō-ji, received the title of *sōjō*, or archbishop (the highest status yet achieved by a Shingon priest), he protested that this title should first have gone to his master, Kūkai. In response the court, in 856, awarded Kūkai the title of *dai-sōjō*, or great archbishop, at that time the supreme rank in the Buddhist hierarchy.

4. Adapted from Arai and Nakajima, *Odaishi-sama*, text for image no. 26.

5. Kitagawa and Tsuchida, *Heike,* 613–15. We are told that by subsequent physical contact with Junyū's hand all the sūtras at his home temple, Ishiyama-dera, became similarly fragrant. And they remain fragrant to the present day. Junyū never fully recovered from his inability to see Kūkai, however. Attributing his failure to some deep personal unworthiness, he later denied his own disciple full priestly status. Kitabatake Chikafusa, *A Chronicle of the Gods and Sovereigns (Jinnō shōtōki)*, trans. H. Paul Varley (New York: Columbia University Press, 1980), 177–78.

6. Buddhist mountain temples were especially prone to devastating fires. For an account of the great fire on Tendai's Mount Hiei in 966 and the long period of reconstruction that followed, see Paul Groner, *Ryōgen and Mount Hiei: Japanese Tendai in the Tenth Century* (Honolulu: University of Hawai'i Press, 2002), 167–89.

7. A further contributing factor to the decision to close the mountain was the revelation that Governor Kagamasa of Kii province, together with his successors in office, had been embezzling Kōyasan's revenue. Insufficient funds were left to support the few priests who could still be housed.

8. Jōyo was his posthumous name. The name he himself assumed was Kishin, "one who prays for parents."

9. Yamamoto, *History*, 128, 138–39. Found today on a central pillar of Kōyasan's Great Gate (Daimon) is a message very similar to Nigai's: "Day by day [in the valley beyond this gate] the gods and Buddhas are never absent." Hinonishi Shinjō, "The *Hōgō* (Treasure Name) of Kōbō Daishi and the Development of Beliefs Associated with It," trans. William Londo, *Japanese Religions* 27, no. 1 (Jan. 2002): 9.

10. See William H. McCullough and Helen Craig McCullough, trans. and notes, *A Tale of Flowering Fortunes* (Stanford: Stanford University Press, 1980), 2: 513.

11. Michinaga expressed the hope that his buried sūtras would "gush forth on their own accord from that very ground" when Miroku, the Buddha of the Future, preached his inaugural sermon there. See Robert F. Rhodes, "Recovering the Golden Age: Michinaga, Jōkei and the Worship of Maitreya in Medieval Japan," *Japanese Religions* 23, nos. 1 and 2 (Jan. 1998): 62. In 1964 several

buried scrolls of scripture were uncovered during excavations for the new Lantern Hall at Kōbō Daishi's tomb. The nun who contributed these scrolls (in 1114) similarly prayed that they remain under Kōbō Daishi's protection until Miroku's arrival. Yamamoto, *History*, 139, 183. Buried sūtras, called *maikyō*, might also be intended for some future time (*mappō*) when knowledge of the Dharma had been corrupted or died out. Or they might serve a future generation that was better able to understand their contents.

12. For a speculative account of Jōyo's revival of Kōyasan and also of Michinaga's visit there, see William Londo, "The 11th Century Revival of Mt. Kōya: Its Genesis as a Popular Religious Shrine," *Japanese Religions* 27, no. 1 (Jan. 2002): 10–40.

13. Kitagawa, *Heike*, 638–41.

14. Kato Shūson, Shirasu Masaka, and Chin Shunshin, eds., *Kōyasan Monogatari* (Tokyo: Sekai Bunkasha, 1989), 60.

15. Burials on the mountain, which began at about this time, also were designed to provide admission to Miroku's heaven. The attendants of Emperor Horikawa (d. 1107), knowing him to be a zealous devotee of Miroku, buried a lock of his hair before Kōbō Daishi's tomb. In 1160, in fulfillment of a deathbed request, the bones of Bifukumon'in, Emperor Toba's favorite consort, were buried on Kōyasan, this in addition to a tomb built for her at the palace.

16. For a general discussion of the hijiri, their lifestyles, their beliefs, and the manner in which the term itself has been employed, see Christoph Kleine, "Hermits and Ascetics in Ancient Japan: The Concept of *Hijiri* Reconsidered," *Japanese Religions* 22, no. 2 (July 1997): 1–46. See also Kuroda Toshio, "Buddhism and Society in the Medieval Estate System," trans. Suzanne Gay, *Japanese Journal of Religious Studies* 23, nos. 3–4 (1996): 312–19.

17. One measure of Amida worship at Kōyasan at this time is the fact that one-third of the mountain's 530 temples had images of Amida as their *honzon*. Source: *Kōyasan-no-Jōdo*, pamphlet published by Kōyasan's Reihōkan museum for a Pure Land exhibit, Summer 1995. For an enumeration of some of the reasons for the rise of the Pure Land cult at Kōyasan, see Joseph Kitagawa, *Religion in Japanese History* (New York and Oxford: Columbia University Press, 1990), 78–79, and notes.

18. See Kitagawa, *Religion in Japanese History*, 79. An English translation of Kakuban's *Go-rin-ku-ji-myō-hi-mitsu-shaku* (*The Illuminating Secret Commentary on the Five Cakras and the Nine Syllables*; also known as *The Secret Meditation on Rapid Enlightenment and Birth in the Pure Land*), which contains Kakuban's argument concerning the Pure Land-Shingon connection, may be

found in Giebel and Todaro, *Shingon Texts*, 239–328. An extensive study in English of Kakuban's life and thought is Henny van der Veere, *A Study into the Thought of Kōgyō Daishi Kakuban, with a Translation of His "Gorin kuji myō himitsushaku"* (Leiden: Hotei Publishing, 2000). For a compact summary of the promotion of the "Shingon *nembutsu*" in the generations following Kakuban, see George J. Tanabe Jr., "Kōyasan in the Countryside: The Rise of Shingon in the Kamakura Period," in *Re-Visioning "Kamakura" Buddhism*, ed. Richard K. Payne (Honolulu: University of Hawai'i Press: 1998), 48–53.

19. During this period Kakuban wrote his famous "Mitsugon-in Confession," a prayer of contrition that is recited as part of the daily service at all Shingi-Shingon temples. The faulty conduct lamented in the confession frequently is interpreted as describing a spiritual laxity common to Kōyasan at the time, a condition Kakuban sought to correct. See Giebel and Todaro, *Shingon Texts*, 251–55, for an English translation.

20. For a discussion and translation of this text, see James H. Sanford, "Amida's Secret Life: Kakuban's *Amida hishaku*," in *Approaching the Land of Bliss: Religious Praxis in the Cult of Amitābha*, ed. Richard K. Payne and Kenneth K. Tanaka (Honolulu: University of Hawai'i Press, 2004), 120–38. See also Inagaki Hisao, "The Esoteric Meaning of 'Amida' by Kakuban," *Pacific World*, New Series, no. 10 (1994): 102–15.

21. In the late sixteenth century Negoro-ji was overrun and almost completely destroyed by an army directed by the national unifier Toyotomi Hideyoshi. Although the temple retains today only a fraction of its past glory, it is still much worth visiting, especially for the Great Stūpa that survived Hideyoshi's attack (a National Treasure with bullet-scarred walls). The burial mound that holds Kakuban's ashes is situated in a quiet area at the rear of the temple grounds. An important temple possession is a statue of Fudō Myō-ō thought to have a dramatic link to Kōyasan. According to tradition this statue originally resided in a Fudō-dō near Kōyasan's Fudō Entrance, a hall to which Kakuban fled for protection on the night of his expulsion. When a pursuing mob broke into the hall, Kakuban, who long since had mastered the powers of Fudō, transformed himself into a statue identical to the one enshrined there. The leader of the mob, faced with twin images of the deity, impulsively stabbed at one with his sword. When blood poured from the wound the leader and his followers left the hall, confident Kakuban had received a fatal injury. But it was the sculpted Fudō, not Kakuban, that had been wounded. Kakuban escaped from the mountain immediately, taking the life-saving statue with him to Negoro-ji, where it still may be visited. The statue is said to have been carved by

Kōbō Daishi. See "Kiri Momi Fudō," *Sei Ai* (Jan. 1996), 4. Also see "Guide to Negoroji," a Negoro-ji visitors pamphlet. For a slightly different version of the story see van der Veere, *Kōgyō Daishi Kakuban*, 42.

22. In 1690, the five hundred and fiftieth anniversary of Kakuban's expulsion from Kōyasan, the imperial court awarded Kakuban the posthumous title of Kōgyō Daishi ("Great Master Who Revived the Teachings").

23. Miyajima had long been associated with Kōbō Daishi, primarily through his having performed austerities on the summit of its Mount Misen.

24. Kitagawa and Tsuchida, *Heike*, 175–76. The *Heike Monogatari*, a prose epic of the Gempei war, is the primary chronicle of Kiyomori's life. The work also reviews much of the life and legend of Kōbō Daishi.

25. Kitagawa and Tsuchida, *Heike*, 368–69.

26. Although the memorial ceremonies were performed by Buddhist priests, the concept of dead spirits seeking vengeance upon the living is derived from Japanese folk belief and is not consistent with orthodox Buddhist thought.

27. Some of Kōyasan's vassals resorted to planting "secret fields" in order to escape paying the mountain's tax demands. See Tanabe Jr., "Kōyasan in the Countryside," 45.

28. The Nichiren presence at Kōyasan is indicated by a granite shaft erected at the end of an obscure lane in Gonomuro-dani. On the shaft is carved the statement, "Memorial site where Nichiren came to study." Also carved there are the seven syllables *Namu myōho renge kyō* ("Homage to the Lotus Sūtra of the Wonderful Law"), a devout recitation of which, according to Nichiren's teaching, guarantees liberation from the cycles of birth and death. Not coincidentally, five small priest lodgings that formerly existed at this site were named Myōchi-bō, Hōchi-bō, Renchi-bō, Kechi-bō, and Kyōchi-bō. The combined initial syllables of the five names form the saving mantra. To the millions of modern followers of Nichiren-shū and Sokka Gakkai, Nichiren is a Buddha and the equal of Shākyamuni. In life he was notorious for his condemnation of Shingon (as well as of nearly every other contemporary Japanese Buddhist sect), once referring to Kōbō Daishi as "a devil." But during his early career, before the *Lotus Sutra* became all in all to him, Nichiren admired Kōbō Daishi and placed esoteric Shingon teachings above even the *Lotus*.

29. At the time of his first pilgrimage to Kōyasan Ippen already was distributing *o-fuda* on which were printed the seven characters *na-mu-a-mi-da-bu-tsu*, a practice he apparently adopted from Kōya-hijiri who distributed similar *o-fuda* printed from wood blocks they claimed had been carved by Kōbō Daishi. See Dennis Hirota, "The Illustrated Biography of Ippen," in *Buddhism in Practice*, Donald S. Lopez Jr., ed. (Princeton: Princeton University Press, 1995), 567–69.

30. Chōgen was a tireless performer of public works. After three visits to China to study Chinese engineering and architecture he was assigned the task of rebuilding Tōdai-ji, destroyed by Kiyomori in the Gempei War.

31. Devices to protect oneself during such years are called *yakudoshi no minzoku*. See Sachiko Misawa Kanai, "Development of the Kobo Daishi Cult and Beliefs in Japan and Their Connection with the Shikoku Pilgrimage," *Young East* 6, no. 2 (Spring 1980), 29–30. The reason for having eighty-eight temples has been attributed by some to the fact that the three major *yakudoshi*—age forty-two for men, thirty-three for women, and thirteen for children—add up to eighty-eight. The number also may be a reference to the eighty-eight delusions that the journey is designed to correct. Even today, in rural Japan, reaching one's eighty-eighth birthday is considered an event of great good fortune, calling for a village-wide celebration.

32. In all likelihood, the full Shikoku pilgrimage route was established well after Kōbō Daishi's time, probably starting out as a modest linkage of several temples in the area of his birthplace at Zentsū-ji. Cape Muroto and Mount Tairyū, locations known to have been used by Kōbō Daishi for the *Gumonji-hō* ritual, presumably were added soon after. Gradually, other sites were included until the full eighty-eight-temple circuit was established. One orthodox view perceives the pilgrimage to be divided into progressive stages of anticipated spiritual transformation. The first series of temples is known as the *dōjō* of awakening faith, the second the *dōjō* of discipline, the third the *dōjō* of enlightenment, and the last the *dōjō* of entering Nirvāna. See Taisen Miyata, *A Henro Pilgrimage Guide to the Eighty-Eight Temples of Shikoku, Japan* (Sacramento: Northern California Koyasan Temple, 1984), 10.

33. A number of other religious bodies also assumed credit for inducing the timely typhoon winds, but none with the credibility accorded to Kōyasan's Nami-kiri Fudō. The statue was appealed to again at the time of the Meiji Restoration and during the two world wars of the twentieth century.

34. The success of Kōyasan's policy of working both sides in the conflict is discussed in Mikael S. Adolphson's *The Gates of Power: Monks, Courtiers, and Warriors in Premodern Japan* (Honolulu: University of Hawai'i Press, 2000), 323–45.

35. Yamamoto, *History*, 150.

36. As a consequence of their suppression very few genuine Tachikawa texts survive into modern times. A detailed account of Tachikawa-ryū's most notorious ceremony, the "Skull Ritual," exists only in a condemnatory document written by an opponent. As described, the practitioner of the Skull Ritual begins by covering a human skull with multiple layers of laquer until it resembles a living head. The skull is then wiped repeatedly with fresh liquid (both

blood and semen) derived from sexual intercourse with a "beautiful and willing woman." One hundred and twenty layers of liquid are specified. During this process, which requires months, the practitioner repeatedly passes the skull through incense while chanting a "spirit-returning" mantra. At night he takes the increasingly lifelike skull into his bed to keep it "gestating." After eight years of ritual prayer and devotion the practitioner may receive certain supernatural powers, the greatest of which is to hear the skull speak. See James H. Sanford, "The Abominable Tachikawa Skull Ritual," *Monumenta Nipponica*, 46, no. 1 (Spring 1991), 1–20. For further information on Tachikawa-ryū, see John Stevens, *Lust for Enlightenment: Buddhism and Sex* (Boston and London: Shambala, 1990), especially pages 80–85. Just how large the Tachikawa movement was, and how genuinely scandalous it may have been, is now difficult to determine. Presumably the teachings got their best hearing in small local settings among the already predisposed (among some hijiri, for example) rather than at major Shingon centers such as Kōyasan and Tō-ji. For suggestions that the influence may have been more widespread, see Susan Blakeley Klein, *Allegories of Desire: Esoteric Literary Commentaries of Medieval Japan* (Cambridge and London: Harvard University Press, 2002), 150–57. There is virtually nothing in orthodox Shingon Buddhism today that could be described as sexually provocative, although some have nominated the "elephant god" Shō-ten (Sk. Ganesha), often depicted in the form of identical elephant-headed human figures locked together in a face-to-face embrace. This image is said to depict the union of the spiritual "soul" of the universe with the universe's primordial material essence—that is, the union of Dainichi of the Diamond Realm with Dainichi of the Womb Realm. Kōbō Daishi usually is credited with the introduction of Shō-ten to Japan, where the god was used as a remover of evil hindrances. See Dwijendra Nath Bakshi, *Hindu Divinities in Japanese Buddhist Pantheon* (Calcutta: Benten, 1979), 38; Benoytosh Bhattacharyya, *An Introduction to Buddhist Esoterism* (Delhi: Motilal Banarsidass, 1980), 118; and Snodgrass, *Matrix and Diamond World Mandalas*, 537–40. A statue of Shō-ten is an important object of worship in Shingon's annual seven-day Mishuhō ceremony at Tō-ji. In this setting the twinned god is discretely covered—or at least it is covered when the public is admitted to the sanctuary at the close of the seven days.

37. Herman Ooms, *Tokugawa Ideology: Early Constructs, 1570–1680* (Princeton: Princeton University Press, 1985), 19.

38. Yamamoto, *History*, 152.

39. James Murdoch, *A History of Japan* (Kobe: Chronicle, 1903), 2: 164.

40. On the destruction of Hieizan see Neil McMullin, *Buddhism and the State in Sixteenth-Century Japan* (Princeton: Princeton University Press, 1984),

145–51, 356, and Michael Cooper, *They Came to Japan: An Anthology of European Reports on Japan, 1543–1640* (Berkeley: University of California Press, 1965), 98–99.

41. McMullin, *Buddhism and the State*, 137–38.

42. Ibid., 213.

43. Such pledges usually ended in oaths of terrible elaboration, something like: *If I violate this pledge, the divine punishment of Brahmā and Indra, of the Four Heavenly Kings, of all the great and small kami of the nation, the kami of the four shrines of Amano and their relatives and attendants, Kōbō Daishi and Kongōsatta, and all the gods of the Dual Mandala will enter through the 84,000 pores of my body, and I shall be in this life afflicted with white leprosy and black leprosy, and in the next life fall into the limitless hell with no opportunity to issue therefrom. Thus I swear.* See Asakawa Kan'ichi, "The Life of a Monastic *Shō* in Medieval Japan," in *Land and Society in Medieval Japan*, ed. Asakawa Kan'ichi (Tokyo: Japan Society for the Promotion of Science, 1965), 184. The above italicized passage was adapted from this source.

44. The size of Nobunaga's army is placed at an astounding, and very questionable, 137,000. Granted, at this time Japan's population was four times England's, and most of the nation's enterprises, whether military, ceremonial, or constructional, seem to have involved large numbers, but 137,000 is excessive if only because of the logistical problems such a number would present. What does seem likely is that Nobunaga, with Kōyasan isolated and without a significant ally, counted on a quick victory.

45. Yamamoto, *History*, 154.

46. Asakawa, "Life of a Monastic *Shō*," 189.

47. For a general discussion of Nobunaga's attack on Kōyasan, see Hotta Shinkai, *Kōyasan: Kongōbuji* (Kōyasan: Gakusei-sha, 1972), 141–50.

48. At this point Nobunaga had achieved domination over thirty-one of Japan's sixty-six provinces.

49. Cooper, *They Came to Japan*, 103.

50. Kōyasan's "ancient domain," or *kyū-ryō*, was a ring of approximately thirty thousand acres that surrounded the summit ridge.

51. So much of Kōyasan was rebuilt under Ōgo that Hideyoshi suggested the mountain be called *Mokujiki no Kōya*, "the Wood-Eating Saint's Kōyasan." McMullin, *Buddhism and the State*, 392.

52. Hideyoshi promised that the metal recovered from the surrendered weapons would be used in the rivets of a gigantic Great Buddha he was constructing in the capital, thus assuring the donors peace in this life and salvation in the next. Mary Elizabeth Berry, *Hideyoshi* (Cambridge and London: Harvard University Press, 1982), 104.

53. The warrior-monks often were described as a bad lot who introduced gambling, thievery, and even murder to the monastery halls. Kōbō Daishi would not have been pleased. Asakawa, "Life of a Monastic *Shō*," 186 n. 78.

54. Berry, *Hideyoshi*, 212.

55. Hideyoshi later had a celebratory dance added to the end of the *Kōya-mōde* drama, a dance he performed himself. Donald Keene, *Some Japanese Portraits* (Tokyo, New York, and San Francisco: Kodansha International, 1978), 68–69.

56. Visitors to Kongōbu-ji's *Yanaginoma* ("Willow Room") will find a sign over the door that tells of Hidetsugu's fate. Hideyoshi is not mentioned, but everyone knows the story. Hidetsugu's place of burial is a remote spot in the woods behind Kōdai-in in Gonomuro-dani. At the modest grave we found coin offerings and a bundle of fresh *Kōya-maki* branches intended to quiet Hidetsugu's still-troubled spirit.

57. Murdoch, *History of Japan*, 2:383–84; George Sansom, *A History of Japan: 1334–1615* (Stanford, Stanford University Press, 1961), 367.

58. Murdoch, *History of Japan*, 2:385–86.

59. In his will Hideyoshi asked that a shrine be built for him in Kyōto next to his own Great Buddha and near to his mausoleum. He asked also that he be designated the nation's primary *daimyōjin* ("great august deity"). See Ooms, *Tokugawa Ideology*, 50. These wishes were carried out, and for a time the shrine, the mausoleum, and the Great Buddha became a pilgrimage center for a daimyōjin cult. But Ieyasu soon put an end to this arrangement and, at his own death, usurped Hideyoshi's claims to divinity. Hideyoshi's Great Buddha fell in an earthquake. All that is left today of Hideyoshi's immense temple (Hōkō-ji), built at enormous expense, is a great bell, which visitors may strike after paying a small fee.

60. Yamamoto, *History*, 155–56.

61. Yamasaki, *Shingon*, 47.

62. Monasticism itself held little interest for the Tokugawa, whose social and political philosophy was almost exclusively Neo-Confucian.

63. David M. Earl, *Emperor and Nation in Japan: Political Thinkers of the Tokugawa Period* (Seattle: University of Washington Press, 1964), 236–37, 87–88, 92.

64. Hotta, *Kōyasan Kongobu-ji*, 170–72.

65. Quoted by James Edward Ketelaar, *Of Heretics and Martyrs in Meiji Japan: Buddhism and Its Persecutions* (Princeton: Princeton University Press, 1990), 33.

66. Quoted by Ketelaar, *Of Heretics and Martyrs*, 43.

67. Helen Hardacre, *Shintō and the State, 1868–1988* (Princeton: Princeton University Press, 1989), 102–103.

68. In 1883 the government allowed the reinstitution of the Mishuhō (short for *Go-shichinichi-no-mishuhō*), but henceforth it had to be held at Tō-ji rather than at the imperial palace. The specific venue there was the Kanjō-in, first built in 1069 and modeled after Hui-kuo's Seiryū-ji in Ch'ang-an. Today the primary Mishuhō participants are the chief priests from each of the major subsects of Shingon, including the Buzan and Chizan branches of Shingi-shingon. The goals of the seven-day ceremony, as defined by Kōbō Daishi, are the promotion of the personal health and safety of the emperor, the preservation of the imperial succession, the peace and harmony of the state, and the fruitful harvest of the farmlands. No outside observers may attend the ceremony, but hundreds of priests, student monks, and laity gather just before noon on the last day (January 14) to watch the final exit of the high priests along an elevated and sanctified white gravel path. Included in this processional is a trunk that contains the reigning emperor's robe, which had been consecrated twice daily during the ceremony. The presence of the robe reflects in part the Japanese esoteric theory that the emperor, the goddess Amaterasu, and the Great Sun Buddha compose a triple alliance of shared divinity, and that the Imperial Law and the Buddhist Law are intertwined and mutually dependent. See David Moerman, "The Ideology of Landscape and the Theater of State: Insei Pilgrimage to Kumano [1090–1220]," *Japanese Journal of Religious Studies* 24, nos. 3–4 (1997): 364–66. At the conclusion of the processional the visitors are invited to make a brief tour of Kanjō-in to view the multiple ceremonial altars and objects of worship.

69. The usual assumption that Emperor Komei's 1866 funeral was entirely Buddhist in nature has been challenged recently by Edmund T. Gilday, "Bodies of Evidence: Imperial Funeral Rites and the Meiji Restoration," *Japanese Journal of Religious Studies* 27, nos. 3 and 4 (2000), 284–89.

70. A retrospective on the Miwa Shrine written in 1873 conscientiously avoids mention of any Buddhist elements in its long history. Hardacre, *Shintō and the State*, 81–82.

71. As a replacement for these lost protectors the Kōyasan administration took the Nami-kiri Fudō from Nan-in temple and installed him in the Garan's Sannō-in, a hall that previously had served as the *haiden* (votive hall) to the Myōjin-sha. In the Myōjin-sha itself were installed sacred Buddhist scriptures brought up the mountain from the "purified" Amano shrine, which had been stripped of all its Buddhist elements. See Reihōkan Museum, *Sacred Treasures of Mount Kōya: The Art of Japanese Shingon Buddhism* (Kōyasan: Kōyasan Reihōkan Museum, 2002), 170.

72. An account of some of the local dynamics of the attempted disentanglement of Buddhism and Shintō is found in Helen Hardacre, *Religion and Society in Nineteenth-Century Japan: A Study of the Southern Kantō Region, Using Late Edo and Early Meiji Gazateers* (Ann Arbor: Center for Japanese Studies, University of Michigan, 2002), 150–212.

73. For a historical analysis of the creation of modern "Shintō" see Sarah Thal, "A Religion That Was Not a Religion: The Creation of Modern Shinto in Nineteenth-Century Japan," in *The Invention of Religion: Rethinking Belief in Politics and History*, ed. Derek Peterson and Darren Walhof (New Brunswick, NJ, and London: Rutgers University Press, 2002), 100–14.

74. When offering itself as the one proper leader in a projected new pan-Asian political economy, the Tōkyō government argued that Japan more than any other nation had shown fidelity to the essence of Asian spiritualism—that is, Japan had embraced and preserved Buddhism.

75. Many Buddhist observers at this time feared that Christianity, with its aura of advanced Western technology, democratic institutions, and achievement in the arts (especially music), was going to pose a greater threat than had Shintō.

76. Toki added that Buddhism had the advantage of embracing a universal principle of "emptiness" (Sk. *shūnyatā*; J. *kū*) that resolved all problems of duality, empirical forms, and conditionality. Back home, the Shingon journal *Dentō* anticipated that the Christians in the Parliament audience would fail to grasp the Buddhist truths that Toki and others were seeking to convey to them. What was needed, the journal suggested, was the introduction to the West of a great Dharma teacher such as Kūkai. The "savior of the Japanese nation" could be the savior of the world. For two helpful accounts of the Parliament, see Ketelaar, *Of Heretics and Martyrs*, 159–64, and Judith Snodgrass, *Presenting Japanese Buddhism to the West* (Chapel Hill and London: University of North Carolina Press, 2003), 198–221. For more on Toki, see Antony Boussemart, "Toki Hōryū (1854–1923), a Shingon Monk and the 1893 Chicago World's Parliament of Religions," *Japanese Religions* 27, no. 2 (July 2002): 179–94.

77. Kato et al., *Kōyasan Monogatari*, 9–10.

78. Hotta, *Kōyasan Kongobu-ji*, 181–90.

79. The priests and monks then living on the mountain numbered about seven hundred.

80. Ironically, although the stated Occupation policy was to eliminate all vestiges of militaristic State Shintō while simultaneously encouraging the rehabilitation of Buddhist organizations, many of the imposed economic reforms—such as rural land reforms, changes in the inheritance laws, the abolition of the custodial forest system, and alteration of the family *danka* requirement—had a seriously damaging effect on temple incomes both at Kōyasan and in the Japan-

ese Buddhist world generally. William P. Woodard, *The Allied Occupation of Japan 1945–1952 and Japanese Religions* (Leiden: E. J. Brill, 1972), 200–201.

81. The Kōyasan Shingon Sect (Kōyasan Shingon-shū) was given its full independence in 1946, one year after the end of the Pacific War. Today the sect is made up of approximately 3,800 affiliated Shingon temples located around the nation and overseas. Every four years a senior priest is elected to serve as administrative head (*kanchō*) of the sect; the *kanchō* also fills the role of "master of [Kōyasan] mountain," or *zasu*. The *hōin*, who is chosen annually to act as Kōyasan's spiritual and liturgical stand-in for Kōbō Daishi, has only ceremonial duties. Today there are in all some forty different Shingon subsects, with three groupings of particular historical importance: (1) the "old teachings" group, with major headquarters at Kongōbu-ji, Tō-ji, Kajū-ji, Daigo-ji, Ninna-ji, Sennyū-ji, and Daikaku-ji; (2) the "new teachings" (or Shingi Shingon) group, with headquarters at Hase-dera and Chishaku-in; and (3) the Shingon Ritsu group with headquarters at Saidai-ji in Nara. Each of the forty subsects recognizes the doctrinal validity of the others. In 1878 the Meiji government ordered that all the Shingon subsects unite under the leadership of Tō-ji ("in the spirit of Daishi"), but this forced administrative unity did not hold.

82. The Kinki area extends from the Kii Peninsula northward to the Sea of Japan and includes Kyōto, Ōsaka, Kobe, and Nara.

83. Ed Readicker-Henderson, *A Traveler's Guide to Japanese Pilgrimages* (New York and Tokyo, Weatherhill, 1995), 125.

CHAPTER 5. COURT OF THE CENTRAL HALLS

1. The term *garan*, which refers to the primary court area of a temple complex, is an abbreviation of the Sanskrit *samgha-ārāma*, literally a garden or place of rest (or of residence) for a group of monks. Inagaki, *A Dictionary of Japanese Buddhist Terms,* 59. For a discussion of the unique layout of the main buildings of Kōyasan's *garan*, including the mandala implications, see David L. Gardiner, "Mandala, Mandala on the Wall: Variations of Usage in the Shingon School," *Journal of the International Association of Buddhist Studies* 19, no. 2 (1996): 245–79. The overall precinct forms a slightly skewed rectangle approximately 350 meters east to west and 175 meters north to south.

2. Present plans call for the rebuilding of the Chūmon during the coming decade.

3. It is 29 meters (96 feet) on each side and 47 meters (157 feet) in height.

4. The *tahō* of *tahōtō* means "many treasures," and alludes to a Buddha of the ancient past named Tahō (Sk. *Prabhūtaratna*) who appears seated in an

immense "Stūpa of Many Treasures" in the eleventh chapter of the *Lotus Sutra*. Tahō Buddha enters the narrative for the purpose of testifying to the truth of Shākyamuni's teaching. The *tō* in *tahōtō* (also the *tō* in Daitō) is an abbreviation for *tōba*, or *sotoba*, a Japanese rendering of the Sanskrit *stūpa*, the name of a style of ancient monument built for deceased persons in India. In its early form the Indian *stūpa* was essentially a dome-shaped memorial monument on top of which was constructed a small terrace and shrine for a relic of the dead. Over this terrace rose a shaft with an honorific stone umbrella to provide symbolic shade for the shrine. This primitive *stūpa* was made of earth, stone, and brick. Its primary detail, the egg-shaped mound (called an *anda*, or egg), represented a kind of earth-womb, an emblem of latent creative power. The terrace and shrine represented a sanctuary lifted above the earth, beyond the cycle of death and rebirth. The umbrella, especially as it later evolved into multiple umbrella disks, represented the Bodhi tree that shaded the meditating Buddha when he achieved Enlightenment. The jewel-shaped object placed above all the disks represented the sun. An alternative symbolic interpretation of the *stūpa* links the solid mound to Mount Sumeru (J. *Shumi-sen*), the cosmic mountain at the center of the universe. The shaft that holds the disks then becomes the central axis of the world. The individual disks (especially when nine in number) become the various heavens or stages of enlightenment, or, especially in Japan, the Five Buddhas and the Four Primary Bodhisattvas. (A simple folk interpretation proposes that the square base represents Shākyamuni's folded robe, the dome his overturned begging bowl, and the spire his walking staff.) A roof was added to the basic Indian *stūpa* by the Chinese. Since the Japanese built their domes not with stone or brick but with vulnerable plaster troweled over a wood frame, they soon chose to add a lower roof and four surrounding walls to protect the lower part of the dome from weathering. Thus, what began in India as a solid earth and masonry mound with an elevated shrine evolved in Japan into a hollow structure with an interior shrine. For a discussion of the evolution of the *stūpa* see Lama Anagarika Govinda, *Psycho-cosmic Symbolism of the Buddhist Stūpa* (Berkeley: Dharma Publishing, 1976). See also Robert Treat Paine and Alexander Soper, *The Art and Architecture of Japan* (Harmondsworth, England: Penguin, 1974), 226–27, and Pierre Rambach, *The Secret Message of Tantric Buddhism* (Geneva and New York: Skira/Rizzoli, 1979), 105–106. For the most thorough discussion in English of the *stūpa's* symbolic richness see Adrian Snodgrass, *The Symbolism of the Stupa* (Ithaca: Cornell Southeast Asia Program, 1985). Today there are seven surviving *tahōtō*-style "pagodas" at Kōyasan. The oldest of these, dating from the thirteenth century, is at Kongōsanmai-in. It is designated a National Treasure. Japan's first *tahōtō*-style pagoda presumably was built by Saichō in 817, but the first grand-scale *tahōtō*, or Daitō, with its two rings of core-supporting columns, was built at Kōyasan. See Alexander Coburn Soper III, *The Evolution of Buddhist Architecture in Japan* (New York: Hacker Art Books, 1978), 195.

5. The "jewel" is shaped somewhat like a Hershey's "candy kiss." A few more specifics about the symbolic features of the Daitō spire (J. *sōrin*). At the base of the spire are successive images of fertility and refreshment: a "dew basin" (*roban*), a downturned bowl (*fukumachi*), and an upturned flower basket (*uke-bana*). Then, at fixed intervals along the shaft are nine "umbrella" rings (*hōrin*) that mark the nine stages of ascending consciousness. Above the rings, near the top of the spire, are three more bowls formed by clusters of lotus petals. Just below the spire's summit is an eight-spoked solar disk, symbol of Sun and Buddha. And above that, the highest man-made object in the Garan, is the flaming jewel, the *nyoi-shu* or *mani-shu* (Sk. *chintāmani*). The message of the jewel is that the Buddha's divine mercy descends upon all.

6. Since it performs only a utilitarian function the lower roof of the *tahōtō* is not counted in the sequence of symbolic shapes.

7. This sitting posture is the *goma-za*, "the posture of the conquest of demons." Snodgrass, *Matrix and Diamond World Mandalas*, 226, n. 24.

8. For an enumeration of all thirty-two physical attributes of a Buddha (the *sanjūni-sō*), including the number of teeth and length of tongue, see Irie Taikichi and Shigeru Aoyama, *Buddhist Images*, trans. Thomas I. Elliott (Osaka: Hoikusha, 1993).

9. The triangle formed by the touching thumbs evokes the *yoni*, the female sexual organ, sign of the Womb that gives birth to the Buddhas and all things else.

10. In order that the worshiper's view of the central Buddha not be blocked, each of the surrounding directional Buddhas has been displaced from his proper compass position.

11. Hōshō is the main object of worship in Shingon's great annual *Go-shi-chinichi-no-mishuhō* (The Latter Seven-Day Rite) held at Tō-ji each New Year.

12. The association of Shākyamuni with the Buddha of the North is almost exclusively a Shingon tradition.

13. Different commentaries assign somewhat different attributes to the various members of the *Gobutsu* assembly. For my discussion I have depended largely on Yamasaki, *Shingon*, 150–51. See also Vessantara [Tony McMahon], *Meeting the Buddhas: A Guide to Buddhas, Bodhisattvas, and Tantric Deities* (Birmingham, UK: Windhorse, 1994), 53–126. For specific *mudrā*, see E. Dale Saunders, *Mudrā: A Study of Symbolic Gestures in Japanese Buddhist Sculpture* (New York: Pantheon, 1960).

14. The Daitō is supported by a virtual forest of pillars. Twenty pillars support the rectangular exterior wall. A circle of twelve pillars support the dome.

Another circle of twelve support the cylinder above the dome. Within this last is a circle of four pillars. Paintings of the sixteen Bodhisattvas (the *Jūroku Daibosatsu*) are mounted on the pillars of the two innermost circles. Ten Bodhisattvas face outward from the central axis of Dainichi Buddha. The remaining six face "forward" (southward) as a concession to the perspective of the worshiper. The artist who produced the painted images in today's Daitō was one of Japan's most celebrated producers of *Nihonga* ("Japanese style painting"), Dōmoto Inshō (1891–1975).

15. Nāgārjuna's influence on Mahāyāna Buddhism is so great that eight major Buddhist schools include him among their patriarchs.

16. The patriarchal line that begins with Nāgārjuna and ends with Kōbō Daishi is called the *denji hasso*. Another line of transmission, the *fuhō hasso*, begins with Dainichi Buddha and Kongōsatta, followed by Nāgārjuna. In order to maintain the magical total of eight patriarchs, this second list excludes Zenmui and I-hsing.

17. Saunders, *Mudrā*, 119–20.

18. Kūkai's beliefs concerning the role of Nāgārjuna in the reception and transmission of the True Teaching are discussed by Ryūichi Abé, *Weaving of Mantra*, 219–35. For other accounts of the Iron Tower legend, see Yamasaki, *Shingon*, 87–89; Soper, *The Evolution of Buddhist Architecture*, 194–96; and Snodgrass, *Matrix and Diamond World Mandalas*, 111–14. Kūkai's narration of the story is found in Alex Wayman and Tajima Ryūjin, *The Enlightenment of Vairocana* (Delhi: Motilal Banarsidass, 1992), 237–38. Amoghavajra's account is in Charles Orzech, "The Legend of the Iron Stūpa," in *Buddhism in Practice*, ed. Donald S. Lopez Jr. (Princeton: Princeton University Press, 1995), 314–17.

19. For brief descriptions of the Kondō built in 1852 see Ernest Mason Satow and A. G. S. Hawes, *A Handbook for Travellers in Central and Northern Japan*, 2nd ed., revised (London: John Murray, 1884), 417–18; T. Philip Terry, *Terry's Guide to the Japanese Empire* (Boston and New York: Houghton Mifflin, 1933), 524–25; and Basil Hall Chamberlain and W. B. Mason, *A Handbook for Travellers in Japan* (London: John Murray, 1907), 376–77. The Kondō's floor plan is found in Rambach, *Secret Message of Tantric Buddhism*, 51. Photographs of the lost Kongōsatta and Fudō Myō-ō sculptures are printed in Sawa Takaaki, *Art in Japanese Esoteric Buddhism*, trans. Richard L. Gage (Tokyo: Heibonsha, 1972), 60–61, plates 62 and 63. All six of the lost sculptures are pictured in *Art Treasures of Kōyasan Temples* (Tokyo: Kokka Publishing Co., 1908), plates 6 and 7.

20. Details of the fire come largely from an interview with Priest/Professor Yamamoto in 1990.

21. A hidden Buddha is called a *hibutsu*.

22. There is a rumor that a craftsman doing repair work some years ago peeked inside the sealed cabinet and saw a held jar.

23. Quoted from *The Secret Key to the Heart Sutra*, Hakeda, *Kūkai: Major Works*, 263. Largely as a consequence of his vow to heal the body and perpetuate life Yakushi became the most prominent Buddha of the Nara and early Heian periods. Yakushi was (and continues to be) the *honzon* of Kūkai's Jingō-ji and Tō-ji temples and Saichō's headquarters temple, Enryaku-ji, on Mt. Hiei. He also was the *honzon* of Prince Shotoku's Hōryū-ji. Of the hundreds of sculptures popularly attributed to Kūkai by far the largest number are of Yakushi. One theory holds that Yakushi was a sort of stand-in for Dainichi in Japan prior to the introduction of Esoteric Buddhism.

24. Sculptor Takamura Kōun appears to have been influenced in this carving by the style of the five ninth-century Kokūzō Bosatsu that survive today at Jingō-ji (all National Treasures). Like the Jingō-ji group the Kōyasan sculpture has a broad face with crescent eyebrows and full cheeks, a short and fleshy neck, and a compact body of almost sensual smoothness.

25. The six paired supernumerary arms brandish a *vajra* bell and *vajra* trident, an arrow and a bow, a *vajra* sword and an elephant goad. The two natural arms are crossed at the wrists with the hands pressed together back to back, little fingers interlocked and index fingers pointing upward. This is the *niwa-in*, or two wings *mudrā*. It gives Gōzanze total mobility in attack.

26. These two Indian gods, now servants in the Buddhist fold, initially had challenged Dainichi's supremacy.

27. Gōzanze Myō-ō's front face is said to express "amorous fury," his left and right faces disgust and anger, his rear face heroism.

28. Yamasaki, *Shingon*, 86–87.

29. Taisen Miyata, *A Study of the Ritual Mudrās in the Shingon Tradition* (Sacramento?: 1984), 121.

30. At the onset of her pregnancy Queen Māyā saw (or dreamed she saw) her future son step from a golden pagoda in the sky and seat himself on the head of a six-tusked white elephant. The elephant descended through the air to her side, at which point Shaka dismounted and "passed into her bosom like a shadow." Alice Getty, *The Gods of Northern Buddhism* (Tokyo: Tuttle, 1962), 16. Each of the elephants of the Fugen sculpture holds a single-pointed *vajra* in its trunk, representing the inflow and outflow of breath that sustains life. The six tusks are thought to demonstrate the power to subjugate the six origins of temptation (the five human senses and the will). For a more detailed discussion of Fugen-enmei's iconography see Snodgrass, *Matrix and Diamond World Mandalas*, 263–67.

31. The two mandalas of the Dual Mandala had separate scriptural origins, the *Taizō-kai* mandala being described in the *Dainichi-kyō* sūtra, the

Kongō-kai mandala in the *Kongōchō-gyō* sūtra. A great deal of extrascriptural imagery also is found in the execution of the two mandalas. The initial close linkage and theoretical fusion of the two probably was the work of Hui-kuo, or perhaps of Hui-kuo and Kūkai in concert.

32. Here in the Golden Hall, as in virtually all Shingon temple sanctuaries, the two mandala scrolls are drawn with paint or colored thread, and displayed vertically. In the earliest period they were laid out horizontally on the ground, and composed of colored powders. In either case the top of the Womb Realm Mandala is understood to point toward the east, the top of the Diamond Realm Mandala to point toward the west.

33. Mixtures of the three primary colors—red, yellow, and blue—together with white and black produce all colors and tones, just as mixtures of the Five Elements produce all the forms of the Dharma World. For a discussion of the symbolism and liturgical use of the five Buddhist colors see Snodgrass, *Matrix and Diamond World Mandalas*, 212–14.

34. Before each altar table is a raised seat (*raiban*) for the presiding priest. To the left of this seat is a small side table (*wakizukue*) that holds a perfume brazier, a serving stick, ceremonial water, and several forms of incense. To the right is a Chinese gong (*kei*), which the priest strikes at appropriate moments in the ritual. In addition to representing the Great Sun Buddha, the altar table's centerpiece evokes the Iron Tower of India that Nāgārjuna entered. It may contain a relic (*shari*) of the historical Buddha. Tradition says that when Shākyamuni was cremated in India his remains filled some forty bushels, providing *shari* for eighty-four thousand memorial stūpas. In theory these memorial ashes can be divided infinitely. See Akiyama Aisaburo, *Pagodas in Sunrise Land* (Tokyo: 1915), 99–100. When no *shari* is available, a copy of a sacred mantra may be substituted, for such a text is understood to be equally a part of the Buddha's body. Historically, Shingon has been the most active of all the Japanese Buddhist sects in the use and manufacture of relics. For the rich history of Buddhist relics in Japan, see Ruppert, *Jewel in the Ashes*.

35. Helpful discussions in English of the Dual Mandala are found in Ishida Hisatoyo, *Esoteric Buddhist Painting*, trans. E. Dale Saunders (Tokyo, New York, and San Francisco: Kodansha International, 1987), 29–65; Yamasaki, *Shingon*, 123–51; Rambach, *The Secret Message of Tantric Buddhism*; Elizabeth ten Grotenhuis, *Japanese Mandalas: Representations of Sacred Geography* (Honolulu: University of Hawai'i Press, 1999), 33–95; Yamamoto Chikyō, *Introduction to the Mandala* (Kyoto: Dōhōsha, 1980); and Snodgrass, *Matrix and Diamond World Mandalas*. The last of these discussions is the most comprehensive, at 841 pages. All six sources have been employed in the presentation that follows.

36. A visitor who wishes to make a close visual study of the Dual Mandala should look at those on display in the Reihōkan museum or, better still, purchase one of several excellent reproductions.

37. The worlds of desire, of form, of non-form (J. *sangai*).

38. The six paths (J. *rokudō*): of the hells, of the hungry ghosts, of animals, of the ashura (Sk. asura; demons), of humankind, of the heavens.

39. The Womb Realm Mandala's full name is *daihi-taizō-shō-mandara*, "Mandara of Birth from the Womb of Great Compassion." Adapted from Snodgrass, *The Matrix and Diamond World Mandalas*, 129. The several courts of the mandala not named above are the Kannon Court, the Vajra Holder's Court, the Wisdom Holders' Court (which includes Fudō Myō-ō and Gōzanze Myō-ō), the Jizō Court, the Jogaishō Court, the Kokūzō Court, and the Soshitsuji Court.

40. Snodgrass, *Matrix and Diamond World Mandalas*, 576.

41. In this reading the five fingers of the left hand may be understood to represent the five fundamental elements (earth, water, fire, wind/air, and space) while the embracing right hand supplies the necessary sixth element: mind or consciousness.

42. For a discussion of the sexual imagery of the *chi ken-in* see Saunders, *Mudrā*, 102–107. Generally speaking, Shingon mandalas and Shingon art contain little of the explicit sexual imagery so characteristic of Tibetan esoteric iconography.

43. The fifth Element, Space, is represented by the painting as a whole.

44. Exoteric chronology holds that each of the three vast eons of time (Sk. *kalpa*; J. *kō*)—that is, of the past, present, and future—has had, or will have, one thousand Buddhas. In this scheme Shākyamuni is the fourth Buddha of the present sub-sub-*kalpa*. Shingon esoteric doctrine, however, largely rejects the *kalpa* concept, emphasizing instead full access to enlightenment in the present moment. Consequently, each of the thousand Buddhas is interpreted as representing an aspect of Knowledge already innate within the body and mind of every being. For a discussion of the thousand Buddhas, see Snodgrass, *Matrix and Diamond World Mandalas*, 634–36. A list of all thousand names can be found in Buddhist scripture.

45. Snodgrass, *Matrix and Diamond World Mandalas*, 708.

46. Inagaki, *Japanese Buddhist Terms*, s.v. "Bonnō soku bodai."

47. Willa Jane Tanabe, "Basic Threads of Shingon Buddhist Art," in *Sacred Treasures of Mount Kōya: The Art of Japanese Shingon Buddhism* (Kōyasan: Kōyasan Reihōkan Museum, 2002), 13.

48. From "A Memorial Presenting a List of Newly Imported Sutras and Other Items" (*Shōrai mokuroku*), in Hakeda, *Kūkai: Major Works*, 145–46.

49. Starting at the interior southeast corner and moving clockwise, the eight painted celebrants of the Kondō are Diamond Perfume, Diamond Dance, Diamond Joy, Diamond Incense, Diamond Flower, Diamond Garland, Diamond Song, and Diamond Lamp.

50. In the previous Kondō, the one that burned in 1926, the wall at the back of the sanctuary was decorated with images of sixteen of Shākyamuni's closest disciples, the so-called *rakan* (Sk. *arhat*; Ch. *lohan*). Since interest in the *rakan* had greatly diminished by the 1920s Kimura was commissioned to replace them with sixteen major figures from the Dual Mandala (plus an earthbound Shākyamuni). Most of Kimura's images appear in the conventional "flat" iconic form, a type of portraiture (known as *kansōzō*) designed to approximate what is observed in an enlightenment experience. In 1935 another work by Kimura was donated to Kongōbu-ji, an exquisite scroll painting of Dainichi Buddha done in gold ink on indigo silk. For a reproduction of this work see Reihōkan, *Sacred Treasures of Mount Kōya*, 70, 160.

51. Actually, one of the four directional Buddhas, Ashuku, is missing. Or so it seems. But then one remembers that the large black space between the second and third panels is the rear side of Ashuku's cabinet on the dais. Thus, Ashuku is fully present but "hidden," just as in the inner sanctuary. Another curious matter is that Fudō Myō-ō and the goddess Benzaiten appear in Shākyamuni's panel. Evidently, Benzaiten has served as the muse of Shākyamuni's long meditation while Fudō has helped him maintain the intensity of his practice. Contemporary Shingon practitioners could do no better than employ the same two divine assistants.

52. The original is now badly deteriorated, with most of its physical detail lost.

53. Quoted by Ian Reader, Esben Andreasen, and Finn Stefansson, *Japanese Religions: Past and Present* (Honolulu: University of Hawai'i Press, 1995), 106.

54. For Shinnyo's life see Nakagawa Zenkyō, *Bhiksu Shinnyo: A Japanese Prince Who Strived to Reach India in Pursuit of Dharma*, trans. Shirotani Mineyasu (Kōyasan: Kongōbu-ji, 1954). A twelve-page pamphlet. Shinnyo is presumed to have founded Shinnō-in temple at Kōyasan, which is next door to Ryūkō-in and near the Miedō. The portrait of Shinnyo in the Miedō shows him wearing a brown robe and holding a string of prayer beads with both hands. He stares straight ahead with a vague, unexpressive face. He had a reputation for modesty, and was referred to from an early age as "the Crouching Prince." He is listed among those who carried Kūkai's body to the mausoleum. We are told that Kūkai habitually bowed three times whenever he walked past the hall where Shinnyo resided.

55. Just beyond the *torii* gate are six foundation stones, the remains of an earlier *torii* that was built in the more complex *ryōbu* style. *Ryōbu* ("dual") *Shintō* refers to the esoteric belief that the native gods—Niu and Kariba, in this instance—are themselves incarnations of Buddhas and Bodhisattvas. The most famous, and most photographed, *ryōbu*-style *torii* in Japan today is the immense offshore gate before Miyajima's Itsukushima Shrine.

56. Residing behind the third door are the spirits of twelve princes and one hundred and twenty attendants who serve Kebi and Itsukushima.

57. That there are only two *katsuogi* indicates that the Myōjin-sha is relatively insignificant in the large shrine system that supports the mythology of the emperor's divine ancestry. The *honden* for the sun-goddess Amaterasu at her primary Inner Shrine at Ise has the maximum number of ten *katsuogi*. The shrine of creator-god Izanagi on Awaji Island has six. Jimmu, Japan's legendary first emperor, has six at Kashihara-jingu. There are five on the Shintō canopy suspended above the *dohyō* at professional *sumo* tournaments (evidence of *sumo's* high status as an imperial sport). The great Izumo Shrine, historically a rival to Ise, has only three. Splendid Kasuga in Nara rates but two. The deified Tokugawa Ieyasu, greatest of the Shōguns, has only two at Nikkō.

58. The liveliest and best-attended event of the year at the Myōjin-sha occurs just an hour before midnight on New Year's eve. At that time a flaming fifteen-foot wooden torch (the *dai taimatsu*) and a giant sacred wand (an outsized *gohei* with eighty-four separate streamers) are carried in procession to the shrine from Ryūko-in, where the torch was lit from the eternal lamp in Ryūko-in's *nyūjō-no-ma*. Several hundred spectators chant the *Hannya-shingyō* as the *gohei* is carried into the shrine proper and placed on Goddess Niu's side porch. Thus, the mountain gods are invited to protect Kōyasan for another year. By tradition the men who carry the torch are entering their forty-second year; they hope their New Year service to the gods will deflect the misfortune that comes with this unlucky age (*yakudoshi*). See Hinonishi Shinjō, author, and Yano Tatehiko, photographer, *Kōyasan-shiki-no-inori* (Kōyasan: ceremonies of the four seasons) (Tokyo: Kabushi Kigaisha Kosei, 1995), 18–23.

59. This theory, which regards native gods as incarnations of Buddhas and Bodhisattvas, also is known as *honji suijaku* ("manifestation from the original state"). By this system Princess Kebi is a manifestation of the Thousand-Armed Kannon Bodhisattva and Princess Itsukushima a manifestation of the Indian river goddess Benzaiten (both of whom appear in the Womb Realm Mandala). Matsunaga Yūkei, "From Indian Tantric Buddhism to Japanese Buddhism," in *Japanese Buddhism: Its Tradition, New Religions and Interaction with Christianity*, ed. Minoru Kiyota (Tokyo and Los Angeles: Buddhist Books International, 1987), 53. Kūkai sometimes is credited with authoring the *ryōbu* theory, as well

as designing the *ryōbu torii*. His presumed enthusiasm for the native gods is conveyed in the following poem, said to have been composed by Kūkai upon his receiving a formal initiation into Shintō from the emperor: "Among various ways to become a Buddha / The most potent way is / Kami-no-michi." See Kitagawa, *Religion in Japanese History*, 63–64, 64 n. 38. George J. Tanabe Jr. generalizes that "the founding of Mt. Kōya was prompted as much by Kūkai's Shinto sentiments for mountain places as by his desire for a quiet place for Buddhist meditation." George J.Tanabe Jr., "Kōbō Daishi and the Art of Esoteric Buddhism," *Monumenta Nipponica* 37 (1983): 410.

60. Katsuno Ryūshin, *Hieizan to Kōyasan* (Tōkyō: Shibundō, 1959), 18–19.

61. Reihōkan, *Sacred Treasures of Mount Kōya*, 169.

62. In the lower half of the painting are seated the princesses Kebi and Itsukushima, the former holding a fly whisk (*hossu*) as her symbol of authority (also a symbol of the Buddhist prohibition against the destruction of life). Itsukushima holds a Japanese lute, the *biwa*, which reminds us of her identification with Benzaiten. Instead of dogs, a pair of Chinese lions are guarding the princesses. They too are chanting the mystic *A-UN*.

63. A further public celebration takes place at a small Myōjin shrine located on a hillside across from Rengejō-in. After formal prayers before the shrine gate (led by Rengejō-in's head priest), representatives of the local festival committee, acting on behalf of the two gods, begin tossing gifts of *mochi* balls (made of pounded steamed rice) down the embankment. Both children and adults scramble to catch the balls. Anyone who retrieves a colored ball receives a further gift, perhaps a brightly colored *furoshiki* (a scarf-like wrapping cloth). That Gonomuro-dani should have its own separate Myōjin shrine is explained by a familiar type of story. In the twelfth century the founder of Rengejō-in, a monk named Gyōshō, was so devoted to the guardian gods that each day he descended the mountain to pay them reverence at their main shrine in Amano village. When Gyōshō became enfeebled with age Kariba-myōjin took pity on him, advising him in a dream to build a shrine close to his own home temple. The succeeding head priests of Rengejō-in have conducted worship ceremonies at this shrine ever since.

64. According to the anonymously written "Tale of Saigyō," the poet demonstrated his determination to leave his family by "mercilessly" kicking his adored four-year-old daughter from the porch of their residence when she tried to stop him. See Meredith McKinney, trans., *The Tale of Saigyō* (Saigyō Monogatari) (Ann Arbor: Center for Japanese Studies, University of Michigan, 1998), 27–28, 81–82. Also Gustav Heldt, "Saigyō's Traveling Tale: A Translation of *Saigyō Monogatari*," *Monumenta Nipponica* 52, no. 4 (1997): 518. Actually,

almost nothing is known about Saigyō's wife and daughters, some historians questioning whether he ever married. The monks of Kōyasan, however, affirm that his daughters became nuns and lived out their lives in the village of Amano at the foot of the mountain. Their humble gravestones are found in the cemetery at Okuno-in. See Kato, *Kōyasan Monogatari*, 97–98.

65. Mezaki Tokue, "Aesthete-Recluses During the Transition from Ancient to Medieval Japan," in *Principles of Classical Japanese Literature*, ed. Earl Miner (Princeton: Princeton University Press, 1985), 173.

66. R. H. Blyth, *Haiku* (Tokyo: Hokuseido, 1949–1952), 1:115.

67. Hanayama, *Understanding Japanese Buddhism*, 204–205.

68. Yamada Shōzen, "Japanese Esoteric Buddhism and the Moon," in *European Studies on Japan*, ed. Ian Nish and Charles Dunn (Tenterden, Kent: Paul Norbury Publications, 1979), 81.

69. Tradition says the *sanko* thrown by Kōbō Daishi previously had been in the possession of the Shingon patriarchs, starting with Nāgārjuna. Chinese scholar-monk Xuan Zang (Hsüan-chuang, 600–664; J. Genjō) is credited with bringing it to China from India. The *sanko* in question survives at Kōyasan today, or at least it is pictured in a museum catalog. See Reihōkan Museum, *Special Exhibition on Reverend Shinzen and Notable Treasures of Kōyasan* (Kōyasan: Kōyasan Reihōkan Museum, 1990), 16.

70. Visitors to Kōyasan who wish protection from *tengu* are invited to pray at a nearby shrine dedicated to Abbot Kakkai (1142–1220?). The Kakkai-sha is located on the side of Henjōmine, one of the eight lotus-petal hills of Kōyasan. See Yamamoto, *History*, 133, and *Sei Ai* (Feb. 1996), 45–47.

71. Chamberlain, *Handbook for Travellers in Japan*, 45.

72. For the penultimate stroke the spacing is lengthened to six intervals. The final two strokes are separated by but one interval. The 4 a.m., 1 p.m., and 11 p.m. ringings are especially important, for they signal the priests that it is time to go to the temple *dan* for private prayer.

73. A human being has six senses (color, sound, smell, taste, touch, and cognition) corresponding to the six organs of eye, ear, nose, tongue, body, and mind, each of which has three natures (good, bad, and neutral). These attributes have both a positive and a negative aspect that can be expressed in each of the three "worlds" of past, present, and future. Thus, the total number of *karma* bonds is a product of 6 x 3 x 2 x 3; that is, 108. There are other explanations for the number 108: the 108 traditional divisions of the year, the 108 types of meditation, the 108 sacred personages in the Kongō-kai mandala, the 108 attributes of the Buddha, the 108 names for the Buddha, the 108 names for Kongōsatta, the 108 bones in the human body. Some commentators suggest that 108 is a convenient expansion of the sacred number 9 (that is, 9 multiplied by 12), or

the mysterious product of number 1 to the first power, number 2 to the second power, and number 3 to the third power. Others propose that the functional number may not be 108 at all, but the universally splendid 100, the extra 8 being an arbitrary add-on to protect the careless bell ringer or bead counter from an inadvertent shortfall. For a summation of several of these theories, see Saunders' *Mudrā*, 174–76, 255–56. If you ask the average Japanese about the matter you likely will be told, simply, "it is a holy number."

74. An even more important ceremony of the New Year (*Shōgatsu*) at Kōyasan is the *Shushō-e*, a solicitation of good fortune for the nation and its citizens. This ceremony is repeated four times: on January 1, 2, and 3 in the Kondō, and on January 5 in the Daitō. Each of these observances begins at 9:00 a.m. The ritual's most dramatic event comes when all the participating priests are given green wooden staffs made of freshly stripped saplings. These staffs are called *Gō-ō-zue*, literally "cow jewel sticks." At the proper moment the staffs are struck on the floor with three loud raps, an action variously interpreted as providing comfort to the spirits of the dead, suppressing the demons who live beneath the earth, and bringing forth in the new year all the riches of the soil (the last seems to be the official understanding). "Cow jewel" refers to a holy stone that grows in the stomachs of India's sacred cows. It is thought to have the power to bestow material wealth. At the conclusion of the last day's *shushō-e* each visitor is given a personal *gō-ō-zue* to take home and place on the family altar. See Hinonishi, *Kōyasan-shiki-no-inori*, 24–32. There is a widespread Japanese New Year custom, known as *hatsumōde*, of making a ceremonial first visit to a Shintō shrine or Buddhist temple (often to both). Two of the most popular *hatsumōde* temples, Shinshō-ji in Narita and Kawasaki Daishi near Tōkyō, are Shingon. Each receives more than three million visitors during the first few days of the New Year. Understandably, remote and chilly Kōyasan is relatively quiet during the New Year holiday. Most of its *shukubō* temples are closed to visitors, the resident monks having been sent home to celebrate with their families. Kōyasan's Annyō-in is an exception. They welcome holiday visitors and hold a wonderfully prayerful and celebratory New Year breakfast that features toasting the coming months with spiced *sake*, eating kelp and black peas for happiness and robustness, and ingesting long strands of *soba* noodles for extending the length of life.

75. The 108-bead Shingon rosary (the *juzu*) also has four extra beads (for a total of 112), one extra bead for each of the directional Buddhas. The entire string represents Dainichi.

76. Hakeda, *Kūkai: Major Works*, 271.

77. The lotus, which reproduces from its own matrix, gives the appearance of spontaneous generation or self-creation. The First Buddha, or Ādi Buddha, often is depicted as a flame rising from a lotus-flower.

CHAPTER 6. THREE MOUNTAIN INSTITUTIONS

1. The Omote-mon is worth examining both for its carvings and for the scores of *sen-ka-ji fuda* pasted on its pillars and walls. *Sen-ka-ji fuda*—literally, "labels for one thousand temples"—are a consequence of an old custom, now outlawed, of pasting a label with one's name and organization at places of pilgrimage. One popular refinement of the fad was to place the label at a maximum height, thus discouraging custodial removal. To achieve this goal some pilgrims carried long jointed poles; others employed a small bag of sand on which they would place a dampened *fuda*, then throw the bag and *fuda* at the highest beam. See Fujiya Hotel, *We Japanese* (Miyanoshita: Fujiya Hotel, 1949), 172. Some of the older and more colorful wood block *sen-ka-ji fuda* are much prized today by collectors.

2. Kyōhōsha, *Kōyasan Kyōhō*, a twice-monthly Kōyasan newsletter (Kōyasan: Kōyasan Kyōhōsha).

3. Shinzen's mausoleum is immediately behind Kongōbu-ji's main hall. His cremated remains were at first marked by a simple burial mound. In 1131 the mound was replaced by a small *tahōtō*-style pagoda, then in 1640 by the memorial hall that exists today. For a detailed history of Shinzen's mausoleum see Reihōkan, *Special Exhibition on Reverend Shinzen,* 36–37, 61–79.

4. Seed letter mandalas are called Dharma Mandalas (J. *hō mandara*). Mandalas with human forms, the most common type, are Great Mandalas (Sk. *mahā mandala*; J. *dai mandara*). Mandalas using symbolic objects (jewel, lotus, wheel, sword, etc.) to represent the sacred persons are Samaya Mandalas (J. *sanmaya mandara*). Mandalas composed of three-dimensional sculptures, or "actsigns," are known as Karma Mandalas (J. *katsuma mandara*). See Rambach, *Secret Message of Tantric Buddhism,* 64, and Yamasaki, *Shingon,* 126–28.

5. For a brief description of the early Daishi-kō see Gerald Cooke, "Traditional Buddhist Sects and Modernization in Japan," *Japanese Journal of Religious Studies* 1, no. 4 (Dec. 1974): 321–25.

6. As carved on the granite slab the "Iroha" poem is an eight-line *waka* with a syllable count of 7, 5, 7, 5, 7, 5. The modern pronunciation, with some consonants voiced, is indicated below (adapted from *Japan: An Illustrated*

Encyclopedia [Kodansha], s.v. "iroha poem"). The English translation is taken from Ryūichi Abé, *Weaving of Mantra*, 392. Although modern scholarship suggests (though not unanimously) that Kūkai neither composed the poem nor invented *hiragana*, the inscription at the Daishi Kyōkai shrine claims he did both, a claim that continues to be embraced by most Japanese.

Iro wa nioedo	Although its scent still lingers on,
chirinuru o	the form of a flower has scattered away.
waga yo tare zo	For whom will the glory
tsune naran.	of this world remain unchanged?
Ui no okuyama	Arriving today at the yonder side
kyō koete	of the deep mountains of evanescent existence
asaki yume miji	We shall never allow ourselves to drift away
ei mo sezu	intoxicated in the world of shallow dreams.

For a general discussion of Japanese death poetry, of which the "Iroha" is the single most famous example, see Yoel Hoffmann, *Japanese Death Poems* (Rutland, VT, and Tokyo: Charles E. Tuttle, 1986).

7. Kōyasan Shingonshū, *Shingon Buddhist Service Book* (Kōyasan: Kōyasan Shingonshū: 1975).

8. The last quoted expression is Kōbō Daishi's. See Morgan Gibson and Hiroshi Murakami, trans., *Tantric Poetry of Kūkai (Kōbō Daishi) Japan's Buddhist Saint, with Excerpts from* The Mahāvairocana Sūtra *and I-Hsing's* Commentary (Bangkok: Mahachulalongkorn Buddhist University, 1982), 23. *A-ji-kan* practitioners are taught that the sound "ah" (written as the Sanskrit *siddham* letter *A*) is the mother of all sound, the vibration that gives rise to the universe. It is the one-syllable mantra of the ungraspable *dharma-kāya*, Dainichi Buddha. All language is derived from it. When Shākyamuni uttered this syllable each of his listeners heard a complete sermon in his or her own native tongue. See Donald S. Lopez Jr., "Introduction," in *Buddhism in Practice*, ed. Donald S. Lopez Jr. (Princeton: Princeton University Press, 1995), 19. *A-ji-kan* practice may take one of several forms. It may emphasize transformation technique, circulation technique, an expansion visualization (where the moon disk, letter *A*, and lotus gradually expand to the dimensions of the universe), a permeation visualization (the light and energy of the *A* enter the body through inhalation of the breath and are exhaled through the skin pores into the universe), or some other method. See Yamasaki, *Shingon*, 154–59. The length of the meditation may vary. When combined with preparatory elements it can run for an hour or more. Often it is shortened to as little as ten minutes, especially if the practitioner is experienced. Most Kōyasan priests set aside about forty minutes for the medita-

tion. A full-scale preparatory sequence may include three prostrations, repetitions of the Universal Homage Mantra (*Om I bend my knees at the feet of all the Buddhas*), repetitions of the mantra *HAŪM*, recitation of the Body Protection Mantra (five times), recitation of the Five Great Resolutions ("Sentient creatures are innumerable; I vow to save them all," etc.), and, finally, one hundred recitations of the five-syllable mantra of Dainichi of the Womb Realm Mandala (*On a-bi-ra-un-ken, ba-za-ra-da-to ban* [*Om* All-Pervading One, Imperishable One]). A similar exercise may close the meditation. These opening and closing elements are not required. Nor need one employ an *A-ji-kan* scroll, for the meditation is primarily an internal visualization. For detailed discussions of the *A-ji-kan*, see Richard K. Payne, "*Ajikan*: Ritual and Meditation in the Shingon Tradition," in *Re-Visioning "Kamakura" Buddhism*, ed. Richard K. Payne (Honolulu: University of Hawai'i Press, 1998), 219–48; Taisen Miyata, ed., *Ajikan: A Manual for the Esoteric Meditation* (Sacramento: Northern California Koyasan Church, 1979); Kūkai's "The Meanings of the Word Hūm," in Hakeda, *Kūkai: Major Works*, 246–62; and Yamasaki, *Shingon*, 159–62, 190–215. For a short history of *siddham* letters see John Stevens, *Sacred Calligraphy of the East*, rev. ed. (Boston and Shaftesbury: Shambhala, 1988), 2–14. For the calligraphy of the Sanskrit *A*, see Takagi, *Mikkyō no hon*, 118, and Stevens, *Sacred Calligraphy*, 42, 59.

9. In the context of esoteric Buddhism the use of *majinai* ("magic rites") does not imply the overturning or frustration of natural laws, as in the Western "miracle." Mystic formulas and the processes of the material world are understood to be in harmony. When the former induce effects in the latter, natural laws are being fulfilled, not annulled. For a discussion of Kōbō Daishi's introduction of *kaji* and its use in curing physical illness in modern-day Japan, see Pamela D. Winfield, "Curing with *Kaji*: Healing and Esoteric Empowerment in Japan," *Japanese Journal of Religious Studies* 32, no. 1 (2005): 107–30.

10. Copy sheets for the *Hannya-shingyō* may be purchased for a nominal amount at the downstairs office. A pamphlet of instruction (Japanese only) is provided, along with a calligraphy brush and equipment for making ink. Also available is a self-inking brush that works much like a felt-tip pen. The calligraphy brush and liquid ink are much preferred, partly for aesthetic reasons, but mostly because the writer's devotional spirit is understood to flow down the arm into the inked tip of the brush and then onto the paper. Calligraphy brushes (*futofude*) are highly esteemed and never discarded casually when worn out. Near the Eireiden in the Okunoin cemetery is a memorial for used brushes in the form of a bronze tower shaped like a gigantic *futofude*. At the foot of the tower stands the goddess Kannon, traditional sponsor of the art of *shodō*, or "Way of Writing."

11. Stevens, *Sacred Calligraphy*, 113–14. Stevens's book includes a *shakyō* manual and Sanskrit, Chinese, Tibetan, Korean, and English versions of the *Heart Sutra*.

12. Hakeda, *Kūkai: Major Works*, 265. For Kūkai's full interpretation of the *Hannya-shingyō*, see his *Hannya shingyō hiken* (Secret Key to the Heart Sutra) in Hakeda, *Kūkai: Major Works*, 262–75. The more complete name of the sutra is *Hannya-haramita-shin-gyō* [Sk. *Prajñā-pāramitā-hrdaya-sutra*], "The Heart Sutra of Perfect Wisdom." Many English translations are available, including some in verse form. The following translation is found in Koyasan Shingonshu, *Shingon Buddhist Service Book*, 20–24:

> When the Bodhisattva Kannon was practicing profound Transcendental Wisdom, he discerned clearly that the five Psychophysical Constituents were empty and thereby became free from all suffering. O Shāriputra, form is emptiness, emptiness is form; form is no other than emptiness, emptiness is no other than form. Of sensation, conception, predisposition, and consciousness the same can be said. O Shāriputra, all things are characterized by emptiness; they are neither born nor do they perish; they are neither tainted nor immaculate; neither do they increase nor decrease. Therefore, in emptiness there is no form, no sensation, no conception, no predisposition, no consciousness; no eye, ear, nose, tongue, body, mind; no form, sound, scent, sensation, objects of mind; no realm of vision . . . no realm of consciousness. There is no ignorance, no extinction of ignorance . . . no old age and death, no extinction of old age and death. There is no suffering, no origination of suffering, no annihilation, no Noble Paths. There is no wisdom and no attainment because there is no object to be attained. The bodhisattva, because of his dependence on Transcendental Wisdom, has no obstacle in mind; because he has no obstacle, he has no fear. Being free from all perverted views, he reaches ultimate Nirvāna. All the Buddhas of the past, present, and future, depending on Transcendental Wisdom, attain perfect Awakening. One should, therefore, know that the *prajñā-pāramitā* is the great mantra, the mantra of great Wisdom, the highest mantra, the peerless mantra, which is capable of allaying all suffering; it is true and not false. Thus, the *prajñā-pāramitā* mantra is to be delivered: *Gate gate pāragate pārasamgate bodhi svāhā.* (Gone, gone, gone beyond, gone altogether beyond, O Awakening, hail!).

The closing *mantra* is recited in its original Sanskrit form, for only then will it have the power to open the chanter's heart to the influence of Perfect Wisdom.

13. The prominence of the Ten Precepts in modern Shingon is due in substantial part to the work of an eighteenth-century Shingon priest and reformer named Jiun (1718–1804). See John L. Atkinson, trans., "The Ten Buddhistic Virtues (Ju-zen-ho-go)" by Jiun of Katsuragi, *Transactions of the Asiatic Society of Japan* 33 (1905): 159–84.

14. Except for two weeks around the time of the New Year the formal Precepts Ceremony is offered daily at the Jukaidō. Those taking the vows often are members of a packaged trip, or perhaps a group returning from the eighty-eight-temple pilgrimage on Shikoku. Walk-ins are welcome. There is a small fee.

15. Quoted by Paul B. Watt, "Eison and the Shingon Vinaya Sect," in *Religions of Japan in Practice*, ed. George J. Tanabe Jr. (Princeton: Princeton University Press, 1999), 89–90.

16. The first precept clearly implies that one will not eat meat nor in any other way willingly contribute to the death of sentient creatures. The tenth precept may be the most problematical, for in the usual Buddhist context the particular false view being condemned is a denial of, or indifference to, the karmic law of cause and effect. To believe in a personal *karma* that accumulates through a multiplicity of previous lives and assigns to every living person circumstances that are by definition morally appropriate is nearly as difficult for the modern Japanese as it is for the modern Westerner. This being the case, even orthodox presentations of the principle of *karma* tend to be reassuring and upbeat. "Not all of what happens is determined by karma. Even if unfavorable karma has caused unhappiness, one shouldn't lose hope. Wish for the best to come. . . . Trust in the Buddha, enjoy work, and delight . . . that one can work. The point is this: One now is living a life that is karmically fair. Knowing this, one has no need to complain about being a victim. One can live with a sound mind, in peace." Oda, *Kaji*, 59.

17. The spring dates are May 3, 4, and 5, the fall dates October 1, 2, and 3. The spring ceremony establishes a bond between the recipient and Dainichi Buddha of the Womb Realm Mandala. The fall ceremony establishes a bond with Dainichi Buddha of the Diamond Realm Mandala. Laity are encouraged to receive both initiations. Initiations are performed continuously from 10:00 a.m. to 3:30 p.m. on the first day of each session, from 8:00 a.m. to 3:30 p.m on the second day, and from 8:00 a.m. to 3:00 p.m. on the final day. The entire ceremony, including the preparatory lecture, takes about one hour. Permissions may be purchased at the Garan information building. The number of people who receive the sacrament each day ranges between seven hundred and twelve hundred.

18. In Shingon mythology Dainichi Buddha administered a similar initiation to Kongōsatta and Kongōsatta in turn administered it to Nāgārjuna in the Iron Tower.

19. See Arai, *Shingon Esoteric Buddhism*, 87.

20. Quoted by Gelfman, "The *Rishukyō* and Its Influence on Kūkai," 209.

21. In earlier Shingon practice the initiated person received as his or her tutelary deity whatever divine personage of the mandala the *shikimi* chanced to fall upon, an encounter presumably determined by the initiate's *karma* and particular spiritual needs. In today's *kanjō* ceremony all the lay initiates are declared to be bonded to Dainichi and receive the same "diamond name," *Henjō-kongō* (Sk. *Vairochana-vajra*). See Snodgrass, *Matrix and Diamond World Mandalas*, 732–33.

22. Terry, *Guide to the Japanese Empire*, 514.

23. *Japan: An Illustrated Encyclopedia* (Kodansha), s.v. "National Treasures."

24. The Reihōkan schedules five different exhibitions each year, often with accompanying catalogues.

25. Photographs of the paintings of Gonzō and Zennyo-ryū-ō are found in Kōyasan Reihōkan, *Special Exhibition on Reverend Shinzen*, plates 5 and 11.

26. The belief at Kōyasan is that this famous *Raigō* was painted at Mt. Hiei and kept there until it was seized during the military assault by Nobunaga in 1571. Sixteen years later, in 1587, the painting was brought to Kōyasan for safekeeping, and it has remained at Kōyasan ever since. Yamamoto, *History*, 174. Prior to the building of the Reihōkan the *Raigō* occasionally was displayed for visitors at Eko-in. This is where French art historian Gaston Migeon judged it to exceed anything done in European sacred art during the same historical period. Gaston Migeon, *In Japan: Pilgrimages to the Shrines of Art*, trans. Florence Simmonds (London: William Heinemann, 1908), 53. An excellent reproduction of the *Raigō* is found in Abeno Ryūsei, Hinonishi Shinjō, Yamamoto Tomonori, and Akimune Masao, *Kōyasan Kongōbu-ji* (Osaka: Sei-eishi, 1983), 77–79.

27. For a photograph of this shrine, see Abeno et al., *Kōyasan Kongōbu-ji*, 72–73.

CHAPTER 7. THE TEMPLE TOWN

1. The traditional choices would be Fudō Myō-ō for the left compartment, Kōbō Daishi for the right compartment, Dainichi Buddha for the center. In this triad Dainichi is recognized as the source of all Wisdom and Compassion. Fudō Myō-ō is honored as the primary protector of the household and the dead. Kōbō Daishi is the mentor and founder of the faith.

2. The origin of Buddhist prayer beads is popularly ascribed to the historical Buddha, who instructed a troubled king to string together 108 berries from

the Bodhi Tree, one berry for each human passion. While using the berries as a counting device the king chanted his devotion to the Three Treasures (the Buddha, the Dharma, the Sangha) ten thousand times. See Saunders, *Mudrā*, 174–77, and Arai, *Shingon Esoteric Buddhism*, 111–12, for general discussions of the *juzu*. Tradition says Kōbō Daishi's *juzu* was a gift from the Chinese emperor, with beads made of berries gathered from Shākyamuni's Bodhi Tree.

3. Today there are eighteen professional firemen who work in two shifts. An immense storage tank embedded in one of the shoulders of Mount Benten provides the town with its water pressure. Other cisterns are spread throughout the valley, including one beneath the Kongōbu-ji parking lot. The Tokugawa mausoleum, the Kongōsanmai-in stūpa, and the Fudō-dō in the Garan are protected by special water cannons. Despite these precautions, however, fire continues to be a major threat to Kōyasan's sacred halls. Three temples burned during our years in Japan. The fire chief acknowledges that there is little hope of putting out a temple fire once it is well started.

4. In fact, Kōyasan's restaurants are no more vegetarian than are the restaurants of other Japanese towns. The grocery stores of the mountain sell meat products. The primary meat market is located near the side entrance to Kōyasan University. Temple meals, of course, are vegetarian, although not all priests are vegetarians, at least not on all occasions. We were told that the laxity in vegetarian discipline began with the arrival of American military inspectors who were assumed to be incapable of surviving on a meatless diet.

5. The pills, which resemble small buttons of black tar, are manufactured at Kōyasan. The major ingredient is *ōbako*, a form of plantain (*Plantago asiatica*).

6. Beautiful Kisshōten is a daughter of the horrific demon Kishibō-jin, who became the "Buddhist madonna" after being transformed from child-eater to child-protector. Here is the mother's story. Due to an evil *karma* Kishibō-jin (literally, "Demon-children-mother Deity"; Sk. Hāritī) developed an irresistible craving for human children, whom she snatched and devoured in order to provide her own demon children with mother's milk. The compassionate Buddha, learning of her craving, weaned her away from this cruel diet by giving her pomegranates to eat. Today Kishibō-jin often is depicted with adoring children in her arms. She has a shrine near Rengejō-in where anxious Kōyasan mothers sometimes leave an offering of pomegranates.

7. Tradition declares that in making the *sake* Lady Tamayori husked each rice grain with her fingernails. The faithful of Jison-in temple in Kudoyama each year hold a commemorative ceremony in which they manufacture "*tsumabiki-no-sake*" ("*sake* made from rice husked by fingernails").

CHAPTER 8. EDUCATING A SHINGON PRIEST

1. Prior to World War II the mountain's Buddhist high school was male only. Even though the school is now coeducational Kōyasan temple families still tend to send their daughters elsewhere, partly because the high school boys have the reputation of being hard to handle, partly because the girls, being ineligible at Kōyasan to succeed as the head priest of the family temple, have different educational objectives. Certain colleges are thought to enhance their attractiveness as marital partners—for priests, for example. The college sometimes is Catholic.

2. Kōyasan University quite consciously seeks to perpetuate the four principles Kūkai enunciated when he founded Shugei-suchi-in in Kyōto in 828: the promotion of communication and coexistence with other cultures, the study of both religious and secular subjects, the admission of both religious and lay students, and the providing of enough economic support to ensure that no student is excluded on purely economic grounds. In addition to the indicated undergraduate programs, the university offers masters and doctoral degrees in both general Buddhism and Esoteric Buddhism. In all there were some twelve hundred students enrolled at Kōdai each year in the 1990s, although the numbers now seem to be decreasing. About one-third of the male students are monks who work in the local monastery temples for room, board, and a small spending allowance. Approximately half of these student monks eventually will become priests. Despite attempts to increase the number of women at Kōdai, at the end of the twentieth century they made up only about 10 percent of the total student body.

3. Sometimes seminary training comes earlier, immediately after graduation from high school, with the university experience coming later.

4. Prior to 1972 women could train individually for the priesthood under the direction of a master at one of Kōyasan's sub-temples. After 1972 an institute specifically for the training of women was established. Nisō Shudō-in was completed in 1987. For a description of the women's program at Nisō Shudō-in see Eko Susan Noble, "The Monastic Experience," in *Buddhism through American Women's Eyes*, ed. Karma Lekshe Tsomo (Ithaca, NY: Snow Lion Publications, 1995), 125–32.

5. For a description of some of the individual rituals, most especially the fundamental Eighteen Stage Practice (*Jūhachidō*) and the Fire Offering, see Yamasaki, *Shingon*, 168–75. For an account of the *Jūhachidō* that includes a translation of the *Jūhachidō Nenju Kubi Shidai* (attributed to Kūkai) see Miyata, *Study of the Ritual Mudrās*. For a general review of the *shido kegyō*, with special emphasis on *goma* training, see Richard K. Payne, *The Tantric Ritual of Japan: Feeding the Gods: The Shingon Fire Ritual* (Delhi: International Academy of

Indian Culture, 1991), 64–94. At the conclusion of *shido kegyō* each student prepares five or more *goma-fuda* boards that testify that the program has been completed successfully. These *goma-fuda* are blessed in the student's final *goma* ceremony, then placed as offerings at Kōbō Daishi's tomb, at the Myōjin-sha, at the Benzaiten and Kōjin shrines, at the temple of the student's *shisō*, and at the student's home temple (if there is one). Further *goma-fuda* may be given to people who have been particularly supportive. On the *goma-fuda* are recorded the religious name of the practitioner, the date, the place of practice (the *dōjō*), a mantra to Fudō Myō-ō (the *honzon* of the *goma*), and a prayer dedicating the *kegyō* to the welfare of the mountain and the benefit of all people.

6. Entsūru-ji is closed to visitors except on Shākyamuni's lunar birthday.

7. The saffron-colored surplice, or *nyohō-e*, is worn over a two-piece brown robe, or, in the case of women, over a two-piece gray/light-blue robe. The *nyohō-e* is a type of *kesa*, and like all other *kesa*, including the student's white apron-style version, it drapes over the left shoulder, leaving the right shoulder free.

8. On every third day of *kegyō* the students add the Okunoin and the forest cemetery to their prayer circuit, starting at the First Bridge (Ichi-no-hashi) and working through a succession of stations to the climax at Kōbō Daishi's tomb.

9. In 825 Chisen, whom Kūkai had been grooming to be his eventual successor, died at Kōyasan while Kūkai was in the capital. Chisen had been a disciple since the age of nine. Wrote Kūkai, "Whether I was in the royal palace or in the rocky mountains, he followed me as if he were my limbs. When I was hungry [he also was] hungry. When I was joyous [he also was] joyous. How could I imagine that he would beg me to carry his coffin in my wagon and give me painful sorrow?" Yamamoto, *History*, 63. The place of burial is marked by a small *gorintō*.

10. The Kōjin shrine, one of Japan's most beautiful mountain shrines, is visited each year by thousands of lay people who travel there by bus from Kōyasan and from several other points of departure.

11. Yamasaki, *Shingon,* 177–81.

12. The gods' "sacred luggage" has been delivered the previous day, lunar September 2. The Japanese lunar year, based on a Chinese calendar adopted in the seventh century, begins between January 20 and February 19 of the solar calendar. Thus lunar dates are some three to six weeks later than solar dates.

13. Hinonishi, *Kōyasan-shiki-no-inori,* 131–36.

14. The debate begins at dusk and concludes the next morning, with a recess between midnight and four a.m. to permit the Ryūgi priest to perform devotions to the gods at his home temple. Formerly, the texts used in the ritual

had to be memorized, but today they are read (after much rehearsal). Lay visitors may observe the ceremony from the Sannō-in porch or from the back of the hall itself. The Sannō-in Rissei has been held yearly since 1406.

15. For details see Hinonishi, *Kōyasan-shiki-no-inari*, 86–87.

16. Few of Kōyasan's rituals tap more deeply into the early history of Japanese Buddhism. See Hinonishi, *Kōyasan-shiki-no-inari*, 96–98; Hanayama Shōyū, ed., *An Introduction to the Buddhist Canon: 139 Buddhist Scriptures*, trans. R. W. Giebel, 2nd ed. (Tokyo: Bukkyo Dendo Kyokai, 1986), 72.

17. The annual installation of Kōyasan's Hōin is a significant news event. At the 1996 ceremony, which installed the 497th Hōin, there were six video cameramen present, among them one from NHK, Japan's national television network.

18. While in office the Hōin continues to reside at his home temple and observes vegetarianism, celibacy, and physical restriction to the mountain.

CHAPTER 9. A PILGRIMAGE THROUGH THE FOREST CEMETERY

1. Each of the five stones has carved on its face the Sanskrit letter for the element it represents: *A, VA, RA, HA, KHA* (Earth, Water, Fire, Wind, Space). These five letters also are the seed letters of the Five Buddhas of the Womb Realm (Dainichi is represented by the Sanskrit *A*). The backside of the *gorintō* is inscribed with a single elongated Sanskrit *VAM* (Consciousness), the seed letter for the Central Buddha of the Diamond Realm. This calligraphic *VAM* is itself composed of five parts, one part for each of the five "material" elements. Thus, the two sides of the *gorintō* are in essence mirror images of one another, just as are the two expressions of the Dual Mandala. See Stevens, *Sacred Calligraphy*, 11, 69. Also see Rambach, *Secret Message of Tantric Buddhism*, 56–57, 60–61. Hakeda offers the following summary of Kūkai's understanding of the six elements: "These Six Great Elements create all Buddhas, all sentient beings, and all material worlds. There is no creator other than the Six Great Elements, which are at once the creating and the created; the Six Great Elements are in a state of perpetual interfusion. Mahāvairocana [Dainichi], consisting of the Six Great Elements, is one without a second and the totality of all existences and movements in the universe. Thus, all diverse phenomena are identical as to their constituents; all are in a state of constant transformation; no absolute difference exists between man and nature; body and mind are nondual; and, therefore, the value of mind is not necessarily higher than that of body." Hakeda, *Kūkai: Major Works*, 89.

2. See Elizabeth Anna Gordon, "Heirlooms of Early Christianity Visible in Japan," *The Tourist* 8 (July 1920): 35; also Elizabeth Anna Gordon, *Symbols of "The Way"—Far East and West* (Tokyo: Maruzen, 1922), 39. A part of the ancient text carved on the Nestorian Stone reads as follows: "There is One who is true and firm, who, himself uncreated, is the origin of origins; who is incomprehensible and invisible, yet ever existing; who, possessing the secret of all things, created all things; who, surpassing all the Holy Ones, is the sole unoriginated Lord of the Universe; he is our triune, unbegotten, true Lord." (Adapted from a translation by Paul Yashiro Saeki, in Jay Gluck et al., *Japan Inside Out* [Ashiya, Japan: Personally Oriented Ltd, 1992], 403.) Mrs. Gordon found in this text much that reminded her of Kōbō Daishi's conception of the Cosmic Buddha. The original Nestorian Stone may be seen today in Xi-an's Shaanxi Provincial Museum. Another replica is in Rome's Vatican Museum. In the year Mrs. Gordon installed the stone at Kōyasan she published in Tōkyō her fullest commentary on the relationship between Christianity and Mahāyāna Buddhism, a book entitled *The Lotus Gospel.* Among the primary correspondences she finds are that the Word (Logos) of Christianity is equivalent to the True Word (*Shingon*) of esoteric Buddhism, that the Sacred Heart of Jesus matches Buddhism's flaming *mani* jewel, and that the Christian anticipation of the Messiah's return equates with the Mahāyāna belief in the future appearance of Miroku Bodhisattva. Kōbō Daishi, she suggests, presently serves as Miroku's John the Baptist. Thus Mahāyāna Buddhism is but Christianity "clad in a Buddhist garb and nomenclature." See Gordon, *The Lotus Gospel: or, Mahayana Buddhism and Its Symbolic Teachings Compared Historically and Geographically with Those of Catholic Christianity*, 2nd ed. (Tokyo: Waseda University, 1920), 264 and "Foreward."

3. For a discussion of the various categories of the dead and especially of Shingon services for the *muen-botoke*, see Richard Karl Payne, "Shingon Services for the Dead," in *Religions of Japan in Practice,* ed. George J. Tanabe Jr., 159–65 (Princeton: Princeton University Press, 1999).

4. Bibs also are offered when one solicits a favor from one of the *gorintō* or statues in the cemetery. An otherwise unremarkable little Jizō memorial just beyond the Tamagawa, popularly known as the Kasa ("Hat") Jizō, has gained the reputation of assisting sufferers from breast cancer. We found twenty-six bibs tied about the chest of that Jizō, and on the ground before it forty-one small gifts. For a discussion of this Kasa Jizō, see *Sei Ai* (March 1995), 47.

5. The controversial notion that the unhappy spirit of a deceased child may seek retribution (*tatari*) against surviving family members is contrary to traditional Buddhist belief, but nevertheless is promoted by many Buddhist temples in Japan. Among recent studies of the issue are Helen Hardacre, *Marketing the*

Menacing Fetus in Japan (Berkeley, Los Angeles, and London: University of California Press, 1997); William R. LaFleur, *Liquid Life: Abortion and Buddhism in Japan* (Princeton: Princeton University Press, 1992); Anne Page Brooks, "*Mizuko Kuyō* and Japanese Buddhism," *Japanese Journal of Religious Studies* 8 (Sept.-Dec. 1981): 119–47; Hoshino Eiki and Takeda Dōshō, "*Mizuko Kuyō* and Abortion in Contemporary Japan," in *Religion and Society in Modern Japan,* ed. Mark R. Mullins, Shimazono Susumu, and Paul L. Swanson (Berkeley: Asian Humanities Press, 1993), 171–90. With regard to the Shingon belief in the sacred nature of human reproduction, see James H. Sanford, "Fetal Buddhahood in Shingon," *Japanese Journal of Religious Studies* 24 (1997): 1–38. Successive stages of embryonic and fetal development are equated with the eight-petaled lotus, the moon-shaped jewel, the *vajra*, the *gorintō*, and the mantra *AUM.* The evolving organism is regarded as inseparable from the sacred body of Dainichi. Later, of course, in adulthood, the human person faces the daunting task of rediscovering his or her own early "fetal Buddhahood."

6. Among the most popular of the warrior dolls (*musha ningyō*) that provide much of the atmosphere for Japan's Boy's Day are grandly accoutered depictions of Kenshin and Shingen. A truly lucky boy will receive as well a replica of Shingen's battle banner with its famous motto, *Fū-rin-ka-zan* ("Wind-forest-fire-mountain"), an abbreviated assertion of *Swift as the wind; silent as the forest; deadly as fire; unshakeable as the mountain.* See Japan Travel Bureau, *Festivals of Japan* (Tokyo: Japan Travel Bureau, 1991), 44–45. The well-known Japanese *samurai* motion picture epic "Heaven and Earth" (*Ten-to-chi-to*, directed by Kadokawa Haruki, 1990) is about the Kenshin-Shingen relationship.

7. See Aubrey S. and Giovanna M. Halford, *The Kabuki Handbook* (Rutland, VT, and Tokyo: Tuttle, 1956), 403–404. The sculpting of the Fudō *honzon* at Shinshō-ji is popularly attributed to Kōbō Daishi.

8. The granite Asekaki Jizō sits in deep shadow behind a heavy wooden grill, so is difficult to see. Tradition says it was chiseled by Kōbō Daishi. Hinonishi Shinjō, *Kōyasan Minzokushi: Okunoinhen* (Tokyo: K. K. Kōsei Shuppansha, 1990), 19.

9. Here, in brief outline, is the love story. Back in the twelfth century a maidservant of the empress named Yokobue fell in love with a highborn young warrior named Tokiyori. When Tokiyori's father forbade the unequal match, the boy, much in love but unwilling to disobey his father, shaved his head and withdrew to a Buddhist temple west of the capital. Lovesick Yokobue followed him there to plead her cause. To escape Yokobue's still-tempting presence Tokiyori then took the ultimate step of going to Kōyasan. Realizing that all chance of a reunion was lost, Yokobue entered a nunnery in Nara. But when this new life failed to end her yearning, she relocated to Amano in the foothills of Kōyasan in

the hope of catching a glimpse of her beloved when the monks took winter quarters there. Several years passed without their meeting, but in time Tokiyori (who was now known by his religious name, Takiguchi) learned that Yokobue was living at Amano and that she was seriously ill. He sent her a message in the form of a poem and she replied, suggesting that their reunion now could occur only in heaven. The following spring, while meditating at Kōyasan's Daien-in, Takiguchi's attention was drawn to the singing of an *uguisu* ("the Japanese nightingale") perched in a plum tree outside the sanctuary door. The bird's music awakened in him intense memories of Yokobue (her name means "flute," an instrument at which she was very skilled). When the singing abruptly ceased Takiguchi went outside and looked into the well beneath the plum. On the bright surface of the water floated the still body of the bird. Knowing now that Yokobue was dead, Takiguchi retrieved the bird's body and placed it inside Daien-in's statue of Amida Buddha. This statue ever since has been referred to as the Yokobue Buddha or the Uguisu Amida. In the temple's sanctuary today hang paintings that tell the story of Yokobue and Takiguchi. Just outside the sanctuary door are a plum tree and a well. (The location of Daien-in has changed since the twelfth century, so the present tree and well at the temple are essentially memorials to Takiguchi and Yokobue.) Takiguchi's life of piety eventually earned him the name of "the Saint of Kōya." He is buried in the Okunoin cemetery. Yokobue's burial place is rumored to be in Amano, but the matter is uncertain. What is certain is that her spirit is united at last with Takiguchi's spirit in the symbolism of Daien-in's Uguisu Amida statue. The best-known version of this famous story is found in Kitagawa and Tsuchida, *Heike*, 609–12. Also see Tamai Kōichiro, *Yokobue Monogatari* (Kōyasan: Daien-in, 1979), 1–13. For a somewhat different narrative account see Yoshiko K. Dykstra and Yuko Kurata, "The *Yokobue-sōshi*: Conflicts Between Social Convention, Human Love, and Religious Renunciation," *Japanese Religions* 26, no. 2 (July 2001): 117–29. In addition to visiting Kōyasan's Daien-in, devotees of the story visit Takiguchi-dera in western Kyōtō (the temple where Tokiyori first attempted to hide from Yokobue) and Hokke-ji in Nara (where Yokobue first served as a nun). Enshrined at the latter temple is a delicate and quite famous statue of Yokobue that is displayed once each year. At Takiguchi-dera they are both represented by statues placed side by side on the temple altar. Yokobue and Takiguchi do not glance at one another, but gaze humbly straight ahead.

10. R[ichard] H. P. Mason and J[ohn] G. Caiger, *A History of Japan* (Tokyo: Tuttle, 1872), 148.

11. The sponsor of the Burmese stūpa is Jōfuku-in, located just east of the central business section of Kōyasan. At Jōfuku-in is a large pagoda-shaped sanctuary and museum, twenty-six years in construction, that memorializes those

who died in Burma and in all other theaters of the war. Among the displays is a large painting of the horrors of the conventional Buddhist hell. Equally disturbing are two large monochrome murals that present the horrendous suffering at Hiroshima and Nagasaki. The shaken visitor is then invited to descend underground, beneath the sanctuary, to a traditional Gokuraku-meguri ("pilgrimage to paradise") and its vision of redemption. See Ueda Tenzui, "Kōyasan and Southern Buddhism," *The Young East* 2, no. 7 (July 1953): 28–29, 49; also see the text of the latest Jōfuku-in temple brochure.

12. The Kōyasan temple priests buried in this area often are given full-body burials, placed in their burial chambers in an upright seated position after the model of Kōbō Daishi's burial.

13. This comparison is from the year 1991, and I have counted the nearby modern Daireien cemetery together with the "new cemetery." Company monuments often honor all deceased employees, not just the company presidents and managers, in which case everyone receives the status of "company ancestor." Typically, once each year a commission made up of high management, middle management, and the most recently bereaved relatives comes to Kōyasan to chant sūtras, burn incense, pronounce eulogies, and ask the dead to protect the company in its future endeavors. For a general discussion of company memorials at Kōyasan see Nakamaki Hirochika, "Memorial Monuments and Memorial Services of Japanese Companies: Focusing on Mount Kōya," in *Ceremony and Ritual in Japan: Religious Practices in an Industrialized Society*, ed. Jan van Bremen and D. P. Martinez (London and New York: Routledge, 1995), 146–58. At least one company extends its memorial policy to the creatures its business exterminates, "the dead termites, past, present, and future." Such a practice is both good Buddhism and good public relations.

14. The Shintō Yasukuni Jinja ("Shrine for Establishing Peace in the Empire") was founded in Tōkyō by Emperor Meiji in 1869 with the intent of deifying those who had died serving the imperial cause during the Meiji Restoration. Later, the shrine was expanded to include the loyal dead from the Russo-Japanese, Sino-Japanese, and Pacific wars, among them the seven Japanese leaders hanged by the International Military Tribunal in 1948. Having one's name enshrined at Yasukuni was promoted by the wartime government as the noblest of goals and the ultimate consolation for an early death. Kamikaze pilots are said to have parted from one another with the cry, "I'll see you at Yasukuni!" or "I'll meet you under the cherry blossoms on Kudan Hill!" (the location of the shrine). Yasukuni remains for many Japanese a troublesome advertisement for military authority and the imperial system. For a detailed recent discussion of the nature and significance of the Yasukuni shrine see John Nelson, "Social

Memory as Ritual Practice: Commemorating Spirits of the Military Dead at Yasukuni Shinto Shrine," *Journal of Asian Studies* 62, no. 2 (May 2003): 443–67.

15. In all, 934 Japanese, the great majority of them officers, were convicted of war crimes by various Allied tribunals and executed by hanging. They outnumbered the executed Germans by a factor of ten. See *Japan: An Illustrated Encyclopedia* (Kodansha), s. v. "war crimes trials."

16. I was the lone non-Japanese present at this dedication, not because of any personal status but because I saw the physical preparations being made the day before, showed interest, and was invited to attend.

17. Hinonishi, *Kōyasan Minzokushi: Okunoinhen*, 114. Also Gardiner, *Kōyasan*, 55.

18. *Haiku* monuments (called *kuhi*) and *waka* monuments (called *kahi*) are found throughout Kōyasan—in the cemeteries, on temple grounds, beside roads and paths. A booklet published by the Kōyasan Tourist Association contains photographs and locations of 121 of these poems carved on stone. See Kōyasan Kankō Kyōkai, *Kōyasan no kahi ya kuhi o tazunete* (Kōyasan: Kōyasan Kankō Kyōkai, 1989). The mountain's stone-carved poems also are the subject of a twenty-seven-article series in Kōyasan Shuppansha's *Sei Ai* ("sacred love") monthly magazine (Jan. 1999 through March 2001).

19. Sansom, *A History of Japan, 1334–1615*, 369.

CHAPTER 10. THE INNER TEMPLE AND KŌBŌ DAISHI'S MAUSOLEUM

1. *Yakudoshi*, or "calamity years," are determined largely by homonymous associations. For example, the word for forty-two (*shi ni*) has the same sound as "to death"; the word for thirty-three (*sanzan*), the unlucky year for women, has the same sound as "birth difficulty." Historically, the Japanese have taken seriously such associations, assigning to the sounds of a number of words the power to affect events, a concept known as *kotodama* (the "soul/spirit of language"). Today few Japanese men and women come to Kōyasan seeking *yaku-doshi-yoke* ("calamity year protection"), but the service remains a minor source of income at many other temples around the country.

2. Both the inexpensive *nōkyō-chō* and the quite elaborate *kakejiku* are on sale here. A *kakejiku* designed for the eighty-eight temple Shikoku pilgrimage typically will have an image of Kōbō Daishi at its center and designated spaces for each of the eighty-eight temple seals. When the pilgrimage is completed, and all the seals collected, the *kakejiku* is mounted on silk and hung in the family

tokonoma where it will serve as an object of devotion and a work of decorative art. Many pilgrims who do the Shikoku pilgrimage get their first and last seals here at Kōyasan's Gokusho. Other locations at Kōyasan also have their special seals, some for established multi-temple pilgrimages. Myō-ō-in (with its "Red Fudō" painting) and Nan-in (with its Nami-kiri Fudō sculpture) are the final stops on a thirty-three-temple Fudō Myō-ō pilgrimage. Fukuchi-in and Kongōsanmai-in are the final stops on a seventeen-temple Aizen Myō-ō pilgrimage.

3. According to legend, the god Bishamon-ten first appeared in Japan in order to teach military tactics to Prince Shōtoku (572–621), a great historical figure and important early advocate of Buddhism. In more recent times, popular veneration of Bishamon-ten has treated him largely as a source of good fortune, in which case the pagoda he holds is presumed to be filled with silver and gold.

4. Daikoku-ten, the leader of the Lucky Seven, is greeted with a traditional New Year's cheer: "He has come! He has come! Leading the gods of luck, Lord Daikoku has come!" Ihara Saikaku, *The Japanese Family Storehouse*, trans. G. W. Sargent (Cambridge: Cambridge University Press, 1959), 168. Saichō, who may have been the first to introduce Daikoku-ten worship to Japan, depicted the god as having three faces. Kōbō Daishi subsequently had a vision of Daikoku-ten with a single face, and it is Kōbō Daishi's image that is the standard today: a chubby man in a soft hat, baggy silk gown, and black boots, carrying a large bag of treasure and a massive magical hammer that produces good fortune. Usually, Daikoku is shown either standing or sitting on two or four rice bales, further symbols of his capacity to provide material abundance. He also may be accompanied by one or more rats, whom he is shown feeding. The Festival of Daikoku is held on the Day of the Rat. A woman may place an image of Daikoku inside a wooden rice measure as a device to promote conception. The clerks at the Gokusho counter sell woodblock prints of Daikoku that follow the single-headed form of Kōbō Daishi's vision. For the rare three-headed image see the "Three-headed Daikokuten" in the Kōyasan Reihōkan, *Sacred Treasures of Mount Kōya*, 132. Directly across the patio from the Gokusho shrine is a stone statue of the god. Shingon theory proposes that Daikoku is a direct manifestation of Dainichi.

5. See Nitobe Inazo, *Bushido: the Soul of Japan* (Rutland, VT, and Tokyo: Tuttle, 1969), 24–25.

6. The vendetta of the forty-seven *rōnin* entered the Japanese Bunraku and Kabuki repertoire as *Kanadehon chūshingura* ("Treasury of loyal retainers of the Iroha poem"), one of the most complex and glorious of Japanese theater pieces. The *kana* in the title refers to the Japanese syllabary of forty-seven sounds popularly attributed to Kōbō Daishi. In some productions the forty-seven *rōnin*, each one wearing one of the forty-seven *kana* on his breast, strike a carefully

arranged pose while crossing Tōkyō's arched Nihonbashi bridge. As viewed from the audience the syllables on their chests spell out Kōbō Daishi's entire *Iroha* poem, an appropriate text in that it affirms the serenity of the *rōnin* as they face death. The courage and loyalty of the forty-seven was evoked often during the Pacific War. In Germany, between 1942 and 1944, with the likelihood of death and defeat increasing almost daily, four different German versions of *Chūshin-gura* were written and performed. See Detlef Schauwecker, "Japan in German Dramas 1900–1945—German Versions of 'Chushingura' in the Nazi Period," *Transactions of the International Conference of Orientalists in Japan* 31 (1986), 70–78.

7. She concluded that it represented a Messianic version of Miroku, a parallel to the "rejected Corner Stone" of Hebrew tradition. Gordon, *The Lotus Gospel*, 205–207.

8. Miroku's Tushita heaven ("heaven of contentment") is the fourth of the six heavens of desire, a migratory realm well below the eternal and immutable world of the Buddhas. It is where all Bodhisattvas reside prior to being incarnated on earth as Buddhas. In the symbolic geography of Kōyasan the Okunoin region, which includes Kōbō Daishi's tomb, is considered a part of Miroku's Tushita paradise. Several scholars have questioned the validity of the traditional Kūkai-Miroku connection, however, arguing that Kūkai focused almost exclusively on the idea of actualizing Buddhahood in one's present life-time and had little interest in the theoretical issue of a future Buddha. See Kiyota Minoru, *Shingon Buddhism: Theory and Practice* (Los Angeles and Tokyo: Buddhist Books International, 1978), 136–37. The suggestion also has been made that the Japanese interest in Miroku as the Buddha-to-Come was inspired primarily by competition with the Christian teaching of a Redeemer who would return in a "Second Coming." Several other locations in Japan are considered likely places for Miroku's first appearance, most famously Mount Kinbu, which is immediately to the south of Yoshino and not far from Kōyasan.

9. Lady Tamayori's remains are believed to be buried beneath Jison-in's shrine to Miroku. Jison-in has its own version of a "Miroku Stone," but one clearly of modern origin.

10. The usual method of this divination is to lift the magical stone, make a wish, then lift it a second time. If the stone has grown lighter in the interval the wish will come true.

11. Professor Hinonishi puts the number of individual lanterns at around twenty-five thousand. Hinonishi, "*Hōgō* of Kōbō Daishi," 12.

12. The lamps associated with Jōyo and Shirakawa may first have been located at the Miedō in the Garan, for not until the middle of the fourteenth century were lantern offerings made primarily at the mausoleum. See Hinonishi,

"*Hōgō* of Kōbō Daishi," 8–13. The longest continuously burning holy fire in Japan is said to be the wood fire that burns under a cauldron of hot water in the Reika-dō of the Shingon temple built near the summit of Mt. Misen on Miyajima in the Inland Sea. Tradition holds that Kōbō Daishi himself first lit this fire when he practiced the *Gumonji-hō* ritual on Mt. Misen in the year 800. Visitors who climb the island mountain today are invited to enter the small, smoke-blackened shelter and dip out some of the sacred hot water for tea.

13. For a full version of Oteru's story see Takano Harume, *Hinjo no itto* (Kōyasan: Kongōbu-ji, 1954). The flame from the Poor Woman's Lamp is "borrowed" on several occasions at Kōyasan. Quite appropriately, it is the source flame for the tens of thousands of memorial candles and lanterns that are lit each year at the time of O-Bon.

14. It is a custom with some pilgrims not to wash these smocks in the belief that the accumulated stains of the journey are sacred. Such a smock would serve as an appropriate attire for the final journey to Nirvāna. For a description of the many special customs of the pilgrimage, as well as specific details about the individual temples, see Miyata, *Henro Pilgrimage Guide*. See also Oliver Statler, *Japanese Pilgrimage* (Tokyo: Charles Tuttle, 1984) and Readicker-Henderson, *Traveler's Guide to Japanese Pilgrimages*, and, most recently, Ian Reader's reflective and information-packed *Making Pilgrimages: Meaning and Practice in Shikoku* (Honolulu: University of Hawai'i Press, 2005). Actually, only a small minority of the Shikoku pilgrims begin and end their pilgrimages at Kōyasan. Further, as we discovered while in Shikoku, some pilgrims are not Shingon Buddhists, and some deny having any particular devotion to Kōbō Daishi. But nearly all acknowledge a "spiritual" motive for the venture. For a discussion of Kōyasan's influence on the Shikoku pilgrimage, see Ian Reader, "Weaving the Landscape: The Shikoku Pilgrimage, Kōbō Daishi and Shingon Buddhism," in *Matrices and Weavings: Expressions of Shingon Buddhism in Japanese Culture and Society,* a Special Issue (October 2004) of *Mikkyō Bunka Kenkyūsho Kiyō* (Bulletin of the Research Institute of Esoteric Buddhist Culture), Kōyasan University, 139–64.

15. The annex, the Kinen-Tōrōdō, is located immediately to the east of the Tōrōdō but at a slightly lower level. It was constructed in 1984, just twenty years after the new Tōrōdō, when available space in the latter began to run out. It has two *honzon*. The *honzon* on the upper floor is especially interesting, for it is a carved figure of Kōbō Daishi holding a small *gorintō* in his left hand instead of the usual string of beads. Since a *gorintō* is the primary attribute of Miroku, the sculpture is known informally as the "Miroku Daishi."

16. The Six Jizō accompany and comfort the spirits of the dead as they journey forward along one of the Six Paths (the *Rokudō*) temporarily assigned to them by their accumulated *karma*: the path of hell, of hungry ghosts, of animals,

of warring *asuras*, of human beings, and of heavenly beings (in Buddhism the heavenly beings are mortal and have sorrows). According to an old custom, before burial the ashes of the deceased are brought before these Six Jizō, at which time the appropriate Jizō begins his comforting duties. A six-sided tower with the Six Jizō is located near the Ichi-no-hashi bridge of the forest cemetery.

17. Kōbō Daishi's spirit is understood to be present simultaneously in the tomb and in Miroku's heaven.

18. Since Kōbō Daishi's time a number of Japanese priest ascetics have entered terminal meditations, and in several instances their mummified bodies continue to be ritually honored and sometimes displayed as living Buddhas. The most famous of these is monk Tetsumonkai at Churen-ji on Mount Yudono in Yamagata Prefecture. See Hori Ichiro, "Self-Mummified Buddhas in Japan: An Aspect of the Shugen-dō ('Mountain Asceticism') Sect," *History of Religions* 1, no. 2 (Winter 1962), 222–42. Hori finds the following details to be shared by all eight of the "mummified Buddhas" of the Yudono branch of the Shingon Shugendō school in Yamagata: (1) each practiced rigorous asceticism, (2) each abstained from cereals during the final preparation, (3) each believed in the *sokushin jōbutsu* doctrine, (4) each took, or received, the addition of *kai* (taken from *Kū-kai*) as a suffix to their Buddhist names. In this context it is well to keep in mind that the *sokushin jōbutsu* doctrine ("becoming a Buddha with one's present body") addresses the question of becoming enlightened during one's present lifetime. It is not concerned with escaping a natural death or somehow perpetuating one's physical being.

19. For some further speculation about the burial and the burial chamber see Shiba, *Kukai the Universal*, 283–88.

20. Only priests with the rank of *jōgō* are permitted to enter the inner precinct to care for these shrines. If we are surprised to find native gods enshrined within an enclosure defiled by death, we need only remind ourselves that Kōbō Daishi is thought to be alive.

21. A common procedure is to have ashes taken to one of Kōyasan's sub-temples where, after receiving ceremonial attention for one or more years, the ashes are deposited in the Nōkotsudō. Alternatively, the ashes may be brought directly to the Lantern Hall for a memorial ceremony, after which they go to the Nōkotsudō.

22. In 1964 another large collection of sūtras, dated 1114, was dug up during the excavation for the Lantern Hall annex. Those scrolls also were taken to the Reihōkan. There are many locations in Japan where sūtras have been buried as an offering to Miroku.

23. On the animals of the Gobyō see Hinonishi, *Kōyasan Minzokushi: Okunoinhen*, 219.

24. Kongōbu-ji, *Odaishi-sama: eienno-inochi* (Honorable Daishi: eternal life) (Kōyasan: Kongōbu-ji, 1982), 52. For an account of a night at the Gobyō in which many ghosts appear (including the ghost of Toyotomi Hideyoshi's nephew Hidetsugu) see the short tale "Buppōsō" in Ueda, *Ugetsu Monogatari*, 139–49.

25. Kōbō Daishi reportedly revealed to Kakukai, the thirty-seventh abbot of Kongōbu-ji, that Kakukai had in his former lives evolved through the following ascending spiritual stages: (1) an ocean clam that overheard the chanting of a Buddhist hymn, (2) an ox that hauled paper used for copying sūtras, (3) a horse that carried devout pilgrims to Kumano, (4) a human being who cared for sacred votive fires, (5) a human being who served as caretaker at Kōyasan's Okunoin. It is by such karmic increments that one gets to be an abbot. Morrell, *Sand and Pebbles*, 119–20.

26. The observation was made by Kōyasan University President Takagi Shingen in a private interview, Nov. 6, 1992. I had asked if he thought the overwhelming attention shown to the Gobyō tended to obscure Kōbō Daishi's central teachings concerning the Great Sun Buddha as expressed by the Daitō.

27. Later in the morning, at 10:30, Odaishi-sama will receive his second and last meal of the day. In accordance with ancient Buddhist custom, no food will be eaten after the noon hour.

28. A *goma* offering is performed daily in the Lantern Hall at the Okunoin. One also is performed on the 1st, 8th, 11th, 18th, 21st, and 28th of each month at the Aizen-dō in the Garan. Additionally, many individual monastery temples make frequent fire offerings.

29. The Shingon fire offering is far more complex than the following abbreviated account suggests. For a fuller description see Payne, *Shingon Fire Ritual,* especially chapters 6, 7, and 9. I have taken some details from Payne. Another useful description is found in Michael Saso, *Tantric Art and Meditation: The Tendai Tradition* (Honolulu: Tendai Educational Foundation, 1990), 1–31.

30. The *goma* fire sometimes is described as requiring no chemical ignition, but as erupting spontaneously as an effect of the *mantra*. See Stuart Picken, *Buddhism: Japan's Cultural Identity* (Tokyo, New York, and San Francisco: Kodansha International, 1982), 70.

31. The most dramatic esoteric ritual of flame and smoke is the *saitō-goma*, an outdoor fire ceremony that involves a large central pyre made of logs and branches, the burning of thousands of *soe-goma-gi*, and a concluding "fire walk" over hot coals. We attended a number of Shingon-sponsored *saitō-goma*, one of them a well-orchestrated event held in a forest clearing adjacent to Kōyasan's Hōki-in temple. The rectangular roped-off area consecrated for the ritual was

perhaps twenty meters on each side, with the observing faithful gathered outside the rope. The *honzon* for this ceremony was a hidden carving of goddess Benzaiten in the form of a coiled white snake with a human head (Byakuja-gyō Uga Benzain-ryū-ō-jin, popularly shortened to Benzai-ryū-ō). This carving, attributed to Kōbō Daishi, formerly had been enshrined on nearby Mount Benten. Presiding at the ceremony were Hōki-in's head priest and his wife, the latter a shamanistic priestess who is a medium for Benzaiten. (In her role as medium, the wife received on the eleventh day of each month, Benten's Day, visitors who came to her to obtain the goddess' help.) Assisting with the *saitō-goma* was a group of men and women whose skills and dress indicated *yamabushi* training and affiliation. At the ceremony's close, after the head priest and the other ritualists had walked down the purifying path of hot coals to pay obeisance to the goddess, virtually all of the several hundred spectators walked down the same path, each seeking the goddess' help with some personal need. For further details concerning the *saitō-goma*, see Paul L. Swanson, "*Shugendō* and the Yoshino-Kumano Pilgrimage," *Monumenta Nipponica* 35, no. 1 (1981): 67–70, and Payne, *Shingon Fire Ritual*, 53–56. For a description of *yamabushi* attire see H. Byron Earhart, *A Religious Study of the Mount Haguro Sect of Shugendō: An Example of Japanese Mountain Religion* (Tokyo: Sophia University Press, 1970), 25–28. Unless a Shingon temple has some connection with the *yamabushi* tradition it is unlikely to offer an outdoor *goma*. While the *saitō-goma* is not a formal part of the *shido kegyō* program, seminary students usually will receive an initiation into the ritual during their training year.

CHAPTER 11. KŌBŌ DAISHI'S BIRTHDAY CELEBRATION

1. This particular year's four maidens represent Kongōbu-ji temple, the local Kiyō Bank, the Kōyasan Tourist Association, and the town of Kōyasan.

2. The Kōdai football team achieved some fame in the 1990s when they were made the subject of a television documentary. With too few players and no proper place to practice, the Ravens were having trouble developing their skills. They had yet to win their first game—in fact, after several years they had yet to score a point. The team has since been disbanded.

3. Kōbō Daishi is understood to have provided Japan with much of the religious basis for its modern environmental movement. For Kōbō Daishi's theories on the environment see Paul O. Ingram, "Nature's Jeweled Net: Kūkai's Ecological Buddhism," *The Pacific World*, New Series, no. 6 (Fall 1990): 50–64.

CHAPTER 12. CELEBRATING
KŌBŌ DAISHI'S *NYŪJŌ* AND
THE "CHANGING OF THE ROBE"

1. The painting also is known as the *Kaihi-no-mie*, or "Picture of the Opening Door."

2. Other paintings of Daishi in *nyūjo* show his hands as they appear in Prince Shinnyo's portrait: a five-pointed *vajra* in the right hand, a string of prayer beads in the left. See for example the hanging scroll "Kōbō Daishi in Eternal Meditation," Reihōkan, *Sacred Treasures of Mount Kōya*, 64.

3. Emperor Daigo is thought to have instructed Abbot Kangen to locate a source of "spiritual water" at Kōyasan, and this well is the result. Tradition also has Kangen founding Hōki-in temple. *Hōki* is the name of the imperial reign at the time Kōbō Daishi was born. Visitors to the chapel often bring containers to fill with water from the well. The water is believed to have medicinal properties that improve the skin and digestive system.

4. The dye, taken from the bark of the *hinoki* tree, turns the silk a rich brownish-red, a color said to symbolize both the power of the sun and the energy of the earth. The floorboards of Hōki-in's garden porch, where the dyeing process takes place, are deeply stained with the color. Both the weaving of the silk and the tailoring of the robe are done in Kyōto.

5. See Satow, *Handbook for Travellers*, 415, and Kanai, "Development of the Kobo Daishi Cult," 23. Some Shingon priests today suggest that the primary basis for the laity's belief in a living Kōbō Daishi is not the demonstrable presence of a living person in the tomb at Kōyasan but rather the fact that Kōbō Daishi is vividly present in their lives, especially when sought through prayer.

6. Details of the *Tsuma-muki-no-ske-kaji* ceremony are found in Hinonishi, *Kōyasan Shiki-no-inori*, 59. Kōyasan's Sambō-in is the venue for the invocation because of the belief that Sambō-in originally was founded at Jison-in by Kōbō Daishi's mother.

7. This reddish-brown robe is not the new one that was enshrined in the Miedō a few weeks earlier at the solar Shō-mieku ceremony. Rather, it is the robe that was given to Kōbō Daishi the preceding year. When the present Hōin retires from office he will keep this older robe as a precious memento of his service.

8. *Ikebana*, the art of flower arrangement (literally, "flowers kept alive"), had its historical origins in the arrangement of flower offerings for Buddhist deities. The art sometimes is referred to as *hana-no-shūkyō*, "the religion of the flower."

9. The twenty-first day of the other eleven months of the year also are sacred days. On these days less elaborate *mieku* ceremonies are held at the Miedō, the Tōrōdō, and at Daishi Kyōkai.

10. Edward Kamens, trans., *The Three Jewels: A Study and Translation of Minamoto Tamenori's* Sanbōe (Ann Arbor: Center for Japanese Studies, University of Michigan, 1988), 312–14. The eighth day of the fourth month also is the anniversary of Shākyamuni's enlightenment. On this day each month a ceremonial observance is held at Kōyasan's Reihokan museum. On the fifteenth of each month an observance of Shākyamuni's death day is held at Kongōbu-ji.

11. The ceremony and events surrounding the *Busshō-e* also are known as the *Hana-matsuri*, or Flower Festival, because of the offering of flowers. In the scroll painting the infant Shaka is shown standing with his right hand pointing toward the heavens, his left hand pointing toward the earth (the posture also assumed by the small statue in the *hanamidera*). He has just announced to the world his status and role in life: "I alone am honored, in heaven and on earth. This triple world is full of suffering. I will be the savior from this suffering." Near the bottom of the scroll a group of earthly creatures, both human and animal, pay adoring tribute. At the top of the scroll celestial figures are descending to give homage. The four guardian kings are kneeling. From the sky directly above Shaka two great cloud-wrapped dragons pour down a perfumed liquid over his body. Queen Māyā (J., Maya), the Buddha's mother, who died shortly after his birth, is not physically present in the painting, but several Shāla trees are shown, one of which she had grasped for balance when delivering her child. We are told that Shaka emerged from his mother's right side "unsullied by the impurity of the mother's womb." See Mary Cummings, *The Lives of the Buddha in the Art and Literature of Asia* (Ann Arbor: University of Michigan Center for South and Southeast Asian Studies, 1982), 111–16.

12. This particular Shingon *Nehan-e*, with its division into four parts, was designed by the Japanese scholar and mystic Myōe Kōben (1173–1232). Shākyamuni is said to have come to Myōe one midnight and described to him his life in four stages. Thus, the four "lectures." The first lecture is the "*Nehan-kōshiki*," a general reflection on the Buddha's entering Nirvāna. The second, the "*Rakan-kōshiki*," praises the sixteen disciples who preserved and followed his teachings. The third, the "*Yui-seki-kōshiki*," pays homage to the historical sites associated with Shākyamuni's life and death. The fourth and last, the "*Shari-kōshiki*," honors the holiness and magical properties of the eighty thousand fragments of Shākyamuni's remains. See Hinonishi, *Kōyasan-shiki-no-inori*, 37. Theologically, the most significant assertion of the chanted lectures is that Shākyamuni, although he complained of a backache and took to his deathbed much as any other mortal might, was in actual fact the eternal Dharmakāya (J. *hosshin*), the absolute Buddha, the consciousness that permeates all things and out of which all things arise. His birth, awakening, and apparent death, therefore, were but expedients ("skillful means"; Sk. *upāya*; J. *hōben*) designed to inspire lethargic

and ignorant human beings into pursuing for themselves the path toward Enlightenment.

13. Shākyamuni lies on a pallet in a grove of Shāla trees, his body on its right side, head pointed toward the north. All his scattered followers, the kings of every nation, the deities of heaven, and every creature of land and sea (except, some say, the cat) are here. This multitude has been drawn to the deathbed by a luminosity given off by the Buddha's golden body. The Buddha's human disciples show profound grief, but the divine Bodhisattvas, because undeceived, are merely watchful. Near the top of the painting is a small second scene, Lady Māyā looking down from heaven at her dying son. Japan's most famous artistic rendering of Shākyamuni's death is the *Shaka-nehan-zu,* or "Shākyamuni in Nirvāna," a National Treasure painted in 1068 and now in the possession of the Reihōkan museum. For a full discussion of this rarely displayed work see Sherwood F. Moran, "The Death of Buddha, a Painting at Kōyasan," *Artibus Asiae* 36 (1974): 97–146. An excellent reproduction is found in Abeno et al., *Kōyasan Kongōbu-ji,* 80–81.

CHAPTER 13. ANNUAL RITUALS FOR THE DEAD

1. The term *bon* is an abbreviation of *urabon,* the Japanese rendering of the Sanskrit *ullambana,* itself a corrupted form of *avalambana*—literally, "hanging [upside] down." The inverted posture depicts the agony of spirits who live in the hell of the *preta,* or "hungry ghosts." It also might suggest the plight of the infant in the womb awaiting yet one more birth in the endless cycle of birth and death. See Inagaki, *Japanese Buddhist Terms,* s.v. "Urabon." The primary ceremonies of Bon are thought to have had their origin in the *Ullambana-sūtra,* in which the Buddha tells a disciple he can liberate his mother from the realm of the *preta* by making food offerings on the fifteenth day of the seventh month. The disciple is so overjoyed by this instruction that he dances in celebration, thus inaugurating (or so it is supposed) the popular folk dance of Bon, the *bon-odori.* During the Edo era the date of Bon was July 15, a month earlier than the present date.

2. The earlier date has two primary benefits. It permits the mountain's young monks to return to their families for the end of this all-important holiday. It also permits Kōyasan's resident priests to conduct private Bon ceremonies for parishioners who live at a distance.

3. Headstrong Kumagai Naozane (1141–1208), a *samurai* hero of the Gempei War, is much celebrated in Kabuki, Bunraku, and Nō drama, as well as

in the prose epic *Heike monotagari*. The signal event of his violent life was his reluctant battle slaying of a young courtier named Taira no Atsumori (1169–1184), a lad who closely resembled Kumagai's own son. Deeply stricken by the fatal encounter, Kumagai put aside his sword and became a Buddhist ascetic, eventually retreating to Kōyasan on the advice of Hōnin, the founder of the Jōdō sect. At Kōyasan Kumagai lived out his life praying for Atsumori's spirit. The two men, Kumagai and Atsumori, are memorialized with identical side by side *gorintō*. According to playwright Zeami (in the Nō drama *Atsumori*) they will be reborn on the same lotus throne in heaven. Royall Tyler, *Japanese Nō Dramas* (London and New York: Penguin, 1992), 48. The Kōyasan temple where Kumagai is thought to have lived is now named Kumagai-ji. It is the only sub-temple on the mountain that has the *ji* designation. Atsumori's severed head is buried at Suma-dera, a famous Shingon temple in Kobe near the beach where the slaying took place.

4. Kenneth Rexroth calls the hugely productive Yosano Akiko (1878–1942) (fifty-five books, seventeen thousand poems, eleven children) "the greatest woman poet of modern Japan, and one of the great feminists in the history of Japanese women." Kenneth Rexroth and Ikuko Atsumi, *Women Poets of Japan* (New York: New Directions, 1977), 179. Totally fearless, Yosano was one of the few who dared speak out against Japan's overseas aggression, most famously in "Kimishini tamau koto nakare" ("My Brother, Don't Waste Your Life in the War"). Today she is presented as a "feminist voice" of Kōyasan, even though during her life she had no particular association with the mountain.

5. This translation of the Light Mantra is adapted from Arai, *Shingon Esoteric Buddhism*, 128.

6. The quoted statement (by Myōe) about the efficacy of the consecrated sand is taken from Mark T. Unno, *Shingon Refractions: Myōe and the Mantra of Light* (Boston: Wisdom Publications, 2004), 212. For more on Myōe's commentary on the relationship of sand, mantra, the remission of sin, and enlightenment, see George J. Tanabe Jr., *Myōe the Dreamkeeper* (Cambridge, MA, and London: Council on East Asian Studies, Harvard University, 1992), 138–41. See also Janet Goodwin, "Shooing the Dead to Paradise," *Japanese Journal of Religious Studies* 16, no. 1 (1989): 65–66. On the specific *Dosha-kaji* ceremony held at Kōyasan, see Hinonishi, *Kōyasan-shiki-no-inori*, 46–47. Despite the continued prominence of the ceremony at Kōyasan (held there since 1896) and at some other Shingon temples, I was told that consecrated sand is rarely used today in Shingon burials.

7. Plot details of the three plays are found in P. G. O'Neill, *A Guide to Nō* (Tokyo and Kyoto: Hinoki Shoten, 1954). See Tyler, *Japanese Nō Dramas*,

183–204, for a full translation of *Matsukaze*. An encounter between a "traveling priest" and a tormented soul is perhaps the most frequently occurring plot device in Nō drama.

CHAPTER 14. LEAVING THE HOLY MOUNTAIN

1. The chapel sometimes is referred to as Kōyasan's Soto-no-Fudō, or "exterior Fudō," for it lies outside the traditional boundary of Kōyasan. It formerly was cared for by Kongōbu-ji, but now is maintained by laity, or so I was told.

2. Stories of suicide and executions attach to this otherwise serene location. The cascade is named Chigo-no-taki, "The Child's Waterfall," presumably in reference to a suicide story.

GLOSSARY OF SELECTED JAPANESE
AND SANSKRIT TERMS AND NAMES

Note: Japanese words are romanized according to the standard Hepburn system, followed by a rendering in Japanese/Chinese characters. Sanskrit words are transliterated according to the simplified system commonly employed in non-specialized texts, followed, where there is a variance, by the standard scholarly transliteration.

ajari (J. 阿闍梨 ; Sk. āchārya, ācārya): "Holy teacher." Title given to priests who have received Shingon or Tendai esoteric initiation. There are two ranks, great *ajari* (J. 大阿闍梨; *dai ajari*) and ordinary *ajari*.

A-ji-kan (J. 阿字観): "Meditation on the Letter A," in which the Sanskrit A (both as sound [*ah*] and in its written form) is perceived to be the uncreated essence of all things, the *Dharma-kāya*, Dainichi Buddha. The most important of many Shingon meditative practices.

Amida-nyorai (J. 阿弥陀如来; Sk. Amitābha ["infinite light"] or Amitāyus ["infinite life"] Tathāgata): One of the five Buddhas of the Diamond Realm, residing in the West and associated especially with compassion. Amida is the primary Buddha in the Pure Land sects, which emphasize Amida's vow to accept into his Gokuraku paradise all who sincerely call on his name.

Ashuku-nyorai (J. 如来; Sk. Akshobhya, Akṣobhya Tathāgata): The name means "immovable." One of the five Buddhas of the Diamond Realm, residing in the East and representing the Wisdom of the Perfect Mirror (that is, seeing all things precisely as they are). Ashuku's primary emblem is the five-pronged *vajra*. In esoteric Buddhism, Yakushi, the healing Buddha, is equated with Ashuku.

a-un (Sk. oṃ; J. 唵, on): Also AUM or OM. A mystic syllable that announces the presence of the absolute in the phenomenal world, the perpetual outward (*a*) and inward (*un*) flow of the progenitive Diamond Breath. At

Kōyasan the sound is "observed" in the open-mouthed and close-mouthed guardian deities at the Great Gate (Daimon) and in the two guardian dogs at the Myōjin-sha. It begins the *darani* of the Diamond Realm. One of the most complex and comprehensive symbols of Hinduism and Buddhism.

Benzaiten (J. 辯才天; Sk. Sarasvatī): Also Benten or Daibenzaiten. A goddess who variously grants wisdom, beauty, wealth, victory, protection from danger, eloquence in speech or music, and other benefits. Derives from an Indian river goddess. Has an eight-armed form and a two-armed form. In the latter form she plays a lute (*biwa*) and appears in the Womb Realm Mandala.

Bodhisattva (Sk.; J. 菩薩, bosatsu): Literally, "enlightenment being." A transcendent being who has attained enlightenment but renounced entry into Nirvāna in order to assist other sentient beings gain enlightenment. Often takes on the suffering of others or transfers own personal merit. Among the most popular are Jizō, Kannon, Fugen, and Kōkuzō. The term also may be applied to a person whose striving for enlightenment is distinguished by altruism.

bon (J. 盆): Japan's major mid-August festival honoring the ancestral dead.

bonnō (J. 煩悩; Sk. klesha, kleśa): "Evil passions" (*karma* bonds) that pollute the human mind and body. Some commentaries hold that there are 108 of these afflictions.

Busshō-e (J. 佛生会): The ceremonial observance of Shākyamuni's birthday, April 8. Also known as the *Hana-matsuri*, or Flower Festival.

Butchō (J. 佛頂; Sk. ushnīsha, uṣṇīṣa): A fleshy protuberance on the crown of the head that indicates the attainment of Buddhahood. One of the thirty-two distinguishing marks (*sanjūni-sō*) on the body of the Buddha.

butsudan (J. 佛壇): A Buddhist altar, most especially in a private home or private quarters of a temple, where family ancestors are enshrined and religious rites performed.

chigo (J. 稚児): A child, especially one who represents a divinity at a festival.

Chō-ishi-michi (J. 町石道): "Chō-stone-path." The primary pilgrimage trail that ascends Kōyasan. Extends from Jison-in near the Kinokawa River to the Daitō at Kōyasan, and thence to Kōbō Daishi's tomb. Named for the stone markers spaced one chō (109 meters) apart along the route.

Dainichi Nyorai (J. 大日如来; Sk. Māhāvairochana [Māhāvairocana] Tathāgata): The Great Sun Buddha. The Essence of the cosmos. Ultimate Reality. All Buddhas and Bodhisattvas, and all their teachings, emanate from Dainichi.

Daishi Kyōkai Honbu (J. 大師教会本部): Daishi Mission Headquarters. A training and worship center at Kōyasan devoted primarily to the laity.

Daishi-tanjō-e (J. 大師誕生会): The "Daishi Nativity Ceremony," held on June 15. Also known as the *Aoba matsuri*, or "Blue (Green) Leaves Festival."

Daitō (J. 大塔): Great Stūpa. At Kōyasan the massive central "pagoda" built in the form of a *tahōtō* ("tower of many treasures"). It enshrines Dainichi Buddha, whose cosmic body it represents. See also *stūpa*.

dan (J. 壇): The square altar table in a sanctuary where the offering rituals are performed. The *dan* for a fire offering is called a *goma-dan*.

Denpō-kanjō (J. 傳法灌頂): The formal "Dharma-transmission initiation" into the esoteric priesthood.

deshi (J. 弟子): A student formally receiving instruction from a teaching priest or master, the *shisō*.

Dharma (Sk.; J. 法, hō): Close to the English word "religion," but with a wider connotation: law, truth, ethics, universal norms. A summational term for principles of conduct that are conducive to good karma. Also used to refer to the totality of Buddhist teaching.

Dharma-kāya (Sk.; J. 法身, hosshin): The transcendent body (*kāya*) of the Buddha that equates with Ultimate Reality, the Essence of the Universe. In Shingon Buddhism this body directly reveals the fundamental esoteric teachings. The two other Buddha bodies are the enjoyment body (Sk. sambhoga-kāya, saṃbhoga-kāya) that enjoys bliss in paradise and the transformation body (Sk. nirmāna-kāya, nirmāṇa-kāya) by which a Buddha appears on earth—Shākyamuni, for example.

dōjō (J. 道場): Literally, "hall of the way." A hall or location reserved for religious practice and the worship of the Buddha.

ema (J. 絵馬): Literally, "horse picture." A small wooden tablet (usually five-sided) with a votive picture on the front and a written appeal on the back. The tablet is hung at the shrine of a *kami* or, more rarely, a Buddhist divinity.

En-no-Gyōja (J. 役行者): En-the-Ascetic (b. 634?). Also known as En-no-Ozunu. A semilegendary Buddhist mountain ascetic believed to have achieved miraculous powers. Patriarch of the mountain sect Shugendō, whose followers are called *yamabushi* ("one who sleeps in the mountains").

Fudō Myō-ō (J. 不動明王; Sk. Achala-vidyā-rāja, Acala-vidyārāja): "Immovable Mantra King." The best known of the myō-ō and, despite his frightening demeanor, among the most beloved and trusted of Japanese Buddhist deities. A direct manifestation and servant of the Great Sun Buddha.

fusuma (J. 襖): An interior screen or sliding door made of two thicknesses of paper stretched over a wooden frame. Usually covered with a painting or decorative design.

garan (J. 伽藍; Sk. saṃghārāma, saṃghārāma): The courts and buildings of a Buddhist temple referred to collectively. At Kōyasan the term is applied to the halls and large court at the original temple location.

gasshō (J. 合掌; Sk. añjali): A gesture of salutation or reverence made by joining one's palms together and placing them before the breast.

Gobutsu (J. 五佛): The comprehensive central "five Buddhas" in esoteric Buddhism. In the Diamond Realm Mandala the *Gobutsu* are depicted with Dainichi in the center surrounded by the four directional Buddhas: Ashuku, Hōshō, Amida, and Fukūjōju. In the Womb Realm Mandala the equivalent directional Buddhas are Hōdō, Kaifuke, Muryōju, and Tenkuraion.

gobyō (J. 御廟): A place of burial. At Kōyasan applied almost exclusively to Kōbō Daishi's mausoleum.

godai-myō-ō (J. 五大明王): The Five Great Kings of Light (or Mantra Holders), each a direct manifestation of one of the Five Buddhas. With fierce demeanor they protect Buddhism, subdue evil, and aid those in search of enlightenment. There are other myō-ō (Sk. vidyārāja) beside the five, most importantly (at Kōyasan) Aizen Myō-ō. The myō-ō occupy their own mansion in the Womb Realm Mandala.

goeika (J. 御詠歌): A choral chanting of sacred songs to the accompaniment of hand bells.

gokuraku (J. 極楽; Sk. Sukhāvatī): "Highest joy." The paradise of Amida Buddha and, by popular extension, any heavenly paradise.

Gokusho (J. 御供所): Offering Hall. The large hall at the Okunoin where various offerings are prepared, including Kōbō Daishi's two daily meals.

Goma (J. 護摩; Sk. homa): The ritual act of burning special votive sticks and other materials as an offering to a deity. The offering may be performed for a wide range of objectives, such as stopping some calamity, destroying evil passions, and gaining enlightenment. A *saitō-goma* is a large-scale outdoor version of the ritual that includes a central pyre of logs and often the burning of thousands of *soe-goma-gi* ("attached-goma-sticks"). A "fire walk" over hot coals usually concludes a *saitō-goma*.

gorintō (J. 五輪塔): Literally, "five-ringed tower." A tombstone made up of five vertically placed stones, each stone carved to represent one of the five elements (earth, water, fire, air, space). The monument as a whole represents both the sixth element, consciousness, and the Dharma body of the Great Sun Buddha.

goryō (J. 御霊): An unquiet or vengeful spirit who may have died unhappily and without receiving appropriate rites. Such a spirit can be pacified through specific ceremonies known as *goryō-e*.

Go-shichinichi-no-mishuhō (J. 後七日の御修法): "Imperial Rite of the Second Seven Days of the New Year." Often shortened to *mishuhō*. Grand ceremony inaugurated by Kōbō Daishi for the purpose of praying for the health of the Emperor and the peace of the nation. Originally held at the Imperial Palace, but now at Tō-ji in Kyōto.

gumonji-hō (J. 求聞持法): A lengthy and demanding ritual practice, dedicated to Kokūzō Bodhisattva, for obtaining an enhanced memory and understanding of the scriptures, thus assisting one toward enlightenment. Performed several times by Kōbō Daishi.

Gyoi-kaji (J. 御衣加持): "Precious Clothes Incantation." The ceremony held at Hōki-in on March 17 during which Kōbō Daishi's new robe and other garments are purified.

haibutsu kishaku (J. 廃仏毀釈): "Abolish the Buddha, destroy Shākyamuni." A slogan of Japan's anti-Buddhist activists during the early Meiji period.

hanamidera (J. 花見寺): A bower of flowers made to shelter a small statue of the infant Shākyamuni or the infant Kōbō Daishi during celebrations of their respective nativities.

Hannya-rishu-kyō (J. 般若理趣經; Sk. Prajñā-pāramitā-naya-sūtra): Often shortened to *Rishu-kyō*. The teaching of perfect wisdom conveyed to Kongōsatta by the Great Sun Buddha. In the Shingon sect the *Rishu-kyō* is chanted each morning as the core sūtra of the *Rishu-zammai-hōyō* service.

Hannya-shin-gyō (J. 般若心經): A very short sūtra (262 characters) that represents the essence of the long Prajñā-pāramitā-sūtra, an expression of the transcendental wisdom of emptiness (Sk. shūnyatā, śūnyatā). Frequently chanted from memory by the laity and often copied for *shakyō*.

Henjō-kongō (J. 遍照金剛): Roughly, "the light that shines everywhere and is as eternal as the diamond." The esoteric name given to Kōbō Daishi by his Chinese mentor, Hui-kuo. Also the esoteric name of Dainichi-nyorai.

henro (J. 遍路): A religious pilgrim.

hibutsu (J. 秘仏): Literally, "secret Buddha." A Buddha image that is hidden permanently or revealed only on special occasions.

higan-e (J. 彼岸会): A Buddhist ceremony for the dead held at the spring and fall equinoxes. *Higan* translates as "the other shore."

hijiri (J. 聖): Itinerant holy men who at times lived in large numbers at Kōyasan (the *kōya-hijiri*) and did much to spread the fame of the mountain and its founder.

hōin (J. 法印): The highest liturgical office at Kōyasan, held for one year by a senior priest who acts as Kōbō Daishi's ceremonial surrogate.

honden (J. 本殿): The main shrine or inner sanctuary where a *kami* is enshrined. A *haiden* is an oratory or hall (or space) for worship that stands in front of a *honden*.

hondō (J. 本堂): The main hall of a temple where the *honzon* is enshrined.

honji suijaku (J. 本地垂迹): The theory that the Shintō gods are incarnations of Buddhist divinities.

honzon (J. 本尊): A temple's principal object of worship.

hotoke (J. 佛): A Buddha. Or an ancestral spirit that after a period of time and with proper ritual support becomes a Buddha. *Hotoke ni naru,* "to become a Buddha," is a polite term for dying.

Hui-kuo (Ch.; J. 惠果, Keika): (746–805) The Chinese mentor to Kōbō Daishi and the seventh of Shingon's Eight Patriarchs of the Propagation of Doctrine.

ihai (J. 位牌): A memorial tablet on which the posthumous name of a deceased person is written.

ikebana (J. 生け花): Literally, "flowers kept alive." The art of flower arrangement, with ancient origins in the practice of preparing flower offerings for Buddhist deities.

Inari (J. 稲荷): Formerly a Japanese god of the rice harvest, but now a god who assists with almost any enterprise. Closely linked to Kōbō Daishi, especially as the primary guardian deity of Tō-ji temple in Kyōto. Also a guardian of Kōyasan.

Iroha-uta (J. いろは歌): The Japanese syllabary ingeniously arranged in a sequence that forms a Buddhist poem. Its composition is popularly attributed to Kōbō Daishi.

Jizō Bosatsu (J. 地藏菩薩; Sk. Kshitigarbha-bodhisattva, Kṣitigarbha-bodhisattva): Literally, "womb of the earth." Popularly venerated as protector of the suffering dead, especially the children. Also protector of travelers. Has the appearance of a simple monk.

Jōdō-shin-shū (J. 浄土真宗): The "True Essence Pure Land Sect" founded c. 1224 by Hōnen's disciple Shinran. Usually referred to as Shin-shū. More revolutionary than Jōdo-shū in that it abandoned the *vinaya* precepts, permitted its priests to live as laymen (get married, eat meat, etc.), and gave less stress to the *nembutsu*. Teaches total dependence on Amida's grace for salvation.

Jōdō-shū (J. 浄土宗): The "Pure Land Sect" founded by Hōnen in 1175. Teaches that anyone who believes in Amida's original vow and recites the *nembutsu* will be reborn in Amida's Pure Land.

Jūjū-shin-ron (J. 十住心論): "The Ten Stages of the Development of the Mind." The title of Kōbō Daishi's discourse on the evolution of human religious thought and temperament from the most primitive stage to the most transcendent.

juzu (J. 数珠): A string of prayer beads. The standard Shingon *juzu* has 108 beads.

kaimyō (J. 戒名): An honorific posthumous name assigned by a priest.

kaji (J. 加持): A transference of the Buddha's compassionate power to provide physical health and peace of mind, usually in association with specific prayers and rituals.

kakejiku (J. 掛け軸): A decorative hanging scroll. At Kōyasan often refers to a long scroll that displays the seals of the eighty-eight temples of the Shikoku pilgrimage.

Kakuban (J. 覺鑁): (1095–1143) A head abbot who did much to revitalize Kōyasan, but was driven from the mountain in 1140 when he attempted to introduce new doctrines. Kakuban's followers later founded the *Shingi* branch of the Shingon Sect.

kami (J. 神): In general use refers to indigenous "Shintō" deities, many of whom were assimilated into Buddhism during the eleventh and twelfth centuries through identification with Buddhist figures. Also may be used to describe any person, object, entity, or place that has a sacred, numinous quality.

kanchō (J. 管長): The chief abbot. The elected superintendent priest of Kōyasan.

kanjō (J. 灌頂; Sk. abhisheka, abhiṣeka): A formal anointing or consecration ceremony that confers important powers.

karma (Sk.; J. 業, gō): A principle of causality that holds that the intention of every thought, word, and deed, whether good or evil, imprints a latent influence on one's life that produces an eventual corresponding effect, often in future lifetimes.

kechien-kanjō (J. 結縁灌頂): A Shingon initiation rite during which a priest or lay devotee is bonded more closely to the Buddha. Among the several ceremonial devices employed are the dropping of a *shikimi* leaf on a mandala while blindfolded and having one's head sprinkled with water.

kegyō (J. 加行): A period of intense practice that the monks and priests of Kōyasan enter from time to time. A formal one-hundred-day *shidō kegyō* is a requirement in seminary training.

kesa (J. 袈裟): An outer vestment worn by priests. Considered a sacred symbol of the priesthood and the Buddhist faith.

kō (J. 講): A lay religious association.

Kōbō Daishi (J. 弘法大師): "Dharma-spreading Great Teacher." Posthumous name awarded priest Kūkai (774–835), founder of the Japanese Shingon sect and the monastery on Kōyasan. See also *Kūkai*.

Kōmyō-shingon (J. 光明眞言): "Mantra of Light." A basic Shingon mantra by which evil karma is destroyed by the light of the Buddha.

kondō (J. 金堂): "Golden hall." The chief hall of a large Buddhist temple compound.

Kongōbu-ji (J. 金剛峰寺): "Diamond Peak Temple." The name selected by Kōbō Daishi for the overall temple-monastery he founded on Kōyasan. The name now usually applies only to the central headquarters temple of the mountain, which also is the headquarters of the international Kōyasan Shingon-shū branch of Shingon.

Kongō-kai (J. 金剛界; Sk. Vajra-dhātu): The "Diamond Realm" that represents the Wisdom aspect of the Great Sun Buddha. Depicted in the Kongō-kai (Diamond Realm) Mandala.

Kōya-maki (J. 高野槙): Japanese umbrella pine. Bundles of this lush, long-lasting, dark-needled pine are sold to visitors for decorating family graves and *butsudan*. Said to contain the spirit of Buddhism.

Kōyasan (J. 高野山): Mount Kōya, named for the elevated level valley (kōya) where the temple monastery is built.

Kūkai (J. 空海): The assigned ordination name of Saeki no Mao (774-835), born in Sanuki Province, Shikoku, founder of the Shingon sect and Kōyasan. The name literally means "sky-sea," but perhaps is better rendered as "the ocean of emptiness." See *Kōbō Daishi*.

kyō (J. 経; Sk. sūtra): A scripture that conveys the Buddha's teaching.

kyōzō (J. 経蔵): A storehouse for Buddhist scripture.

Mahāyāna (Sk.; J. 大乗, Daijō): Literally, "the Great Vehicle (of salvation)." The dominant form of Buddhism in China, Tibet, Korea, and Japan, and therefore often referred to as the Northern School. Emphasizes the Bodhisattva ideal of renouncing Nirvāna in order to work for the enlightenment of all people. Usually teaches that earthly desires, when properly redirected, are inseparable from enlightenment. The contrasting term *Hīnayāna* (Sk.; J. shōjō; literally, "small or lesser vehicle" of salvation), once a common description of southern Buddhism, is now largely avoided.

mandala, maṇḍala (Sk.; J. 曼荼羅, mandara): A visual representation of the forces—Buddhas, Bodhisattvas, and other divine beings—that make up the cosmic order. Esoteric mandalas usually follow the model of the ground plan of a symmetrical palace with a square central court and exterior entrances in each of the four directions. Used as aids in various rituals and as objects of meditation.

mani-shu (J. 摩尼珠; Sk. chintāmani, cintāmaṇi): A sacred globular gem with a pointed top, often surrounded by flame, that represents the Buddha and his teaching. May be equated with the *nyoi-shu*, a symbol of Bodhichitta, the compassion that impels one to seek enlightenment for the sake of all living beings. Is the primary emblem of the Daitō at Kōyasan.

mantra (Sk., J. 眞言, shingon): "True word." A mystical syllable, word, or phrase, usually chanted, employed to concentrate the mind and effect spiritual and temporal change. Mantra made up of longer verses are called *darani* (J. 陀羅尼; Sk. dhāranī, dhāraṇi).

mappō (J. 末法): The final period of the decay of the Dharma during which people find it all but impossible to understand or practice Shākyamuni's teachings, and therefore are in need of an easier path to salvation. In Japan *mappō* was thought to have begun in 1052. The concept is important in Pure Land Buddhism but generally rejected by Shingon.

miedō, or mieidō (J. 御影堂): "Hall of the honorable portrait." A hall where an image (usually a painting) of a noble priest or founder of a temple is enshrined.

Mikkyō (J. 密教): Literally, "esoteric (secret, hidden, difficult, profound, mystical) doctrines." Contrasted with *kengyō*, "exoteric doctrines." According to tradition the esoteric doctrines were made known by Dainichi, the Dharmabody Buddha, and subsequently transmitted through a succession of receiving patriarchs (Kongōsatta, Nāgārjuna, etc.). After surfacing in India in the seventh and eight centuries, Mikkyō was carried to China in the eighth, then introduced to Japan as Shingon Esoteric Buddhism in the ninth by Kōbō Daishi. Mikkyō also was incorporated into Tendai by Saichō and others. Sometimes referred to as *Mantrayāna, Vajrayāna,* and *Tantrayāna.*

mikkyō-no-hana (J. 密教の花): Esoteric flower arrangement.

mikoshi (J. 神輿): An ornate covered litter for transporting a deity from one location to another.

Miroku (J. 弥勒; Sk. Maitreya): The Buddha of the future, now dwelling in the Tushita heaven (Sk. Tuṣita; J. 兜率天, Tosotsu).

mokujiki (J. 木喰): "Wood-eating." An ascetic practice limiting the diet to fruit, berries, and nuts, all of which grow on vines and trees, and abstaining from rice and other grains.

mudrā (Sk.; J. 印相, inzō): Literally, "sign." Symbolic poses of the hands and fingers used in conjunction with *mantras* during meditation. Specific *mudrā* usually are associated with the enlightenment or vows of a particular Buddha, Bodhisattva, or other divinity. Mudrā were introduced to Japan by Kōbō Daishi and are employed primarily by followers of Shingon and Tendai.

muen-botoke (J. 無縁仏): The forgotten or "unconnected" dead who have no one to mourn for them or perform rituals in their behalf. Gravestones of the *muen-botoke* are called *muen-tō.*

myōjin-sha (J. 明神社): Shrine for a "bright kami" or deity. The term usually implies a shrine where the deity is thought to be a combined *kami* and Buddha (or Bodhisattva).

Nāgārjuna (Sk.; J. 龍樹, Ryūju): (c. 150–c. 250) One of the chief philosophers of Mahāyāna Buddhism and the first of Shingon's Eight Patriarchs of the Propagation of Doctrine. Legend has Nāgārjuna receiving the basic esoteric sūtras in a miraculous Iron Tower in southern India.

naijin (J. 内陣): Literally, "inner section." The inner sanctuary of a *hondō* where the *honzon* and altar are located and where the rituals are performed. The *gejin*, or outer section, is primarily a gathering place for those witnessing the ceremony.

Nehan-e (J. 涅槃会): Ceremonial commemoration of Shākyamuni's entering Nirvāna (Feb. 15).

nembutsu (J. 念仏): Literally, "thinking of the Buddha." Usually refers to the chanted invocation "namu-Amida-butsu" ("I take refuge in Amida Buddha") with the intention of gaining rebirth in Amida's western paradise after death. A practice of the various Pure Land sects.

Nirvāna (Sk. Nirvāṇa; J. 涅槃, Nehan): Literally "extinction," but more accurately a mode of blissful existence that is free from the effects of karma and change. In esoteric Buddhism the emphasis is on union with the universal wisdom and compassion of Dainichi, the cosmic Buddha, and consequently on continued service to others.

nō (J. 能): Noh drama. A highly stylized poetic dance-drama, often employing masks, that originated in the fourteenth century. Nō plays frequently address Buddhist themes.

nōkotsudō (J. 納骨堂): A special temple hall for the interment of cremated remains.

nōkyō-chō (J. 納経帳): An album carried by pilgrims in which the stamp or seal of each visited temple is entered.

nyonin-kinzei (J. 女人禁制): "No women allowed." The policy of excluding women from sacred areas or areas reserved for male religious practice.

Nyonin-Kōya (J. 女人高野): "Kōya for Women." Shingon temples specially dedicated to providing women with the religious training and experience denied them by their exclusion from Kōyasan.

nyūjō (J. 入定): Literally, "entering into meditation (Sk. samādhi)." At Kōyasan the term is applied especially to the meditation Kōbō Daishi entered at the end of his life and which he still sustains at his place of burial.

o-fuda (J. お札): A type of talisman purchased at a temple or shrine that brings good luck or wards off bad influences. Usually a flat, slightly-tapered piece of wood stamped with the temple/shrine name and wrapped in white paper.

ōhiroma (J. お広間): The grand room. A large public room in a temple where major gatherings and ceremonies are held.

okunoin (J. 奥の院): An especially sacred "inner hall or sanctuary" located in a remote area of a temple property. At Kōyasan the Okunoin is composed of Kōbō Daishi's mausoleum, the dozen or so halls and residences that support the ceremonial observances at the mausoleum, and the forest cemetery through which pilgrims make their approach.

Rishu-zammai-hōyō (J. 理趣三昧法要): The primary morning ceremony at most Shingon temples, used for such purposes as venerating the *honzon*, healing the sick, and assisting the dead. Central to the ceremony is the chanting of the *Hannya-rishu-kyō*.

rokudai (J. 六大): The Six Elements (earth, water, fire, air, space, and consciousness) that are the basic ingredients of the universe. The six fully interpenetrate one another, thus supporting the essential unity of temporal phenomena and unchanging ultimate reality (that is, the unity of the Womb and Diamond Realms).

Ryōbu-mandara (J. 兩部曼荼羅): The "Dual Mandala" made up of the Kongō-kai and Taizō-kai mandalas. Although each mandala emphasizes a different aspect of Dainichi Buddha, the two are fully equivalent.

Ryōbu Shintō (J. 兩部神道): "Two-sided" or "Dual" Shintō, which holds that the indigenous gods of Japan are manifestations of various Buddhist divinities. For example, the sun deity Amaterasu of Ise Jingū is a manifestation of Dainichi Buddha. The theory is associated especially with Shingon.

Saichō (J. 最澄): (767–822) Founder of the Japanese Tendai sect (Ch. *T'ien-t'ai*) and of Enryaku-ji temple on Mount Hiei near the capitol. Posthumously named Dengyō Daishi.

saisen bako (J. 賽銭箱): The donation boxes found in front of nearly all Shintō and Buddhist shrines.

samādhi (Sk.; J. 定, jō): Meditation. The condition of mind that is reached through meditation. See also *nyūjō*.

sannō (J. 山王): Mountain king or mountain god.

Senshū-gakuin (J. 専修学院): The one year "Specialization School" at Kōyasan for training male priests in ritual practice. Women attend the Nisō-gakuin.

settai (J. 接待): An offering made to a pilgrim (henro).

shakujō (J. 錫杖): Literally, "copper staff." A monk's wooden walking staff with a top of loose metal rings that rattle. The approaching noise warns ground insects and other creatures away or, alternatively, awakens them from illusory dreams. Commonly held by images of Jizō, En-no-Gyōja, and Kōbō Daishi when he appears as a traveling monk.

Shākyamuni, Śākyamuni (Sk.; J. 釋尊, Shakamuni, Shaka, Shakuson): Literally, "Sage of the Shaka Clan." Epithet for the historical Buddha and founder of Buddhism who lived in India around 500 BCE.

shakyō (J. 写経): The religious practice of sūtra copying.

shari (J.; Sk. sharīra, śarīra): A relic, especially of the Buddha.

shido kegyō (J. 四度 加行): "Preparatory Fourfold Enlightenment Practice." An intense one-hundred-day practice that is part of Kōyasan's seminary training.

shikimi (J. 樒): The *illicium religiosum*, or star anise. A native evergreen shrub dedicated to the Buddha and employed in the *kechien-kanjō* ceremony. Also pronounced *shikibi*.

shinbessho (J. 真別処): An isolated residence or hermitage. At Kōyasan it is the popular name for Entsūritsu-ji, a remote, deep woods training center for priests.

Shingon-shū (J. 真言宗): Literally, "True Word Sect." The school of Esoteric Buddhism systematized by Hui-kuo and Kōbō Daishi and introduced to Japan by Kōbō Daishi in the early ninth century. Kōyasan Shingon-shū is the branch of Shingon with headquarters at Kongōbu-ji.

shisō (J. 師僧): A teacher priest who gives religious instruction and guidance to a student disciple (J. 弟子, *deshi*).

shōji (J. 障子): Sliding screens of one thickness of undecorated, white, semi-opaque paper stretched over a wooden lattice. Designed to admit a soft light through windows and doorways while providing privacy.

Shōjin-ryōri (J. 精進料理): Literally, "a diet in pursuit of enlightenment." The temple diet; vegetarian, with some further restrictions. The term also implies the proper method of preparing and arranging food.

Shō-mieku (J. 正御影供) "Exact Day Ceremony of the Sacred Portrait." Ceremonial commemoration of the anniversary of Kōbō Daishi's entering into his final meditation. Observed both on the solar anniversary (March 21), when the primary venue is the Tōrōdō, and on the lunar anniversary (21st day of 3rd lunar month), when the primary venue is the Miedō.

shōmyō (J. 声明): The chanting of Buddhist hymns and verses. A major religious practice and area of study.

Shugei-shuchi-in (J. 綜藝種智院): Innovative school founded by Kōbō Daishi in 828 near Tō-ji in the capital. Also the name of the present-day college at Tō-ji.

Shugyō Daishi (J. 修行大師): A popular devotional image of Kōbō Daishi showing him with a walking staff, a sedge hat, and wearing pilgrim dress.

shukubō (J. 宿坊): Quarters at a temple reserved for guests and pilgrims.

shumi-dan (J. 須彌壇): A dais for a Buddhist image, named after the central cosmic mountain, Mount Sumeru (J. 須彌山, Shumi-sen), that supports both the earth and paradise.

sōhei (J. 僧兵): Low ranking monk soldiers attached to many Japanese temples from the latter half of the tenth century to the end the sixteenth.

sokushin jōbutsu (J. 即身成仏): "Becoming a Buddha with one's present body." Perhaps the most fundamental doctrine of Shingon Buddhism.

sōrin (J. 相輪): The spire at the top of a stūpa or "pagoda."

stūpa (Sk.; J. 塔, tō): Originally, in India, a dome-shaped structure placed over the remains of the historical Buddha and other saints, but which subsequently evolved into forms variously emphasizing a dome-shaped core, the base terraces, or a multistoried tower, etc. The primary examples of the *stūpa* at Kōyasan are the great central Daitō and the several smaller but similarly designed *tahōtō*. All have a square base story above which is a residual dome, a large upper roof, and a multi-ringed spire. All enshrine Buddhas and are venerated as symbols of Ultimate Reality. Miniature *stūpas* containing relics or a selection of scripture, and representing Dainichi Buddha, are placed at the center of Shingon altar tables. Gravestones in the form of *gorintō* also are a type of *stūpa*, as are the wooden memorial *sotoba* placed at graves. See also *daitō*.

sugi (J. 杉): The Japanese cedar. *Cryptomeria japonica.* Japan's largest conifer and Kōyasan's most prominent and dramatic tree. Small *sugi* branches are used to make *hanamidera* bowers and are placed in rows (*sugi* lines) to establish ceremonial paths and set off sanctified areas. The bark sometimes is used for incense.

Taizō-kai (J. 胎藏界; Sk. Garbha-dhātu): The "Womb Realm" representing the Great Sun Buddha's unfolding Compassion that nurtures all phenomena, providing every sentient being with the inherent capacity to attain enlightenment. Depicted in the Taizō-kai (Womb Realm) Mandala.

temizuya (J. 手水屋): A basin of running water at the entry to a shrine or other sacred area for the ritual cleansing of one's hands and mouth.

tengai (J. 天蓋): A canopy, usually golden, that hangs above the altar and major sacred images in a temple. A symbol of the glories of paradise.

tengu (J. 天狗): A mysterious creature of Japanese folklore with a long beak, wings, and the body of a man. Or, if of higher rank, a long nose, red face, and holding a fan made of feathers. Usually resides in the upper branches of *sugi* groves in the mountains, perhaps guarding a nearby treasured object. Tengu traditionally are mockers of priests and Buddhism, but not at Kōyasan.

tōba (J. 塔婆; Sk. stūpa): A memorial tablet in the form of a thin slat of wood cut in the profile of a *gorintō* on which has been placed the Buddhist name (*kaimyō*) of the deceased person.

Tōdai-ji (J. 東大寺): "Great East Temple." An imperial temple founded near the Nara capital in 741 that became the headquarters of all provincial temples during the Nara Period. Was the location of the nation's first official Buddhist *kaidan* (ordination platform) and the possessor of the colossal bronze statue of the Great Sun Buddha known as the Daibutsu. Kōbō Daishi served as Tōdai-ji's administrative director for three years.

Tō-ji (J. 東寺): "East Temple." Headquarters of the Tō-ji branch of Shingon-shū. Founded in the imperial capital (Heian-kyō/Kyōto) in 796 and later developed by Kōbō Daishi into a major esoteric Buddhist center.

tokonoma (J. 床の間): A decorative alcove in a Japanese room that typically includes a slightly raised floor, a hanging scroll, and an arrangement of flowers. Treated as a sacred space.

tōrōdō (J. 灯籠堂): "Lantern hall." At Kōyasan the large veneration hall that faces Kōbō Daishi's mausoleum and is filled with memorial lanterns.

tsuya (J. 通夜): An all-night vigil or meditation. *Tsuya-dō*, halls set aside for such vigils, are found at some temples along pilgrimage routes.

ūrnā, ūrṇā (Sk.; J. 白毫相, byakugō-sō): A clockwise curling tuft of hair on the forehead between the eyes of a Buddha or Bodhisattva. The tuft emits the light of spiritual insight.

vajra (Sk.; J. 金剛, kongō): Indra's thunderbolt modified and used by esoteric Buddhism as a symbol of indestructible truth, the essence of everything that exists. Often translated as "diamond" or "adamantine." As a ritual instrument the *vajra* takes the form of a bolt with one (J. 壱股杵, *dokko-sho*), three (J. 三股杵, *sanko-sho*), or five (J. 五股杵, *goko-sho*) prongs at either end. A version with five prongs at one end and a bell at the other is called a *goko rei* (J. 五股鈴). Kōbō Daishi holds a *goko* in his right hand in Prince Shinnyo's iconic painting. The *goko* is the primary emblem of Kōyasan's Golden Hall.

yakudoshi (J. 厄年): The unlucky years in a person's life (age forty-two for a man, thirty-three for a woman), for which one is advised to seek exorcism at a shrine or temple. A folk belief rather than a Buddhist belief.

Yakushi-nyorai (J. 薬師如来; Sk. Bhaishajya-guru, Bhaiṣajya-guru Tathāgata): Medicine-Master Buddha or Buddha of Healing. The Buddha of the Land of Emerald in the east who vowed to cure disease. In esoteric Buddhism is identified with Ashuku-nyorai of the Diamond Realm Mandala. See *Ashuku-nyorai*.

Zentsū-ji (J. 善通寺): Located at the site of Kōbō Daishi's childhood home, also the largest and most important temple on the Shikoku eighty-eight-temple pilgrimage. Allegedly founded by Kōbō Daishi in 806 and named after his father; thus the first Shingon temple.

SOURCES CITED

Abé, Ryūichi. *The Weaving of Mantra: Kūkai and the Construction of Esoteric Buddhist Discourse*. New York: Columbia University Press, 1999.

Abe Zentei. *The Life of Kōbō Daishi*. Osaka: Bukkyosha, 1939. (First published in 1912 by Kōyasan Sanmitsu Association.)

Abeno Ryūsei, Hinonishi Shinjō, Yamamoto Tomonori, and Akimune Masao. *Kōyasan Kongōbu-ji*. Osaka: Sei-eishi, 1983.

Adolphson, Mikael S. *The Gates of Power: Monks, Courtiers, and Warriors in Premodern Japan*. Honolulu: University of Hawai'i Press, 2000.

Akiyama Aisaburo. *Pagodas in Sunrise Land*. Tokyo: 1915.

Arai Shōhei, lyricist. "Nyonin-michi." Melody by Suzuki Jun. Recorded by singer Tagawa Toshimi.

Arai Yūsei, author, and Nakajima Kimi, illustrator. *Odaishi-sama: A Pictorial History of the Life of Kobo Daishi*. Translated by Hiroshi Katayama et al. Osaka: Kōyasan Shuppansha, 1973.

Arai Yusei. *Shingon Esoteric Buddhism: A Handbook for Followers*. Translated by George Tanabe, Seichō Asahi, and Shoken (Ana) Harada. Edited by Eijun (Bill) Eidson. Kōyasan and Fresno: Kōyasan Shingon Mission, 1997.

Ariyoshi Sawako. *The River Ki* (Kinokawa). Translated by Mildred Tahara. Tokyo, New York, and San Francisco: Kodansha International, 1980. (First published in 1959.)

Asakawa Kan'ichi. "The Life of a Monastic Shō in Medieval Japan." In *Land and Society in Medieval Japan*, ed. Asakawa Kan'ichi, 163–92. Tokyo: Japan Society for the Promotion of Science, 1965.

Astley-Kristensen, Ian, trans. *The Rishukyō*. Tring, UK: Institute of Buddhist Studies, 1991.

Atkinson, John L., trans. "The Ten Buddhistic Virtues (Ju-zen-ho-go)" by Jiun of Katsuragi. *Transactions of the Asiatic Society of Japan* 33 (1905): 159–84.

Bakshi, Dwijendra Nath. *Hindu Divinities in Japanese Buddhist Pantheon*. Calcutta: Benten, 1979.

355

Berry, Mary Elizabeth. *Hideyoshi*. Cambridge and London: Harvard University Press, 1982.

Bhattacharyya, Benoytosh. *An Introduction to Buddhist Esoterism*. Delhi: Motilal Banarsidass, 1980.

Blyth, R. H. *Haiku*. 4 vols. Tokyo: Hokuseido, 1949–1952.

Boussemart, Antony. "Toki Hōryū (1854–1923), a Shingon Monk and the 1893 Chicago World's Parliament of Religions." *Japanese Religions* 27, no. 2 (July 2002): 179–94.

Bownas, Geoffrey. *Japanese Rainmaking, and Other Folk Practices*. London: Allen and Unwin, 1963.

Brooks, Anne Page. "*Mizuko Kuyō* and Japanese Buddhism." *Japanese Journal of Religious Studies* 8 (Sept.-Dec. 1981): 119–47.

Chamberlain, Basil Hall, and W. B. Mason. *A Handbook for Travellers in Japan*. London: John Murray, 1907.

Cooke, Gerald. "Traditional Buddhist Sects and Modernization in Japan." *Japanese Journal of Religious Studies* 1, no. 4 (Dec. 1974): 267–330.

Cooper, Michael. *They Came to Japan: An Anthology of European Reports on Japan, 1543–1640*. Berkeley: University of California Press, 1965.

Cummings, Mary. *The Lives of the Buddha in the Art and Literature of Asia*. Ann Arbor: University of Michigan Center for South and Southeast Asian Studies, 1982.

Daitō Shuppansha. *Japanese-English Buddhist Dictionary*. Revised edition. Tokyo: Daitō Shuppansha, 1991.

Dan Furuya. *Kōyasan: sanjō toshi*. Ōsaka: Nambā Shuppan, 1983.

Dystra, Yoshiko K., and Yuko Kurata. "The *Yokobue-sōshi*: Conflicts Between Social Convention, Human Love and Religious Renunciation." *Japanese Religions* 26, no. 2 (July 2001): 117–29.

Earhart, H. Byron. *A Religious Study of the Mount Haguro Sect of Shugendō: An Example of Japanese Mountain Religion*. Tokyo: Sophia University Press, 1970.

Earl, David M. *Emperor and Nation in Japan: Political Thinkers of the Tokugawa Period*. Seattle: University of Washington Press, 1964.

Faure, Bernard. *The Power of Denial: Buddhism, Purity, and Gender*. Princeton and Oxford: Princeton University Press, 2003.

Fowler, Sherry D. *Murōji: Rearranging Art and History at a Japanese Buddhist Temple*. Honolulu: University of Hawai'i Press, 2005.

Frédéric, Louis. *Buddhism*. Translated by Nissim Marshall. Paris and New York: Flammarion, 1995.

Fujiya Hotel. *We Japanese*. Miyanoshita: Fujiya Hotel, 1949.

Fukurai Tomokichi. *Clairvoyance and Thoughtography*. London: Rider and Co., 1931.

Gardiner, David L., trans. *Koyasan*. A guide book. Kōyasan: Kongōbu-ji, 1992.

———. "Kūkai's View of Exoteric Buddhism in *Benkenmitsu nikyōron*." *Mikkyō Bunka Kenkyūsho Kiyō* [Bulletin of the Research Institute of Esoteric Buddhist Culture] 5 (March 1992): (202)-(161).

———. "Mandala, Mandala on the Wall: Variations of Usage in the Shingon School." *Journal of the International Association of Buddhist Studies* 19, no. 2 (1996): 245–79.

———. "Transmission Problems: The Reproduction of Scripture and Kūkai's 'Opening' of an Esoteric Tradition." *Japanese Religions* 18, no. 1 (Jan. 2003): 5–68.

Gelfman, Thomas Wayne. "The *Rishukyō* and Its Influence on Kūkai: The Identity of the Sentient Being with the Buddha." PhD diss., University of Wisconsin-Madison, 1979.

Getty, Alice. *The Gods of Northern Buddhism*. Tokyo: Tuttle, 1962.

Gibson, Morgan, and Hiroshi Murakami. *Tantric Poetry of Kūkai (Kōbō Daishi) Japan's Buddhist Saint, with excerpts from* The Mahāvairocana Sūtra *and I-Hsing's* Commentary. Bangkok: Mahachulalongkorn Buddhist University, 1982.

Giebel, Rolf W., and Dale A. Todaro, trans. *Shingon Texts* (by Kūkai and Kakuban). Berkeley: Numata Center for Buddhist Translation and Research, 2004.

Gilday, Edmund T. "Bodies of Evidence: Imperial Funeral Rites and the Meiji Restoration." *Japanese Journal of Religious Studies* 27, nos. 3 and 4 (2000): 273–96.

Gluck, Jay, Sumi Gluck, and Garet Gluck. *Japan Inside Out*. Ashiya, Japan: Personally Oriented Ltd, 1992.

Goodwin, Janet. "Shooing the Dead to Paradise." *Japanese Journal of Religious Studies* 16, no. 1 (1989): 63–80.

Gordon, Elizabeth Anna. "Heirlooms of Early Christianity Visible in Japan." *The Tourist* 8 (July 1920): 19–41; (Sept 1920): 113–20.

———. *The Lotus Gospel: or, Mahayana Buddhism and Its Symbolic Teachings Compared Historically and Geographically with Those of Catholic Christianity*. 2nd ed. Tokyo: Waseda University, 1920.

———. *Symbols of "The Way"—Far East and West*. Tokyo: Maruzen, 1922.

Govinda, Lama Anagarika. *Psycho-cosmic Symbolism of the Buddhist Stūpa*. Berkeley: Dharma Publishing, 1976.

Grapard, Allan G. "Patriarchs of Heian Buddhism: Kūkai and Saichō." In *Great Historical Figures of Japan*, ed. Murakami Hyoe and Thomas J. Harper, 39–48. Tokyo: Japan Culture Institute, 1978.

Groner, Paul. *Ryōgen and Mount Hiei: Japanese Tendai in the Tenth Century*.

Honolulu: Kuroda Institute Book, University of Hawai'i Press, 2002.

———. *Saichō: The Establishment of the Japanese Tendai School.* Berkeley: Berkeley Buddhist Studies Series, 1984.

Hakeda, Yoshito S., trans. *Kūkai: Major Works, Translated, with an Account of His Life and a Study of His Thought.* New York: Columbia University Press, 1972.

Halford, Aubrey S., and Giovanna M. Halford. *The Kabuki Handbook.* Rutland, VT, and Tokyo: Tuttle, 1956.

Hanayama Shōyū, ed. *An Introduction to the Buddhist Canon: 139 Buddhist Scriptures.* Translated by R. W. Giebel. 2nd edition. Tokyo: Bukkyo Dendo Kyokai, 1986.

Hanayama Shōyū et al., eds. *Understanding Japanese Buddhism.* Tokyo: Japan Buddhist Federation, 1978.

Hardacre, Helen. *Marketing the Menacing Fetus in Japan.* Berkeley, Los Angeles, and London: University of California Press, 1997.

———. *Religion and Society in Nineteenth-Century Japan: A Study of the Southern Kantō Region, Using Late Edo and Early Meiji Gazateers.* Ann Arbor: Center for Japanese Studies, University of Michigan, 2002.

———. *Shintō and the State, 1868–1988.* Princeton: Princeton University Press, 1989.

Heine, Steven. "Sōtō Zen and the Inari Cult: Symbiotic and Exorcistic Trends in Buddhist and Folk Religious Amalgamations." *Pacific World,* New Series, no. 10 (1994): 75–101.

Heldt, Gustav. "Saigyō's Traveling Tale: A Translation of *Saigyō Monogatari.*" *Monumenta Nipponica* 52, no. 4 (1997): 467–521.

Hinonishi Shinjō. "The *Hōgō* (Treasure Name) of Kōbō Daishi and the Development of Beliefs Associated with It." Translated by William Londo. *Japanese Religions* 27, no. 1 (Jan. 2002): 5–18.

———. *Kōyasan Minzokushi: Okunoinhen* (Kōyasan Folklore: Okunoin). Tokyo: KK Kōsei Shuppansha, 1990.

Hinonishi Shinjō, author, and Yano Tatehiko, photographer. *Kōyasan-shiki-no-inori* (Kōyasan: ceremonies of the four seasons). Tokyo: Kabushi Kigaisha Kosei, 1995.

Hirota, Dennis. "The Illustrated Biography of Ippen." In *Buddhism in Practice,* ed. Donald S. Lopez Jr., 563–77. Princeton: Princeton University Press, 1995.

Hoffman, Yoel. *Japanese Death Poems.* Rutland, VT, and Tokyo: Charles E. Tuttle, 1986.

Hori Ichiro. "Self-Mummified Buddhas in Japan: An Aspect of the Shugen-dō ('Mountain Asceticism') Sect." *History of Religions* 1, no. 2 (Winter 1962): 222–42.

Hoshino Eiki and Takeda Dōshō. "*Mizuko Kuyō* and Abortion in Contemporary Japan." In *Religion and Society in Modern Japan*, ed. Mark R. Mullins, Shimazono Susumu, and Paul L. Swanson, 171–90. Berkeley: Asian Humanities Press, 1993.

Hotta Shinkai. *Kōyasan: Kongōbuji*. Kōyasan: Gakusei-sha, 1972.

Ihara Saikaku. *The Japanese Family Storehouse*. Translated by G. W. Sargent. Cambridge: Cambridge University Press, 1959.

Ikeda Genta. *Kōbō Daishi Takahatsu no shi: Gonzō Daitoku*. Nara City: Nanto Daian-ji, 1977.

Inagaki Hisao. *A Dictionary of Japanese Buddhist Terms*. 3rd ed., with supplement. Kyoto: Nagata Bunshodo, 1988.

———. "The Esoteric Meaning of 'Amida' by Kakuban." *Pacific World*, New Series, no. 10 (1994): 102–15.

Ingram, Paul O. "Nature's Jeweled Net: Kūkai's Ecological Buddhism." *Pacific World*, New Series, no. 6 (Fall 1990): 50–64.

———. "The Power of Truth Words: Kūkai's Philosophy of Language and Hermeneutical Theory." *Pacific World*, New Series, no. 7 (Fall 1991): 14–25.

Irie Taikichi and Shigeru Aoyama. *Buddhist Images*. Translated by Thomas I. Elliott. Osaka: Hoikusha, 1993.

Ishida Hisatoyo. *Esoteric Buddhist Painting*. Translated by E. Dale Saunders. Tokyo, New York, and San Francisco: Kodansha International, 1987.

Iwahashi Tetsuya. *Ningyo-kō: Kamuro Karukaya-dō-no-hihō* (Mermaid study: a hidden treasure of Kamuro Karukaya-dō). Kamuro Karukaya-dō Hozonkai, 1992.

Jaffe, Richard M. *Neither Monk Nor Layman: Clerical Marriage in Modern Japanese Buddhism*. Princeton and Oxford: Princeton University Press, 2001.

Japan Travel Bureau. *Festivals of Japan*. Tokyo: Japan Travel Bureau, 1991.

Kamens, Edward, trans. *The Three Jewels: A Study and Translation of Minamoto Tamenori's Sanbōe*. Ann Arbor: Center for Japanese Studies, University of Michigan, 1988.

Kanai Sachiko Misawa. "Development of the Kōbō Daishi Cult and Beliefs in Japan and Their Connection with the Shikoku Pilgrimage." *Young East* 6, no. 2 (Spring 1980), 12–37.

Kasahara Kazuo, ed. *A History of Japanese Religion*. Translated by Paul McCarthy and Gaynor Sekimori. Tokyo: Kosei, 2001.

Kato Shūson, Shirasu Masaka, and Chin Shunshin, eds. *Kōyasan Monogatari* (The Story of Kōyasan). Tokyo: Sekai Bunkasha, 1989.

Katsuno Ryūshin. *Hieizan to Kōyasan*. Tōkyō: Shibundō, 1959.

Keene, Donald. *Some Japanese Portraits*. Tokyo, New York, and San Francisco: Kodansha International, 1978.

Kenkyusha. *Kenkyusha's New Japanese-English Dictionary.* Koh Masuda, editor in chief. 4th edition. Tokyo: Kenkyusha, 1974.

Ketelaar, James Edward. *Of Heretics and Martyrs in Meiji Japan: Buddhism and Its Persecutions.* Princeton: Princeton University Press, 1990.

"Kiri Momi Fudō." *Sei Ai* (Jan. 1996), 4.

Kitabatake Chikafusa. *A Chronicle of the Gods and Sovereigns (Jinnō shōtōki).* Translated by H. Paul Varley. New York: Columbia University Press, 1980.

Kitagawa, Hiroshi, and Bruce T. Tsuchida, trans. *The Tale of the Heike.* Tokyo: University of Tokyo Press, 1975.

Kitagawa, Joseph M. *On Understanding Japanese Religion.* Princeton: Princeton University Press, 1987.

———. *Religion in Japanese History.* New York and Oxford: Columbia University Press, 1966, 1990.

Kiyota Minoru. *Shingon Buddhism: Theory and Practice.* Los Angeles and Tokyo: Buddhist Books International, 1978.

Klein, Susan Blakeley. *Allegories of Desire: Esoteric Literary Commentaries of Medieval Japan.* Harvard University Asia Center for the Harvard-Yenching Institute. Cambridge and London: Harvard University Press, 2002.

Kleine, Christoph. "Hermits and Ascetics in Ancient Japan: The Concept of *Hijiri* Reconsidered." *Japanese Religions* 22, no. 2 (July 1997): 1–46.

Kodansha. *Japan: An Illustrated Encyclopedia.* Tokyo: Kodansha, 1993.

Kokka Publishing Company. *Art Treasures of the Koyasan Temples.* Tokyo: Kokka Publishing Company, 1908.

Kongōbu-ji. *Kongōbu-ji.* A 36-page booklet. Kōyasan: Kongōbu-ji, 1983.

Kongōbu-ji. *Odaishi-sama: eienno-inochi* (Honorable Daishi: eternal life). Kōyasan: Kongōbu-ji, 1982.

Konishi Jin'ichi. *The Early Middle Ages.* Translated by Aileen Gatten. Vol. 2 of *A History of Japanese Literature,* ed. Earl Miner. Princeton: Princeton University Press, 1986.

Kōno Seikō and F. M. Trautz, trans. *Der Grosse Stūpa auf dem Kōyasan.* Kōyasan: 1934.

Kōyasan. An occasionally published bulletin in English. Department of Foreign Mission, Kongōbu-ji, and Department of Education, Shingon Mission of Hawaii.

Kōyasan Daigaku. *Kōyasan Daigaku, '90.* An informational brochure published by Kōyasan University.

Kōyasan Kan'kō Kyōkai. *Kōyasan no Kahi ya Kuhi o Tazunete* (A visit to the waka and haiku stone monuments of Kōyasan). Kōyasan: Kōyasan Kan'kō Kyōkai, 1989.

Kōyasan Shingonshū. *Shingon Buddhist Service Book.* Kōyasan: Kōyasan Shingonshū: 1975.

Kuroda Toshio. "Buddhism and Society in the Medieval Estate System." Translated by Suzanne Gay. *Japanese Journal of Religious Studies* 23, nos. 3–4 (1996): 287–319.

Kyōhōsha. *Kōyasan Kyōhō.* A twice-monthly "Kōyasan Newsletter." Kōyasan: Kyōhōsha.

LaFleur, William R. *Liquid Life: Abortion and Buddhism in Japan.* Princeton: Princeton University Press, 1992.

Lamers, Jeroen P. *Japonius Tyrannus: The Japanese Warlord Oda Nobunaga Reconsidered.* Leiden: Hotei Publishing, 2000.

Lloyd, Arthur. *The Creed of Half Japan: Historical Sketches of Japanese Buddhism.* London: Smith, Elder, 1911.

Londo, William. "The 11th Century Revival of Mt. Kōya: Its Genesis as a Popular Religious Shrine." *Japanese Religions* 27, no. 1 (Jan. 2002): 10–40.

Long, Susan Orpett. "Becoming a Cucumber: Culture, Nature, and the Good Death in Japan and the United States." *Journal of Japanese Studies* 29, no. 1 (Winter 2003): 33–68.

Lopez, Donald S. Jr. "Introduction." In *Buddhism in Practice*, ed. Donald S. Lopez Jr. Princeton Readings in Religions series. Princeton: Princeton University Press, 1995.

Ludvic, Catherine. "From Sarasvatī to Benzaiten." PhD diss., University of Toronto, 2001.

MacWilliams, Mark. "Living Icons: *Reizō* Myths of the Saikoku Kannon Pilgrimage." *Monumenta Nipponica* 59, no. 1 (Spring 2004): 35–82.

Mason, R[ichard] H. P., and J[ohn] G. Caiger. *A History of Japan.* Tokyo: Tuttle, 1872.

Matisoff, Susan. "Barred from Paradise? Mount Kōya and the Karukaya Legend." In *Engendering Faith: Women and Buddhism in Premodern Japan*, edited by Barbara Ruch, 463–500. Ann Arbor: Center for Japanese Studies, University of Michigan, 2002.

Matsunaga, Alicia. *The Buddhist Philosophy of Assimilation: The Historical Development of the* Honji-Suijaku *Theory.* Tokyo: Sophia University, 1969.

Matsunaga, Daigan, and Alicia Matsunaga. *Foundation of Japanese Buddhism.* 2 vols. Los Angeles and Tokyo: Buddhist Books International, 1974, 1976.

Matsunaga Yūkei. "From Indian Tantric Buddhism to Japanese Buddhism." In *Japanese Buddhism: Its Tradition, New Religions and Interaction with Christianity*, ed. Minoru Kiyota, 47–54. Tokyo and Los Angeles: Buddhist Books International, 1987.

McCullough, Helen Craig, trans. *The Taiheiki: A Chronicle of Medieval Japan.* Rutland, VT, and Tokyo: Charles Tuttle, 1979.

McCullough, William H., and Helen Craig McCullough, translation and notes. *A Tale of Flowering Fortunes.* 2 vols. Stanford: Stanford University Press, 1980.

McKinney, Meredith, trans. *The Tale of Saigyō* (Saigyō Monogatari). Ann Arbor: Center for Japanese Studies, University of Michigan, 1998.

McMullin, Neil. *Buddhism and the State in Sixteenth-Century Japan.* Princeton: Princeton University Press, 1984.

Mezaki Tokue. "Aesthete-Recluses During the Transition from Ancient to Medieval Japan." In *Principles of Classical Japanese Literature*, ed. Earl Miner, 151–80. Princeton: Princeton University Press, 1985.

Migeon, Gaston. *In Japan: Pilgrimages to the Shrines of Art.* Translated by Florence Simmonds. London: William Heinemann, 1908.

Miyake Hitoshi. *Shugendō: Essays on the Structure of Japanese Folk Religion.* Ann Arbor: Center for Japanese Studies, University of Michigan, 2001.

Miyasaka Yushō. *Ningen no shujusō: Hizō hōyaku* (The various aspects of man: the precious key to the secret treasury). Tokyo: Tsukuma Shobō, 1967.

Miyata, Taisen, ed. *Ajikan: A Manual for the Esoteric Meditation.* Sacramento: Northern California Koyasan Church, 1979.

———. *A Henro Pilgrimage Guide to the Eighty-Eight Temples of Shikoku, Japan.* Sacramento: Northern California Koyasan Temple, 1984.

———. *A Study of the Ritual Mudrās in the Shingon Tradition.* Sacramento?, 1984.

———, trans. and annotator. *The Way of Great Enjoyment: Mahā-sukha-vajra-amogha-samaya-sūtra (Prajnā-pāramitā-naya).* Sacramento: Northern California Koyasan Temple, 1989.

Moerman, David. "The Ideology of Landscape and the Theater of State: Insei Pilgrimage to Kumano [1090–1220]." *Japanese Journal of Religious Studies* 24, nos. 3–4 (1997): 347–74.

Moran, Sherwood F. "The Death of Buddha, a Painting at Kōyasan." *Artibus Asiae* 36 (1974): 97–146.

Morrell, Robert E. *Sand and Pebbles* (Shasekishū): *The Tales of Mujū Ichien, A Voice for Pluralism in Kamakura Buddhism.* Albany: State University of New York Press, 1985.

Mosher, Gouverneur. *Kyoto: A Contemplative Guide.* Rutland, VT: Tuttle, 1964.

Murdoch, James. *A History of Japan.* 3 vols. Vol. 1. Kobe: "Chronicle," 1910. Vol. 2. Kobe: "Chronicle," 1903. Vol. 3. London: Kegan Paul, Trench, Trubner, 1926.

Nagasaka Yoshimitsu. *Junrei Kōyasan* (Kōyasan pilgrimage). Shinchosha, 1990.

Nakagawa Zenkyō. *Bhiksu Shinnyo: A Japanese Prince Who Strived to Reach India in Pursuit of Dharma*. Translated by Shirotani Mineyasu. Kōyasan: Kongōbu-ji, 1954. A 12-page pamphlet.

Nakamaki Hirochika. "Memorial Monuments and Memorial Services of Japanese Companies: Focusing on Mount Kōya." In *Ceremony and Ritual in Japan: Religious Practices in an Industrialized Society*, ed. Jan van Bremen and D. P. Martinez, 146–58. London and New York: Routledge, 1995.

Nelson, John. "Social Memory as Ritual Practice: Commemorating Spirits of the Military Dead at Yasukuni Shinto Shrine." *The Journal of Asian Studies* 62, no. 2 (May 2003): 443–67.

Nitobe Inazo. *Bushido: the Soul of Japan*. Rutland, VT, and Tokyo: Tuttle, 1969.

Noble, Eko Susan. "The Monastic Experience." In *Buddhism through American Women's Eyes*, ed. Karma Lekshe Tsomo, 125–32. Ithaca, NY: Snow Lion Publications, 1995.

Oda Ryuko. *Kaji: Empowerment and Healing in Esoteric Buddhism*. Tokyo: Kinkeizan Shinjo-in Mitsumonkai Publishing, 1992.

Okamura Keishin. "Kūkai's Philosophy as a Mandala," *The Eastern Buddhist*, New Series 18, no. 2: 19–34.

Omori Jisho. *Doctrine of Water: An Introduction and Guide to Bentenshu Faith*. Translated by Satoshi Tatsumi. Ibaraki City: Bentenshu Kyomuka, 1971.

Ooms, Herman. *Tokugawa Ideology: Early Constructs, 1570–1680*. Princeton: Princeton University Press, 1985.

O'Neill, P. G. *A Guide to Nō*. Tokyo and Kyoto: Hinoki Shoten, 1954.

Orzech, Charles D. "The Legend of the Iron Stūpa." In *Buddhism in Practice*, ed. Donald S. Lopez Jr., 314–17. Princeton Readings in Religions series. Princeton: Princeton University Press, 1995.

———. "Seeing Chen-yen Buddhism: Traditional Scholarship and the Vajrayāna in China." *History of Religions* 29 (1989): 87–114.

Paine, Robert Treat, and Alexander Soper. *The Art and Architecture of Japan*. Harmondsworth, England: Penguin, 1974.

Papinot, E. *Historical and Geographical Dictionary of Japan*. Rutland, VT: Charles E. Tuttle, 1972.

Payne, Richard K. "*Ajikan*: Ritual and Meditation in the Shingon Tradition." In *Re-Visioning "Kamakura" Buddhism*, ed. Richard K. Payne, 219–48. Honolulu: University of Hawai'i Press, 1998.

———. "Shingon Services for the Dead." In *Religions of Japan in Practice*, ed. George J. Tanabe Jr., 159–65. Princeton: Princeton University Press, 1999.

———. *The Tantric Ritual of Japan: Feeding the Gods: The Shingon Fire Ritual*. Delhi: International Academy of Indian Culture, 1991.

Petzold, Bruno. "Japanese Buddhism: A Characterization, Part 6 (Kōbō Daishi)." In *Mikkyō: Kōbō Daishi Kūkai and Shingon Buddhism,* a Special Issue (October 1990) of *Mikkyō Bunka Kenkyūsho Kiyō* (Bulletin of the Research Institute of Esoteric Buddhist Culture), Kōyasan University, 59–86.

Picken, Stuart. *Buddhism: Japan's Cultural Identity.* Tokyo, New York, and San Francisco: Kodansha International, 1982.

Ponsonby-Fane, Richard. *Studies in Shinto and Shrines.* Kyoto: Ponsonby Memorial Society, 1962.

Rambach, Pierre. *The Secret Message of Tantric Buddhism.* Geneva and New York: Skira/Rizzoli, 1979.

Reader, Ian, Esben Andreasen, and Finn Stefansson. *Japanese Religions: Past and Present.* Honolulu: University of Hawai'i Press, 1995.

Reader, Ian. *Making Pilgrimages: Meaning and Practice in Shikoku.* Honolulu: University of Hawai'i Press, 2005.

———. "Weaving the Landscape: The Shikoku Pilgrimage, Kōbō Daishi and Shingon Buddhism." In *Matrices and Weavings: Expressions of Shingon Buddhism in Japanese Culture and Society,* a Special Issue (October 2004) of *Mikkyō Bunka Kenkyūsho Kiyō* (Bulletin of the Research Institute of Esoteric Buddhist Culture), Kōyasan University, 139–64.

Readicker-Henderson, Ed. *A Traveler's Guide to Japanese Pilgrimages.* New York and Tokyo: Weatherhill, 1995.

Reihōkan Museum. *Kōyasan-no-Jōdo.* Kōyasan: Reihōkan Museum, Summer 1995.

———. *Kōyasan-no-nyorai-zō* (Figures of Nyorai [Tathāgata] at Kōyasan). Special Exhibition No. 17 of the Grand Treasure at Kōyasan. Kōyasan: Reihōkan Museum, 1996.

———. *Sacred Treasures of Mount Kōya: The Art of Japanese Shingon Buddhism.* For Exhibition held at Honolulu Academy of Arts, September 1 to November 10, 2002. Kōyasan: Reihōkan Museum, 2002.

———. *Special Exhibition on Reverend Shinzen and Notable Treasures of Kōyasan.* 11th Exhibition of the Grand Treasury of Kōyasan. Kōyasan: Reihōkan Museum, 1990.

Rexroth, Kenneth, and Ikuko Atsumi. *Women Poets of Japan.* New York: New Directions, 1977.

Rhodes, Robert F. "Recovering the Golden Age: Michinaga, Jōkei and the Worship of Maitreya in Medieval Japan." *Japanese Religions* 23, nos. 1 and 2 (Jan. 1998): 53–71.

Ross, Catrien. *Supernatural and Mysterious Japan: Spirits, Hauntings, and Paranormal Phenomena.* Tokyo: Yenbooks, 1996.

Rouzer, Paul. "Early Buddhist Kanshi: Court, Country, and Kūkai." *Monumenta Nipponica* 59, no. 4 (Winter 2004), 431–61.

Ruppert, Brian D. "Buddhist Rainmaking in Early Japan: The Dragon King and the Ritual Careers of Esoteric Monks." *History of Religions* 42, no. 2 (Nov. 2002), 143–74.

———. *Jewel in the Ashes: Buddha Relics and Power in Early Medieval Japan.* Cambridge and London: Harvard University Press, 2000.

Sanford, James H. "The Abominable Tachikawa Skull Ritual." *Monumenta Nipponica* 46, no. 1 (Spring 1991): 1–20.

———. "Amida's Secret Life: Kakuban's *Amida hishaku.*" In *Approaching the Land of Bliss: Religious Praxis in the Cult of Amitābha*, ed. Richard K. Payne and Kenneth K. Tanaka, 120–38. A Kuroda Institute Book. Honolulu: University of Hawai'i Press, 2004.

———. "Fetal Buddhahood in Shingon." *Japanese Journal of Religious Studies* 24 (1997): 1–38.

Sangharakshita [Dennis Lingwood]. *The Eternal Legacy: An Introduction to the Canonical Literature of Buddhism.* London: Tharpa Publications, 1985.

Sansom, George. *A History of Japan, 1334–1615.* Stanford: Stanford University Press, 1961.

Saso, Michael. *Tantric Art and Meditation: The Tendai Tradition.* Honolulu: Tendai Educational Foundation, 1990.

Satow, Ernest Mason, and A. G. S. Hawes. *A Handbook for Travellers in Central and Northern Japan.* 2nd ed., revised. London: John Murray, 1884.

Saunders, E. Dale. *Mudrā: A Study of Symbolic Gestures in Japanese Buddhist Sculpture.* New York: Pantheon, 1960.

Sawa Takaaki. *Art in Japanese Esoteric Buddhism.* Translated by Richard L. Gage. Tokyo: Heibonsha, 1972.

Schauwecker, Detlef. "Japan in German Dramas 1900–1945—German Versions of 'Chushingura' in the Nazi Period." *Transactions of the International Conference of Orientalists in Japan*, no. 31 (1986): 70–78.

Schumann, H. W. *The Historical Buddha.* Translated from German by M. O'C. Walshe. London, New York, etc.: Arkana, 1989.

Sei Ai. Monthly magazine published by Kōyasan Shuppansha.

Shaanxi Travel and Tourism Press. *Handbook for Xi'an.* Shaanxi Travel and Tourism Press, 1988.

Shiba Rotaro. *Kukai the Universal: Scenes from His Life* (Kūkai no Fūkei). Translated by Takemoto Akiko. New York: ICG Muse, 2003.

Smyers, Karen A. *The Fox and the Jewel: Shared and Private Meanings in Contemporary Japanese Inari Worship.* Honolulu: University of Hawai'i Press, 1999.

Snodgrass, Adrian. *The Matrix and Diamond World Mandalas in Shingon Buddhism.* New Delhi: International Academy of Indian Culture and Aditya Prakashan, 1997 (reprint).

———. *The Symbolism of the Stupa.* Ithaca: Cornell Southeast Asia Program, 1985.

Snodgrass, Judith. *Presenting Japanese Buddhism to the West.* Chapel Hill and London: University of North Carolina Press, 2003.

Soeda Ryūshō and Miyatake Mineo. *Odaishi-sama wa Ikiteiru* (Odaishi-sama is still living with us). Tokyo: Linden, 1996.

Sonoda Kōyū. "Kūkai." In *Shapers of Japanese Buddhism*, trans. Gaynor Sekimori; ed. Yusen Kashiwahara and Koyu Sonoda, 39–51. Tokyo: Kōsei Publishing Company, 1994.

Soper, Alexander Coburn, III. *The Evolution of Buddhist Architecture in Japan.* New York: Hacker Art Books, 1978.

Statler, Oliver. *Japanese Pilgrimage.* Tokyo: Charles Tuttle, 1983.

Stevens, John. *Lust for Enlightenment: Buddhism and Sex.* Boston and London: Shambala, 1990.

———. *The Marathon Monks of Mount Hiei.* Boston: Shambala, 1988.

———. *Sacred Calligraphy of the East.* Rev. ed. Boston and Shaftesbury: Shambhala, 1988.

Suzuki, Beatrice Lane. *Impressions of Mahayana Buddhism.* Kyoto: Eastern Buddhist Society, 1940.

Swanson, Paul L. "*Shugendō* and the Yoshino-Kumano Pilgrimage." *Monumenta Nipponica*, 35, no. 1 (1981): 55–84.

Takagi Toshio. *Mikkyō no hon.* Books Esoterica, vol. 1. Tōkyō: Takagi Toshio, 1992.

Takano Harume. *Hinjo no itto.* Kōyasan: Kongōbu-ji, 1954.

Takano Shunme. *Nyonindō no Yurai* (The origin of Nyonindō). 28 pages. Kongōbu-ji, 1981.

Tamai Kōichiro. *Yokobue Monogatari.* A pamphlet. Kōyasan: Dainen-in, 1979.

Tanabe, George J., Jr. "The Founding of Mount Kōya and Kūkai's Eternal Meditation." In *Religions of Japan in Practice*, ed. George J. Tanabe Jr., 354–59. Princeton: Princeton University Press, 1999.

———. "Kōbō Daishi and the Art of Esoteric Buddhism." *Monumenta Nipponica* 37 (1983): 409–12.

———. "Kōyasan in the Countryside: The Rise of Shingon in the Kamakura Period." In *Re-Visioning "Kamakura" Buddhism*, ed. Richard K. Payne, 43–54. Honolulu: University of Hawai'i Press, 1998.

————. *Myōe the Dreamkeeper*. Cambridge, MA, and London: Council on East Asian Studies, Harvard, 1992.

Tanabe, Makoto, and Kris K. Shibuya. *An Exploration of Historic Kobe*. Kobe: Shimbun Shoin, 1985.

Tanabe, Willa Jane. "Basic Threads of Shingon Buddhist Art." In *Sacred Treasures of Mount Kōya: The Art of Japanese Shingon Buddhism*, 12–17. Kōyasan: Kōyasan Reihōkan Museum, 2002.

ten Grotenhuis, Elizabeth. *Japanese Mandalas: Representations of Sacred Geography*. Honolulu: University of Hawai'i Press, 1999.

Terry, T. Philip. *Terry's Guide to the Japanese Empire*. Boston and New York: Houghton Mifflin, 1933.

Thal, Sarah. "A Religion That Was Not a Religion: The Creation of Modern Shinto in Nineteenth-Century Japan." In *The Invention of Religion: Rethinking Belief in Politics and History*, eds. Derek Peterson and Darren Walhof, 100–14. New Brunswick, NJ, and London: Rutgers University Press, 2002.

Tokutomi Ganryū. *Karukaya Dōshin to Ishidōmaru*. Pamphlet available at Karukaya-dō.

Tyler, Royall. *Japanese Nō Dramas*. London and New York: Penguin, 1992.

Ueda Akinari. *Tales of the Spring Rain*. Translated by Barry Jackman. Tokyo: Japan Foundation, 1975.

————. *Ugetsu Monogatari*. Translated and edited by Leon Zolbrod. Tokyo: Charles E. Tuttle, 1977.

Ueda Tenzui. "Kōyasan and Southern Buddhism." *The Young East* 2, no. 7 (July 1953): 28–29, 49.

Unno, Mark T. *Shingon Refractions: Myōe and the Mantra of Light*. Boston: Wisdom Publications, 2004.

Urakami Ryako. "Introduction to Shingon Buddhism." Lecture given at Symposium on the Cross-Cultural Cooperation Based on Religion and Science, Bangkok, Thailand, Dec. 8–10, 1995.

Ury, Maran, trans. "Recluses and Eccentric Monks: Tales from the *Hosshinshū* by Kamo no Chōmei." *Monumenta Nipponica* 27, no. 2 (1972): 149–73.

Vandercammen, Jan. *A Legendary Guide of Osaka*. Osaka: Osaka Shunjūsha, 1995.

van der Veere, Henny. *A Study into the Thought of Kōgyō Daishi Kakuban, with a translation of his* Gorin kuji myō himitsushaku. Leiden: Hotei Publishing, 2000.

Vessantara [Tony McMahon]. *Meeting the Buddhas: A Guide to Buddhas, Bodhisattvas, and Tantric Deities*. Birmingham, UK: Windhorse, 1994.

Watsky, Andrew M. *Chikubushima: Deploying the Sacred Arts in Momoyama Japan*. Seattle and London: University of Washington Press, 2004.

Watt, Paul B. "Eison and the Shingon Vinaya Sect." In *Religions of Japan in Practice*, ed. George J. Tanabe Jr., 89–97. Princeton: Princeton University Press, 1999.

Wayman, Alex, and Ryūjin Tajima. *The Enlightenment of Vairocana*. Delhi: Motilal Banarsidass, 1992.

Weinstein, Stanley. "The Beginnings of Esoteric Buddhism in Japan: The Neglected Tendai Tradition." *Journal of Asian Studies* 34, no. 1 (Nov. 1974): 177–91.

Winfield, Pamela D. "Curing with *Kaji*: Healing and Esoteric Empowerment in Japan." *Japanese Journal of Religious Studies* 32, no. 1(2005): 107–30.

Woodard, William P. *The Allied Occupation of Japan 1945–1952 and Japanese Religions*. Leiden: E. J. Brill, 1972.

Yamada Shōzen. "Japanese Esoteric Buddhism and the Moon." In *European Studies on Japan*, ed. Ian Nish and Charles Dunn, 77–83. Tenterden, Kent: Paul Norbury Publications, 1979.

Yamamoto Chikyō. *History of Mantrayana in Japan*. New Delhi: International Academy of Indian Culture, 1987.

———. *Introduction to the Mandala*. Kyoto: Dōhōsha, 1980.

Yamaoka Sohachi, chief editor. *The Water for the Thirsty: The Life of Lady Chiben Who Lives in Love*. Tokyo: Dainichi Publishing Company, 1982.

Yamasaki Taikō. *Shingon: Japanese Esoteric Buddhism*. Translated and adapted by Richard and Cynthia Peterson. Edited by Yasuyoshi Morimoto and David Kidd. Boston and London: Shambhala, 1988.

Yamashina Yoshimaro. *Birds in Japan: A Field Guide*. Tokyo: Tokyo News Service, 1961.

INDEX

Abé, Ryūichi, 288n65, 288n67, 304n18

Abe Zentei, 283n26, 286n50, 287n54, 289n75

abortion, issue of. See *mizuko*

Adolphson, Mikael S., 295n34

Aizen-dō (in Garan), 332n28

Aizen Myō-ō, 165, 224

Aizen Myō-ō Seventeen Temple Pilgrimage, 327n2

A-ji-kan meditation (Letter A meditation): instruction in, 170, 314n8; variations of, 314n8

Ajima ("Taste-testing") Jizō, 201, 237

Akechi Mitsuhide: assists with destruction of Mt. Hiei, 97; assassinates Oda Nobunaga, 100–101; is defeated by Toyotomi Hideyoshi, 100–102; *gorintō* of in forest cemetery, 208, 263

Akiyama Aisaburo, 306n34

Akuno Shizuka, 12, 276n20

altar (*dan*): design of, 139–40; instruments of, 25, 306n34; as mandala of the Five Buddhas, 140; relic within, 306n34

Amano (village), 60, 81, 286n51, 324n9

Amaterasu (sun goddess): ancestor of first emperor, 1; as cognate of Dainichi, 271n1; as sharer of divinity with emperor and Great Sun Buddha, 299n68; visited at Ise by Meiji emperor, 115

American Occupation after World War II, effects of, 300n80

Amida Nyorai: image of in Daitō, 127–28; in "Descent of Amida" (scroll painting), 179–80, 318n26; as *honzon* of Eireiden, 212; as *honzon* of Rengejō-in, 17, 25; *mudrā* of, 127; popularity of on Kōyasan, 292n17; in Pure Land faith, 83; uguisu Amida at Daien-in, 324n9

Amoghavajra (Shingon patriarch), 33, 42–43, 130

Annyō-in (Kōyasan): affiliates with Ashikaga clan, 93; celebration of New Year at, 312n74

Aoba-matsuri ("Green Leaves Festival"). See Kōbō Daishi's birthday celebration

Arai Yūsei, 279n13, 291n4, 337n5

Araki Murashige, 98

Ariyoshi Sawako, 12

Asakawa Kan'ichi, 297n43, 298n53

lung temple of KD's death, 74
Jimmu (emperor): founder of nation, 1; grandson of Amaterasu, 1
ji-nai-machi ("town within the temple"). *See* temple town
Jinken Keihatsu Shirīzu (publication), 162
Jison-in: supply temple and winter retreat for Kōyasan, 3, 81; center for cult of Lady Tamayori, 273n8
Jiun (precepts reformer), 317n13
Jizō Bodhisattva, 6, 330n16. *See also individual Jizō*: Ajima ("Taste-testing") Jizō; Asekaki ("Perspiring") Jizō; Kasa ("Hat") Jizō; Kazutori ("Number-counting") Jizō; Mizumuke ("Water-splashing") Jizō; Nakayoshi ("Bosom-friend") Jizō; O-take Jizō; Oyako-Jizō; "Rouged Jizō"; San-hei Mizuko Jizō: Six Jizō
Jizō-ji (in Shiide village), 3, 272n3
Jōdo-shū (Pure Land school): the *nembutsu* of, 83; role of Amida Buddha in, 83; conflict with Shingon at Kōyasan, 83–85
Jōfuku-in (Kōyasan): World War II memorial pagoda at, 325n11; murals of Hiroshima and Nagasaki at, 325n11
Johō (Kōyasan ascetic), story of, 155–56
Jōkyō, 76
Joya-no-kane ("watch night bell" of the New Year), 158
Jōyo (Kishin Shōnin): reopens Kōyasan, 80–81; eternal lamp of, 80, 81; death of, 81; portrait of in Miedō, 148
Jūjū-shin-ron ("The Ten Stages of the Development of the Mind," by

Kūkai), 67–70, 289nn68–70
Junna (emperor), 63, 67, 70
Junyū, 79, 291n5
juzu. *See* prayer beads
Juzu-ya Shirobei (prayer bead shop): merchandise of, 184–85; selecting prayer beads at, 184–85

Kadonomaro. *See* Fujiwara Kadonomaro
Kagemasa (governor of Kii), 291n7
kaimyō (posthumous Dharma name), 279n13
kakejiku (scroll for collection of temple seals), 219, 226, 327n2
Kakkai, 156, 311n70
Kakkai-sha, 311n70
Kakuban (Kōgyō Daishi): early training, 84; assigned leadership at Kōyasan, 85; attempts synthesis of Amida worship and Shingon, 84; builds Daidenpō-in and Mitsugon-in, 84; flees Kōyasan, 85, 293n21; present reputation of, 86; writings of, 85, 292nn18–20; posthumous title of, 294n22; memorial of in Kōyasan's forest cemetery (Mitsugon-dō), 210, 263
Kakushin, 90
kalpa, 307n44
Kamakura government: introduction of feudalism, 86; effects on Kōyasan, 88–89
kamikaze ("divine wind"), 16, 92
kamikaze pilots: memorial at Kōyasan, 202–3; association with Yasukuni Jinja (Tōkyō), 326n14
Kamiya (village), 7, 277n21
Kammu (emperor), 39
Kamuro (village), 2–3

Printed in Great Britain
by Amazon